Gert-Jan van der Heiden, George van Kooten, and Antonio Cimino (Eds.)
Saint Paul and Philosophy

Saint Paul and Philosophy

―

The Consonance of Ancient and Modern Thought

Edited by
Gert-Jan van der Heiden, George van Kooten,
and Antonio Cimino

DE GRUYTER

ISBN 978-3-11-054319-3
e-ISBN (PDF) 978-3-11-054746-7
e-ISBN (EPUB) 978-3-11-054805-1

Library of Congress Cataloging-in-Publication Data
A CIP catalog record for this book has been applied for at the Library of Congress.

Bibliografic information published by the Deutsche Nationalbibliothek
The Deutsche Nationalbibliothek lists this publication in the Deutschen Nationalbibliografie;
detailed bibliografic data are available on the Internet at http://dnb.dnb.de.

© 2019 Walter de Gruyter GmbH, Berlin/Boston
This volume is text- and page-identical with the hardback published in 2017.
Cover image: Caravaggio (1571-1610), Conversion on the Way to Damascus, Wikimedia,
CC-PD-Mark.
Printing and binding: CPI books GmbH, Leck
♾ Printed on acid-free paper
Printed in Germany

www.degruyter.com

Acknowledgments

This volume is the result of the project "Overcoming the Faith-Reason Opposition: Pauline *Pistis* in Contemporary Philosophy." We are grateful to the Netherlands Organisation for Scientific Research (NWO) for funding this project as part of the NWO Free Competition for the Humanities (project no. 360–25–120). For an overview of this project and of the ensuing publications, see the website: http://www.nwo.nl/onderzoek-en-resultaten/onderzoeksprojecten/i/21/8121.html.

We would like to thank the Center for Contemporary European Philosophy of Radboud University, Nijmegen, as well as the Faculty of Theology and Religious Studies of the University of Groningen for hosting this project. We also gratefully acknowledge the help received from Suzan Sierksma-Agteres in preparing this volume for publication.

It is with great sadness that we must report the death of one of our contributors, Professor Françoise Frazier, who deceased on December 14, 2016. We were very impressed by the erudition and warm interest with which she participated in our conference, and are very proud that her contribution in English to our volume will make her scholarship more widely accessible for non-Francophone readers.

Table of Contents

Gert-Jan van der Heiden, George van Kooten, and Antonio Cimino
Introduction: On the Philosophical Affiliations of Paul and Πίστις —— 3

Part I. Philosophical Portraits of Paul and Πίστις

Andrew Benjamin
Reading, Seeing and the Logic of Abandonment: Rembrandt's *Self-Portrait as the Apostle Paul* —— 21

Jeffrey Bloechl
The Invention of Christianity: Preambles to a Philosophical Reading of Paul —— 47

Ben Vedder
Heidegger's Hermeneutics of Paul —— 67

Ezra Delahaye
The Philosophers' Paul: A Radically Subversive Thinker —— 81

Peter Zeillinger
Disillusioning Reason—Rethinking Faith: Paul, Performative Speech Acts and the Political History of the Occident in Agamben and Foucault —— 95

Gert-Jan van der Heiden
On What Remains: Paul's Proclamation of Contingency —— 115

Part II. Paul and Πίστις in the Greco-Roman World

George van Kooten
Paul's Stoic Onto-Theology and Ethics of Good, Evil and "Indifferents": A Response to Anti-Metaphysical and Nihilistic Readings of Paul in Modern Philosophy —— 133

Teresa Morgan
Narratives of Πίστις in Paul and Deutero-Paul —— 165

Françoise Frazier
Returning to "Religious" Πίστις: Platonism and Piety in Plutarch and Neoplatonism —— 189

Suzan Sierksma-Agteres
The Metahistory of Δίκη and Πίστις: A Greco-Roman Reading of Paul's "Justification by Faith" Axiom —— 209

Anders Klostergaard Petersen
Paul's Use of Πίστις/Πιστεύειν as Epitome of Axial Age Religion —— 231

Part III. The Political Theologies of Paul

Marin Terpstra
The Management of Distinctions: Jacob Taubes on Paul's Political Theology —— 251

Carl Raschke
Paul as Political Theologian: How the "New Perspective" Is Reshaping Philosophical and Theological Discourse —— 269

Holger Zaborowski
Church, Commonwealth, and Toleration: John Locke as a Reader of Paul —— 283

Antonio Cimino
Europe and Paul of Tarsus: Giorgio Agamben on the Overcoming of Europe's Crisis —— 297

Ward Blanton
The Invisible Committee as a Pauline Gesture: Anarchic Politics from Tiqqun to Tarnac —— 309

Gert-Jan van der Heiden and George van Kooten
Epilogue: Saint Paul and Philosophy—The Consonance of Ancient and Modern Thought —— 325

Index of Ancient Sources —— 351

Index of Names and Subjects —— 361

List of Abbreviations

For the references to books of the Bible, we use the following abbreviations:

Gen.	*Genesis*
Deut.	*Deuteronomy*
Jer.	*Jeremiah*
Hab.	*Habakkuk*
Mal.	*Malachi*
Matth.	*Matthew*
Mark	*Mark*
Luke	*Luke*
Acts	*Acts*
Rom.	*Romans*
1 Cor.	*1 Corinthians*
2 Cor.	*2 Corinthians*
Gal.	*Galatians*
Eph.	*Ephesians*
Phil.	*Philippians*
Col.	*Colossians*
1 Thess.	*1 Thessalonians*
2 Thess.	*2 Thessalonians*
1 Tim.	*1 Timothy*
2 Tim.	*2 Timothy*
Tit.	*Titus*
Philem.	*Philemon*
Heb.	*Hebrews*

Gert-Jan van der Heiden, George van Kooten, and Antonio Cimino

Introduction: On the Philosophical Affiliations of Paul and Πίστις

From July 2012 until October 2016, philosophers from Radboud University, Nijmegen, and theologians from the University of Groningen worked together on a project entitled "Overcoming the Faith-Reason Opposition: Pauline *Pistis* in Contemporary Philosophy." During several seminars in the course of the project and one concluding international conference in June 2015, the members of the research team discussed the various aspects of this topic with experts from the field of philosophy, classical studies, and theology. They examined the meaning and impact of the notion of πίστις (faith, conviction, or belief) in the letters of the apostle Paul, in the Greco-Roman world he inhabited, and in the present-day philosophical interpretation of these letters. The results of these discussions are presented in this volume that gathers together sixteen essays as well as a concluding discussion of the implications of the essays for the general line of inquiry of this project as a whole. To introduce these essays and the goal of this volume, we will first explicate the underlying premises of the research project "Overcoming the Faith-Reason Opposition" and subsequently indicate how the essays contribute to this project.

In contemporary debates on the place of religion in society and on the relation between religion and science, the parties often play the card of the (in)famous opposition—more than a mere distinction—between faith and reason. Perhaps one reason that this opposition is stressed is that it is embraced by the two extreme, opposing parties in the debate: Both the protagonists of fundamentalist forms of religion and the protagonists of what one might term "Enlightenment fundamentalism" (which is indeed thus termed in the Dutch societal debate) propagate the concept of a faith that excludes reason, and a reason that excludes faith. Hence, these opposing parties share an opinion about what faith and reason are, but, by identifying themselves exclusively with either faith or reason, they exclude the possibility of a genuine debate with the other party. The conjunction "faith *and* reason" is actually treated as the disjunction "*either* faith *or* reason," as if these two terms set up a dualism. Yet, it remains to be seen whether such a dualism or opposition is sustainable from both a theological and a philosophical point of view. When we consider the origins of the notion of faith, is it indeed the case that it excludes every form of rationality? And when we look at philosophical accounts of reason, do they indeed exclude every form of faith?

To address these questions, it might not be too far-fetched to turn to one of the main religious sources in the history of Christianity, the letters of Paul, and to examine how he uses the language of πίστις as a determining factor in his letters. In fact, the choice to adopt Paul's letters as point of departure was inspired by two important developments taking place in philosophy and theology today. The first concerns the increasing attention to Paul's letters in present-day continental philosophy. The second concerns the rise of a new paradigm in Pauline studies in theology. Both of these developments suggest that the interpretation of Paul's letters has much in store for a reassessment of the importance, meaning, and impact of Paul's notion of faith and its relation to reason. Where the development in continental philosophy gives rise to the question of how πίστις influences present-day conceptions of reason and rationality, the development in biblical scholarship prompts the question of how ancient philosophy and its rationality influenced Paul's notion of πίστις. It is particularly exciting to see what happens when we bring these two developments into dialogue and observe how they cross-pollinate each other. Let us therefore briefly outline the questions these two developments inspire.

Paul in Continental Philosophy. Since the 1990s, the interpretation of Paul's letters has become a booming business in continental philosophy. One of the reasons why this interest grew up in the 1990s may be found in the publication of at least four important books. The foremost of these is perhaps Heidegger's "Introduction to the Phenomenology of Religion," an interpretation of Paul's letters which, though it presents lecture series dating back to 1920–1921, was published only in 1995. Given the importance of Heidegger's work for the field of continental philosophy as a whole, it would hardly be surprising that such a publication turned the attention of the philosophers to Paul. Yet this was not all. Two years earlier, in 1993, Jacob Taubes's philosophical legacy and his testimonial regarding the importance of Paul for his work, which he presented just before his death in Berlin in 1987, was published under the title *The Political Theology of Paul*. This text makes Paul a major point of reference in the pivotal discussions on political theology. In the same decade, in 1997, Alain Badiou's *Saint Paul* was published. Badiou presents Paul not so much in his Lutheran-Kierkegaardian guise as the one who offers a theological account of the individual's salvation, but rather as the one who forges the notions of universalism and equality. Discussing, interpreting, and criticizing insights from Heidegger, Taubes, and Badiou, at the close of the decade, in 2000, Giorgio Agamben published yet another interpretation of Paul entitled *The Time That Remains*. If we view these developments together with reflections on Paul from other authors who determine the debate in continental thought—such as Stanislas Breton, Gianni Vattimo, Jacques Derrida, Paul Ricoeur, Jean-François Lyotard, and Slavoj Žižek, to mention but a few—it is hardly surprising that in the succeeding years Paul's letters turned out to have a remarkable fecundity in philosophy, inspiring a vast and ongoing discussion between philosophers, philosophers of religion, and theologians.[1]

Interestingly enough, in many, if not all, of these philosophical readings, Paul's notion of πίστις plays a pivotal role. In fact, as the reader will find in the essays of this volume, it is exactly the notion of πίστις that provides present-day philosophers with the means to reinterpret concepts such as truth, subjectivity, universality, and temporality. Given the perceived opposition between faith and reason, is it not striking that philosophers reinterpret πίστις to rethink their fundamental concepts? What does this imply for their account of reason and rationality and philosophy itself? Inspired by this question, we may wonder *why* these philosophers reinterpret Paul's conception of πίστις, and *how* they do so. In light of the essays presented here, it may be helpful to distinguish two motives. First, contemporary thought is clearly motivated by a critique of metaphysics and its specific forms of rationality, which also impacts our scientific and institutional practices. One of the concerns of present-day philosophy is that, although these forms of rationality are a strong factor in many of our practices, Paul's notion of πίστις contests these forms and offers alternative perspectives. Second, these ontological, or metaphysical, considerations are very often—but not always—elaborated in terms of their consequences for political theology or political ontology. Especially πίστις in its relation to trustworthiness, fidelity, and conviction proves to be an important source of inspiration for these more political theoretical reflections; another important concept is the specific ethos or attitude to the world this notion inspires, as articulated for instance in Paul's formula ὡς μή ("as not" or "as if not"). As one might expect, the Pauline reflection on the law and the difference between the law of works and (the law of) faith also has a particular bearing on these politically inspired interpretations of Paul.

Paul in New Testament Studies and Classical Studies. The second development is taking place at the interface between New Testament research and classical studies, including ancient philosophy. Recent research findings confirm not only that Christian origins take shape in the Greco-Roman world, in which there is a continuity between religious philosophy and philosophical religion, but also

---

[1] See, for example, Caputo and Martín Alcoff, *St. Paul among the Philosophers*; Loose, *The Apostle Paul in Modern Philosophy*; Blanton and de Vries, *Paul and the Philosophers*; Frick, *Paul in the Grip of the Philosophers*.

that Christianity in its early stages can be understood and was practiced as a philosophy in the ancient sense of the word. As we can glean from the letters of Pliny the Younger, Christianity, unlike early Judaism and Greco-Roman religion, ends the ritual-cultic practice of animal sacrifice and provides a strongly ethical religion. Recent results of New Testament research show in particular that ancient philosophical thinking, both Platonic and Stoic, had a huge impact on Paul's letters and on the meaning of the terms he uses to understand reality.

Due to these developments in biblical scholarship, a new paradigm in Pauline studies is taking shape, and many of the following essays contribute to its elaboration. In this new paradigm, Paul is approached as a Jew from the Greco-Roman period who read the Greek translations of Hebrew texts and was in full interaction with contemporary Greek discourse. Paul's background in Tarsus, a city celebrated by Strabo for its philosophical, rhetorical, and educational training, underpins his profound acquaintance with ancient education. The essays related to this line of inquiry focus on Paul's usage of πίστις language and his interaction with Greco-Roman schools of thought.

Finally, from the perspective of present-day philosophy, these developments in New Testament scholarship are important for the discussion of in what sense the philosophical readings are attuned to New Testament scholarship, and to what extent the kinship that today's philosophy discovers in Paul's letters is confirmed by other scholarship. It is the goal of this volume to address these issues and to show, by bringing the individual contributions of this volume into discussion with each other in an extended epilogue, the deep consonances between the ancient thought of Paul, its world, and the thought of today. Clearly, when we speak of consonances, we are not referring to a complete overlap. Rather, what we are interested in is showing which particular motifs, themes, and notions allow for a fruitful dialogue between ancient thought and modern thought, without losing sight of the important dissonances and differences there will always remain. The attention for the resonances, consonances, cross-fertilizations, and dialogues with ancient thought is because only they allow us to capture the significance of Paul's ancient texts for philosophy today.

To do justice to the diversity of directions in which the interrogation of Paul, his πίστις language, and his affiliation with present-day philosophy can lead us, we have divided this volume into three parts. The first part displays a number of philosophical portraits of Paul as painted in philosophy today, with a particular eye to the notion of πίστις. The second part discusses Paul's letters and πίστις in a Greco-Roman context. The third part discusses the political theology that philosophers find in Paul.

Part I. Philosophical Portraits of Paul and Πίστις

Western history has produced many images of Paul. Different interpretations and reinterpretations of Paul appear in different periods, and each brings its own application of Paul to the time in which he is read. Perhaps, if one were to attempt the impossible task of pointing out one shared characteristic of these many images, interpretations, and applications, one could quote Simon Critchley: "Saint Paul is trouble. It is simply a fact about the history of Christian dogma that a return to Paul is usually very bad news for the established church."[2] Yet perhaps even this attempt is not simply descriptive but mainly reflects the interest in Paul as offering a political theology that places the establishment under threat and pressure. Therefore, it might be worthwhile to pause a little first to consider more closely the portraits that are painted, which notions they highlight in Paul's letters, and in light of which concepts the philosophers appropriate these notions and let them resonate with their own systematic philosophical concerns. In particular, it is important for the purpose of this volume to capture the color in which they paint Paul's notion of πίστις, and how it can offer an alternative to the forms of rationality and concepts the philosophers want to call into question, such as truth, law, necessity, and (the onto-theological) God. Philosophers find these alternatives in Paul's description of the καιρός or of the attitude of the ὡς μή; in accounts of Paul's God favoring what is not (τὰ μὴ ὄντα) over what is (τὰ ὄντα); in the universality of this God, as professed in the famous phrase "neither Jew nor Greek"; and in the importance of the conversion of the self, and so on. Following the hermeneutic adage that interpretation is always also application, one might perhaps suggest that for these philosophers, interpreting Paul is nothing but the contestation of certain philosophical concepts. The essays that follow will show why this is so.

In the opening essay "Reading, Seeing and the Logic of Abandonment," Andrew Benjamin investigates the significance of images of Paul and strikingly notes that "every image of Saint Paul is an attempt to singularize or at the very least to secure an identity, and thus an identity as a singularity, for Paul. Paul as image therefore continues to stage, in different ways and with different emphases, the network of relations of which Paul, his image, is always the after-effect." Benjamin explores this impact of the image by seeing, contemplating, and reading a number of paintings of Paul with special attention to Rembrandt's *Self-Portrait as the Apostle Paul*. In particular, he discusses how the play of light in some of these paintings stages the fundamental moment of Paul's conversion, as Ben-

---

2 Critchley, *The Faith of the Faithless*, 155.

jamin interprets: "The lit face is therefore the sign of conversion." Yet, unlike what authors such as Badiou seem to suggest, this conversion does not come out of nowhere. It entails, and can only occur in accordance with, an implied logic of abandonment, of a turning away from the past so that the converted face can show itself as and in light. With this first exploration of what it means to offer an image of Paul, and to paint his picture, this volume turns to fifteen images, sculpted or painted with the tools of theology, philosophy, and philology, to deepen our understanding of Paul, the importance of his letters, and in particular the specific sense of his account of faith.

The first engagement with present-day readings of Paul is by Jeffrey Bloechl, who in his article entitled "The Invention of Christianity" examines Paul as the first theologian of the Church, who thus invented Christianity. The Christianity that Paul invents in his preaching is born first in his heart, and moreover according to a violence that is well known. What could have prepared Paul for the event on the road to Damascus, and how should we later interpret it? What concepts today, after his singular experience and the urgent preaching gave rise to a worldview, best enable us to hear some of what Paul heard and wished to have repeated in the life of faith? Such questions, as Bloechl explains in his contribution, point beyond, or rather beneath the systematic explanations—dogmatic and speculative—that would have us render the meaning of faith in scientific propositions. Philosophers have their own reasons for contesting the reign of science, and some have appealed to Paul for material support (for instance, Agamben and Badiou). Others, however, have aimed first to simply understand Paul on his own terms (for example, Heidegger and Breton). Bloechl addresses the question of which philosophy hearkens most closely to the experience of Paul, and how its thinking meets the words that pass between the voice heard from on high and the voice in which it is announced.

In "Heidegger's Hermeneutics of Paul," Ben Vedder meticulously analyzes Heidegger's interpretation of Paul. To that end, he first discusses Heidegger's concern with facticity, and the way he sees the need of a philosophy that is connected with and emerges out of human facticity. This leads to a philosophy that tries to avoid petrified concepts and is a-theistic in principle. According to Heidegger, classical philosophy is not able to do justice to human facticity and historicity. Thus, the question imposes itself of how a philosophy has to be in order to make human facticity understandable. For Heidegger, as Vedder indicates, the early Christian texts of Paul are an expression of the experience of this human facticity. Especially the notion that Christ will come like a thief in the night expresses the unpredictability of the future. Subsequently, the question is raised whether an atheistic philosophy can understand religion. For Heidegger, an atheistic philosophy is the only possibility, and this also applies to the philosophy of religion. The unpredictability of the future is also expressed in early Christianity in those passages where Paul writes about the "as not." The "as not" expresses that humans live not as completely open to the unpredictable future but still have to use concepts that are framed already beforehand. This means that human self-understanding remains always a vulnerable and broken understanding. This, as Vedder argues, applies also to the hermeneutics of religion.

In "The Philosopher's Paul," Ezra Delahaye looks at the so-called turn to Paul in contemporary continental philosophy. The question he asks is: Why do these philosophers read Paul? Even though there were a multitude of other circumstances that led these philosophers to Paul, Delahaye focuses exclusively on the philosophical problems that are addressed by these philosophers through Paul. After dividing the philosophers who deal with Paul into groups that have similar theoretical motives, Delahaye argues that there are two main approaches to Paul in contemporary philosophy: the universalist approach and the ontological approach. The main difference between these groups can be understood through the Pauline texts that serve as their reading key, that is, Gal. 3:28 and 1 Cor. 7:29–31. Delahaye goes on to show how Badiou, as the representative of the universalist approach, reads Paul as a political thinker based on Gal. 3:28. The representative of the ontological approach, Agamben, centers his reading of Paul on 1 Cor. 7:29–31 and the ontological interpretation of this text. This brings us, as in the text by Vedder, to the important theme of the ὡς μή, the "as (if) not," to which some of the philosophers who read Paul, such as Heidegger and Agamben, pay special attention and tribute. Both the universalist and the ontological approach, as Delahaye claims, ultimately read Paul as a political ontological thinker, who re-grounds the political order in a renewed ontology.

In "Disillusioning Reason—Rethinking Faith," Peter Zeillinger analyzes how Agamben's book on Paul paved the way for some of his later works, such as *The Sacrament of Language*. These texts focus on specific performative gestures and their efficacy in juridical, political, and religious contexts. Starting from Agamben's reading of Paul's understanding of faith and its specific messianic temporality, Zeillinger shows how the performative gestures of faith correlate to early cultural practices of establishing social and political bonds. These analyses are connected to Agamben's important allusions to the later works of Foucault and his research on the early Christian practices of penance, as well as to Agamben's later elaborations on the structure of the oath and its relationship to the cultural and social development of man. By these reconstructions, Zeillinger reveals— with Agamben and Foucault—the eminent role that performative gestures like πίστις, *fides*, confession, and the oath played in the development of Occidental culture and political history. In this way, the acts of faith are absolved from their restriction to the realm of religion and their opposition or even contradiction to reason. Especially the structure of the specific temporality attached to *performativity*, which Paul identifies as messianic, attests to the efficacy of speech acts for the establishment of social and political bonds.

In "On What Remains," Gert-Jan van der Heiden shows how the senses of crisis, transformation, and contingency that mark the present-day philosophical interest in Paul can be traced in the philosophical readings of Paul's accounts of time, law, and world—and especially in their accounts of Paul's almost nihilistic language concerning the end of time, the universal condemnation of the law, the passing away of the world, and the description of himself as the waste of the world. If time, law, and world are marked by a crisis and are coming to an end (or being transformed), two questions arise, which determine the order of this article: First, what remains of time, law, and world in and by this ending? Second, what type of comportment, attitude, or ethos allows the believer to have a sense of, or access to, what remains of time, law, and world? The latter question delves into the nature and the meaning of the notion of faith, or πίστις, since faith is the word that characterizes this comportment, or ethos, of the believers. Van der Heiden addresses these questions in three steps. First, he discusses the specific conception of time as a time of urgency or emergency. Subsequently, he shows in relation to *Romans*, in which sense this account of urgency affects what humans *can do* (or cannot do). Finally, he shows what this urgency means for what humans or the world *can be* (or cannot be) according to Paul; he explicates this in relation to his comments on the form of this world, τὸ σχῆμα τοῦ κόσμου τούτου, and some other τοῦ κόσμου-formulas as used in *1 Corinthians*.

Part II. Paul and Πίστις in the Greco-Roman World

What happens to our understanding of Paul if we approach him in light of his own historical context and follow up on the recent research? This research suggests that the Greco-Roman world does not know the same strict opposition between philosophy and religion, as we tend to maintain today, but rather displays a continuum between religious philosophy and philosophical religion. Given this more open relation between philosophy and religion, it makes sense to compare the content of Paul's letters to the philosophical schools of his time. What does such a comparison reveal? The essays collected in the second part of this volume show us possible answers to this question. In particular, they disclose this question in relation to Paul's πίστις language, and explore the influences of and affinities with his surrounding schools, such as the Stoic and Neoplatonic schools. In addition, these essays offer a first indication of how this approach to Paul gives rise to questions concerning the present-day philosophical readings of Paul.

The first essay of this second part, "Paul's Stoic Onto-Theology and Ethics of Good, Evil and 'Indifferents'" by George van Kooten, exemplifies what types of questions these might be. Van Kooten's essay constitutes an important transition and confrontation between the present-day philosophical portraits discussed in the first part and the particular perspectives one may open up on Paul by positioning him more strongly in his Greco-Roman context. Van Kooten discusses the characterization of Paul as an anti-philosopher and messianic nihilist by modern philosophers such as Badiou, Agamben, and Taubes. These philosophers focus mainly on passages in *1 Corinthians*. Whereas they show themselves sensitive to philosophically relevant sections in this letter, the current article challenges their far-reaching interpretations by exploring the similarities of these Pauline passages with the discourse of ancient philosophers, notably the Stoics. Differently from Badiou, who interprets 1 Cor. 2:1–5 (with its disapproval of "persuasive words of wisdom") as an anti-philosophical passage, this article views Paul's criticism as directed not against philosophy but against the sophists who championed effective rhetoric instead of truth. And in contrast with Badiou's interpretation of 1 Cor. 1:26–29 as an anti-onto-theological reflection about "the things that are not" (τὰ μὴ ὄντα) which God preferred over "the things that are" (τὰ ὄντα), it actually seems that Paul shares the ontology of the Stoics, who believe that all things emerge from God and return to God, just as Paul states. Paul does not believe that the universe has been created from nothing but rather, in Stoic fashion, that it emerged from God himself. Finally, in contrast with Taubes and Agamben, who see Paul's "nihilism" at work in his statements in 1 Cor. 7:29–31 about performing particular actions "as (if) not" (ὡς μή) performing them, Van Kooten seeks to understand this passage against the background of the Stoic theory of the so-called ἀδιάφορα: the things that are morally indifferent and located between absolute good and absolute wrong. In this way, the author shows that Paul is not nihilistic but rather merely indifferent about certain things, although he does articulate his preferences. He is not anti-philosophical, but actually draws on the philosophical criticism of the sophistic movement. Finally, he is not anti-onto-theological either, but rather deeply convinced that the whole of reality is grounded in God.

In "Narratives of Πίστις in Paul and Deutero-Paul," Teresa Morgan argues that a narrative of the analysis of πίστις in *1 Thessalonians*, *Galatians*, *Ephesians*, and *1* and *2 Timothy* "helps to reveal the subtle variations and, in some cases, evolutions of thinking in early churches about Christ, salvation, and the nature of the new divine-human community on earth." Combining these five letters, Morgan shows how "πίστις language is used to tell stories about the relationship between God and Christ and God, Christ and humanity; about the working of God's mercy, salvation, and the restoration of the faithful to righteousness; about the appointment of apostles to preach the gospel and their relationship with those they preach to; about how the faithful are chosen to accept the apostles' preaching; about how community members should live and relate to one another; about how traditions and writings are authorized as objects and tools of πίστις." This indicates that the use of πίστις language by Paul and his followers cannot be properly understood from the distinction between faith and reason. Rather, in addition to the concern of present-day philosophers with, for instance, the structure of the oath and the particular comportment of the believers to the world, Morgan shows that once one approaches the narratives in which πίστις figures, it becomes clear that πίστις language functions on many different levels. Πίστις is not only a theological notion, but also a term with ethical and ecclesiological connotations, informing the developing structure and life of churches. As Morgan concludes, "It is hard to conceive of any other lexical family in Greek that could have captured all these stories and bound them together into one grand, complex, (more or less) integrated system of thought and practice."

In "Returning to 'Religious' Πίστις," Françoise Frazier deepens and extends the discussion on the meaning and importance of πίστις language in the ancient world by discussing how Plutarch's successors use this language and by comparing the use of πίστις in Neoplatonism and Plutarch. This essay continues her previous studies on "religious" πίστις in Plutarch, which show that for Plutarch πίστις does not yet indicate "suprarational faith," that his use of the word still remains close to Plato's, and that for all Middle-Platonists πίστις remains at the level of δόξα. For the comparison between Neoplatonism and Plutarch, two aspects need to be taken into account, as Frazier shows. As far as the intellectual and doctrinal aspect (i.e., Platonism) is concerned, the case of Plotinus emerges as particularly illuminating: Πίστις does not mean "suprarational faith" in the *Enneads* either. Πίστις appears, with πιστεύειν, in the ascension of the soul, which may be compared to the philosophical approach of the Intelligible in Plutarch. Whereas Plotinus thinks the soul can join the Intelligible because the One has replaced it as an unattainable Absolute, for Plutarch contemplation is still impossible here below. As a consequence, the second, existential aspect—"Piety"—requires another Neoplatonist: not Plotinus, for whom philosophy and piety are one and the same, but rather his disciple Porphyry and, after him, Iamblichus and Proclus, who trace a spiritual itinerary through the triad (or the tetrad) πίστις, ἔρως, ἀλήθεια (and ἐλπίς). In Plutarch, these elements are not yet linked together, but ἐλπίς, associated with joy and a mystic imagery (borrowed from Plato and still used by Neoplatonists), suggests that God's presence may be felt already in this world. By following this line of thought, Frazier reinterprets important themes and imageries that are used throughout the history of Platonism and thus situates Plutarch more precisely in this movement.

Suzan Sierksma-Agteres continues the inquiry into the πίστις language in Paul's letters by connecting it to the language of δίκη, which appears not only in Paul's justification by faith, for instance, but can also be traced in many other ancient sources. In line with the title of her contribution, "The Metahistory of Δίκη and Πίστις," she explores how the axiom of justification by faith is not so much concerned with an atemporal care for the individual sinner, as the traditional Lutheran interpretation has suggested. Rather, first, it is concerned with the universal application of this justice, now transcending ethnic boundaries as emphasized by the so-called New Perspective, and, second, it belongs to a particular understanding of history. Greco-Roman "metahistorical," grand narratives show a widespread belief in an initial golden age of divine rule, followed by a period of retreat of virtues and moral decline, sometimes including utopian, universalistic visions of a return of the days of faith and justice. A similar metahistorical discourse can be discerned in Paul's *Romans*. Moreover, Sierksma-Agteres's semantic research confirms the proximity of justice and faith as virtues of high regard in Greco-Roman sources. This ethical approach to justice is further developed by the Platonic concept of an internal law, identified as a divinely given "mind" or "measure." In *Romans*, these findings resonate with the moral reform of the mind according to the "measure of faith" (Rom. 12:1–8). Hence, as the author shows, Pauline justice can be argued to be deeply universal, ethical, and participational in nature. Moreover, by emphasizing the twofold dimension of Paul's axiom of the justification of faith—universalizing and belonging to a metahistory—Sierksma-Agteres succeeds in offering both a historical context for, and a historical critique of Badiou's insistence on Paul's universalism and its relation to the notion of faith.

By focusing on "Paul's Use of Πίστις/Πιστεύειν as Epitome of Axial Age Religion," Anders Klostergaard Petersen alludes to an old debate that has harassed the study of biblical studies, classics, and the history of religion: the Judaism–Hellenism discussion. Despite the immensely influential book *Judentum und Hellenismus* by Martin Hengel, in which he once and for all undermines the dichotomic manner of formulating the relationship between the two entities, much of this debate lingers on in different repercussions of the binary scheme in which the gain of the one is understood to imply the loss of the other. Petersen targets this debate by focusing on the question of Paul's use of πίστις and πιστεύειν, which has also come to play a dominant role in current scholarship. However, he localizes the discussion in a far wider frame of reference than is traditionally done. He does so by pursuing the question of the meaning of the terms in the context of cultural evolution, with a special focus on the transition from archaic to axial age types of religiosity. Needless to say, this is a moot theoretical perspective that has not previously been applied to the field of late Second Temple Judaism. Yet, Petersen shows that much can be gained—both at the theoretical, methodological, modular, and empirical level—by endorsing such an approach.

Part III. The Political Theologies of Paul

The question of the politics that Paul inspires is vast and has many different answers. The interest in political theology, revived by Taubes in relation to Paul's letters, seems to determine the course—or at least a part of the course—of the important texts by Agamben, Badiou, Taubes, and Žižek, affecting the themes of messianism and sovereignty. The interest in Paul's discovery of universalism and equality gives rise to unexpected alliances and is argued to be at the core of both Badiou's communism and, more recently, Siedentop's liberalism (and both Agamben and Siedentop argue that the Pauline inheritance that should be revived has come to us through the Franciscan order—another unlikely alliance).[3] Yet, as in the case of more ontological considerations, Paul's letters are open to different accounts of what a political theology looks like and what makes it a *political* theology. In this sense, it is better to speak of political *theologies*, with different repercussions for the mode of political action to which they inspire. Moreover, these different political theologies bring into play a particular sense of faith: as fidelity and conviction, on the one hand, or more as oath and veridiction on the other. In a certain sense, the essays of this part expand on the themes and concepts introduced in the first part and apply them to more or less concrete political circumstances or phenomena.

The idea that Paul offers a political theology was developed by Jacob Taubes in *The Political Theology of Paul*. In "The Management of Distinctions," Marin Terpstra raises the question whether it is justified to depict Paul's letters as an example of political theology, as Jacob Taubes did in his Heidelberg lectures on *Romans*. As Terpstra suggests, the justification lies in the fact that as a founder of non-Jewish "Christian" communities Paul had to act as a politician. Yet, he was a politician of a special kind, one who claimed to be called by God (or

---

[3] See Siedentop, *Inventing the Individual*.

Christ) to be a spiritual leader with the task of establishing a new people. To clarify what this implies and means, Terpstra discusses the way Paul manages distinctions—between Jews and non-Jews, between followers of Christ and those who adhere to the status quo, and so on—as well as the impact of Paul's theology on these distinctions. In fact, as Terpstra argues, this impact is to be found in an intensification of distinctions. In its extremes, this intensification leads to the distinction between friend and enemy. By way of this possible consequence Taubes's reflections on political theology are connected with Carl Schmitt's use of the term "political theology." As Terpstra shows, it turns out that Paul's political theology cannot be taken in the sense in which Roman intellectuals already used the term (namely, as state cult), but points in another direction, namely, towards a messianic subversion of the state. Terpstra concludes his essay with a comment on what Taubes called the "Gnostic temptation" hidden in this reversed political theology.

In "Paul as Political Theologian," Carl Raschke explores how the so-called new perspective of Paul, focusing on the Jewish context of the apostle's writings and exemplified in the biblical scholarship of N.T. Wright and others, has profound implications for contemporary political theology. Raschke gives careful consideration to an important book by the American theologian Theodore Jennings, *Outlaw Justice*, and compares Jennings's approach with key contemporary European philosophical ventures in recent decades, which aim to reinterpret Paul and Jewish eschatology in political terms. Raschke argues that the central term δικαιοσύνη in Pauline soteriology is also a fundamental concept for the ancient theory of the πόλις. Where Plato, in the *Republic*, seeks to explicate the integral relationship between the soul and the well-ordered πόλις in accordance with the notion of δικαιοσύνη, Paul follows a comparable trajectory in setting forth the theme of participation "in Christ" as an existential as well as a socio-normative project. In this way, Raschke shows how the considerations we encounter in Sierksma-Agteres's essay can be taken up in the context of a reading of Paul inspired by Derrida. It is this unique, tensive relationship between the two meanings of the word δικαιοσύνη—both ethical and political—that not only makes Paul intelligible in a whole new way within his own historical setting, but re-contextualizes him as an important figure—as Jennings discerns—for political thinking through the ages. Raschke can thus begin to re-conceive Paul's *Romans*, especially, not only as an ongoing polemic against Judaism and paganism, but as a "radical political theology" that confronts and critiques the apparatus of the imperial state itself. As Raschke concludes, just as the Roman conqueror, in bringing the benefits of imperial rule, establishes δικαιοσύνη, so does Christ in not succumbing to crucifixion and death: God, through his suffering servant, has triumphed over all the erstwhile "visible" and "invisible" would-be sovereigns of the *saeculum* itself, the "rulers of this age," including Caesar.

Paul, as Holger Zaborowski argues in his "Church, Commonwealth, and Toleration," is not only a source of inspiration for the left-wing, post-modern accounts of politics and political theology, as can be found in thinkers as diverse as Agamben, Badiou, Taubes, and Žižek, but also an important source of inspiration for modernity, in particular for modern political liberalism, and for John Locke as one of its fathers. Zaborowski goes on to show this by interpreting Locke, specifically his *Letter Concerning Toleration*. The author argues that "even though the biblical passages do not justify his arguments strictly speaking and play a rather illustrative role in the context of his argumentation, Locke does not merely pay lip service to the New Testament, but tries to do justice to its teaching from a philosophical position." Locke's account of the difference between Church and commonwealth, in particular, may be understood in light of the Pauline heritage. As Zaborowski argues: "It is clear that Locke's definition of the church and of the commonwealth, as defined in the *Letter*, shows striking parallels to the view of Paul as explained by Locke. There can be, therefore, no doubt about a distinctly Pauline dimension of Locke's political thought. One could argue, of course, that he reads his own political philosophy into Paul's *Romans*. ... It seems more plausible, however, that he was truly inspired by Paul." Zaborowski concludes his essay with a question concerning the necessity of a political theology for liberalism today.

In "Europe and Paul of Tarsus," Antonio Cimino turns to the political implications of Agamben's reading of Paul, but this time in relation to the current crisis and the future of Europe. Cimino concentrates on a recent interview given by Agamben, in which the Italian philosopher analyzes the current European political and social crisis and sketches his own solution to it. Remarkably, Agamben's analysis relies on concepts and frameworks he outlines not only in some of his major works—such as *Homo Sacer* and *State of Exception*—but also in his book on Paul. In this context, the Pauline notion of the ὡς μή plays a pivotal role, since it helps Agamben to delineate a new alternative to the logic of sovereignty that dominates European modernity and the current political shape of Europe. Cimino singles out the theoretical frameworks that implicitly underlie Agamben's diagnosis of Europe's crisis and shows some problematic aspects of it. In this connection, he attempts to show the extent to which the politics of the ὡς μή—albeit outlined by Agamben in a philosophically original and provocative way—does not constitute a feasible solution that can break the logic of sovereignty.

With "The Invisible Committee as a Pauline Gesture," Ward Blanton introduces a rather different aspect of the political implications of Paul in telling the story of the French collective Tiqqun, or the Invisible Committee, and its political manifestos, such as *Introduction to Civil War*, *This is Not a Program*, and *The Coming Insurrection*. As Blanton shows, these manifestos demonstrate "strong affinities with recent philosophical work on Pauline messianism." And he asks: "How has it gone unnoticed that their efforts to render a protreptic or conversionistic call to a radical politics are, in central and serially repeated respects, articulated through a Pauline legacy, especially the Pauline legacy as read through the messianic Paulinism of Giorgio Agamben (for instance, *The Time that Remains*)?" In the essay that follows, Blanton not only informs the reader about the Tarnac events and the particular political response to this French collective, but also explains in which sense the thought of this collective is Pauline as well as inspired by Francis of Assisi—much like the work of Agamben. Finally, Blanton shows how these Pauline resonances are first and foremost concerned with retrieving Paul's πίστις: "In the end, the struggle to invent a contemporary Paulinist gesture will have been then about the preservation or recuperation of a messianic πίστις."

By Way of Conclusion

For the reader of the different essays in this volume, it will become increasingly clear that they demand at least one additional reflection. How do the essays of the first, second, and third part relate to each other? How do the concepts introduced in the first part connect with the description of the πίστις language and the positioning of Paul in a Greco-Roman context to which the second part is devoted? And in what sense can the political theologies under discussion in the third part be connected to ethical or political concerns in the Greco-Roman period? Or perhaps more importantly: to what extent does taking Paul's own historical circumstances and culture into account improve our understanding of the Pauline influence on the political theologies that concern philosophers today? Or should we rather say that this influence is to be understood solely in terms of the effective history of Paul's letters in Western culture? Or yet again, is this a false dichotomy since, after all, the present-day historical and theological accounts are also formed by the same effective history? Most importantly of all, what, when reflecting on the collection of essays we present in this volume, can we say about the crucial themes and concepts by which Paul's letters prove their philosophical and theological fecundity today? An attempt to answer these questions will be offered in the epilogue, "Paul and Philosophy: The Consonance of Ancient and Modern Thought," in which Gert-Jan van der Heiden and George van Kooten reflect on and connect the essays collected in this volume in order to explicate the deep consonances they reveal between ancient and modern thought. Based on the individual contributions, the epilogue will show which motifs, themes, and notions serve as the building blocks of these consonances.

References

Blanton, Ward, and Hent de Vries, eds. *Paul and the Philosophers*. New York: Fordham University Press, 2013.
Caputo, John D., and Linda Martín Alcoff, eds. *St. Paul among the Philosophers*. Bloomington, IN: Indiana University Press, 2009.
Critchley, Simon. *The Faith of the Faithless: Experiments in Political Theology*. London: Verso, 2012.
Frick, Peter, ed. *Paul in the Grip of the Philosophers: The Apostle and Contemporary Continental Philosophy*. Minneapolis, MN: Fortress Press, 2013.
Loose, Donald, ed. *The Apostle Paul in Modern Philosophy*. Bijdragen 70, no. 2 (2009).
Siedentop, Larry. *Inventing the Individual: The Origins of Western Liberalism*. Cambridge, MA: Harvard University Press, 2014.

Part I. **Philosophical Portraits of Paul and Πίστις**

Andrew Benjamin
Reading, Seeing and the Logic of Abandonment: Rembrandt's *Self-Portrait as the Apostle Paul*

Abstract: In this essay, Andrew Benjamin investigates the significance of images of Paul. The author striking notes every image of Saint Paul is an attempt to singularize or at the very least to secure an identity, and thus an identity as a singularity, for Paul. Consequently, Paul as image therefore continues to stage, in different ways and with different emphases, the network of relations of which Paul, his image, is always the after-effect. Benjamin explores this impact of the image by seeing, contemplating, and reading a number of paintings of Paul with special attention to Rembrandt's *Self-Portrait as the Apostle Paul*. In particular, he discusses how the play of light in some of these paintings stages the fundamental moment of Paul's conversion, as Benjamin interprets: "The lit face is therefore the sign of conversion." Yet, unlike what authors such as Badiou seem to suggest, this conversion does not come out of nowhere. It entails, and can only occur in accordance with, an implied logic of abandonment, of a turning away from the past so that the converted face can show itself as and in light. With this first exploration of what it means to offer an image of Paul, and to paint his picture, this volume turns to fifteen images, sculpted or painted with the tools of theology, philosophy, and philology, to deepen our understanding of Paul, the importance of his letters, and in particular the specific sense of his account of faith.

1

What is an image of Saint Paul? Even if this question is addressed, if only initially, within the space opened by the suspension of the question of the image as it occurs within Paul's own writings, what continues to insist is the presence of Paul. To return to the beginning therefore: What is identified within an image of Paul? Once the image becomes the locus of consideration, what cannot be avoided is the question both of the image and the way that examination is itself to be understood.[1] As a beginning there is Paul. Hence, the answer to the ques-

---

[1] The status of the image remains a question that continues to attract considerable attention.

tion of the name's identity, the name Paul, necessitates developing the logic within which this particular name appears. While that name generates an inevitable conflict concerning its precise determination, it is also the case that the name provides a setting within which that conflict can occur. Indeed, conflict, which is the result here of Paul's indeterminate presence, is created by a setting that nonetheless yields forms of coherence. Coherence is not a mere formal quality of a work. Coherence marks the necessity that images have an ideational content; a content that is itself staged by the work of paint thus color, line, light, etc. One works with and through the other. In sum form is always informed.² Within such a setting every image of Paul is an attempt to singularize or at the very least to secure an identity, and thus an identity as a singularity, for Paul. Paul as image therefore continues to stage, in different ways and with different emphases, the network of relations of which Paul, his image, is always the after-effect.

Rubens' early painting *The Conversion of Saint Paul* (1602; Fig. 1) presents Paul—constructs Paul thereby allowing Paul to figure—through its creation of the space of "conversion."³ Within it the motif of Paul takes on a determined quality.⁴ Paul's image cannot be thought other than in relation to light. Light, which is the work of paint and thus paint's formal presence, brings with it the question of what precisely informs form. Here, in Rubens' painting the light beneath the Christ figure dramatizes the dark within which "Paul" is located. In moving from the dark to the light, Saul will become Paul. The event within

---

For a survey of recent investigations see the papers collected in the volume Alloa, *Penser l'image*. See in addition the philosophical and historical study of the image in Lechte, *Genealogy and Ontology of the Western Image*.

2 This is the point at which to note the distance that this paper attempts to stage, albeit *sotto voce*, from the analysis of Rembrandt that occurs in Riegl, *Das holländische Gruppenporträt*. Riegl is interested in the structure of the content of images. However, that content is purely formal. Thus, when he argues that he is not in tested in the "*Was*" but rather his interest lies "*im Wie der Darstellung*" (ibid., 245), this "*Wie*" (How) is simply a formal presence. It is neither a presence in which form is informed nor one in which form's relation to a "beholder" (*Beschauer*) involves a complex set of relations such that there cannot be mere seeing and thus mere beholding.

3 For a discussion of this painting and its contextualization within a larger history of European painting see, Müller Hofstede, "An Early Rubens Conversion of St Paul." The work is currently in the Courtauld Gallery.

4 I have developed the term "motif" in my *Art's Philosophical Work*. In sum, a motif is a figure or term that is repeated within a range of images in which while what is repeated is the same, the sameness in question allows for differences. Hence the motif of Paul allows for his presence to be repeated, and for that presence to have coherence even if there are important differences within the motif's repeated presence. Equally, the motif of the book will allow for a sense of difference that has a more profound effect.

Figure 1. Peter-Paul Rubens (1577–1640), *The Conversion of Saint Paul* (1602). Vaduz, Lichtenstein. The Princely Collections, Vaduz-Vienna. Oil on oak panel, 72 x 103 cm. © 2017. Liechtenstein, The Princely Collections, Vaduz-Vienna/Scala, Florence.

art's work is held by—if not structured by—a relation between light and dark. In other words, the painting allows a motif of Paul to figure, a motif that is positioned within and as the work of art. Unseated from his horse, his having fallen he becomes, as a result, the presentation of a state that presages. No longer standing he will be able to stand again (and anew). Standing no longer as Saul, a positioning within the context of the painting that is the fallen state, the state that is obscured, he will, nonetheless, come to stand. That standing, which has to be understood as an emergence into being, (interplaying *stare* and *stand*) is an emerging from that which obscures. Light is directed from the figure of Christ standing forth from the dark of the clouds within a form of radiance and illumination that is not just carried by the body of the horse directly beneath him, the direction of the traces of light is itself repeated by the direction taken by the horse's twisting head.[5] They reinforce each other creating what here is light's overall force. Color and movement combine. This combination, thus this moment within the work's work, is interrupted by the color of the cloak worn by the boy trying to subdue the horse from which Saul has fallen. Not only does the color as present recall the color of the cloak worn by the Christ figure, it is also the case that this interruption stops the play of light that would have reached the body of Saul. That body is obscured. As a result, it is darkened. And yet, light plays on his face. This is the decisive point since it allows the now lit face to rise from obscurity while maintaining its relation to the obscure. One works with the other. As a consequence, it is as though his lit face is rising from the obscurity. The lit face is therefore the sign of conversion. Recalled here is of course the other Paul, Paul the writer of text, and thus recalled with that name is the decisive passage from *2 Corinthians* in which what is central is the lit face of Christ:

> For God, who said, "Let light shine out of darkness," made his light shine in our hearts to give us the light of the knowledge of God's glory displayed in the face of Christ. (ὅτι ὁ Θεὸς ὁ εἰπών Ἐκ σκότους φῶς λάμψει, ὃς ἔλαμψεν ἐν ταῖς καρδίαις ἡμῶν πρὸς φωτισμὸν τῆς γνώσεως τῆς δόξης τοῦ Θεοῦ ἐν προσώπῳ Χριστοῦ.)[6]

Paul's face is not the face of Christ. (In addition, in these lines there is no statement of a Pauline conception of the image even though, as will be developed at a later stage, the use of the term "glory (δόξα)" refers to the setting in which it does occur.) Rather the lit face is always already related to the face of Christ. As is

---

5 Burckhardt describes Christ appearing "as a rent in the night sky" (Burckhardt, *Recollections of Rubens*, 84).
6 2 Cor. 4:6; the textual reference is here Acts 9:1–22.

clear, what is central to that face is God's "glory (δόξα)." The latter has to be identified with its presence in the lit face. Hence Paul's face is glorified. This is form informed. Moreover, this is what it means, in this context, for the face of Paul to appear; appearing as an emerging, thus appearing to stand over Saul. The prone figure has therefore a doubled presence insofar as Paul's conversion is Saul's abandonment. Here it is essential to be clear. The contention is that there cannot be one without other. Conversion and abandonment are interconnected. Hence what is at work is what might best be described not as a conversion but more accurately as a logic of abandonment in which that conversion is inscribed. That logic constructs the Pauline event.[7] The event is anoriginally doubled; abandoning leaves its traces in the identity it founds and that identity has to be understood as related to the abandoned *as* abandoned. The event that is founded in the case of Rubens' painting is given in the face; the face is marked in advance therefore by its having a foundational position.

The form of complexity present in Rubens' scene of conversion is however not there in Caravaggio's painting—a work with the "same" set of relations—which is located in the Cerasi Chapel in the Church of Santa Maria del Popolo in Rome, namely the *Conversion on the Way to Damascus* (1601; Fig. 2).[8] In this particular painting whilst there is the work of light, light works in another way. Form is informed differently. What is of significance therefore is how the differences in question are to be understood. The work of light within Caravaggio's painting is such that Saul is already Paul. The motif of Paul figures differently precisely because the work of light stages a transition that has already taken place. What occurs here is a different point in the overall narrative. This is the light that dominates. The entire body is lit. Obscurity therefore has a different role. In Rubens' painting the body of Paul was divided. Here in Caravaggio's the division is located elsewhere. Rather than the body of Saul/Paul being a divided and thus present as a transitional body, in this instance division as the work of light only really pertains to the man holding the horse. In this painting of triumphant conversion, he is no longer part of Paul's accompaniment (even though he is accompanying Paul). He is both there and not there. Retained as aban-

---

[7] The argument is that the event in question is not a singularity. It is always doubled. The argument therefore is pitted against Badiou's interpretation of Paul. One that has to neglect the implicit abandoning that is inscribed in the act of conversion. Badiou's universalism cannot think the complexity at work in the logic of abandonment. See Badiou, *Saint Paul.*

[8] In Parmigianino's drawings of *The Conversion of St Paul* (1527–30) (specifically the ones in the Courtauld Collection, Princess Gate Collection, 360) precisely because the specificity of the medium—drawing as opposed to painting—hands and thus modalities of touch, rather than the interplay of color and light, play the effecting role. Again, there is another motif of Paul.

Figure 2. Caravaggio (1571–1610), *Conversion on the Way to Damascus* (1601). Rome, Italy. Church of Santa Maria del Popolo. Cerasi Chapel. Oil on canvas, 230 x 175 cm. © 2017. Photo Scala, Florence/Fondo Edifici di Culto – Ministero dell'Interno.

Figure 3. Rembrandt Harmensz. van Rijn (1606–1669), *Self-Portrait as the Apostle Paul* (1661). Amsterdam, the Netherlands. Rijksmuseum. Oil on canvas, 91 x 77 cm. © Public domain.

doned he becomes therefore what might be described as the figure of abandonment. It is as though Rubens is more concerned with the way the logic of abandonment has constructed the motif of Paul, rather than with its triumphant after-effect. And yet, it is not as though the after-effect is itself unaffected by the presence of that logic. Indeed, if it can be argued that the motifs of Paul are produced by that logic's work, then what gives ideational coherence to these paintings of Paul is way the work of that logic acquires specificity. (This has to be the case since at play here is a logic that does not have an already determined and thus singular form.) Hence in Caravaggio's painting the event cannot be seen except in relation to the ineliminability of the obscured figure who is present and thus who is the presence of the abandoned. Caravaggio's painting retains the abandoned by positioning it within obscurity—leaving it there, positioning it, *qua* figure, within the necessity of its own abandonment and thus its already having been abandoned.

The complex logic of abandonment, which is the Pauline event, sets the scene allowing for an approach to another motif of Paul, specifically, here, Rembrandt's *Self-Portrait as the Apostle Paul* (1661; Fig. 3).[9] Not only is the image of Paul fundamental, what cannot be avoided is the link established by Rembrandt between that image (Paul) and his own self-image. Rembrandt continued to paint himself. Self-portraiture forms a fundamental part of his overall project.[10] If there is a final point that needs to be made prior to turning to Rembrandt then it concerns how the formal arrangement of the figures within a painting is to be understood. While there may be a compositional set of relations that might establish an affinity between Caravaggio and Rembrandt on the one hand, and while therefore there may be a commensurability of project between paintings of Paul in both Rubens and Caravaggio on the other, the overriding interpretive claim is that despite the presence of purely formal relations once there is an insistence on art's material presence, that is as a beginning the work of color, line, light, and so on—and working with the assumption that it is art's material presence and thus its mattering that produces meaning, form endures as informed—then what emerges as of interest are the differences that the image of Paul creates; in other words, the creation of the discontinuous continuity of Paul as motif. It is within that setting that the particularity of Rembrandt's Paul appears.

---

9 The argument that the painting is Paul was established in the early 20th century by Schmidt-Degener and Valentiner. The argument had to do with the presence of what H. Perry Chapman describes as Paul's "traditional attributes." For an extended discussion of this evidence and then an interpretation in light of it see Chapman, *Rembrandt's Self-Portraits*, 121–28.

10 The significance of this painting for a general consideration of self-portraiture has also been noted by Douglas P. Lackey in "Rembrandt and the Mythology of the Self-Portrait."

Part of the argument to come is that in Rembrandt's Paul the logic of abandonment, while present, is staged in terms of a complex of relations between seeing, reading and blinding.

2

It is always a question of what is seen. And yet, once posed as a question, seeing as a question, then its contents, the set of demands that are being made and which pertain to the seen, are far from as clear as may first have appeared. The painting—*Self-Portrait as the Apostle Paul*—is seen.[11] Viewing occurs. Viewing takes place within it. Paul/Rembrandt looks out. He looks out seeing. He lifts his head from a book that is, as a consequence, within the staged set of relations that comprise this particular painting, no longer seen. What is seen, viewed, stages a relation to seeing even though what counts as seeing is problematized and as a result emerges as a question. The presence of a book that had been seen, is now—in the "now" of the painting—no longer seen; the status and nature of this book becomes a locus of inquiry and thus are a setting to which a return must be made. As his head looks out seeing has a relation to the not seen. The face is given within that relation and thus given with the staging of the logic of abandonment. The anoriginal complexity of seeing occurs in this "now," the "now" that is simultaneous with the turn of the reader's head leading him to look out, to move, that is from reading to seeing. What has to be taken up is the possibility of this "now": In other words, the question at hand concerns the possibility of a pure now in which there is just a body that turns or moves. With the head having turned, what would have been the book's solicitation and thus its presence as a site of reading are, for its now putative reader, no longer in play. And it is this "no longer," that is itself a temporal marker that forms part of the "now." One cannot be separated from the other. The "now" is equally the "no longer." That is what is seen. As a consequence, what is raised is the complex way the work of art, as part of its work, registers time. At the beginning, therefore, the possibility of a pure now is undone. What this means is that any original singularity which would have included, the singular now, the exclusivity of movement, gesture, facial expression, and so on,

---

11 Importantly, Steven Goldsmith has also identified Pauline impulse in this painting in "Almost Gone." The argumentation presented here however is different. As he writes: "His *Self-Portrait as the Apostle Paul* (Fig. 2), like *Bartholomew* signed and dated 1661, seems to espouse the Pauline doctrine of salvation by grace alone, available even to a feeble old man surprised to receive it" (ibid., 411).

have become impossibilities. All are produced, all have the quality of after-effects, all are informed, none therefore can have the quality of original singularity.

In looking at the canvas, ascribing to the canvas the quality of its being a scene of looking, a scene to be looked at, and thus seen, the book which within the canvas is unseen comes to be seen; seen by looking. What is seen therefore is the scene of the refusal to open the space in which seeing and reading would coincide; a coincidence that would have the quality of an opening due to the interplay between reading and deliberation. In the *Self-Portrait as the Apostle Paul* they coincide no longer. In other words, what is refused is not just seeing. What is in fact refused is the transformation of seeing into reading. Reading is abandoned. Indeed, it is possible to go further and argue that the entire painting is preoccupied with the undoing of reading in the wake of the centrality of seeing. The painting stages the relation between seeing and reading. The presentation of one is always already the presentation of the other. However, it is an undoing—one with its own triumphant consequences—that the very structure of the painting both allows and refuses at the same time. Their simultaneity comprises the effective presence of the logic of abandonment. Moreover, it is this logic which, of course, reinforces the refusal of both an unfettered allowing and a pure now, precisely because it comprises the work's work.

It is not as though a concern with reading and the presentation of the book as either read or unread were unfamiliar topics for Rembrandt. (While the book and questions of reading figure within the history of art, here the presence of the motif of reading will be restricted to Rembrandt. There is within the space opened by that name an already prominent set of relations.) It is also clear from *Musical Company* (*Family Allegory*) (1626) that Rembrandt knew how to present books. Within that particular painting books are open. While one clearly contains musical notation, another is a standard work which, because of what appears to be the decoration and size of the opening word or letter, would seem to indicate the presence of a work written in either Dutch or German. In addition, the latter work is not in two columns. Rather, the page contains a single column that is to be read from left to right. There are at least two further works by Rembrandt that are relevant here. The first is *An Old Woman Reading* (1631; Fig. 4) while the second is *Jeremiah Lamenting the Destruction of Jerusalem* (1630; Fig. 6). The first is a scene of actual reading, with all the consequences that this actuality will entail, while the second involves the book which, within the setting created by the painting, remains unread. Pursuing the motif of reading will allow for a return to the presence of Rembrandt as Paul.

An Old Woman Reading is not simply important because the woman in question is taken to be the prophetess Hannah or that she is reading Hebrew and thus

Figure 4. Rembrandt Harmensz. van Rijn (1606–1669), *An Old Woman Reading, Probably the Prophetess Hannah* (1631). Amsterdam, the Netherlands. Rijksmuseum. Oil on panel, 60 x 48 cm. © Public domain.

the locus of her engagement is the Hebrew Bible (as opposed to either an ignored book, or the Book as the synthesis of both "Testaments").[12] Of significance is the location of each of these elements as themselves produced by the work of light. Hannah reads from a darkened position. She reads into the light. What is lit is the book. What is clear therefore is that here in this particular work reading and seeing coincide. She looks down. It is as though the physical space between the face and the book is closing as a consequence of the persistence of the act of reading. The presence of her right hand on the page underscores the intensity of the act. She is steadying herself. Her eye is adjusting continually as the page is held in place. The importance of the book is the result of light. All that is present is text. The relationship is to text. Her interiority, if access is thought to have been effected by her face, has to be understood in relation to the practice of reading. *Pace* Riegl there can be no pure state of *Aufmerksamkeit*.[13] She is not merely attentive. Furthermore, there cannot be any sense of interiority that takes place at a distance from that act; an act that can be named and which has to be understood as the act of reading that is itself the displacement of the centrality of seeing. Here seeing is reading.[14] Within the context of this work this is what being attentive means. The act of reading therefore mediates in advance both claims about interiority and claims about the nature of the face. Faces are at work. Here is a face that is reading. To continue the position sketched above, her head's presence as a face, is mediated in advance by its incorporation into that activity. While the bonnet has clear contextual references, that it reflects light underscores the face's presence within the process of reading. She is the reader incarnate. The face cannot be extracted as a singular site. Her interior world is given within the exteriority of the act that defines her. She reads. Moreover, she reads from the dark. What is read—the book—has become the place of light. If light is linked to "God's glory," then here the locus of glory has another place. It is the book not the face. Hence here the nature of the book—the motif of the book—is fundamentally different.

One clear point of contrast is of course Gerard Dou's *Old Woman Reading* (1631–32; Fig. 5). What she is reading is straightforward. It can be seen. *Luke* is open at the beginning of Chapter 19. While the temptation is to stay with the text of the Gospel—and read it—there is another relation that opens up the

---

[12] On the question of the presence of "Hebrew" within the corpus of Rembrandt's paintings see Alexander-Knotter, "Rembrandt's Hebrew."

[13] For a discussion of this aspects of Riegl's work see: Olin, "Forms of Respect." Heuer, "'Hundreds of eyes.'"

[14] I have taken up the relation between seeing and reading in the context of Philo, see "Barring Fear."

Figure 5. Gerard Dou (1613–1675), *Old Woman Reading* (c. 1631–32). Amsterdam, the Netherlands. Rijksmuseum. Oil on panel, 71.2 x 55.2 cm. © Public domain.

concerns of the image. That other relation is the presence of Luke within the history of painting. Luke as the patron saint of painting inscribes the centrality of painting into the work's work.[15] It is brought into the frame; painted to be seen. Painting is present firstly as the image within the book. Then by the presence of the name "*Luce*" painted onto the book's page. Finally, the connection between Luke and the painting as whole reinforces its presence as art's work. Taken together they are integral to the way in which the work stages itself as art. A process that can be can be called *art's self-staging*. Hence, what cannot be precluded is the possibility that in Gerard Dou's painting centrality should be given to the relation between the eye and the image rather than the eye and the text. As a result, the link between Luke, the presence of an image within the text and thus the move from reading to seeing predominates. If the work's attempt to inscribes the primacy of seeing and therefore the primacy of immediacy as central, leaving aside the extent to which such a project could be viewed as successful in its own terms, then seeing predominates. The result would be clear. Reading would only ever be secondary. Moreover, and as with the text being read, both would have been literalized. The literalization of the book is equally the literalization of its content. The book would then no longer be a locus of deliberation. What is taking place in Rembrandt's *An Old Woman Reading* is radically different.

In the case of *An Old Woman Reading* while the image draws the eye in, the text, present within the frame, demands the mediated activity of reading. If such a characterization is accurate then Rembrandt's work, which is itself already an image insofar as it is the work of art, constructs both a direct site of reading, though equally is the setting in which reading becomes a form of seeing. As such it opens the work to being seen within the structure of mediation and not immediacy. It invites, in other words, a reformulation of seeing in which seeing becomes reading. Seeing in this context therefore is not secondary to reading. This is what is seen. While this may appear a simple contradiction, it opens up another possibility namely that the image, the painting, now demands what might be described as a non-imagistic account of its own presence. It is this possibility, the possibility in which the image becomes a locus of work rather than a making present, that needs to be pursued. Pursuing it is essential as reading, now in this extended sense, will complicate the logic of abandonment. While another return to Rembrandt's Paul awaits, there is still an additional preliminary step. It is not just that consideration needs to be given to another book, once given what will be reinforced is the impossibility of there being the book as an

---

15 I have discussed the significance of Luke in the context of Jan Gossaert's painting of Luke in "On the Image of Painting." For a further discussion of the historical issues raised by this painting see Owens Schaefer, "Gossaert's Vienna 'Saint Luke painting'"; and Olds, "Jan Gossaert's 'St Luke Painting the Virgin.'"

enforcing singularity. The complications intrinsic to the motif of the book need further amplification. What matters now is the presence of the book, the motif of the book, in *Jeremiah Lamenting the Destruction of Jerusalem* (Fig. 6).

Figure 6. Rembrandt Harmensz. van Rijn (1606–1669), *Jeremiah Lamenting the Destruction of Jerusalem* (1630). Amsterdam, the Netherlands. Rijksmuseum. Oil on panel, 58 x 46 cm. © Public domain.

In the painting of Jeremiah lamenting, the book is present in a number of different ways. There is a book to Jeremiah's right. While he is cast in light the book remains in the shadows. It is there without light. One the book's side is the hand-written word "*Bibel*." It appears on the top edge. The book therefore is the Book. And yet, there is an immediate question that arises. What particular instance of the Book is it? It cannot be the Torah or even the Old Testament, as neither would have been referred to by the singular term "Bible." Clearly, however, the word *Bibel* is used to name the book that Jeremiah might have read. Consequently, that Book is both named and misnamed in advance. Even accepting this delimitation of the Book—or book—as points of departure what is significant here is that as Jeremiah looks away what then becomes clear is that the Book that Jeremiah could have read offers neither solace nor a source of understanding. The painting stages the limits of the Book that is simultaneously the Book's delimitation as a book. In its having become just a book any possible connection therefore between Book and life and thus what might also be thought in terms of law and life in which the Book is the locus of law, the living out of which would have become the definition of life, is resisted by the separation between affect and the Book.[16] (This is, after all, the Pauline imperative.) It would be as though the Book were not itself a source of an understanding of affect; as though, moreover, Jeremiah had not lamented; as though, finally, that lamentation is not to be thought in terms of a complex set of relations to the law; the latter being the actual province of the Book. It might be added here that lamentation rather than a locus of pure affect only exists because of its relation to the law. Lamenting betrays the exigency of the law and thus a breach in the real. This

---

16 The relationship between law and life and the incorporation of one within the other—transfiguring thereby what is understood by both law and life—is the moment at which law would be linked to deeds. This linking plays a fundamental role both in Rosenzweig's critique of Buber and more importantly in his own conception of the law. The point is made by Rosenzweig in the following terms: "Whatever can and must be done is not yet deed, whatever can and must be commanded is not yet commandment. Law [*Gesetz*] must again become commandment [*Gebot*], which seeks to be transformed into deed at the very moment it is heard" (Rosenzweig, "The Builders," 84). In addition, as has been mentioned, integral to the Pauline event, though here articulated within what has been called the logic of abandonment is the literalization of the law such that it is possible for the law to have a relation of non-relation to life. I have discussed this aspect of Paul in an examination of Giorgio Agamben's interpretation of Paul: see "The Inoperative Jew: Agamben's Paul." In addition, there is another sense in which the link between words and deeds is recast in ways that the relation between them is central such that it cannot be the deed alone that matters (equally word cannot exist as an end in itself.) At stake here is the relation between λόγος and ἔργα in Xenophon. To this end see the interchange between Hippias and Socrates in the *Memorabilia*, 4.4.10 – 18.

exigency and thus the doubling of betrayal are the elements that complicate any claim about the singularity of the "now" and thus the possibility of a locus of pure affect.

What is of significance however is the way lament is presented. Here it is essential to recall that the predicament of the Israelites in relation to God, as recounted in Jeremiah, has a number of different permutations. One of the predominating themes is that God has been "forsaken." To forsake ('âzab) defines a specific negative form of relationality. Note the following formulation that occurs at Jer. 2:19: "Have you not brought this on yourselves by forsaking (עָזְבֵךְ) the Lord your God when he led you in the way?" Once the direct context is distanced and the problem that emerges is allowed to attain a form of abstract generality then another question emerges: that is, what is it like not to "forsake"? While it might be tempting to evoke a form of remembrance it is far more likely that what is at stake is that form of return in which a relation is either retained or recovered. In either instance once relationality is defined in terms other than those of forsaking, then relationality has to be understood as inscribed within whilst sustaining a continuity of practices. And it should be added that they are what will have become possible as the result of a form of return. The process of returning—*Teshuvah*—involves the recognition of a mode of life that is itself orientated by "truth," "justice" and "holiness"; in other words, as orientated by law and thus by the Book as the locus of law.[17] This is after all part of the argumentation of Jer. 4:1. While what is at work is a set of concerns that are intrinsic to fundamental elements of Jewish thought, what is of interest here is that they stage a set up that occurs in the book of Jeremiah. Again, this is not to deny that they occur elsewhere; nonetheless, what is of significance is their specific location in *Jeremiah*. As such they provide the setting in which to approach Rembrandt's painting *Jeremiah Lamenting the Destruction of Jerusalem* in terms of its centrality for these concerns.

What is clear, as has been suggested, is that the figure of Jeremiah laments. Lamenting occurs here such that Jeremiah remains oblivious both to the cause of the lament, which has already been identified as the existence of the law, and that as a result the site that yields a way into that exigency and thus an engagement with lament, namely the Book as the locus of law, remains closed to him. The pressure of his arm which, while supporting his head, pushes into the book causing it to bend reinforces both his detachment and thus his indifference. The peculiarity of that indifference underscores his presence. Of equal significance is

---

[17] For a discussion of some of the elements proper to this concept in the broader context of Jewish theology see, Petuchowski, "The Concept of 'Teshuvah.'"

the direction of his eyes. It is not as though they seek an answer in the Book or posit the Book as a possible locus of engagement. That the Book as the locus of law, named in the painting, not as Torah but as *Bibel*, a naming therefore that is, as has already been noted, a misnaming, remains closed. The consequence of this positioning of the book, the book as motif, is that it cannot provide a way through lament even though lament originates in the law. Jeremiah remains uncomprehending. Moreover, as present here lament become a *huis clos*. And yet, the contention has to be that quite literally, the possibility of another way cannot be seen. Gershom Scholem in writing on lament locates a strategy of engagement. He opens up the possibility that Judaism is able, "as it overcame myth, and forbade magic, to absorb lament within itself (*die Klage in sich aufnehmen*)."[18] Were that absorption to be possible seeing would have to have been displaced by reading; Rembrandt's Jeremiah would have to become his Hannah.

3

Rembrandt's relation to Judaism is a well worked field.[19] Equally, Rembrandt's concern with Paul has its own constancy. As a motif, Paul reappears in both a 1629 drawing and a number of paintings.[20] As a result what is opened up, as a possible field of investigation, is the presentation of another instance of Paul as motif. However, precisely because there are different Pauls within Rembrandt's corpus the question of how Paul's presence is to be understood has to be made more precise. Hence, in this instance, as has already been indicated, one particular painting is being maintained as the locus of investigation, namely, *Self-Portrait as the Apostle Paul* (1661). And it should be noted in advance that the presence of this "as" which while fundamental to the argumentation to be presented here has already attracted a great deal of attention. Moreover, it is this "as" that allows a link between painting as a practice and the writings of Paul to be established.[21] The additional opening point to note is that since

---

18 Scholem, *Tagebücher. 1917–1923*, 133.
19 Nadler, *Rembrandt's Jews*. See in addition, Zell, "Eduard Kolloff and the Historiographic Romance of Rembrandt and the Jews."
20 I have discussed the 1629 drawing towards the end of this paper.
21 Christopher Braider has discussed the significance of this "as" (Braider, "The Fountain of Narcissism"). Braider's paper is central to the attempt to secure the link between Rembrandt and Paul. In addition, Braider also refers to Caravaggio in the presentation of his overall argument. While Braider's paper is an indispensable contribution in its own right, the project of po-

what is at stake is a self-portrait, then not only is the process of painting implicated, of equal importance are the questions that pertain to the possibility or impossibility of self-presentation. (The "self" of self-portraiture endures as a question.[22]) Nonetheless, given that the locus of investigation is the work of art it cannot be the case that a painting exemplifies (positively or negatively) a text. The image remains an image. The work of art is the place of art as work. Writing has a fundamentally different nature. Hence, rather than assume that the connection between art and text allows for a simple oscillation between them—an oscillation that would have elided their difference within the attempt to secure a connection—a way in has to be found that preserves their difference and yet which allows that difference to become productive. What this means here is that a specific mode of relationality needs to be sought. In this instance, a way in occurs by taking seriously the conception of the image staged in Paul's writings. This is the opening that has to be developed.

The point of departure is the famous passage from *2 Corinthians* in which a link between blindness and the negative instance of belief is presented with exacting concision. The significance of this passage can be found in its evocation of "the image of God" and the creation of human in God's image. The latter has to be understood as an evocation of the position announced in Gen. 1:26, even if the conception of "image" in the latter text is fundamentally transformed in the process.[23] In 2 Cor. 4:4 Paul writes the following:

> The god of this age has blinded the minds (ἐτύφλωσεν τὰ νοήματα) of unbelievers (τῶν ἀπίστων), so that they cannot see the light of the gospel that displays the glory of Christ (τὸ μὴ αὐγάσαι τὸν φωτισμὸν τοῦ εὐαγγελίου τῆς δόξης τοῦ Χριστοῦ), who is the image of God (ὅς ἐστιν εἰκὼν τοῦ Θεοῦ).[24]

The passage cited above precedes the one from *Corinthians* that has already been noted. Reiterated in both is the formulation "the glory of Christ" (τῆς δόξης τοῦ Χριστοῦ). In the latter Christ is "the image of God." In the former the "glory of God" registers in "the face of Christ." A position that is reiterated in Col. 1:15. In that context Christ "is the image of the invisible God" (ἐστιν εἰκὼν τοῦ

---

sitioning the Pauline event within the logic of abandonment and then locating that logic within two these works marks the point of genuine differentiation.

22 While not necessarily endorsing the detail of the argument for a problematization of the self-portrait in general and Rembrandt's in particular see, Derrida, *Mémoires d'aveugle*.
23 For an extended discussion of the different ways in which the *imago dei* can be understood in the context of Genesis see Lorberbaum, *In God's Image*.
24 2 Cor. 4:4.

Θεοῦ τοῦ ἀοράτου).²⁵ Therefore there is the image and thus the making present of that which is not present ("invisible," ἀοράτου). While acknowledging from the start the importance of these formulations within the history of Christianity, what is of direct interest here is that in both instances there is a making present. Christ as "image" is present. He is God's image. He is a presence to be seen and what is seen is "glory."²⁶ The "glory" that is displayed "on the face of Christ." Christ therefore is not just the image. Rather the point is that he is an image to the extent that the image is understood as a making present to be seen. However, this is the point at which the complication introduced by the logic of abandonment has to be noted. Once the work of this logic is followed, which is itself a necessity since it yields seeing in its overcoming of reading, then seeing is no longer a form of presencing that stands on its own. Seeing is not pure, which in this context means that this making seen—the image as there to be seen—cannot be understood if its relation to blinding is not included.

Belief (or faith, that is, πίστις) is already that which marks both the overcoming of law and the move to Christ. Hence the importance of the formulation πίστις Χριστοῦ such that what is always involved is "faith in Christ" who is the "image of God."²⁷ This set up brings faith or belief into a constellation with seeing and the figure of Christ. What occurs at the center of that constellation is an image which is seen. Expressed in the terms at work here what this entails is that seeing has overcome the necessity to read. Here is the point at which the disjunction insists. The object of belief is not the object that is read. The former must be seen, and the temporality of seeing differs radically from the temporality of reading. Indeed, it might be that the continuity of time gestured at by the positioning and function of Hannah's hand in *An Old Woman Reading* reinforces the nature of the differences. Her hand is there on the page prolonging the act. Underscoring both the continuity of reading and thus reading's inherent mediacy. Mediated by the processes of interpretation and then the ensuing and necessary deliberations to which both acts give rise, reading is inextricably bound up both with the activity of judgment and thus also with the impossibility of its necessary literalization. Reading however cannot be separated from the law. Though more emphatically it pertains to the locus of the law, namely the Book. The law is read. (Reading in this now quite extended sense.)

---

25 Col. 1:15.
26 While it cannot be pursued here it nonetheless need to be noted that δόξα is a translation of the Hebrew *kabod*. There is an important thinking of the "glory" of God in Torah. For a discussion of the latter see Sommer, *The Bodies of God and the World of Ancient Israel*.
27 This is a formulation that appears in a number of Paul's text. See Gal. 2:16, 20 and 3:22; Rom. 3:22, 26; Phil. 3:9; cf. Eph. 3:12.

What this means is that to the extent that seeing is the overcoming of reading and that seeing obviates the need to read, the related position is always going to be that once articulated within the logic of abandonment the condition of seeing—that is, of not reading—is its co-presence with blinding. Blinding and seeing are held together within a version of the logic of abandonment. Blinding therefore is a necessary component of the move away from the book and towards the locus of faith/belief. Moreover, to the extent that the argument is made that blinding and seeing are related, it is fundamental that inscribed into the process is the presence of those whose fail to see. This is the point that, as noted above, has already been made by Paul when he suggested that, "the god of this age has blinded the minds (ἐτύφλωσεν τὰ νοήματα) of unbelievers (τῶν ἀπίστων)." Blinding has both a literal as well as a figural register. It is in relation to the position argued here that Augustine is able to suggest in his *Contra Faustum Manichaeum* that:

> For among all of their anointed ones the Jews also searched for their redeemer the one who was to save then. But they were blinded by the secret justice of God (*excaecati occulta iustitia Dei*).[28]

The blinding of the Jews is the position that while fundamental to certain elements of the argumentation of Augustine comes to be played out in the history of European art in relation to the figure *La Synagoga*.[29] Equally, it is there, for example in Pascal's argument advanced in the *Pensées* that not only were the Jews blind "it is this very refusal which is the foundation of our belief."[30] Equally for Bossuet in his *Discour sur l'histoire universelle* (1681) blindness and deafness were the cause of the "ruin" of the Jews.[31]

---

28 Augustine, *Contra Faustum Manichaeum*, 12.44. It needs to be noted that Augustine's relation to Judaism is more complex than this passage indicates. For an interpretation of Augustine that highlights thus complexity see, Fredriksen, *Augustine and the Jews*.
29 There is an extensive literature on *La Synagoga*. The foundation text is probably Blumenkranz, *Le juif médiéval au mirroir de l'art Chrétien*. The most important recent contribution to this discussion—precisely because of the detail of its architectural history is Rowe, *The Jew, The Cathedral and the Medieval City*.
30 This is the position that occurs in the *Penseés*, no. 273. The text cited is in Pascal, *Oeuvres Complètes*, 536.
31 Bossuet, *Discour sur l'histoire universelle*, 225–26.

4

As Paul, Rembrandt looks out. He turns looking out. This looking out continues to attract attention, as does the fact that he looks. There is a face looking. The portraits of this period, especially those by Rembrandt, have been described as residing "on a knife's edge between poignant humanity and mere plasticity." For the same author, the face of Paul stands for "a promotion of a face into light and grace."[32] Equally it is possible to argue that in Rembrandt, especially in his portrait of Moses, the face "dominates a visual field" and yet the contention here is always going to be that despite a potential ambiguity, a face can never be a locus of pure ambiguity. Once this latter position can be substantiated then there is, for example, a problem when Joseph Koerner argues that the

> face in Rembrandt acquires its meaning only within the essential obliqueness of its message, and within the dangerous probability that this message will be believed but totally misunderstood.[33]

What has to be refused is the evocation of "humanity" as though faces were not always already implicated in that complex determination of human being that resisted the possibility that what was "pure" in humanity could ever be represented as such. Equally, it would be false to argue that Rembrandt's concern was to "disclose to us our human limitations."[34] Terms such as "us" and "human" in such contexts are produced, they do not have an original significance.

Looking out occurs within what has already been identified as the logic of abandonment. As a result, looking out is to look up from reading. If the complexity of looking, seeing and reading were to be given their full force then what would occur is a restaging of a concern with both subjectivity and interiority. It is not that subject positions are determined such that there is the absence of any form of indeterminacy. Rather the claim is that neither indeterminacy nor ambiguity can be pure. Moreover, while the nature of Paul's face alters precisely because it is also a self-portrait that complexification of the subject posi-

---

32 Goldsmith, "Almost Gone," 416.
33 Koerner, "Rembrandt and the Epiphany of the Face," 32. See in addition Benjamin Binstock's discussion in "Rembrandt's Paint" of this aspect of Koerner's argument.
34 The latter position concerning this "us" is the conclusion reached by Margaret Deutsch Carroll in her analysis of Rembrandt's painting of Aristotle. In this regard see Deutsch Carroll, "Rembrandt's 'Aristotle,'" 55. I have tried to argue for a more complex interpretation of the face in the context of Dürer, see Benjamin, *Of Jews and Animals*, Chapter 4.

tion is nonetheless still inscribed within the logic of abandonment. "Obliqueness" and "ambiguity" should not be confused with indeterminacy.

In Rembrandt's 1629 drawing of Paul, while it may have been thought that the Saint is meditating, it is clear that his eyes are still held by the text. He is reading. And yet he is turning to read. While his body is facing away from the object being read his head is turned. He looks down and is reading. Having turned away he is turning back. There is of course the other possibility. Namely, that he has turned back one more time to a text that while past—seeing may have already supplanted reading—it is still the case that as a text it exerts a hold. Here there is a genuine ambiguity. Moreover, it may be that this now precise because delimited ambiguity has a structuring effect on the self-portrait under consideration. Though were that to be the case, it would be an ambiguity that occurred in reverse. Insofar as in looking away there is the possibility, as the book is open, still open, that it is still being read. And the heart of both moments—in part constitutive of the twofold possibility—is the non-necessity of the book as a site of reading. Moreover, it is the very structure of ambiguity that has the effect of constituting the book as mere book in literalizing reading both are positioned as having a non-necessary relation to life. Only when the book is coterminous with its stated presence—its literalization—does it close down the need for deliberation. This is the book that in its separation from life is "dead." What is meant by non-necessity therefore is the externalization of the book as book, and thus its non-presence as that which would define life. This non-necessity was captured in the conception of the book that was at work in the image of Jeremiah lamenting. Counter posed to such a conception of the book is the one being read by Hannah. The latter eschews the logic of abandonment the former is structured by it.

Finally, what then of the work as a self-portrait? The question to be addressed to any self-portrait concerns the conception of the self within it. Rather than continue with the assumption that a self-portrait is premised on a necessary impossibility, (without for a moment questioning the implicit truth of such a claim) the argument is going to be that once self-presentation involves the identification of that self with Paul then not only does that stage a particular relation to the image and thus is integral to the way the work presents itself as art—its being art as inscribed into its work as the work of art—it is equally the case that Paul's particularity has to be the locus of engagement. Here particularity means the motifs of Paul within Rembrandt's continual return to this figure. The Paul of the 1661 self-portrait exists as much within the frame that holds him, as he does in relation to the continuity of Rembrandt's concern both with Paul and the motif of reading. If any of these elements is a singularity it is because it exists within the network of relations, which here comprises, at the very minimum seeing, reading, blinding, that constitutes them as such. With the frame, there is a genuine ambiguity. While the interplay of reading and seeing prevail reading is literalized in the process. However, its consequences are precise. In the same way as self-presentation is impossible if the self were thought to have been presented completely—not only does Freud's discovery of the unconscious endure, Kantorowicz's discovery of the two bodies of the king continues to have extension—that insistent ambiguity, even an insistent "obliqueness" always has specific determinations.[35] Pursuing those determinations here would need to begin with Paul's turban. The thickness of the paint when contrasted with other elements calls attention to the work of paint as that which produces the image. Equally, the turban in pulling the hair back has exposed the face to light. The lit face becomes an after-effect of the way the turban is at work within the frame. The turban in allowing the face to be lit entails that the effect of the turban cannot be disassociated from the way light works to mark the conversion. Conversion is articulated within the logic of abandonment. The lit face therefore has to be located not just as connected to the ambiguity of the reading seeing relation but to the effect of that ambiguity, namely the literalization of the book and thus the staged separation of the relationship between the Book (thus law) and life. Conversion is the end of one life and the beginning of another. To begin however is to have abandoned. This is what is seen.

References

Alexander-Knotter, Mirjam. "Rembrandt's Hebrew." *Jahrbuch der Berliner Museen* 51 (2006): 25–32.
Alloa, Emmanuel, ed. *Penser l'image*. Dijon: Les presses du réel, 2010.
Badiou, Alain. *Saint Paul: La fondation de l'universalisme*. Paris: PUF, 1997.
Benjamin, Andrew. "The Inoperative Jew: Agamben's Paul." In *Place, Commonality and Judgment: Continental Philosophy and the Ancient Greeks*, by Andrew Benjamin, 136–59. London: Continuum, 2010.
Benjamin, Andrew. *Of Jews and Animals*. Edinburgh: Edinburgh University Press, 2010.
Benjamin, Andrew. "On the Image of Painting." *Research in Phenomenology* 41, no. 2 (2011): 181–205.
Benjamin, Andrew. *Art's Philosophical Work*. London: Rowman and Littlefield, 2015.
Benjamin, Andrew. "Barring Fear: Philo and the Hermeneutic Project." *Epoché* 20, no. 2 (2016): 307–26.

---

[35] Kantorowicz, *The King's Two Bodies*.

Binstock, Benjamin. "Rembrandt's Paint." *RES: Anthropology and Aesthetics* 36 (1999): 138–65.
Blumenkranz, Bernard. *Le juif médiéval au mirroir de l'art Chrétien*. Paris: Études Augustiniennes, 1966.
Bossuet, Jacques-Bénigne. *Discour sur l'histoire universelle*. Paris: Garnier Flammarion, 1966.
Braider, Christopher. "The Fountain of Narcissism: The Invention of Subjectivity and the Pauline Ontology of Art in Caravaggio and Rembrandt." *Comparative Literature* 50, no. 4 (1998): 286–315.
Burckhardt, Jacob. *Recollections of Rubens*. London: Phaidon Press, 1950.
Chapman, H. Perry. *Rembrandt's Self-Portraits: A Study in Seventeenth-Century Identity*. Princeton, NJ: Princeton University Press, 1990.
Derrida, Jacques. *Mémoires d'aveugle: L'autoportrait et autres ruines*. Paris: Réunion des Musées Nationaux, 1991.
Deutsch Carroll, Margaret. "Rembrandt's 'Aristotle': Exemplary Beholder." *Artibus et Historiae* 5, no. 10 (1984): 35–56.
Fredriksen, Paula. *Augustine and the Jews: A Christian Defense of Jews and Judaism*. New York: Doubleday, 2008.
Goldsmith, Steven. "Almost Gone: Rembrandt and the Ends of Materialism." *New Literary History* 45, no. 3 (2014): 411–43.
Heuer, Christopher P. "'Hundreds of eyes': Beyond Beholding in Riegl's 'Jakob van Ruysdael' (1902)." *Journal of Art Historiography* 9 (2013): 2–14.
Kantorowicz, Ernst H. *The King's Two Bodies: A Study in Mediaeval Political Theology*. Princeton, NJ: Princeton University Press, 1999.
Koerner, Joseph Leo. "Rembrandt and the Epiphany of the Face." *RES: Anthropology and Aesthetics* 12 (1986): 5–32.
Lackey, Douglas P. "Rembrandt and the Mythology of the Self-Portrait." *The Philosophical Forum* 37, no. 4 (2006): 439–55.
Lechte, John. *Genealogy and Ontology of the Western Image and its Digital Future*. London: Routledge, 2012.
Lorberbaum, Yair. *In God's Image: Myth, Theology, and Law in Classical Judaism*. Cambridge: Cambridge University Press, 2015.
Müller Hofstede, Justus. "An Early Rubens Conversion of St Paul: The Beginning of His Preoccupation with Leonardo's Battle of Anghiari." *The Burlington Magazine* 106, no. 732 (1964): 94–106.
Nadler, Steven. *Rembrandt's Jews*. Chicago: University of Chicago Press, 2003.
Olds, Clifton. "Jan Gossaert's 'St Luke Painting the Virgin': A Renaissance Artist's Cultural Literary." *Journal of Aesthetic Education* 24, no. 1 (1990): 89–96.
Olin, Margaret. "Forms of Respect: Alois Riegl's Concept of Attentiveness." *The Art Bulletin* 71, no. 2 (1989): 285–99.
Owens Schaefer, Jean. "Gossaert's Vienna 'Saint Luke painting' as an early reply to protestant Iconoclasts." *Notes in the History of Art* 12, no. 1 (1992): 31–37.
Pascal, Blaise. *Oeuvres Complètes*. Edited by Louis Lafuma. Paris: Seuil, 1963.
Petuchowski, Jakob J. "The Concept of 'Teshuvah' in the Bible and the Talmud." *Judaism* 17, no. 2 (1968): 175–85.
Riegl, Alois. *Das holländische Gruppenporträt*. Wien: WUV-Universitätsverlag, 1997.

Rosenzweig, Franz. "The Builders: Concerning the Law." In *On Jewish Learning*, edited by N.N. Glatzer, 72–94. Madison, WI: University of Wisconsin Press, 1955.

Rowe, Nina. *The Jew, The Cathedral and the Medieval City: Synagoga and Ecclesia in the Thirteenth Century*. Cambridge: Cambridge University Press, 2011.

Scholem, Gershom. *Tagebücher. 1917–1923*. Frankfurt am Main: Jüdischer Verlag, 2000.

Sommer, Benjamin D. *The Bodies of God and the World of Ancient Israel*. Cambridge: Cambridge University Press, 2009.

Zell, Michael. "Eduard Kolloff and the Historiographic Romance of Rembrandt and the Jews." *Simiolus: Netherlands Quarterly for the History of Art* 28, no. 3 (2000–2001), 181–97.

Jeffrey Bloechl
The Invention of Christianity: Preambles to a Philosophical Reading of Paul

Abstract: It is true that Paul is not the Messiah, but his prophet. Yet he receives a revelation for which there is not yet either stable understanding or conceptual articulation. As the first theologian of the Church, it is thus Paul who invents Christianity. But before this could be a matter of labor with concepts, it had already been a powerful experience that called for them. The Christianity that Paul invents in his preaching is born first in his heart, and moreover according to a violence that is well known. What could have prepared Paul for the events on the road to Damascus, and how are we able to later understand them? What concepts today, after his singular experience and the urgent preaching gave rise to a worldview, best enable us to hear some of what Paul heard and wished to have repeated in the life of faith? Such questions point beyond, or rather beneath the systematic explanations—dogmatic, speculative—that would have us render the meaning of faith in scientific propositions. Philosophers have their own reasons for contesting the rule of science, and some have appealed to Paul for material support (e.g., Agamben, Badiou). Others, however, have aimed first to simply understand Paul on his own terms (Heidegger, Breton). Which philosophy hearkens most closely to the experience of Paul? And how does its thinking meet the words that pass between the voice heard from on high and the voice in which it is announced?

Philosophers have never been without reasons for taking an interest in Paul. He is many things at once, yet urgently above all else the one thing that his faith in Jesus Christ confers on him. His preaching is at once familiar to those who know something of the Pharisaic preoccupation with law, and yet purports to open a way beyond the law. Whether or not it truly invents Christianity or only sharpens and adapts what Christ has always meant, it is proclaimed with a scope and, in that sense an ambition, such as that part of the world and its traditions had not seen before. According to what is likely the best known passage from the letters,

---

Scholarship on Paul is immense and diverse. For an understanding of the letters especially in historical, cultural and religious context, I have relied mainly on Koester, *Paul and His World*. My understanding of Paul's theology has drawn mainly on Dunn, *The Theology of the Apostle Paul*. The present work extends that of two previous texts: "Call and Conversion on the Road to Damascus," and "Law and Love According to Paul and Some Philosophers," the 2013 Simone Weil Lecture at the Australian Catholic University.

DOI 10.1515/9183110547467-004

Christ makes it such that we are neither Jew nor Greek, slave nor free, and male nor female (Gal. 3:28)—all of which implies, for Christ and for the preacher who identifies with him, a spiritual authority that is delivered from sufficient height as to reach everyone equally and at once. Perhaps emperors and tyrants had previously dreamed of claiming this kind of authority by force and bloodshed. Paul is capable of imagining a conquest that would occur in the soul. All of what it is for anyone to be human—in the world, among things, with others, before a god—would henceforth have a single meaning. History has not yet delivered its verdict on this idea, but its appearance constitutes a veritable "torsion" by which everything that came before is gathered together into a single vision that, once it has appeared, can neither be contained in something greater nor simply reversed and forgotten.[1] It is not certain whether our collective attempt to understand Paul will contribute to the working out of his original intention, or to the chastening of its ambition.

1 Paul Before He Preached

We should not forget that the oldest canonical Christian text that has been securely dated is Paul's *1 Thessalonians*.[2] Almost certainly written by 54 CE, what we call *1 Thessalonians* is also known to be Paul's first letter, and thus his first surviving effort at preaching his vision of faith in the God of Jesus Christ. To be sure, Paul was by then well aware of the details of Jesus's life, teaching, death and resurrection, but he had come by this in the form of narratives that would not be set down as what became the four canonical Gospels until another few decades had passed. And, of course, he would have been able to refine his sense of the facts in discussion with the original disciples Peter and James, who

---

[1] This word comes from the philosophy of history proposed by Voegelin, and it is of course his interpretation of Paul that I have in mind in this passage. See Voegelin, *Order and History*, 239–60.

[2] There are only two other significant candidates. It is thought that the "Q-source" for the gospels of Matthew and Luke may have been in circulation as early as 50 CE. The existence of this text, apparently a collection of sayings, is only strongly hypothetical, according to careful readings of *Matthew*, *Luke* and their one known and available source, *Mark*. In any case, there is no known copy. A small minority of scholars also set a date of approximately 50 CE for the Διδαχή, essentially a series of instructions on Christian (largely, sacramental) life. Some of the Church Fathers refer to the Διδαχή as early as the fourth century CE, but copies of the text had long disappeared until one was discovered in the late nineteenth century, in Constantinople. The majority of biblical scholars agree that the text was written after the emergence of the idea of a single authoritative gospel message (διδαχή: by the gospel).

he had met by 35 CE, a few years after his famous vision of the resurrected Christ when on the road from Jerusalem toward Damascus. All of this is to say that Paul's letters appear chronologically between Jesus himself and the canonical Gospels in which most believers first encounter him.³ Indeed, there is even some symmetry about this. *1 Thessalonians* was written about twenty years after the crucifixion, and about twenty years before the composition of the first such gospel, widely thought to be that of Mark, in roughly 72 CE.

Paul's only theme is the life of faith. As the spiritual and moral leader of the communities to whom he addresses himself, he develops his theme in a discourse of preaching and thus with a claim to authority. Needless to say, this is a claim that requires some justification. Paul does not hesitate to offer it. To the Galatians, he mentions the approval of Peter, James and, later, John, who had been taught by Jesus in person. They had heard the content of his preaching and recognized the grace that had been given to him (Gal. 2). But there is more. Whereas they could rely on experiences of Jesus in flesh and blood, his faith neither had nor needed any support from events visible according to the order of this world. Paul would have us see in this a sign of particular election. What the original disciples saw he had no need of, and what he saw they did not see. This is said perhaps more pointedly to the Corinthians: what he saw was Jesus after his death (1 Cor. 9), which is also to say after the Ascension in which Jesus ceased to be visible in ordinary terms. It is this special revelation, moreover, that furnishes him with the meaning of the "gospel" (εὐαγγέλιον) that he preaches (Gal. 1:12).

Perhaps inevitably, the question of Paul's vision of the life of faith, of his gospel, is led back to the question of the revelation (ἀποκαλύψεως) that is its source and principle. But this only raises further questions, since as everyone knows the revelation itself arrived all at once and overturned some of Paul's most fervent beliefs. Paul's first and in fact most detailed account is given in his *Galatians*, a full two decades after the event itself:

---

3 I am mindful of the scholarly distinction between "Paul's letters" and the "Pauline letters." The former group, comprised of texts about which there is considerable agreement that Paul himself is the author, includes: *1 Thessalonians, Galatians, 1 Corinthians, 2 Corinthians, Philippians, Philemon,* and *Romans*. Scholars disagree as to whether some of the six remaining letters have also been written, wholly or in part, by Paul, but they do recognize theological consistency throughout, hence the designation "Pauline." In the vast majority of my references, in this essay, I restrict myself to letters generally accepted as having been written by Paul himself (on some occasions with the help of *Timothy*), but on a few occasions, I do make exceptions.

> I did not receive [the gospel] from any man, nor was I taught it, but it came through a revelation of Jesus Christ. For you have heard of my former life in Judaism, how I persecuted the church of God violently and tried to destroy it; and I advanced in Judaism beyond many of my own age among my people, so extremely zealous was I for the traditions of my fathers. But when he who set me apart from before I was born and had called me through his grace, was pleased to reveal his Son to me, in order that I might preach him among the Gentiles, I did not confer among flesh and blood. (Gal 1:11–16)[4]

The Lukan author of *Acts*, writing about five decades after the event (and more than two decades after Paul's death), provides us with two accounts, first in the third person and later in a version that quotes Paul as he speaks just before his arrest in Jerusalem:

> Now as he journeyed he approached Damascus, and suddenly a light from heaven flashed about him. And he fell to the ground and heard (ἤκουσεν) a voice saying to him, "Saul, Saul, why do you persecute me?" And he replied, "Who are you, Lord?" And he said, "I am Jesus, whom you are persecuting: but rise and enter the city and you will be told what you are to do." The men who were traveling with him stood speechless, hearing (ἀκούοντες) the voice but seeing (θεωροῦντες) no one. Saul arose from the ground; and when his eyes were opened, he could see nothing; so they led him by the hand and brought him into Damascus. And for three days he was without sight and neither ate nor drank. (Acts 9:3–9)

> As I made my journey and drew near to Damascus, about noon a great light from heaven suddenly shone about me. And I fell to the ground and heard (ἤκουσα) a voice saying to me, "Saul, Saul, why do you persecute me?" And I answered, "Who are you, Lord?" And he said, "I am Jesus of Nazareth whom you are persecuting." Now those who were with me saw (ἐθεάσαντο) the light but did not hear (ἤκουσαν) the voice of the one speaking to me. And I said, "What shall I do, Lord?" And the Lord said to me, "Rise, and go into Damascus, and there you will be told all that is appointed for you to do." (Acts 22:6–10)

The two passages from *Acts* include a complication that Paul does not mention to the Galatians: not everyone present saw and heard the same things, or rather not everyone saw and heard everything. Paul saw a light from heaven, heard a voice, and knew it to be that of Jesus. His companions either saw the light and heard a voice, but saw no speaking person (Acts 9), or else saw the light but did not hear the voice (Acts 22). What was the experience of Paul's companions? It would teach us nothing at all about Paul's distinctive experience if we were to conclude only that Acts 9 and 22 are inconsistent and therefore, together, indecisive. But we may instead take the somewhat more promising view that the

---

[4] See 1 Cor. 15:2–8. All New Testament passages are taken from Nestle and Aland, *Greek-English New Testament*, which adopts the Revised Standard Version of the English translation.

difference between hearing the voice but not seeing the one who spoke (Acts 9) and not hearing the voice at all (Acts 22) comes down to the difference between two ways of hearing without truly understanding. In the narrative provided in Acts 9, it would thus be said that Paul's companions did hear a voice but somehow did not know its true source. Perhaps they did not even know it to be personal, but in any case they did not know it to be that of Jesus. And in Acts 22, Paul himself would tell us in a different way what is nonetheless essentially the same thing: his companions did not hear the voice of Jesus, though perhaps as far as he is concerned they heard nothing at all.[5] This of course raises the question of how it is that the only one of the group departing from Damascus who saw, heard and understood was specifically Paul. Nothing in the text suggests that he would have been uncommonly disposed to recognize and understand Jesus.

We may leave it to the theologians to speculate on God's reasons for such dramatic intervention in human affairs. Let us instead start with an interest in the nature and formation of the soul who will have undergone it. Who was this Paul who heard and saw Jesus on the road to Damascus, and whose understanding of what was said to him took the form of a gospel for all nations?

What Paul mentions only briefly, modern scholarship has explored in some detail. The man who would commit nearly all of his adult life to preaching that Jesus Christ had come and would come again for all human beings of good will had previously persecuted those who believed in Jesus with an intensity nourished by unusual religious zeal. While still in his late teens, he had left Tarsus for Jerusalem as a Pharisaic Jew whose commitment to the law took the form of particular adherence to a personal master. After four years spent applying himself to memorizing and understanding the entirety of the law, he emerged as a fledgling authority in his own right. It is uncertain whether he formally committed to a single master during those years of study, but in Acts 22:3 we do hear him report that while in Jerusalem he studied "at the feet of Gamaliel." Rabban Gamaliel the Elder had an immense influence during this period, in part because his teaching went beyond interpretation of the law to include an instruction by example that could involve virtually anything that he was seen to do. This had the effect of requiring any other teacher, and indeed any fledgling student, to take

---

5 In further support of this way of resolving the apparent contradiction between these two verses, I note that according to Liddell and Scott the root of the Greek word translated in both verses as "hear" (ἀκούω) can also mean "understand," particularly when, as in the case of Acts 22, the voice puts one in the accusative ("the voice speaking to me [...] the Lord said to me").

account not only of his scholarly work but also his every public act.⁶ Little is known of his specific teachings, but it is tempting to suppose that a particular judgment that is presented in Acts would have caused Paul some scruple in his persecution of the followers of Jesus. Learning that a group of Pharisees wished to put to death some of the apostles, Gamaliel is said to have spoken regretfully about other such events in recent times and taught that "in the present case I tell you, keep away from these men and let them alone; for if this plan or this undertaking is of men, it will fail; but if it is of God, you will not be able to overthrow them. You might even be found opposing God!" (Acts 5:38–39). Still, the fact that no such incident is recorded in any Jewish sources opens the way to some doubt about its authenticity, and one might well agree with Helmut Koester that such an expression of tolerance in fact makes it quite unlikely that the Paul we know would have been drawn to Gamaliel at all. The most one can say with confidence is that were Gamaliel to have made such a public statement, Paul would almost surely have heard of it.⁷

A more reliable record of Gamaliel's teaching appears in the *Mishnah*, where he is said to advise, "Secure a teacher for yourself [in religious questions], hold yourself far from doubt, and do not often give a tithe according to general valuation."⁸ For present purposes, the emphasis on finding a teacher is especially interesting. Even supposing that Paul will have stayed clear of Gamaliel himself, the advice, no doubt well known in Jerusalem, is likely to have resonated with him. As we have already noted, it is plainly consonant with the main lines of the Pharisaic Judaism to which he fervently adhered, and indeed specifically if a teacher was known to be capable of preserving the contours of the law. But more so, whereas in earlier times religious authority was invested in the role of judgeship, by the first century of the Common Era that role, along with kingship and ritual priesthood, had fallen into some decline. When we add to these developments the fact that already before this period it had become widely

---

6 The nature and impact of this teaching is expressed in the Talmud, where it is stated that when Gamaliel died "the honor [i.e., outward example] of the Torah ceased, and purity and piety became extinct" (*Sotah* 15.18).

7 Koester is less convincing when he proposes to reject the entire account of Paul's relation to Gamaliel given in *Acts*, largely because it will have said that, "Paul grew up in Jerusalem and studied there with the famous Rabbi Gamaliel I" (Koester, *Introduction to the New Testament*, 107). Here is what Acts 22:3 reports Paul saying: "I am a Jew, born at Tarsus in Cilicia, but brought up (ἀνατεθραμμένος) in this city [Jerusalem] at the feet of Gamaliel." To be sure, the verb ἀνατρέφω does suggest a sense of lineage and upbringing, but this is not necessarily a matter strictly of one's childhood home or early education. Nothing prevents us from understanding "brought up" in the moral and religious sense of the English "formation" or German *Bildung*.

8 *Pirkei Avot* 1.16.

thought that the age of the prophets had ended sometime around the fifth century before the Common Era, we have little difficulty surmising that Jewish life was more intent than ever on the preservation and application of law.[9] Accordingly, it does not reach far to think that at this time a Pharisaic Jew such as Paul would have had at least some positive disposition toward the appearance of a teacher who proposes to deepen one's relation to the law, no doubt both in mind and in practice.

Jesus of Nazareth was of course such a person. Is it necessary to repeat what is said about the law in his Sermon on the Mount (Matth. 5–7; cf. Luke 6:20– 36)? Uncertainty about the relation between that teaching and the anterior Jewish understanding surely was as great then as it is even now. The early followers of Jesus did not themselves know whether they remained in continuity with the Jewish faith of their births, or were separated from it by their faith in Jesus. Whenever and wherever their preaching seemed to indicate the latter, they were at minimum ostracized. This is hardly unexpected, and it underscores what is likely the real stake between Paul and those who he pursued with vengeance: a correct understanding of the law and God's righteousness. This is evidently how to understand the martyrdom of Stephen, where Paul, at that point still called Saul, is first encountered. A discourse that Stephen intends as an awakening of the Jewish people to the God of Jesus Christ takes the form of a lengthy characterization of their history as a record of selfish or slow-witted rejection of the prophets—whereupon, with Saul consenting, Stephen is stoned (Acts 7:53).

Now this much requires us to think that Saul was vehemently opposed to any attempt by the early followers of Jesus to disavow or break up the integrity of the law, as if all that had previously been taught and practiced either had always been in error or had been wholly discredited by something new. But it leaves open the possibility that he might eventually accept Jesus in a manner that does not take such a strictly negative view of the Jewish law. And in that case, his response to what he saw and heard on the road to Damascus would not be *conversion* so much as free *commitment* to a call toward greater realization of what God wills for us. As it happens, the scriptural accounts tell us precisely

---

9 It is widely thought that Malachi was the last of the prophets in Judaism, and sometimes suggested that he was conscious of the possibility that there would be none after him. By the time of Paul, roughly five centuries had passed since the book of Malachi had been composed, and indeed there had been no new prophets widely recognized by the Jewish people. However, many Christian interpreters take Malachi's promise that the prophet Elijah would return to announce the "coming of the great and dreadful day of the Lord" (Mal. 4:5) as referring to John the Baptist and Jesus Christ.

this. Saul is accused (he has been persecuting Jesus), and he is offered a higher path—moreover, this does not merely promise sanctification, but calls for an extraordinary mission.

None of this should lessen our sense of the drama on the road to Damascus, but instead draw particular attention to the personal encounter at its heart. We have already seen that in Gal. 1, Paul underlines it as the defining feature of his calling: God revealed to him his Son, and thereupon was everything decided. It is one thing to suppose, as we have done thus far, that Paul likely was disposed by certain elements in his own Jewish faith to see and understand the call of a teacher intent on an elevated relation to the divine will. It is another to gain some insight into the act and perspective by which that call becomes the defining feature of an entire life, as it surely did by the time of Paul's mission to the nations. By what commitment to Jesus Christ does that mission involve a new relation to the law?

The question at once provides any serious reading of Paul with its essential focus, and admits of two distinct approaches. One possibility would be to begin from the side of Paul's sense of a personal relation with Jesus Christ. This evident locus of this approach would be his numerous references to living "in Christ" (ἐν Χριστῷ; for instance, Rom. 8:1). Forms of this expression appear in all of the Pauline letters except *Titus*, and most often are exhortative in nature. The faithful are called to an identity and a path that is already known to the one who does the calling—which is to say that the passages that call and exhort find their center of gravity in the elevated experiences of the preacher himself. And indeed, Paul does not hesitate to make such claims. Their apogee is not to be overlooked. In *2 Corinthians*, he refers to a rapture that conducted him even beyond identification with his own body:

> I know a man in Christ (ἐν Χριστῷ) who fourteen years ago was caught up into the third heaven—whether in the body or out of the body I do not know, God knows. And I know that this man was caught up (ἁρπαγέντα) into Paradise—whether in the body or out of the body I do not know, God knows ... (2 Cor. 12:2–3)

This passage and others (for instance, 1 Cor. 14:18) famously led Albert Schweitzer to conclude that Paul's expression "in Christ" denotes a generally "mystical" form of participation. For Schweitzer, "'being in Christ' corresponds to, and as a state of existence *takes the place of* being in the flesh," and this transformation is found *in statu nascendi* already among the newly baptized.[10] The life of active faith would open itself to a new identity received from Christ and enacted in con-

---

[10] Schweitzer, *The Mystical Theology of Paul the Apostle*, 127, 115–16 (emphasis added).

stant intimacy with him. This interpretation does have the merit of drawing into a comprehensive account of the Pauline letters passages that one might otherwise wish to consider inessential and extravagant. Yet not every passage calling for participation in the life of Christ requires an appeal to Paul's mystical experiences. Thus, for example in *1 Thessalonians*, Paul contemplates the second coming of Jesus Christ, and extols a readiness for that moment:

> ... we who are alive, who are left, shall be caught up together (ἁρπαγησόμεθα) with [those who had already died] in the clouds to meet the Lord in the air; and so we shall always be with the Lord [...] So then let us not sleep, as others do, but let us keep awake and be sober [...] And we exhort you, brethren, admonish the idlers, encourage the fainthearted, help the weak, be patient with them all. (1 Thess. 4:17, 5:6 and 5:14)

Here, of course, the vision is robustly eschatological, so that incorporation of one's personhood into that of Christ is promised specifically in the form of what is always still to come. And the fact that one must wait, or better anticipate, requires the cultivation of practices that immediately imply a theory of community. This suggests a somewhat different sense of participation, and no doubt a somewhat different sense of the body of Christ than is profiled by an emphasis on mystical intimacy. Is there a necessary contradiction between the two? It is not impossible that when Paul invokes a community to which each person belongs uniquely and indispensably, he has done nothing more than "democratized" the heart of his own mystical experience: Jesus Christ calls each person singularly to himself, and the universality of this singular calling is the condition of genuine plurality.[11] This much is still in keeping with the biblical experience of kinship: to live in Christ is to live as children of God. This can also be expressed in the register of metaphysics: to participate in the body of Christ is also to belong together.

But what is the nature of this belonging? And what then of the community in which it is enacted—the community in which life in Christ must somehow also inform a life among one's fellow believers? What does faith enjoin for our relations with one another? Such questions cannot be pursued without careful reflection on the law. This would be the focus of a second approach to reading Paul. And this second approach has attracted the interest of some recent philosophers.

---

[11] I borrow the thought of a "democratization of mysticism" from Marguerat, *Paul in Acts and in His Letters*, 175–76, citing Luz, "Paulus als Charismatiker und Mystiker."

2 Paul between Jerusalem and Rome

Though it has seemed certain that Paul's formation as a Pharisaic Jew led him to considerable interest in the question of the law, we find that in his letters he develops the theme only gradually. *1 Thessalonians* commits only two final chapters to some general remarks concerning moral life. *2 Thessalonians* preaches that love of God is fulfillment of the law, but leaves unsettled the question of whether or quite how the law might nonetheless continue to serve. In 1 Cor. 5–7, the moral dimension of a life making ready for the second coming is developed in considerable detail, with prescriptions concerning various features of the life of the flesh. But this letter also contains Paul's remarkable image of the church of God as the body of Christ (1 Cor. 12:12–30), in which moral action is no longer overridingly a matter of readiness for the second coming of Jesus, but equally a matter of relations among members of the community. The image goes far to avoid reducing order in the lives of the faithful to the dictates of a worldly political hierarchy. Plainly, it is the resurrected Christ and not some worldly potentate who is the head. This means both that the community as such transcends its existence as a worldly totality, and that each part has a unique importance secured outside and beyond its place in any such totality. In this much, the image is much in keeping with the idea, itself thoroughly eschatological, that Christ's reign and whatever it holds in store for the faithful are not merely of this world. It is also easily joined to the gospel accounts of Jesus's temptation in the desert, where he makes it clear that he is not intent on a kingdom of this world (Matth. 4, Luke 4).

Of course, it is not at all certain that the people in Corinth would have heard these things, and in any case Paul's concern for them was not restricted to spiritual matters alone. His intention was not only to help them understand the community centered on Jesus, but also to clearly distinguish it from, specifically, the very different community centered on Rome that had to be reckoned with. This introduces an interesting complication to his attempt to articulate the Christian relation to law: Paul's faith in Christ simultaneously not only conducts him through and beyond his previous Pharisaic Jewish conception of law, but also holds open an essential distance from the political conception enforced especially by Rome.

What does it mean to be part of the body of Christ? It is to participate in the life in which each person belongs to all the others and gives oneself to all the others, just as Jesus himself belongs to each and all and gives himself to each and all. This would be the social and political expression of the love that Paul calls ἀγάπη, and indeed in the "more excellent way" (1 Cor. 12:31) by which we might understand what is meant by life in the body of Christ. From this there follows a lengthy attempt to characterize love: patient and kind, it "bears all things, believes all things, hopes all things, endures all things" (1 Cor. 13:7)— in other words, places the one who loves second to the one who is loved, and this by virtue of the example and the promise of Jesus who is Christ for the believer. This, then, is the "law of Christ" (Gal. 6:2), a law not written according to the desires of the flesh or norms of particular communities. It is a law beyond law, a law that renders inoperative the law that only prohibits and thereby incurs wrath and resentment, and that transcends the limits of a law that binds together only those who belong to a people or a nation. With regard to the Jewish law— and this most assuredly comes first, at least as far as Paul is concerned—those who give themselves in faith to Jesus Christ are "discharged from the law (κατηργήθημεν ἀπὸ τοῦ νόμου)" (Rom. 7:6). And to be sure, the call to ἀγάπη discharges one from the law not in the sense of annulation or rejection but fulfillment, as realization of what obedience to the law has always sought (Gal. 5:14, Rom. 13:8; cf. Matth. 22:40). As for Roman law, it would seem that if the law that transcends all worldly laws is defined by a call to ἀγάπη, then the attempt to preach it, and to convene the community in which all members would live by it, is political strictly to the degree that any disavowal of politics is nonetheless, or still, a political gesture.[12]

Has it been made sufficiently clear to us what would define the community of a love that transcends law? An insistently political discourse has thought to advance our understanding by opposing it to any possible totality. Agamben

---

[12] This is the point of application for Jacob Taubes's thoroughly political reading of *Romans*, in which Paul will have at once declared war on Rome and positioned himself as the rightful heir to Moses. To sure, between Rome and Moses, it is undoubtedly a question of the law, and from a depth that Taubes as much as anyone has helped us to explore. But as Christians necessarily contend, Paul addresses himself to Roman and Mosaic law only on the condition of a faith in Jesus Christ as God by which alone, he claims, the law may be transcended. Yet this objection is not without its own complexity. On one hand, it is not evident that the theological notion of an "obedience of faith" is only a "polemical variant of obedience of laws," as Taubes contends (*The Political Theology of Paul*, 14). When a Christian theologian like Karl Rahner defines faith by *obedientia*, he emphasizes its root sense of receptivity to a revelation that is heard (*ob-audire*). Perhaps this suggests an argument for the distinctiveness of a receptivity that is not, contrary to Taubes's usage, immediately juridical and political (see Rahner, *Hearer of the Word*; and Rom. 1:15 and 16:26). On the other hand, it should not be assumed too quickly that Paul himself ever truly refers to Jesus as God. Within the limits of the one letter to which Taubes confines himself, the passage in question must be Rom. 9:4: "They [my brethren, my kinsmen by race] are Israelites, and to them belong the sonship, the glory, the covenants, the giving of the law, the worship and the promises." For an account of the exegetical difficulties and debate, see Dunn, *The Theology of Paul the Apostle*, 255–57.

works from a conviction that the State is by definition and in all cases a repository of oppressive force, with the law as its violent extension into human life. Subjectivity is this subjection to the law, but pristine life is found at the underside of every system of norms. Agamben's interest in Paul lies mainly with the "messianic time" by which a hoping being is oriented to a futurity that exceeds that of the not-yet-now. Messianic life is life that always already refuses any order by aiming beyond it, and thus life whose temporality comprises its uniqueness. Paul will have discovered this in himself thanks to his encounter with Jesus, and then proclaimed it as the general condition for all human life. In turn, Agamben proposes to liberate the bare form of messianic life by way of a general critique of politics, and conversely to take it as the basis from which to criticize any and all order that would impose limits on it. It should not pass notice that none of this requires recourse to the Jesus in whom Paul invests his very identity, since it will suffice simply that Paul has seen what he has seen. Agamben is far from unaware of this. Indeed, in his "commentary" on *Romans*, he dissociates Paul's use of the word χριστός from any necessary reference to the person named Jesus.[13] The hydraulics of this shift are striking. As Paul is raised in importance, Jesus is lowered, and since there is no pretense that Paul himself is in any sense divine the messianic uniqueness of Jesus is thus evacuated, through him, into all humanity. The result is a plurality that verges on atomism.

As for the moral life that this would involve, Agamben considers it to lie in the possibilities opened up by a realization that in our original condition, as bare life, we are not reducible to the identity imposed on us by the State. He is thus takes Paul's advice to live "as if not" (ὡς μή) attached to the world (for instance, 1 Cor. 7) as a call to liberation from the law, rather than according to the eschatological vision we found in Paul's own texts. For Agamben, activity in accord with the conditions of messianic life is activity neither subject to the law nor defined by an urge to negate it. Of course, this suggests that individual life is essentially decentered except or until it submits to totalization. Here, then, is another claim that claims the support of Paul's preaching and yet opposes it on a central matter: for Agamben, salvation is in fact liberation, and the political significance of Pauline Christianity lies essentially in promoting it. This is not without an equally striking implication for the law. According to Agamben, when Paul speaks of being "discharged from the law," we are to understand that this would take the form of messianic life acting in full agreement with its own original innocence with respect to any order. At that level, or in that condition, we are without law, *anomial*. And yet in all cases the law has already been imposed.

---

13 See Agamben, *The Time that Remains*, 15–18.

Love, such as Agamben is interested in it, would then lie in an emancipatory dissent from the law that imposes order and identity, so that it is one and the same thing to withdraw from the law and to open oneself to the uniqueness of each life that it suppresses. Here then the result is a moral practice that appears subservient to political intervention, or else is indistinct from it. And it goes without saying that openness to the uniqueness of bare life falls well short of the active commitment invested in what Paul means by ἀγάπη. In the Pauline letters, love goes out toward one's fellow human being in her specificity, in order to positively transcend the limits of the law.

On some of these points, Badiou's political reading of Paul is to be preferred. Like Agamben, Badiou comes to Paul from an interest in liberating us from totalization. And whereas Agamben envisions a plurality of messianic lives, Badiou contends, at slight but important distance from him, that radical and irreducible particularity is in fact the universal condition of our humanity. His attempt to verify such a claim centers on an attempt to account for newness, as the index of particularity, without reducing it to a variation or improvisation on what is already familiar. Thus, particularity is disclosed in events of newness that are, however, quickly absorbed into the pattern of what is already familiar, and in that sense old. In the terms of Badiou's ontology, "event" therefore signifies the eruption of newness into the domain of "being," where it appears and is named. But this can make a lasting difference only if the interrupting event is named in a manner that does not immediately falsify it by submitting it to what would become a subsequent totalizing interpretation. According to Badiou, history does include instances in which an event has been named without submitting it to totalization, and their presence in our cultural memory raises the possibility of awakening humanity to its fundamental particularity.[14] He finds one such instance in Paul's fidelity to the event that is Jesus as Christ.

This is already enough for us to understand that Christianity is of interest to Badiou only in its structure, and not with regard to its specific content. As he reads Paul, the letters depict Jesus as Christ insofar as Jesus interrupts the familiar cadence of being as it had been defined by Jewish and Roman law. Or, again in the terms of his ontology, Paul "names" the Christ-event in a manner that makes it available to us by invoking a faith that cannot be reduced to adherence to any worldly principles or set of laws. As one might expect in such an argument, what thus "relieves us of the law" is said to be the promise of a resurrec-

---

14 These principles are elaborated in Badiou, *Being and Event*. In a brief chapter on Pascal, Badiou develops a conception of the "Christ-event" that anticipates a central feature of his interpretation of Paul. See, e.g., ibid., 214, 218, 220.

tion that defies all worldly order.¹⁵ Hence is Badiou content to agree with many theologians that the resurrection is neither verifiable nor falsifiable. But as far as he is concerned this does not matter, and in fact it is strictly in accord with the very nature of an event to defy assimilation to what is already known.¹⁶

This once again grants Paul an importance that rivals that of Jesus, since the event becomes an event in the fullest sense—it becomes available to us in a stable form that can truly make a difference—only through the genius of the Pauline discourse. Interestingly, Badiou is nonetheless willing to think that its origin does lie in Paul's sense of a privileged relation with Jesus. But this is once again a matter only of structure, rather than any appreciation of theological or existential elements. And on closer inspection, this is also the site of a subtle but important difference with Agamben. In order for Agamben's Paul to call us to the messianicity of bare life, he will have heard a call from beyond every order, or else the call is only another feature of some order. Badiou has the somewhat different notion that Paul succeeds in making available the Christ-event only to the degree that he manages to make it available without submitting its newness to the regime of laws already prevailing wherever he preaches. Thus, for Agamben, Paul's preaching consists essentially in *witness* to the underside of the law, but for Badiou that preaching is defined by an active *refusal* that turns us fully against the law. If Agamben understands Paul, and all human life, as fundamentally ano*nomial, Badiou has in view a conception of subjectivity that is instead actively *anti*nomial. Concerning *Paul himself*, let us simply note that he considers Christ to be the "fulfillment" (τέλος) of the law (Rom. 10:4)—a notion that is difficult to reconcile with claims that the law suppresses life or opposes it in a manner that requires revolt. This is already enough to make it quite clear that the plurality of those whose faith transcends conformity to law is not the plurality of those whose suffering urges withdrawal from law, and not the plurality of those whose outrage would have them refuse it.

Badiou's position does flirt with atomism to the degree that it aims at a particularity anterior to any unity, but this is partly addressed by his philosophy of the event. In his work on Paul, the event is assimilated to the Christian notion of grace. The notion is found to operate on two levels. There is the Christ-event itself, in which a radically new content is received and preached without submitting it to the prevailing order. There is also the gift of oneself to another who is transformed by it in what Badiou is willing to recognize as neighbor-love. In both cases, there is absolute freedom of movement, and unqualified breach of every

---

15 Badiou, *Saint Paul*, 48. The expression is evidently a rendering of the Pauline καταργεῖν.
16 Ibid., 45.

horizon. Radical difference is crossed and lives are joined in the birth of meaning. But also in both cases, the original initiative must await completion in an interpretation and response. Just as the Christ-event stood in need of the Pauline discourse, so the act of selfless love awaits pure accession by the beloved. It remains for the one to whom it is given to carry out the labor required in order to fulfill what then truly qualifies as grace. But herein lies a serious problem, for according to the dictates of Badiou's central concepts, love is complete only when and if it is registered in a manner that breaks fully with any prior understanding. Whether this is a matter of responding to God or to a loving friend, it would mean, in the final instance, addressing oneself to what one knows only as *not me*. This would be to conduct oneself to great distance from what we have found in Paul's own texts. It would also be to accept as the course of love what could not confidently attempt more than the refusal of everything that has been gathered first to oneself. But then it is not clear that such a love could ever be more than the simple—and rather empty—contrary of self-love.

Now as problematic as these two appropriations of Paul clearly are, they serve well to bring out the revolutionary force of the call for an experience of community and moral life that would not be answerable to strictly political authority even while nonetheless staking a claim over how we are to comport ourselves in this world. Or better, precisely because they do so far and yet prove unable to admit the vital and active nature of a love in which Paul's own vision would be actualized, they beg the question of a Pauline politics of love taken simply on its own terms. The question is more than historical, as if seeking nothing more than a fair account and equal time for Paul himself. We also owe it to the presence of the philosophers in this discussion that we may wonder whether Paul might even have a better account of some important matters.

3 Paul and the Community of Love

The most familiar reading will suffice to frame some concluding thoughts. Matters have become clear enough for us to recognize two guidelines along which to pursue an account of Paul's conception of the community of a love, *before and apart from any need to profile it in an explicitly political manner*. On one hand, we have recurred more than once to what may now be called the Christological "fulcrum" by which Paul arranges concepts and deploy images in the service of his mission.[17] Whatever else it means for him to live "in Christ," it always marks the

---

[17] I take this expression from Dunn, *The Theology of Paul the Apostle*, 722–29.

center of gravity for our being before God and with others. On the other hand, we have already found in 1 Cor. 12 a rich text in which Paul speaks quite explicitly about community without an overriding interest in promoting the quintessentially political development of hierarchy and authority. We have just seen where the latter interpretation concludes, and what it costs. All of this returns us to the question of just what Paul does intend, or what he has in view, such as he is led to speak of the community in terms of a body and its members? We find an interesting answer to this question if, disabused of the political interpretation, we attend to the fact that Paul's imagery of body and members appeals directly to our physical, even sensuous nature, as perhaps as what is most familiar to us. What we then hear is a call most urgently to a transformation of our basic attitude and orientation in the world—again, before any question of the possible ramifications for politics. Many scholars of Paul will find this way of reading the passage rather evident, as they will the claim that it is confirmed specifically by the recourse to imagery that probably registered powerfully with the Corinthians, and indeed to any human being: our struggles with what in the vernacular we still call "the flesh." Paul's conception is uncommonly rich. His word "flesh" designates something like a dynamism of human being by which we are attached to the world and everything in it—and to that degree precisely not to the God of Jesus Christ. We are helped to understand the proper depth of this idea in Eph. 2:11–12, where the focus is once again on our unity and distinctiveness as members of one body:

> ... remember that at one time you Gentiles in the flesh [....] were at that time separated from Christ, alienated from the commonwealth of Israel, and strangers to the covenant of promise, having no hope and without God in the world (ἐλπίδα μὴ ἔχοντες καὶ ἄθεοι).

Here the important point lies not to so much in a contrast between the earlier faithlessness of the Gentiles with their subsequent, true faith in Christ, as in a manner of distinguishing a way of life captivated by the flesh from another way of life that becomes possible to the degree that one is free of that captivation. What is it to be a Gentile? In *Ephesians*, it is to be not only without affiliation to the "commonwealth" (πολιτείας) of Israel, but also to be "separated" (ἀπηλλοτριωμένοι) from Christ, and therefore without kinship to the covenant of promise given first to the Jews and, in their line, to the followers of Jesus. To be Gentile in this sense—to be Gentile "in the flesh"—is to be without hope (ἐλπίδα) and thus, ultimately, *without God in the world*. The Greek word for this phrase is somewhat tighter than the translation indicates (it is also unique in all of the Pauline writings): to be Gentile in the flesh is to live in a world that is ἄθεος. To be sure, when the letter refers to "Gentiles in the flesh" (ἔθνη ἐν σαρκί) one has the impression that a specific group of people is singled out; yet the manner in which this is done plainly indicates a much more general possibility for the human condition. Otherwise, the very aim of preaching to the Gentiles at all makes little sense. They were "Gentiles by birth," as some translations have it, but this circumstance clearly does not rule out another, more spiritual possibility defined by faith in Christ. And this other possibility would be reached by opening oneself to a promise unforeseeable from within the horizon defined by flesh.

Conversely, the call to a new attitude or orientation would seem bound to entail another horizon entirely. Furthermore, as the phenomenologists have reminded us, a horizon is not merely a frame or sphere within which to know something; before that, more fundamentally, it is an openness that is always defined by the particular mood through which we see whatever appears there. At the psychological level, the world and everything in it appear differently to us when we are depressed than they do when we are happy. Each mood thus seems to attune our world in a manner that other moods do not.[18] This can also be said of moods, attunements and horizons that define entire ways of life, and not only psychological outlooks. With regard to the Pauline notions that preoccupy us here, the horizon that belongs to the way of life that is captivated by the flesh would proceed from a distinctive mood that is defined by its own attunement—and all of this would give way to a different mood defined by a different attunement belonging to the life of faith in Christ (joy, for example). It probably goes without saying that for the one who comes to believe in Christ the world appears in a new light.

Let us consider for a moment the nature of our relations to the flesh and the world as they appear from the perspective of Paul's mission. Captivated by the flesh, we take the world to be the first and last condition of our being, so that what appears to us shows up solely in the light of our interest, and we take ourselves to be the focal point of its meaning. Insofar as we are committed to faith in Christ, those relations are opened up to admit a higher relation with God. This cannot mean that we no longer are in the world, and not even that the faithful would be immune to a recurrent impulse to seize upon the world or parts of the world as if they come before God. It makes better sense to think that the flesh is *transformed* in faith, rather than being simply extinguished by it. When we mortals might strip off our old nature, or old self, and put on the new (Col. 3:10–11), we do not kill the flesh, but sanctify it. The flesh is, as it were, inscribed in another register, so that the visceral dimension of our being is also more than vis-

---

[18] See Heidegger, *Being and Time*, § 29.

ceral. Simone Weil captures this well when in her effort to understand Paul's notion of the old and new self she juxtaposes Phil. 3:19 and Col. 3:12: there are those among us who are captivated by the flesh, and "whose God is in their belly," and there are others who embrace Christ and "put on, thus, bowels of mercy."[19]

Now this manner of taking up the old into the new also defines a Pauline relation to the law that is not simply, as the more strictly political reading is in danger of suggesting, a rejection of one authority in favor of higher one, even if at the end of the day it would turn out to lie among one's own inner capacities. When Paul speaks negatively about the law, he generally has in mind law in the sense of letter and judgment, which is to say the law by which sin is defined by transgression of explicit prohibitions. Such a law, or perhaps better, such a *relation to* the law is deficient in two respects. As Paul himself helps us to see, it leaves us perpetually confronted with our own incapacity to fully justify ourselves—that is, confronts us with our everlasting sinfulness, so that we are at risk of losing hope. But we might add that it also leaves the law itself exposed to the strange possession by the flesh that issues in moral perversion: the moral masochist, for example, has taken possession of the law in the form of enjoying its severity. Yet for all of this, our relation to the law can also be positive. The law can educate and instruct us in a righteousness that goes farther than refraining from transgression. Far from overlooking this, Paul seems to have it presently in mind when he insists on the holiness of the law (Rom. 7:12) and makes clear that he himself does not propose to abolish the law but only to properly uphold it (Rom. 3:31). We have already taken notice of what this means in the form of Paul's reference to the law of Christ. Christ enjoins us to love God and love one another, as the foundation on which rests the law of the patriarchs and prophets. One loves one's neighbor not beyond all limits and without reason, but immediately and essentially as who he is, before and beyond what one may otherwise want from him.

The Christological specification of this thought is well known. For Paul, it is the self-emptying Christ who introduces us, in recognizable terms, to the God who is unconditional love. It is also well known that the love of one another for which the Christian community is so frequently noted is incomprehensible apart from a belief in each member that God loves her specifically, personally as herself. And this, let us note, leaves us philosophers to consider the thought

---

19 Weil, *Notebooks of Simone Weil*, 209–10. We are accustomed to audacious language from Weil, but in the present case she merely sides with an older tradition for which conversion to spirit must entail drama for the body.

that genuine plurality and a notion of absolute goodness are not necessarily opposed. To the contrary, one might even entertain the possibility that each necessarily implies the other.

References

Agamben, Giorgio. *The Time that Remains. A Commentary on the Letter to the Romans.* Translated by Patricia Dailey. Stanford, CA: Stanford University Press, 2005.
Badiou, Alain. *Saint Paul: The Foundation of Universalism.* Translated by Ray Brassier. Stanford, CA: Stanford University Press, 2003.
Badiou, Alain. *Being and Event.* Translated by Oliver Feltham. London: Continuum, 2005.
Bloechl, Jeffrey. "Call and Conversion on the Road to Damascus. An Exercise in the Hermeneutics of Surprise." In *Surprise: An Emotion*, edited by Anthony J. Steinbock and Natalie Depraz. Dordrecht: Springer, forthcoming.
Dunn, James D. G. *The Theology of the Apostle Paul.* Grand Rapids, MI: Eerdmans, 1998.
Heidegger, Martin. *Being and Time.* Translated by John Macquarrie, and Edward Robinson. London: SCM Press, 1962.
Koester, Helmut. *Introduction to the New Testament. Volume 2. History and Literature of Early Christianity.* Berlin: De Gruyter, 2000.
Koester, Helmut. *Paul and His World: Interpreting the New Testament in Its Context.* Minneapolis, MN: Fortress Press, 2007.
Liddell, and Scott, *A Greek-English Lexicon.* Oxford: Oxford University Press, 1945.
Luz, Ulrich. "Paulus als Charismatiker und Mystiker." In *Exegetische und theologische Studien. Gesammelte Aufsätze II*, edited by Traugott Holtz, 75–93. Leipzig: Evangelische Verlaganstalt, 2010.
Marguerat, Daniel. *Paul in Acts and in His Letters.* Tübingen: Mohr Siebeck, 2013.
Nestle, E., and K. Aland, eds. *Greek-English New Testament.* Stuttgart: Deutsche Bibelgesellschaft, 1990.
Rahner, Karl. *Hearer of the Word.* New York: Continuum Press, 1994.
Schweitzer, Albert. *The Mystical Theology of Paul the Apostle.* London: Black, 1931.
Taubes, Jacob. *The Political Theology of Paul.* Translated by Dana Hollander. Edited by Aleida Assman and Jan Assmann in conjunction with Horst Folkers, Wolf-Daniel Hartwich, and Christoph Schulte. Stanford, CA: Stanford University Press, 2004.
Voegelin, Eric. *Order and History. Volume IV. The Ecumenic Age.* Baton Rouge, LA: Louisiana State University Press, 1974.
Weil, Simone. *Notebooks of Simone Weil.* Translated by Arthur Wills. London: Routledge, 2004.

Ben Vedder
Heidegger's Hermeneutics of Paul

Abstract: This essay follows Heidegger's interpretation of Saint Paul. First I present Heidegger's concern with facticity and the way he sees the need of a philosophy that is connected with and comes forward out of human facticity. This leads to a philosophy that tries to avoid petrified concepts and is a-theistic in principle. Classical philosophy is not able to do justice to human facticity and human historicity. Therefore, the question arises of how a philosophy has to be in order to make human facticity understandable? For Heidegger, the early Christian texts of Saint Paul are an expression of the experience of human facticity. Especially the notion that Christ will come like a thief in the night expresses the unpredictability and the suddenness of the future. This also raises the question of whether an atheistic philosophy can understand religion. For Heidegger, an atheistic philosophy is the only possibility for philosophy, also for a philosophy of religion. The unpredictability of the future is expressed in early Christianity also there where Paul writes about the "as if not." The "as if not" expresses that humans live not as completely open to the unpredictable future but still have to use concepts that are framed already on forehand. This means that human self-understanding remains always a vulnerable and broken understanding. This applies also to the hermeneutics of religion.

1 How to Understand Heidegger's Hermeneutics of Paul?

Insofar philosophy asks for presuppositions, it might be understood as a philosophical hermeneutics. Can we read Heidegger's explication of the letters of Paul as a hermeneutics of religion? Can an atheistic philosophy understand religion? To this Heidegger answers unequivocally: "Philosophy, in its radical, self-posing questionability, must be atheistic as a matter of principle."[1] Moreover, according to Heidegger, the ultimate is not found in a highest being but in the facticity of

---

[1] Heidegger, *Phenomenological Interpretations of Aristotle*, 148. We are referring here mainly to Heidegger, *The Phenomenology of Religious Life*. This is a translation of Heidegger, *Phänomenologie des religiösen Lebens*. The first part of this book, "Introduction to the Phenomenology of Religion" presents the text of a lecture course by Heidegger presented in Freiburg during the winter semester of 1920/21 and the summer semester of 1921.

DOI 10.1515/9183110547467-005

life, and this should be approached as the ultimate. Of old, philosophy was not involved with factical life and factical experience of life. "Insofar as philosophizing transcends factical experience, it is characterized by the fact that it deals with higher objects and the highest of them, with the 'first and ultimate things.'"[2] But the specificity of Heidegger's approach is that he does not want a theoretical approach of the factical experience of life, although the theoretical is understood as the highest attitude in normal philosophy. Heidegger's opinion is that the factical experience of life is the beginning and end of philosophy. This also holds for a philosophy of religion.

According to Heidegger the relation between metaphysics and religion is no longer obvious. They are even expressly separated. From the beginning of his lecture course "Introduction into the Phenomenology of Religion," he understands the historical as a core phenomenon of religion. In this lecture course Heidegger presents an explication of the basic event of the Christian experience of life, as it appears in the letters of Paul. He especially pays attention to 1 Thess. 4 and 5. In this earliest writing of the New Testament a decisive moment of the Christian experience of life becomes visible by the question of the second coming of Christ. Christ comes suddenly like a thief in the night, as Paul writes: "for your yourselves know perfectly well that the day of the Lord comes like a thief in the night" (1 Thess. 5:2).[3] Heidegger was strongly touched by this unpredictability, this suddenness, for which one should wait in a sober way, which he interprets in terms of the καιρός. The kairological characteristics of time that speaks from this passage determine time as something that cannot be calculated or mastered. Rather, by the future, the time of καιρός presents a threat. It belongs to the history of the actualization of life, which cannot be objectified.[4] In the moment of καιρός one can lose one's life; therefore, life as a whole is at stake here. Every attempt to master or to control this moment is a failure of the attitude with which it has to be encountered.

It is important to find in factical experience of life motives for the self-understanding of philosophy. Out of this self-understanding the task of a hermeneutics of religion can appear. For Heidegger, this is drenched in the problem of historicity. Here also is the danger to fall into the objective world of science because there is the tendency in philosophy to withdraw from historicity. It seems that one wants to defend oneself as it were against history. For a philosophical approach this is even more problematic because philosophy of old tried to get

---

2 Heidegger, *Phenomenology of Religious Life*, 11.
3 We see this as well in the synoptic gospels, cf. Matth. 24:42–44; Luke 12:39ff., Mark 13:33–37.
4 Pöggeler, *Der Denkweg Martin Heideggers*, 36.

rid of history and not to sink into it by looking for eternal truth. The protection takes place mainly by neutralizing it as an object. It becomes an object in which one is theoretically involved.

The theoretical attitude is an attitude, which tries to keep away from history and defends oneself against it. Nevertheless, this protection against history leads to insight in the meaning of historicity. The possibility appears to resist the attitude of theorizing historicity and to bring to light the true unrest of life. One has to try to reveal the phenomenon of worry in factical life.[5]

In order to do this Heidegger develops a specific terminology for the phenomenological approach in order to resist the theoretical approach of historicity. He introduces the concept of the formal indication. It belongs to the theoretical aspect of phenomenology: "The problem of the '*formal indication*' belongs to the 'theory' of the phenomenological method itself; in the broad sense, to the problem of the *theoretical*, of the theoretical act, the phenomenon of *differentiating*."[6] The formal indication however is as an attitude different from the theoretical attitude. Philosophy as theoretical attitude is not suitable to thematize history and religion with respect to factical life. In this article, I will deal with the technical explications of this notion of the formal indication. But I might try to show the difference with the theoretical approach. In a theoretical approach of, for example, love, it is possible to write a book about it even if you never had the experience of loving someone. On a personal level love is then meaningless. This is what Heidegger tries to avoid in his approach, because you understand this approach only out of and within a concrete life experience, out of and within a factical situation. The word "love" is meaningful because you have the experience of loving someone. You know what the word love means out of your own life experience: you know perfectly well what love means out of your own life experience. Based on that you can share that experience and that kind of knowledge with others. This "knowing perfectly well" refers to the situational facticity out of which you or we understand something.

Therefore, according to Heidegger, philosophy itself with its theoretical approach is a problem. We continue to question the specific way of thinking that should be adopted in philosophy because this questioning itself is part of philosophy as such. Heidegger writes: "Philosophy's constant effort to determine its own concept belongs to its authentic motive."[7] The question of what philosophy

---

5 Heidegger, *Phenomenology of Religious Life*, 35.
6 Ibid., 38.
7 Ibid., 7.

is, is a question that every philosopher needs to keep asking himself. This is the reason why Heidegger feels free to develop his own approach.

The answer cannot be given by giving a description of models of philosophy, be they past or present. Nor is it a question of the actual state of affairs in philosophy. According to Heidegger the way in which we philosophize, with the entire conceptual framework of philosophy, as we know it, produces an approach that blocks the very entrance to really authentic philosophy. The conceptual framework itself stands in the way of authentic philosophy. In Heidegger's opinion, philosophy has to start from "the situation of understanding" of the philosopher. But he is also of the opinion that philosophy, as a theoretical framework, hinders access to the situation of understanding. This makes the question of method a very important one in philosophy.

In order to philosophize authentically, the right entrance to the situation of understanding needs to be found. Once we really start looking at it we see that philosophy is an activity; it is something we do or perform. We learn what philosophy is by performing the activity of philosophizing. It is a way of being. The way of being from which we start to philosophize—this is the "situation" of our philosophy—Heidegger calls "facticity." We philosophize from our factical situation. In a certain sense, this word preludes to what Heidegger will interpret as "historicality." Philosophy belongs to the facticity of life in so far as it tries to find its own situation of understanding; philosophy has to clarify the facticity of life. In asking about the specific nature and task of philosophy, the philosopher also has to query the way of being of factical existence itself. To clarify philosophy, it is necessary to clarify factical life, because from there we can get insight into the factical situation of philosophy. Philosophy becomes, as it were, an introduction to the factical experience of life.[8] The philosophical entrance to life and the facticity of life are interconnected in Heidegger's analysis.

Thus, philosophy starts from factical life; it is a way of being of factical life, but it also returns to factical life, because factical life is a subject of philosophical query. Factical life has to be understood from the experience of life, but the experience of factical life is oriented and explicated in different directions. Heidegger writes:

> Philosophy's departure as well as its goal is factical life experience. If factical life experience is the point of departure for philosophy, and if we see factically a difference in principle between philosophical and scientific cognition, then factical life experience must be

---

[8] Cf. Kisiel, "Die formale Anzeige," 30.

not only the point of departure for philosophizing but precisely that which essentially hinders philosophizing itself.[9]

Philosophy as a way of being of factical life, is hindered by a tendency which is characteristic of factical life. Because in factical life there is the tendency to start with concepts that are already there and easy to understand. Factical life is that from which philosophy springs, but it is at the same time that which hinders and blocks situational philosophy.

What is this hindering and blocking tendency of factical life? To understand this, it is important to see in what way exactly we are familiar with philosophy. It is familiar to us as a discipline at the university, as a part of our cultural heritage, as a complex of values and ideas, and as a critical method to discern sense and non-sense. In the word "philosophy" a lot of different activities come together. In general, philosophy is present for us in a rather obvious way. This obvious presence is an indication of the way in which we have philosophy at our disposal. But it goes beyond this, for it is within the framework of this obvious philosophy that we set out to understand life and ourselves. As a result, the way we understand ourselves is never itself discussed and criticized. Factical life is understood within a conceptual framework that is not neutral; it has an effect and an orientation. The question now is what is the orientation, which underlies philosophical discourse.

The way we philosophize shows that we are dealing with a theoretical relation to an object. This theoretical relation is embedded in the experience of factical life. It is not only the theoretical relation that is embedded in it, but also our actions, our dreaming, feeling, and so on. These relations cannot be understood without entities to which they are related. All these relations can only be understood from their orientation towards an entity. If we abandon this orientation towards entities, we are left with an abstraction, which owes its existence to this primarily given orientation. When we speak of "subject" and "object," we are making such an abstraction. Heidegger does not reject this theoretical and abstract orientation, but he sees a more dominant and fundamental relation to entities in man, which he indicates as "care."

It is especially the theoretical relation to entities that hinders the possibility of understanding the facticity of life, because the relations we have in our factical life are not primarily theoretical. Humans have relations with other beings through seeing, feeling, smelling, loving, and so on. This is what a phenomenological approach always emphasizes. Philosophy, however, is completely occu-

---

[9] Heidegger, *Phenomenology of Religious Life*, 11.

pied by its commitment to the object, and because of that the way in which it actualizes this relation remains completely hidden. Factical life and authentic philosophy are always actualized; it is precisely this basic feature of philosophy that is blocked by a theoretical and conceptual approach. As in this paper I write something about Heidegger, and the reader as subjects are reading about that something as an object about which I am writing now. The reader is not directed to or concentrated on the fact that he performs the act of reading and that I as a writer perform the writing. The act of reading and the act of writing disappear in the subject matter I am writing about.

Thus, the hindrance is due to the way we have philosophy at our disposal in our everyday and factical life. In everyday life, there is a tendency for people to be absorbed in the world, in entities and in all the "urgent" things of life. The thoughtless adopting of conceptual frameworks also belongs to these "urgent" and "important" things. This thoughtless adoption of the conceptual framework of "traditional" philosophy blocks the practice of authentic philosophy from the factical situation of life.

2 Understanding Religion Out of Facticity

Heidegger's quest for human existence in its facticity and historicality breaks the classical image of philosophy in which concepts and theories are supposed to describe and lead to an understanding of life as it is. Facticity and fragility of human existence cannot be understood by obvious and familiar concepts. Philosophy itself is situated in this fragility and facticity, which is something that is easily forgotten. Especially in the familiar philosophical concepts, Heidegger sees the possibility that philosophy may be isolated from the situation. This means that philosophy is in constant danger of getting totally absorbed in its theoretical approach.[10] The facticity of human existence in its quest for the real life, employing familiar concepts and frameworks again and again, demands a specific philosophical approach. Normally we understand human life through concepts, but in this conceptual approach the subjective actualization of understanding is not understood. This situational actualization, however, should be the original phenomenon to be studied in philosophy, if we ask what philosophy is all about. This situational actualization cannot be understood through objective concepts, because in objectifying it, we turn it into an

---

10 Ibid., 43–44.

object, which an actualization can never be. The formal indication points at that which we must actualize in our situational understanding of the world.

With philosophy, understood as formal indication, Heidegger does not want to remove the hindrances that are in philosophy to understand the facticity of life, but he wants to recognize it as a hindrance. In recognizing the blockade, the philosophical concepts make visible an entrance to something they hide. This is specific for the formal indicating philosophy; the concepts are fragile and provisional (*vorlaüfig*). This emerges out of the fragility of life itself. The fragility and provisional nature of the factical and historical life are continued in the fragility and provisional nature of the formal indicating philosophy. Life is the factical historical life; it is about the actualization of this pro-visional life, that one cannot understand with totalizing concepts. This is the basis on which Heidegger tries to overcome the onto-theological structure of Western Philosophy. The philosopher has to take care not to answer the quest for life too fast with a crystal-clear insight. It is his task to keep the question open. Therefore, Heidegger writes: "The formal indication renounces the last understanding that can only be given in genuine religious experience."[11]

What is, in this respect, Heidegger's relation to religion? As a philosopher, who is involved in factical life he sees factical life in religion, the religion in which he grew up. That is part of the situation in which he lives. He is as a philosopher in the community of the university. The a-priori is the earlier situation in which he is; the *a priori* is not a general essential structure of philosophical concepts, or of God.

Heidegger asks what the specific approach has to be of philosophy of religion when it is phenomenology of religion. It has to be a philosophy of facticity. Religion has to be understood out of facticity. This phenomenology is not so much directed to its object, religion, but to philosophy that in its actualization uses certain pre-occupations. Phenomenology destructs philosophy and its framework; this is its specificity so that religion can be understood in its situation. Phenomenology has to keep an eye on the pre-occupation in connection with its history. The pre-occupation stands in the way of an original understanding, especially when it refers to historical matters. He writes this in 1922: "The very idea of philosophy of religion (especially if it makes no reference to the facticity of the human being) is pure nonsense."[12]

Philosophizing out of your own facticity makes clear why Heidegger analyzes Paul with regard to the facticity of human being. This stems from Heideg-

---
11 Ibid., 47.
12 Heidegger, "Phenomenological Interpretations with Respect to Aristotle," 393, footnote.

ger's position. He does not approach it according to the lines of dogmatic or systematic theology or of settled historic research. He is aware of his situation. Therefore, he can write that there is a certain prejudice based on a pre-giveness in relation to Christianity. This prejudice or thrownness is part of the pre-structure of understanding as Heidegger works it out in *Being and Time* later on. It is Heidegger's factical situation. Therefore, he writes in his lecture course:

> Real philosophy of religion arises not from preconceived concepts of philosophy and religion. Rather, the possibility of its philosophical understanding arises out of a certain religiosity—for us, the Christian religiosity. Why exactly the Christian religiosity lies in the focus of our study, that is a difficult question; it is answerable only through the solution of the problem of the historical connections. The task is to gain a real and original relationship to history, which is to be explicated from out of our own historical situation and facticity. At issue is what the sense of history can signify for us, so that the "objectivity" of the historical "in itself" disappears. History exists only from out of a present. Only thus can the possibility of a philosophy of religion be begun.[13]

This approach should not see history as an independent process that develops its own meaning. Therefore, Heidegger starts from his Christian religiosity, which he does not refer to the concept of God as the ultimate, but to human facticity and historicity as the ultimate.

Heidegger formulates the following basic determinations as object of his philosophy of religion. They are not theses that have to be proved afterwards. They are phenomenological explications: "1) Primordial Christian religiosity is in factical life experience. It is such experience itself. 2) Factical life experience is historical. Christian experience lives temporality as such."[14] ("To live" understood as *verbum transitivum*.) These are the presuppositions with which Heidegger reads Paul. These basic determinations have to be seen formally; in the beginning one lets them be unstable in order to safeguard them during the phenomenological analysis. In the end the phenomenological explication unfolds the ontology that is implied in this religious experience.

---

13 Heidegger, *Phenomenology of Religious Life*, 89.
14 Ibid., 55.

3 Heidegger's Interpretation of Paul's Letters to the Thessalonians

In his interpretation of the letters to the Thessalonians, Heidegger sees the experience of facticity and the historicality as expressed and articulated in early Christian life.[15] Early Christian life is exemplary, because the orientation of this life is directed towards the actualization of life as historical. The factical situation of life appears in Paul's appeal to the community of faith of the Thessalonians. Paul's appeal is an appeal to Christian life. Paul's letter is a proclamation (preaching), in the form of an announcement to the Christians of Thessaloniki. This proclamation can be understood as a relation; it concerns a public announcement of a specific content. The proclamation as a relation is an announcement of a certain person to an audience. The important thing, however, is not to see the proclamation as a relation with a content as a message about an object, with which you can agree or not, but as an actualization or a performance. Heidegger's interpretation of the proclamation in the letters of Paul aims at the actualization and performing of what is the message of the proclamation. This approach has a number of important consequences, especially with respect to the way in which the preacher and that which is being preached must be understood. From the perspective of the theoretical subject—object approach, the preacher is the announcing person and that which is preached is the announced content. In this case, it concerns two entities between which a relation exists. But when the preaching is understood as actualization, then the preacher and the preached content are understood as moments of the preaching that expresses a situation of concern.[16] It is not just a message to which you can listen; it is a message that you perform. "You know perfectly well," and so on. Phenomenological understanding is determined by the actualization of the spectator. This actualization of the spectator refers to the situation from which the spectator speaks. This situation is of vital importance for understanding. This means one only understands what is said in the proclamation if one shares in the performing of waiting for the second coming of Christ; otherwise you do not perfectly know.

---

15 *1 Thessalonians* is important for an analysis of the early Christian experience of life, because it is the oldest New Testament writing; it is probably written in Corinth between 50 and 52 after Christ. The authenticity is not questioned, this in contrast to *2 Thessalonians*, according to historical critical exegesis.
16 Heidegger, *Phenomenology of Religious Life*, 57.

Paul experiences himself as a fellow sufferer and as a member of the community of faith in Thessaloniki. This is the situation from which he speaks. The need from which Paul speaks, the situation of the preacher, cannot be isolated from that on which he speaks: the preached content. The need Paul finds himself in and from which he speaks, as well as the second coming of Christ as the content of which he speaks, are moments of the preaching as actualization. This he shares with the situation of the community of Thessaloniki. The crucial question now is: How are we to understand the second coming of Christ as a moment of actualization or as a moment of performing historical life? From the perspective of the content of the message, the second coming of Christ is the content of an image that refers to something that will happen in the future. In order to understand this, it is explicated that both the coming and that in which the coming will take place—time—are represented as beings (entities) that are present at hand. The message is meaningful in so far as it refers to a moment in the future. Thinking then means having or creating presentations. A presentation is filled with a content, which refers to something that will happen in the future.

However, Paul does not pay attention to this aspect. Not because he does not know about it, but because his concern is not with a coming that will happen at a certain time. Paul writes: "For you know perfectly well that the day of the Lord comes like a thief in the night" (1 Thess. 5:2). This knowing refers to the way this coming should be expected and the way this future appears. It is therefore that Paul opposes two groups of people and two ways of living. Those who see the second coming of Christ as something that will happen at a certain time. This way of living is one that looks for certainty and peace; it is the life of those living in darkness because they do not have the brightness of authentic knowing. They do not know that Christ comes like a thief in the night. Members of the other group are those who know about the second coming of Christ as something indeterminate and they live in unsteadiness and uncertainty. According to Heidegger, this is a moment of the actualization and performing of historical live.

Actualization is connected with facticity as the situation in which this process of understanding takes place. It is important to understand the actualization from the perspective of the facticity of human existence. This is the point where the two opposite ways of living become explicit. The apostates do not accept the truth; they see the coming as something that will happen in the expected future. In Heidegger's view, this means that they connect the meaning of the proclamation with a certain objectified moment in the future and thus turn away from the actualization of factical and historical life. This turning to the content of the world implies a turning away from the actualization of life. The apostates think that they can wait till the second coming of Christ. (We see this phenomenon in certain sects, that go to a mountain in order to wait for the end of the world.) The true Christians, however, are tuned to the uncertainty of the second coming of Christ; they understand it as an indication for the way they have to live. This makes them awake and open to the unexpected. The true Christians give up the second coming of Christ as a certain content in a future moment. In this situation, facticity and historicality are not neutralized. The apostates think they can wait till the second coming of Christ. Heidegger interprets the coming as an indication of factical and historical existence. But how pure one can anticipate or wait for the unforeseeable second coming of Christ?

It is a fact that man can never give up the meaningful world in which he lives. Factical life means being absorbed by the world. Being-absorbed-by means being oriented to entities which appear meaningful. This does not change in Christian life. But if the perspective of content is given up, the "empty content" can indicate the way in which Christians live their life. What is coming is not an expected moment in the future. Christian life is a devotional standing before God, which has to be actualized again and again. In and by this actualization, Christian life is historical. Christians are those who relate to the world "as if they do not."[17] For this Heidegger quotes from Paul's *1 Corinthians*:

> What I mean my friends, is this: the time we live in will not last long. While it lasts, married men should be as if they had no wives; mourners should be as if they had nothing to grieve them, the joyful as if they did not rejoice; those who buy should be as if they possessed nothing and those who use the world's wealth as if they did not have full use of it. (1 Cor. 7:29–31)

This "as if they do not" does not mean that the Christian has to give up his relations to the world. It belongs in Heidegger's view, to the facticity of life that it is absorbed in the world. It is impossible for the Christian to have other than worldly relations. This ὡς μή refers to the actualization of life. Christian and with that human facticity cannot be experienced from the content of the message. Christian understanding is not in the *representation* of God or of the second coming of Christ, nor does the essence of Christian life lie in preaching as doctrine, dogma or a theoretical view. This "as if not" refers to the fact that factical live is broken. Because the all-embracing tendency towards entities that is so typical of theoretical representation, never disappears. As a result of this brokenness the actualization of factical life can become visible. It means that a pure anticipation on the second coming of Christ in an undetermined moment is not possible. Hence, this turning does not mean that the theoretical approach as a way of caring can be eliminated. It is not possible for Christian life to be lived purely in ac-

---

17 Ibid., 85–86.

tualization. But from the conversion to God the fragility of Christian life becomes visible. This fragility is typical of authentic Christianity, which, according to Heidegger, points to the facticity of human existence. Heidegger writes:

> Christian life is not straightforward, but is rather broken up: all surrounding world relations must pass through the complex of enactment of having-become, so that this complex is then co-present, but the relations themselves, and that to which they refer, are in no way touched.[18]

Living a Christian life means understanding the fragility of life and this implies being aware of the discrepancies of the different orientations of factical life. In the final analysis, factical life is this discrepancy of orientations, which for the most part is not visible. If the orientation on the content is the meaningful one in its orientation on meaningful entities, then the consequence is that the orientation on the performing of historical life is directed to "something meaningless." It is not by chance that later on Heidegger will speak of "no-thing."

In usual understanding, human being is supposed to live in *meaningfulness* that is and has been the adagio of normal life till this day. The same goes for philosophy and science. The statements made there have to be meaningful and correct. In everyday life and in everyday philosophy, man is concerned about this correctness. Therefore, there will always be some relation with our daily concerns.[19] This means that I always remain connected to theoretical concepts when I am explicating live and or other realities. Every interpretation as an explication is a broken and fragile proposal.

In order to make this fragility visible, philosophy has to withdraw from this absorbing content orientation. To this end, it looks for a place from where this all-embracing character of speaking and appearing of beings can be experienced. If the all-embracing character of our concern with contents resisted every possible access to itself, this would make philosophy impossible. The question of the possibility of (authentic) philosophy depends on the possibility of finding a place from where the orientation of factical life can be understood. Understanding our encompassing relation to the world means that this is seen from another perspective that is not intentionally directed to a worldly content. This "from another position or perspective," Heidegger sees exemplary in the historical figure of the second coming of Christ.

The authentic anticipation into an undetermined future is for Heidegger a philosophical possibility to transcend the all-encompassing relation to worldly

---

18 Ibid., 86.
19 Ibid., 10.

things. The "as if not" could be translated as "it is not this, but something different."

Whenever this fragility of factical life is misunderstood because of the tendency to objectivity, the essence of the facticity of human life is misunderstood. The question however is how Heidegger understands this within the horizon of his philosophy of the facticity of life. The first answer has to be that Heidegger formalized the basic Christian experience of life. He does not choose a position with respect to its content, but investigates only the sustaining conditions of possibility of such an experience of life. In Heidegger, it is all about the conditions of possibility of facticity, which are determined in a formal way.[20] He never confirms the possible concrete interpretation with regard to its content. What happens with regard to the content in the moment of καιρός is something that can never be deduced. Only the un-deducible facticity is able to encounter the sudden of the καιρός.

Heidegger gives up the question of what is presupposed in early Christian experience of life from the side of the content of faith. This means that the formal structure of temporality is separated from the content of Christianity. The formal indications have to be repeatable without co-actualizing the act of faith.[21] Heidegger repeats this in his analysis of the φρόνησις.[22] This implies that the content of faith is neutralized, and this implies also an understanding of religion in which the theological metaphysical framework of understanding has left the scene.

For Heidegger, it is not about the faith of the Thessalonians, and certainly not about the content of their faith. He is involved in the experience of historicity, which is implied in this faith and the ontology implied in this experience if historicity. However, it is to question whether this experience of historicity is given in this way as well-separated from this content. It is a fact that it is given in this way and that it implies such an experience of historicity as is presented here. It is the unpredictability of history with respect to the Christian's hope for the second coming of Christ. It refuses every calculative control; this waiting time is oriented towards a suddenly breaking-in event, which al the predictable, certain and unthreatened nullifies. Human being lives and dies towards a not objectifiable fu-

---

20 See Lehmann, "Christliche Geschichtserfahrung," 135.
21 Jung, *Das Denken des Seins*, 53.
22 See Heidegger, "Phenomenological Interpretations with Respect to Aristotle." When Heidegger was asked to apply for a job in Marburg and Göttingen in 1922, the problem was that he had not published that much. The only publications were his dissertation and his *Habilitationsschrift*. To solve this problem, he was asked to write some of his ideas and his plans for the future.

ture. Values, contents of meaning and totalities cannot be deduced from this experience of time as if they belong to eternity.[23]

Can we say that the expecting of the second coming of Christ belongs to the domain of religious behavior? Is Heidegger making religious behavior understandable? In what sense is this a theology? In what sense this is hermeneutics of religion? Does Heidegger really need Paul in showing this specific intentionality towards the future? Is there still a religious intentionality after Heidegger's hermeneutics of religion and what could be the difference with Hegel's notion of overcoming or sublating? Questions that arise out of Heidegger's approach and hermeneutics of Paul, which I cannot answer here.

References

Heidegger, Martin. "Phenomenological Interpretations with Respect to Aristotle." *Man and World* 25 (1992): 358–93.
Heidegger, Martin. *Phänomenologie des religiösen Lebens*. Edited by Matthias Jung, Thomas Regehly, and Claudius Strube. Frankfurt am Main: Klostermann, 1995.
Heidegger, Martin. *The Phenomenology of Religious Life*. Translated by Matthias Fritsch and Jennifer Anna Gosetti-Ferencei. Bloomington, IN: Indiana University Press, 2004.
Heidegger, Martin. *Phenomenological Interpretations of Aristotle: Initiation into Phenomenological Research*. Translated by Richard Rojcewicz. Bloomington, IN: Indiana University Press, 2008.
Jung, Matthias. *Das Denken des Seins und der Glaube an Gott: Zum Verhältnis von Philosophie und Theologie bei Martin Heidegger*. Würzburg: Königshausen & Neumann, 1990.
Kisiel, Theodor. "Die formale Anzeige: Die methodische Geheimwaffe des frühen Heidegger." In *Heidegger—neu gelesen*, edited by Markus Happel, 22–40. Würzburg: Königshausen & Neumann, 1997.
Lehmann, Karl. "Christliche Geschichtserfahrung und ontologische Frage beim jungen Heidegger." *Philosophisches Jahrbuch* 74 (1966): 126–53.
Pöggeler, Otto. *Der Denkweg Martin Heideggers*. Pfullingen: Neske, 1963.
Strolz, Walter. "Martin Heidegger und der christliche Glaube." In *Martin Heidegger und der christliche Glaube*, edited by Hans-Jürg Braun, 25–57. Zürich: Theologischer Verlag, 1990.

---

23 Strolz, "Martin Heidegger und der christliche Glaube," 28.

Ezra Delahaye
The Philosophers' Paul: A Radically Subversive Thinker

Abstract: This article examines the so-called "turn to Paul" in contemporary, continental philosophy: Why do continental philosophers read Paul? After dividing the philosophers who deal with Paul into groups which have similar philosophical motives, the author argues that there are two main approaches to Paul in contemporary philosophy, the universalist approach and the ontological approach. Delahaye, then, argues that the main difference between these groups can be understood through the Pauline text which serves a reading key for the members of these groups, these texts being Gal. 3:28 and 1 Cor. 7:29 – 31.

Delahaye elaborates on the differences in these groups by taking the most well-known philosopher of each group and analyzing how they start from the above-mentioned Pauline texts in their analysis of Paul. Delahaye shows how Badiou—the representative of the universalist approach—reads Paul as a political thinker based on Gal. 3:28. Badiou, then, develops this towards an ontology of the event. The representative of the ontological approach—Agamben—centers his reading of Paul on 1 Cor. 7:29 – 31 and the ontological interpretation of this text. Agamben, then, develops this ontology into political ontology in his reading of Paul. Both approaches, then, ultimately read Paul as a political ontological thinker. A thinker who tries to reground the political order in a renewed ontology. Delahaye's conclusion is that the main philosophical reason these philosophers read Paul is that Paul allows them to overcome contemporary, political problems by renewing and re-grounding ontology.

1 Introduction

Since the late 1990s a number of influential philosophers have started to read the letters of Paul. In this paper, I want to ask the question: "Why?" Why are the philosophers reading Paul? The answer to that question will turn out to be that Paul is a radically subversive thinker and this allows the philosophers to rethink the status quo. This question can be understood in multiple ways. It can be read as "Why read Paul at all?"; "Why read Paul and not another part of the Bible?"; or "Why do philosophers read Paul?" Even though all three questions are valid questions, I will only discuss the latter question in this paper.

The answer to this question is fairly straightforward when you answer it for one philosopher, but it becomes exceedingly difficult when you try to answer it for all the thinkers who turn to Paul at once. However, this is the more interesting question. A number of philosophers from all kinds of different backgrounds have all turned to reading Paul at generally the same time. It has become a philosophical trend and we can only explain this trend on philosophical grounds. So, what are the philosophical grounds this disparate group of philosophers has for turning to Paul all at roughly the same time.

I will approach this question in three steps. I will begin by clarifying which philosophers we are actually talking about. The group of philosophers who have written on Paul is quite extensive by now, but this group can be classified into three groups of reading Paul. Thereafter, I will take one philosopher of each of these groups to be exemplary for that school and then discuss how they read Paul based on which Pauline passages are the key texts for that "school." Finally, I will establish to which philosophical problems reading Paul in this way leads and then I will be able to show that the reason the philosophers read Paul is the dual problem of politics and ontology.

2 On Method

Before discussing the three groups of philosophers who interpret Paul, I first need to make a few preliminary remarks about the method I will use to group these philosophers together and to define these groups. The philosophers I will focus on in this categorization are Nietzsche, Heidegger, Taubes, Breton, Lacan, Žižek, Badiou, Deleuze, Agamben, Ricoeur, Boyarin, Freud, and Benjamin. The latter two do not discuss Paul themselves, but they are drawn into this discussion by other authors. The reason I discuss these authors and not others is that these thinkers are the most influential and original interpreters of Paul in this contemporary philosophical turn. I will group these philosophers into three neat groups based on how they read Paul. Of course, there are overlapping problems and arguments between the different groups, and there are thinkers who don't really fit at all, such as Ricoeur.[1] My proposed grouping, however, will be able to uncover why the philosophers started reading Paul.

The first group is actually not really a part of this contemporary turn to Paul. It is the reading of Paul that Nietzsche developed in *The Antichrist*. In *The Antichrist*, Nietzsche exposes Paul as thinker of the institutionalized church. Paul

---

1 Ricoeur, "Paul the Apostle."

converted Jesus' original teaching into a church, which emphasizes an immortal afterlife at the expense of this life. According to Nietzsche, Paul denies life itself.[2] This is, ironically enough, also the way Paul has been interpreted by the churches for centuries. The only meaningful difference between Nietzsche's interpretation of Paul and the way the churches understood Paul is that Nietzsche evaluated Paul's founding of the Christian religion as something negative, whereas for the churches it was obviously a positive occurrence. Deleuze's reading of Paul also belongs to this group, because it is not so much a reading of Paul as it is a reading of Nietzsche.[3]

The reason that this group does not belong to the contemporary turn is twofold. Firstly, it is not contemporary. Nietzsche's *The Antichrist* precedes most of the other readings of Paul by about a hundred years. Secondly, and more importantly, Nietzsche does not belong to the contemporary turn, because he reads Paul in a completely different way. For Nietzsche, Paul is the thinker of the status quo; he is the great priest. Whereas for the other two groups Paul is a radical thinker who subverts the established order of which Nietzsche accuses him of establishing. Furthermore, and this is quite telling, each and every one of the contemporary philosophers dealing with Paul who explicitly addresses Nietzsche's reading rejects it as the example of how one should not read Paul.[4]

The second group emphasizes, in a very general sense, Paul's anthropology. The focus of these authors lies on one verse in Paul's letters, Gal. 3:28, in which Paul states that positive identities such as Jew and Greek no longer exist. The philosophical theme the philosophers find in these texts is the question of universality. In Paul, they find a way to rethink universality. This is a universality which stems from a new anthropology. In Paul, they find a way to think a new universal humanity.

The philosophers who belong to this group come from a variety of backgrounds, but they all address this problem. The most influential part of this group—people like Žižek and Badiou—draw on the psycho-analytic tradition to think a universal humanity through Paul.[5] They mostly base themselves on the work of Lacan, who in seminar VII commented on Paul's *Romans*, but they also explicitly draw Freud's engagement with religion into this discussion.[6] Also belonging to this group is Breton, who develops the question of the Pauline

---

2 Nietzsche, *The Anti-Christ*, 39.
3 Deleuze, "Nietzsche and Saint Paul."
4 Heidegger, *The Phenomenology of Religious Life*, 86; Badiou, *Saint Paul*, 71; Taubes, *The Political Theology of Paul*, 79.
5 Badiou, *Saint Paul*; Žižek, *The Ticklish Subject*; Žižek, *The Puppet and the Dwarf*.
6 Lacan, *The Seminars of Jacques Lacan, VII*.

universal humanity by reading Paul from his own religious background. Breton emphasizes the allegorical nature of Paul's letters. Through the allegory, Breton claims, Paul is able to expand God's promise to his people in the Old Testament to a universal promise to all people.[7] I will call this second group the universalist approach to Paul. The philosopher who will serve as the exemplar of this group is Badiou, because Badiou most explicitly addresses the question of Paul's universalist humanity.

The third group is, again very roughly speaking, more ontological. In both the second and the third group ontology and anthropology are rethought through Paul. The second group, however, starts in anthropology, whereas the third group starts in ontology. The key text for this third group is 1 Cor. 7:29 – 31. These verses are explained in terms of the end of verse 31 in which Paul states that the form of the world is passing away. The world itself is changed. This shift in the world changes the way life is lived. The main philosophical themes that are expanded upon by the philosophers of this group are temporality, comportment and the world.

Similarly, the philosophers who belong to the second group come from a range of different backgrounds. Agamben and Taubes use the work of Benjamin and Schmitt to read Paul as a Marxist, Jewish thinker. Agamben even goes so far as to claim that Benjamin was actually a Pauline thinker.[8] In this approach to Paul they develop a novel reading in which the law is interpreted as the central, ontological category in Paul. The law structures the world. This, in turn, leads to a new comportment. From a different perspective, Heidegger also focuses on these themes. Heidegger, who starts from Paul's conception of himself and his own life, finds a new life shaped by temporality in Paul.[9] I will call this group the ontological approach to Paul. The most typical philosopher for this group is Agamben, because Agamben combines the Jewish, messianic reading of Taubes with the focus on temporality of Heidegger.

The question is, however, whether representatives can do justice to an entire group of philosophers? Obviously, the philosophers in the groups are all very different and there will be many aspects which these philosophers discuss, which are not covered by a representative. All these philosophers, however, take an approach which falls under one of these groups. Even though the specific way of going about it differs, the central point they want to make and how they make it is highly similar. Similar enough, at least, for my purposes: a representative

---

7 Breton, *A Radical Philosophy of Saint Paul*.
8 Agamben, *The Time That Remains*, 140 – 41; Taubes, *The Political Theology of Paul*.
9 Heidegger, *Phenomenology of Religious Life*, 55.

can do justice to their basic motive in reading Paul. Because even though all these philosophers discuss Paul differently, their reading is basically concerned with one of the two texts mentioned above.

Now a further question can be raised, namely why can Badiou and Agamben do justice to their respective groups as representatives? Why these two and not others? I have two reasons for this decision. Firstly, both Badiou and Agamben are the most influential philosophers within their groups. Their two books are interestingly enough what made both Badiou and Agamben, as well as the philosophical turn to Paul well-known to a broader philosophical audience. Secondly, Badiou's and Agamben's works combine most, if not all of the elements which are part of their groups. Badiou shares the psycho-analytic background with Žižek and Lacan, but also takes many philosophical points from Breton. Similarly, Agamben is heavily indebted to both Taubes and Heidegger in his reading of Paul. Because of these two reasons Badiou and Agamben are best suited to be the archetypes for the universalist and the ontological approaches.

In this paper, I will not discuss the Nietzschean reading of Paul any further. Instead I will focus solely on the other two groups, because—as I have argued—I do not believe the Nietzschean reading belongs to the contemporary turn to Paul. Although I have named the two groups the universalist and the ontological group, there is no strict divide in topics. As we shall see the topics of universalism, ontology and many others are present in both groups. In this paper, I will be unable to discuss all these topics. Rather, I will focus on Badiou and Agamben as representatives of the two groups. In these two authors, I will focus on the question of how they read Paul and to what end.

3 The Universalist Approach

The representative for the universalist approach is Badiou. As I have mentioned the central text in the Pauline oeuvre for this group is Gal. 3:28. The question, then, is: what role do these texts play for Badiou? In the very first chapter of *Saint Paul,* Badiou comments on Gal. 3:28, which reads: "There is no longer Jew or Greek, there is no longer slave or free, there is no longer male and female; for all of you are one in Christ Jesus." In this text Badiou finds Paul's political potential. Paul's thinking can overcome any and every form of identity politics which characterizes our contemporary societies. Badiou mentions France as a specific example in this context since it is a country dominated by the dichotomy between the French and the rest in an ever-increasing way.[10] Paul's thinking can break with our concept of identity, which is our central political concept.[11] It is with this reference to Gal. 3:28 that Badiou begins his book. Similarly, in the very last chapter of the book Badiou takes up this theme, which he calls the traversal of differences, again. This Pauline idea is the guiding principle for Badiou's enquiry into the Pauline letters.

Merely stating that there is no longer Jew or Greek is easy. The question is: how does Badiou ground this statement philosophically through his engagement with Paul? According to Badiou Paul is the poet-thinker of the event.[12] Paul thinks about the event and how this works. This event is the ground for Paul's traversal of differences in Gal. 3:28. What is the event? The event in Paul's life was his experience on the road to Damascus. This encounter with Christ mimics the founding event, that is: the resurrection.[13] Here Badiou evokes, but does not explicitly address his own theory of the event, which he establishes in his other works.[14] After his experience Paul becomes an apostle, someone who testifies about the event from his own position as a subject.[15]

Badiou understands the event Paul experienced against the background of Paul's discussion of the Jew and the Greek. When Paul describes or discusses the world he only ever mentions two subsets of people: Jews and Greeks.[16] All the people in the world are contained in this dichotomy. Obviously, Badiou states, Paul knew that there were more ethnicities then Jew and Greek and that the world is much more complex. So why, then, Badiou asks, does Paul only mention these two?[17] Badiou's answer to this is that Jew and Greek do not denote specific cultural groups with beliefs and identities, but rather two *regimes of discourse*.[18]

Even though these two regimes of discourse are almost polar opposites—the Greek being a discourse of totality and the Jew being a discourse of the exception—these two discourse are actually both discourses of mastery. They both seek to control reality.[19] Paul instates a third, Christian discourse against these two. This

---

10 Badiou, *Saint Paul*, 9.
11 Ibid., 11.
12 Ibid., 9.
13 Ibid., 17.
14 Badiou, *Being and Event*; Badiou, *Logics of Worlds*.
15 Badiou, *Saint Paul*, 18.
16 Ibid., 40.
17 Ibid.
18 Ibid., 40–41.
19 Ibid., 42.

discourse overcomes the Jew and the Greek discourses by inverting their idea of power and control. Badiou mentions 1 Cor. 1:17–29 explicitly in this context.[20] That which is not overturns that which is and places language in a deadlock.

How does the event bring about this inversion? The event is nothing. At least it is nothing for the Jew and the Greek. The event is inexpressible in the language of the Jewish and Greek discourses. They cannot acknowledge it, because it overturns their mode of thinking. Because of this, the event can also not be known. There is no language and no concept for it in the discourses of mastery. The event demands its own discourse. The event, then, is radically and necessarily subversive. It can never be subsumed under the ruling discourse, because a ruling discourse is always a discourse of mastery.

How does the event do this? The event breaks the ruling discourse by establishing a truth. Badiou defines truth as a universal singularity.[21] Firstly, truth is singular. Badiou defines the singular as "neither structural, nor axiomatic, nor legal."[22] The truth is not an expression of a more general structure of something else, nor is it the basic agreement upon which one can build a system. The truth does not follow pre-defined rules. It is not founded on anything which came before it. Truth is the radically new.[23] Something which could not have been thought before the event and therefore has to exist completely independently from all prior entities.

Secondly, truth is universal. The truth does not need any prior identity to do its work, nor does it create a new identity. Because of the novelty of the truth, it is clear that it cannot depend on any prior identity. The truth is available to everyone, not just people who had a certain identity. Because the truth cannot depend on any identity, it can also not depend on an identity it creates itself. As such, the truth has to be universal.[24]

There is much more to be said about Badiou's exposition of the event in Paul. For the present purpose, however, I just want to look at how this theory of the event can ground Gal. 3:28 philosophically. As we have seen, the event is universal. How should this universality be understood? The opposite of Badiou's concept of universality is not particularity. It is not a matter of the all against the part. Rather, the universal is a singular universal. It is open to all,

---

20 Ibid., 46.
21 Ibid., 14.
22 Ibid.
23 It is strange that Badiou does not mention Gal. 6:15, in which Paul speaks about the new creation. Badiou claims that Paul develops an ontology of the new and this text could easily be read to support this claim.
24 Badiou, *Saint Paul*, 14.

but can only happen in a specific context. How does this lead to grounding Gal. 3:28?

The resurrection, which is the truth of the event, could only happen within the Greek and the Jewish discourses. This does not mean that the event depends on either the Jewish or Greek discourse, but the resurrection is an event which breaks with the Greek and Jewish thinking in terms of mastery.[25] Why does the resurrection break the discourses of mastery? Because the discourses of mastery are the thinking of death. Why death? Badiou does not mean biological death, nor does he mean death as being-towards-death, that is: as denoting human finitude.[26] Rather, death denotes a slavery to the law, rules and the flesh.[27] The point for Badiou is that death is the figure of ultimate mastery over life.

The Greek and Jewish discourses exert mastery over life by assigning a place in the universal totality to everything there is. A Jew is a Jew, because that is his assigned place, the same goes for the Greek. The resurrection overcomes this thinking of mastery and as such the assigned places are negated. This way of thinking which assigns to everything its place disappears after the event.

The universality Paul proclaims is based on a completely new figure of thinking which completely overcomes all figures of mastery. This means that all identities are negated and subsumed in the truth of the event, which does not lead to a new positive identity. Paul is a thinker of universalism, which for Badiou means that every difference is negated. Badiou's Paul is a subversive thinker, because the event Paul proclaims overcomes each and every individual difference and every thing's assigned place. In short, the event breaks with every status quo.

4 The Ontological Approach

The central text for the ontological approach to Paul is 1 Cor. 7:29–31. This text plays a central role in the argumentation for the philosopher who serves as an archetype for this group, Agamben. The text reads as follows:

> I mean, brothers and sisters, the appointed time has grown short; from now on, let even those who have wives be as though they had none, 30 and those who mourn as though they were not mourning, and those who rejoice as though they were not rejoicing, and those who buy as though they had no possessions, 31 and those who deal with the

---

25 Ibid., 71.
26 Ibid., 73.
27 Ibid., 59.

world as though they had no dealings with it. For the present form of this world is passing away.

This text in all its complexity essentially says one thing: life has changed, because the shape of the world will soon pass.

Agamben's entire book on Paul can be read as an interpretation of these verses. Even though Agamben explicitly deals with the first ten words of *Romans*, he explains these words mostly in terms of this text from *1 Corinthians*. With regards to Agamben's reading of this text, one can raise two questions: what does this passing of the form of the world entail and how is life changed because of it.

Agamben understands the form of the world in relation the fourth word of *Romans:* κλητός, "called."[28] Agamben connects the word calling through Luther and Weber to our word profession.[29] What he establishes in this reading is that calling was not an exclusively, religious term for Paul. Rather, every condition in which one lives, be it a profession, a religion or even a gender, has been ordained by God. The concept of calling denotes in Agamben's reading of Paul the simple fact that the order of the world is as it is because it was decided upon by God's law. Agamben bases himself on 1 Cor. 7:17–22 for this.[30]

The form of the world is such that everything can be neatly separated based on these callings. The law, which is the logic of the world, is a principle of division.[31] The law divides everything in terms of dichotomist clusters. Everything is either a Jew or a non-Jew and a Greek or a non-Greek, but also a chair or a non-chair. This might seem a trivial, but it has great consequences. If one thinks in this way, everything can be fully described in terms of these identities. There is no in-between. For every identity marker, you can say if something has it or not. Because of the law of the excluded third, this logic can describe everything, but also assign everything to its "proper" place. This is the logic of the world for Paul, the ontology underlying the experience of reality in his day.[32]

Of course, this is not what Paul himself believes. Rather, it is the situation of living under the law. The law which has been suspended by the arrival, death

---

[28] Agamben, *The Time That Remains*, 23.
[29] Ibid., 22.
[30] Ibid., 19.
[31] Ibid., 47.
[32] Although Paul was himself not a philosopher, it is very plausible that Paul at least had a background knowledge about philosophy. There are many reasons to believe that Paul had some kind of education, so it is safe to assume that Paul also had a basic understanding of how people thought about the order of the world in his day. See, for example, Malherbe, *Paul and the Popular Philosophers*.

and imminent return of the Messiah. Unlike Badiou, Agamben hardly develops a theory of the event in relation to Paul. Agamben only discusses the event itself in relation to temporality.[33] What is more important for the present purpose is what happens after the event, namely the revocation of every worldly calling.[34]

The messianic event revokes every condition through the ὡς μή. Ὡς μή is a formula which Paul uses repeatedly in 1 Cor. 7:29–31, but which Agamben elevates to the status of a technical, messianic term.[35] Through the messianic event every condition is called towards the ὡς μή, meaning "as not." What is the sense of this term for Paul?

The ὡς μή is applied to every calling by the messianic event. It denotes that every condition is pushed towards its own negation.[36] After the messianic event those who are weeping are as not weeping. Similarly, Jews are as not Jews and Greeks are as not Greeks. The "as not" is not a negation. The conditions do not disappear.[37] Neither is it an "as if not." It is not a matter of acting *as if* these conditions do not matter.[38] The as not revokes the separating power of every condition.

Worldly conditions are instated by the law. The law is nothing more than a principle which installs divisions. Through the operation of the messianic event this law is suspended and every condition is lived as not. The key term for the suspension of the law in Paul is the Greek verb καταργεῖν.[39] Agamben discusses this term extensively in relation to the potentiality-act pairing of Greek metaphysics. Καταργεῖν means taking the act out of the law, thereby returning it to potentiality.[40] This leads to a situation in which the law still exists, but is no longer operative. This is what happens in the ὡς μή.

Through the messianic event the principles of separation are overcome and the laws that separate are suspended. Because the ὡς μή does not entail a negation, however, the conditions affecting people are not destroyed. Even after the messianic event, people are still Jews or Greeks. Similarly, tables are still tables. Their identities are not changed. What is changed, however, is how identities work. Even though a Jew is still a Jew, this is no longer determining for identity.

---

33 Agamben, *The Time That Remains*, 69.
34 Ibid., 14.
35 Ibid., 24.
36 Ibid.
37 Ibid.
38 Ibid., 35.
39 Ibid., 95.
40 Ibid., 97.

Being a Jew or being a table can no longer be a principle of separation. How is this possible?

What the messianic event overcomes is not the content of the law, but rather the way the law works. As we have seen, the law is based on the principle of non-contradiction. The law separates, because it can divide everything according to its dichotomist mechanisms. The messianic event negates exactly this. After the event the remnant is introduced into every identity.[41] The remnant is "the impossibility for the part and the all to coincide with themselves or with each other."[42]

Every identity makes a division. This division instates a group of people having this identity. This group is nothing more than the sum of all the people who have this identity. Similarly, each person or object can be expressed as a list of identities. The essence of this person or object is, however, the list of identity markers. Everything is exactly its identity, nothing more and nothing less. The messianic event breaks with this logic by instating a remnant into every identity. The remnant is that core within each identity which always eludes definition. It is the "yes, but …" which follows every determination. When someone says: "that person is a writer," someone can always respond with: "yes, but she is also … ." Similarly, no group can ever be exhausted by its parts. This is the case, because there is a remnant in every condition, which says that someone is this condition, but always not entirely.

There is much more that can be said about this, but this is how Agamben develops a new ontology based on 1 Cor. 7. The claim of this paper, however, is not that the philosophers are interested in Paul, because of his ontological potential, but because of his political potential. So, how does this ontology lead to a rethinking of politics?

This is quite an easy question to answer. After the messianic event groups are no longer defining for identity. This means that even though someone is still a Jew, this no longer defines him. However, Agamben explicitly rejects the universality of Paul. This does not mean that Paul's message is not for all. It is for all, because exclusion itself becomes impossible when identity is suspended. This does not mean that all differences are negated and subsumed under one universality.[43] Rather, the differences remain, but they are no longer determining. They still exist, but in a different way.

---

41 Ibid., 55.
42 Ibid.
43 Ibid., 52.

5 Conclusion

Up until this point I have divided the philosophical turn to Paul into three groups, two of which operate under the same premise that Paul is interesting for philosophy. These two groups, which I have called the universalist approach and the ontological approach, are represented by Badiou and Agamben. Thereafter, I have established how Badiou and Agamben read Paul based on the Pauline verses which are central to their endeavors. These texts serve as reading keys for the philosophers and guide them in their dealing with Paul. The point I want to make, however, is that the philosophers who turn to Paul are interested in Paul, because of his political potential. I have yet to make this point. To make this point, I have to take one more step. I have to compare the two groups and see in which ways their projects are similar.

Obviously, it is very strange and intellectually dangerous to think that one is able to say anything meaningful about such a disparate group of philosophers based on a very one-sided reading of two of those philosophers. Why, then, do I think I am able to do it?

In the discussion of the work of Badiou and Agamben I only told a very particular story, namely the story of how they explain the key Pauline text. In Badiou's case we have seen that he takes a text which has a strong universalist connotation and then explains the ontology behind that text. It is very easy to see how his book is structured around that text, seeing as how he begins and ends his book with a discussion of it. In Agamben's case we have seen quite the opposite. He starts with a text in which Paul discusses what turns out to be an ontological problem. Through the new ontology he finds in Paul, Agamben discusses what the political consequences are when you adopt this ontology. Although the exact approach differs in each case, this is exactly what the philosophers in each group try to do.

So, how can we then evaluate these two approaches? Even though these two groups start in a completely different place, they end up with the same Paul, namely Paul as a thinker of a new political ontology.[44] Thinkers of both groups realize that ontology and politics cannot be separated. Furthermore, all of these thinkers read Paul as someone who opposes and rejects the status quo, be it religious dogmatism or the legal order of the state. So, why Paul? Because the phi-

---

[44] Heidegger is an exception in this regard, because he is not interested in the new politics which follow from Paul's ontology. However, the political consequences can and should still be drawn.

losophers' Paul is a radically subversive thinker and because of his new ontology, he also gives philosophers the means to rethink contemporary politics.

References

Agamben, Giorgio. *The Time That Remains: A Commentary on the Letter to the Romans*. Translated by Patricia Dailey. Stanford, CA: Stanford University Press, 2005.
Badiou, Alain. *Saint Paul: The Foundation of Universalism*. Translated by Ray Brassier. Stanford, CA: Stanford University Press, 2003.
Badiou, Alain. *Being and Event*. Translated by Oliver Feltham. London/New York: Continuum, 2005.
Badiou, Alain. *Logics of Worlds*. Translated by Alberto Toscano. London/New York: Continuum, 2009.
Breton, Stanislas. *A Radical Philosophy of Saint Paul*. Translated by Joseph N. Ballan. New York: Columbia University Press, 2011.
Deleuze, Gilles. "Nietzsche and Saint Paul, Lawrence and John of Patmos," In *Paul and the Philosophers*, edited by Ward Blanton and Hent de Vries, 381–94. New York: Fordham University Press, 2013.
Heidegger, Martin. *The Phenomenology of Religious Life*. Translated by Matthias Fritsch and Jennifer Anna Gosetti-Ferencei. Bloomington, IN: Indiana University Press, 2004.
Lacan, Jacques. *The Seminars of Jacques Lacan: Ethics of Psychoanalysis*. Edited by Jacques Alain-Miller. Translated by Dennis Porter. New York: W. W. Norton & Company, 1997.
Malherbe, Abraham J. *Paul and the Popular Philosophers*. Minneapolis, MN: Fortress Press, 1989.
Nietzsche, Friedrich. *The Anti-Christ, Ecce Homo, Twilight of the Idols. And Other Writings*. Translated by Judith Norman. Cambridge: Cambridge University Press, 2005.
Ricoeur, Paul. "Paul the Apostle: Proclamation and Argumentation." In *Paul and the Philosophers*, edited by Ward Blanton and Hent de Vries, 256–80. New York: Fordham University Press, 2013.
Taubes, Jacob. *The Political Theology of Paul*. Translated by Dana Hollander. Edited by Aleida Assman and Jan Assmann in conjunction with Horst Folkers, Wolf-Daniel Hartwich, and Christoph Schulte. Stanford, CA: Stanford University Press, 2004.
Žižek, Slavoj. *The Ticklish Subject: The Absent Centre of Political Ontology*. London/New York, NY: Verso, 2000.
Žižek, Slavoj. *The Puppet and the Dwarf: The Perverse Core of Christianity*. Cambridge, MA: The MIT Press, 2003.

Peter Zeillinger
Disillusioning Reason—Rethinking Faith: Paul, Performative Speech Acts and the Political History of the Occident in Agamben and Foucault

Abstract: Agamben's book on Paul, *The Time that Remains*, initiated some of his later works, especially *The Sacrament of Language*, *The Power and the Glory,* and the reflections on his method of "philosophical archeology" in *Signature of All Things*. These books all focus on performative gestures and their efficacy in juridical, political, and religious contexts. Starting from Agamben's reading of Paul's understanding of faith (πίστις) and its specific "*messianic* temporality," the article shows how the performative gestures of faith correlate to early cultural practices of establishing a social and political bond. The close reading of πίστις in Paul also follows Agamben's hints to the late Foucault and his research on the early Christian practices of penance (ὁμολογία, ἐξομολόγησις, ἐξαγόρευσις) and include also Agamben's later elaborations on the structure of the oath and its relationship to the cultural and social development of man ("anthropogenesis"). By these historical (archeological) reconstructions the article aims to contribute to the project of overcoming the traditional opposition of reason and faith. It reveals the eminent role that performative gestures like πίστις, *fides,* confession and the oath have played for the development of Occidental culture and political history. Thereby the acts of faith are freed of their restriction to the realm of religion and their opposition or even contradiction to reason. Especially the structure of the specific temporality attached to *performativity*—a temporality that Paul identifies as "*messianic*"—attests to the efficacy of performative speech acts for the establishment of social and political bonds.

1 Prologue: Reason and Faith, Ability/Status vs. Relation/Performance

In order to contribute to a project that aims to overcome the traditional opposition of reason and faith, let me at first address a rather general question: If there is reason, what would be the meaning of faith?[1] It is not so much concepts and definitions, which are of interest in this respect, but rather the opposition itself between reason and faith that seems to characterize the tradition of Occidental Philosophy—at least in the "Modern Age" (*Neuzeit*). Is it a contradiction that is at stake here, or another kind of relation? Are reason and faith related to each other at all? In the following, I will focus only on the second part of the couple "reason and faith." I will do this in the context of contemporary philosophies, though I have to face a specific burden in speaking here not only as a philosopher but also as a Christian theologian. It will always be quite easy to question the talk of a theologian, assuming that s/he might simply be referring to an unquestionable religious experience or some sort of revelatory source. Therefore, the following readings will only make sense in the given context of this project if they are taken as strictly *philosophical* readings.

In order to circumscribe the traditional tension between "reason" and "faith," I will propose a tentative and even very rough distinction, which is not intended to define anything but to give a first hint that may initiate a deeper discussion afterwards. Therefore, let me claim that in the Occidental culture and tradition the concept of "reason" has most of the time been assigned to the "internal" realm of "thinking" whereas faith is always related to the "external" realm of language. The Greek and Latin terms that refer to reason—such as νοῦς, φρόνησις, διάνοια, ἐπιστήμη, σοφία or (in Latin): *ratio, intellectus, mens, animus,* and *spiritus*—all have to do with a sort of "inner" ability of the human, or the Gods, or the Cosmos. Whereas faith—though at first sight also belonging to an "inner" realm of the human (but interestingly not of the Gods or the Cosmos)—is intrinsically tied to a form of "expression." Faith is always "expressed" in some way. To "have faith" is thereby always related to an *expression* or performance of this faith. This comes down to a first thesis that has to be proved in the following: Faith only exists in form of an expression—be it verbal or non-verbal. And as each human expression takes the form of "language," one can say: Faith belongs to the realm of language (as expression), it is a form of being related to some kind of otherness, something outside or exterior to the self. While *reason belongs to the "inner" realm of thinking* (regardless of the way in which one may want to describe this realm), *faith belongs to the realm of language as ex-pression*; while reason names an ability or status of the self, for instance as *animal rationale*, faith on the other hand only exists as a perform-

---

[1] The following article is a revised version of a talk presented at Radboud University, Nijmegen, on September 16, 2013 in the context of the research project "Overcoming the Faith-Reason Opposition: Pauline *Pistis* in Contemporary Philosophy."

ative act, as expression of a specific relationality. This distinction, which does not form a contradiction but a specific differentiation, marks the background of my readings of contemporary philosophers reading Paul. But it also sketches how the topic of faith—especially in the work of Agamben—may be referred back to the project of rethinking the traditional occidental opposition between faith and reason. Therefore, rethinking faith in the way contemporary philosophers do, also affects the understanding of reason and its boundaries.²

With this kind of description one can approach the discourses of contemporary philosophers who refer to Paul and to the Greek notion of πίστις by asking: How do these texts—the contemporary discourses as well as those traditional texts they try to interpret—refer to faith as language, as a linguistic act, as a "speech act"? And how do they thereby overcome the boundaries of reason and its restriction to the realm of the "internal"?

2 Setting the Stage with Agamben: Paul's Time of the Messianic

Agamben's reading of Paul is set in the context of his interest in a specific form of temporality which he calls—with reference to Christian theology—*messianic time*. Of course, he isn't arguing for an inner-religious theological discourse. Rather, he focuses on the consequences of these discourses on temporality for the understanding of politics and the potentialities of the political. This can be shown with reference to the very beginning of his commentary on *Romans:* "First and foremost, this seminar proposes to restore Paul's Letters to the status of the fundamental messianic text for the Western tradition."³ For Agamben, the messianic *message* as such amounts to a rethinking of the temporality of presence and thereby to a rethinking of the foundations and motifs for public and therefore political acting. It is this interest in the specific *messianic* temporality that is central for Agamben's reading of Paul:

> [W]e are confronted with an aporia that concerns the very structure of messianic time and the particular conjunction of memory and hope, past and present, plenitude and lack, ori-

---

2 Of course, in the given list of philosophical terms related to reason, one important term is missing: λόγος. And in fact, it is the only term being related to reason *and* speech (language) as well. At this point, I leave open the question of how this ought to be interpreted. But even this exception has never questioned the traditional opposition between reason and faith, *forum internum* and *externum*, or thought and linguistic expression.
3 Agamben, *The Time That Remains*, 1.

gin and end that this implies. The possibility of understanding the Pauline message coincides fully with the experience of such a time [...]. The restoration of Paul to his messianic context therefore suggests, above all, that we attempt to understand the meaning and internal form of the time he defines as *ho nyn kairos*, the "time of the now." Only after this can we raise the question of how something like a messianic community is in fact possible.[4]

Interestingly, the last sentence of this paragraph is missing in the published Italian version (2000) as well as in the German translation (2006) of the text. It sounds like a proleptic clarification—as a later addendum either by the author himself or someone else during the process of translation. Regardless of how it may have come to this supplementary remark, it makes clear what may follow from Agamben's analysis of *messianic* time in Paul: The possible emergence of a specific form of community, appointed as *messianic*, a title that should not prematurely be confined merely to a theological or religious discourse. The envisaged correlation between the specificity of a messianic understanding of time and the foundation of a certain form of community should be kept in mind for the following reading of Agamben's text.

Agamben's commentary, which follows a seminar he offered, is split into six parts, corresponding to the seminar's days, each focusing on some terms of the first ten words of Paul's *Romans*. However, there are two days, the last two days of the seminar, in which he focuses on the same phrase, namely εἰς εὐαγγέλιον θεοῦ, thereby assigning to it a specific weight for his argument. It is also this phrase that names the context of Agamben's elaborations on faith (πίστις). At the beginning of the Fifth Day, he analyzes the meaning of the Greek preposition εἰς, insofar as it expresses a certain kind of relation. It "signals a general movement towards something," as Agamben writes.[5] In addition, he highlights the fact that the τέλος of this relation, in Paul's phrase the εὐαγγέλιον, itself marks a reference, an announcement, and a "joyful message." "The term signifies both the act of announcing, and at the same time, the act of announcement."[6] All these relations, the announcement itself as well as Paul's being separated (ἀφωρισμένος) *for* (εἰς) this announcement are founded in the *messianic* content of the joyful message, that is, the already-having-been-come of the Messiah. Agamben makes clear that the εὐαγγέλιον is not a reference to some future. Instead, the message of an "apostle" strictly differs in this respect from any kind of prophetic saying:

---

4 Ibid., 1–2.
5 Ibid., 88.
6 Ibid., 89.

> Just as the apostle differs from the prophet, so does the temporal structure implied by his *euaggelion* differ from the temporal structure of prophesy. The announcement does not refer to a future event, but to a present fact. "*Euaggelion*," Origen writes, "is either a discourse [*logos*] which contains the presence [*parousia*] of a good for the believer, or a discourse which announces that an awaited good is present [*pareinai*]."⁷

For Paul, this message (that the awaited future has already become present) seems to fundamentally change his relation to the world, to his being in the world and to his acting within the world. The temporal message of the *presence* of the messianic has, for Paul, changed the position of the self. This is the context Agamben's reading of Paul is interested in, and it is exactly this context where he also brings the notion of πίστις into play:

> The problem regarding the meaning of the term *euaggelion* is inseparable from the problem in the meaning of the term *pistis*, "faith," and the implied *parousia*. What is a *logos* that can enact a presence for whomever hears it and believes?⁸

3 Agamben's Reading of Paul's Πίστις

Having summarized the context of Agamben's interest in Paul as it structures his seminar on the prescript of *Romans*, I will now turn to a crucial passage of his elaborations towards the end of the book. The whole Sixth Day can be seen as a set of various comments on the meaning of "faith," insofar as this term names and expresses a specific understanding of social and political practices. Agamben thereby invokes many references to specific political and juridical features within the culture of Antiquity and Late Antiquity that reveal an interesting subtext of the development of the Occidental tradition. Unfortunately, for the most part, his short hints leave the readers to their own further research on these themes. I will therefore try to follow some of the strands Agamben mentions by including some of his own later works as well as the works of some of his authors of reference, especially Foucault.

First of all, it is worth noting that Agamben's reading of Paul finally comes down to an analysis and a rediscovery of the significance of faith for the traditions of the Occident. As we will see, not the religious aspects of faith are of interest here, but rather the consequences for the foundations of a community. Agamben closely follows this specifically juridical strand in the meaning of

---

7 Ibid.
8 Ibid.

faith throughout the final chapter of the seminar. The juridical aspect is revealed by the specific performativity of the linguistic acts of faith, which are therefore compared to the performative aspects of oaths and other linguistic gestures. At the end of a section entitled "The Word of Faith" that opens up Agamben's final line of thought regarding Paul, we can read:

> The belief in the heart [this is Paul's definition of πίστις, PZ] is *neither a holding true* [which would simply mark an individual thought and conviction that would not necessarily have to be expressed, PZ], *nor* the description of *an interior state*, but a justification [I want to emphasize here the juridical context of this term, PZ]; only the *professing of the mouth* accomplishes salvation. [This is a reference to Rom 10:9, introducing the key term ὁμολογία, PZ] Neither a glossolalia deprived of meaning, nor mere denotative word, *the word of faith enacts its meaning through its utterance.* When thinking of the nearness of the mouth and heart, we have to venture something like a performative efficacy ["Wirkung," PZ] of the word of faith realized in its very pronouncement.⁹

Although this is not the right place to fully explicate the context of this passage, one can clearly see that Agamben—with reference to Paul—here refers to the act of faith as some sort of speech act. Only two pages further we find a corresponding section, dedicated explicitly to the *"performativum fidei,"* to the performative character of faith that closes the seminar.¹⁰ Of course, "performativity" also implies an act of *ex-pression*. All the general remarks and structural relations that I have suggested in my prologue are assembled in this passage. Therefore, one should read it very thoroughly. What is at stake here for Agamben? Unfortunately, his texts rarely name their motifs and objectives. For the most part, Agamben simply performs an "archeological reading," leaving it to his readers to draw consequences from it.¹¹ Therefore, I will start by summarizing some of the key terms and important historical references of this decisive section of the seminar,

---

9 Ibid., 131. Italics by Peter Zeillinger. Rom. 10:9 reads, as quoted in and commented by Agamben: "Because if you confess (ὁμολογεῖν, literally, 'to say the same thing') Lord Jesus with your mouth, and believe in your heart that God raised him from the dead, you will be saved" (ibid., 130).
10 The closing section of the book, entitled "Threshold or *Tornada*," which is already placed outside of the Six-Day-Seminar, offers no new readings of Paul but compares his performative thinking of the messianic with the "weak messianic power" *(schwache messianische Kraft)* in Benjamin's *Über den Begriff der Geschichte*. This comparison may confirm the observation that the performativity of faith at the end of the seminar expresses the outcome of Agamben's readings of Paul and has marked the "threshold" for further considerations.
11 On the meaning of "Philosophical Archeology" for Agamben see Agamben, *The Signature of All Things*, 89.

as they contribute to envisaging a broader context for Agamben's interest in Paul's approach to faith.

a. Foucault's reading of early Christian practices of penance. Agamben centers his comments on the *performativum fidei* on some references to the late works of Foucault and his readings of the early Christian practices of penance in the second and third century. But why does he do so? The text itself does not give many hints here. Agamben contents himself to naming an—at the time of the publication of his seminar, in 2000, still unpublished—seminar-course by Foucault at the Catholic University of Louvain in 1981.[12] Fortunately, one can follow and reconstruct the crucial terms and concepts to which Agamben refers also in other later texts by Foucault.

As quoted above, Agamben points out that faith, for Paul, consists in a speech act, a ὁμολογεῖν, which "signifies saying the same thing, making one word agree with another (hence, contractual agreement), or making it agree with a given reality (for example, in the correspondence between *logoi* and *erga*, 'words' and 'works')."[13] Faith performs an act of confession, faith in itself is performative, it is a *profession of faith*. In this context, Agamben refers to Foucault's late investigations on the early Christian practices of penance. These Christian practices were specified by a slightly different term, namely ἐξ-ομο-λόγησις. Again, I emphasize here the prefix ἐξ-. This term simply means "confession." There is no semantic difference to ὁμολογία with the exception of this reference to an exteriority marked by the prefix ἐξ-. The decisive point of this Christian addition of the prefix becomes clear when one of the Church-fathers, namely Tertullian, translates ἐξομολόγησις into Latin as *"publicatio sui,"* "to

---

12 See Agamben, *The Time That Remains*, 133. In fact, at the time of the seminar Agamben's references were no more but one of the very rare hints to this course by Foucault. (See also the references in Raffnsøe, Gudmand-Høyer, and Thaning, *Foucault*, 388, whose authors had obviously joined Foucault's talks and quote from their own notes.) Although the seminar at Louvain has meanwhile been published in English (see Foucault, *Wrong-Doing*), this article will not simply refer to it but reconstruction of Foucault's arguments itself. Sources for this reconstruction were several shorter works and talks of Foucault (especially in the United States during his latest phase of research), and the (Christian) traditions from Late Antiquity itself, which formed the basis for Foucault's own readings. A summary and reconstruction of the research of Foucault's later works (showing surprising tensions with the topics of his published books during his lifetime), especially regarding the "pastorate" and the early Christian practices of penance (which mark, for Foucault, the starting point for the development of the "Occidental subject") can be found in Zeillinger, "Das christliche 'Pastorat.'"
13 Agamben, *The Time That Remains*, 130.

publish oneself."¹⁴ The Christian ὁμολογεῖν/ἐξ-ομολογεῖν, therefore, was not merely to be taken as a simple personal statement with no further consequences, but rather as the expression of a specific relation to the public or to a certain community. In this specific sense, with the addendum of the prefix ἐξ, ἐξομολόγησις was used as the technical term for the early Christian practices of penance, which were established to renew the relation between the individual and the community of the ἐκκλησία. (Note again the prefix ἐξ- in ἐκ-κλησία, an old term of Greek politics meaning those who are "called *out*" to take responsibility for the πόλις, that is, the community they live in.) But why did Foucault have such a lively interest in the correlation of the speech act of the ἐξομολόγησις and the thereby established relation between the individual and the community? A closer look at those early Christian practices may be helpful to understand why Agamben shares this interest. The process of penance and reintegration of the individual consisted of three succeeding parts: Firstly, the act of publicly confessing ones sins in front of the community or the bishop; secondly, a long period of certain dramatic acts of penance, in which the penitent had to publically present himself in sackcloth and ashes, should not wash himself and was obliged to do charitable work for the community; and in the third and final act, the penitent had to express—again, in public—a formal "confession of faith" by which he got reintegrated into the community. The interesting point here is that all these three quite different phases and acts—the public confession of one's sins, the acts of penance, and the final confession of faith—are signified by the *same* term, namely ἐξομολόγησις. Obviously, all of them were considered to be part of one and the same performative act of expressing the Christian faith of the individual in order to be approved by the community and the person becoming a part of the community again. The speech act of publicly revealing one's self (especially with regard to one's faults that have endangered the cohesion of the community), the obligation of the self to this cohesion, and the affirmation of the principles which express the original shared experience, have to be understood as expressions of the same relation. This performative re-establishment of a persistently endangered relation marks the main point for Agamben's interest in this process. Foucault's interest goes even further. He locates, in the act of the individual who publicly confesses the inner structure of his self (with regard to the cohesion of the community), the beginning of the emergence of the occidental subject. In this *publicatio sui* (ἐξομολόγησις), Foucault no longer finds the Stoic efforts of perfecting one's self in order to improve one's behavior with regard to the polis or a pre-given natural, cosmological, met-

---

14 Tertullian, *De paenitentia* 10.1.

aphysical or communal order or harmony.¹⁵ Instead, he emphasizes the struggle to publicly identify oneself with one's self. In the practice of ἐξομολόγησις, one has to become aware and publicly express who one really is.¹⁶

Agamben's short reference to Foucault's late research opens up a wide field of consequences with regard to the development of the Occidental culture. For example, Foucault elaborated that the Christian practices of penance finally became the model for the historical development of the act of confession in court in the twelfth and thirteenth century, displacing the traditional practice of the ordeal. But all of this cannot be elaborated here. Instead, I want to emphasize the correlation of Agamben's reading of πίστις in Paul and his reference to Foucault's interest and remarks on the early Christian practices of penance. The summary of Foucault's lecture from 1980 in Paris, whose topics came close to the talks in Louvain mentioned by Agamben, expresses this correlation quite well:

> A study of *exomologēsis* shows that this term is often employed in a very broad sense: it designates an act meant to reveal both a truth and the subject's adherence to that truth; to do the exomologesis of one's belief is not merely to affirm what one believes but to affirm the fact of that belief; it is to make the act of affirmation an object of affirmation, and hence to authenticate it either for oneself or with regard to others. Exomologesis is an emphatic affirmation whose emphasis relates above all to the fact that the subject binds himself to that affirmation and accepts the consequences.¹⁷

Agamben's summary of Foucault's talk expresses the same:

> This act [of faith or confession, PZ] constitutes something like a performative, since, through confession, the subject is bound to the truth itself [let me emphasize this reference

---

15 Foucault analyzes these efforts especially in his readings of Seneca: Foucault, "About the Beginning of the Hermeneutic of the Self," 206–10.
16 In Christian practices of the fifth and sixth centuries, Foucault traces another version of this kind of subjectification: the ἐξαγόρευσις (note again the prefix ἐξ-) observed in Christian monasteries. This ἐξαγόρευσις (from Latin *manumissio*, which originally signified the public release of slaves *out onto the agora* in Greek and Roman law) was also part of a specific act of penance, though this time the sinner did not confess in public, but only to a single person, e.g. the abbot of the monastery. But again, the main point of this confession was the exposure and hence the recognition of the "inner truth" of the self. This kind of self-awareness was considered to be a relief and became—from the twelfth and thirteenth centuries on—the main model for truth-procedures in the juridical, political, scientific, psychological and finally psychoanalytical contexts of the Occident. Cf. ibid., 220–22 and Foucault, *Wrong-Doing*, 163 ff.
17 Foucault, "On the Government of the Living," 81–82.

to a bond and commitment here, PZ] and changes his relation to others in addition to himself.[18]

This bond between the subjectivized self and its linguistic forms of expression corresponds to the meaning of faith that Agamben finds in Paul's writings according to the quote already presented above: "[T]he word of faith enacts its meaning through its utterance. When thinking of the nearness of the mouth and heart, we have to venture something like a performative efficacy of the word of faith realized in its very pronouncement."[19] Let me, as a first conclusion, therefore emphasize the central but obviously twofold core of the meaning of faith: On the one hand, the linguistic performance decenters the self from any closed identity by publicly revealing its "inner truth." Even if this revelation is based on error or lie, the linguistic act nevertheless reveals, to the subject itself as well as to the community in the very moment of becoming aware of this fact, who the subject is. Agamben's reference to the Christian practices of penance thereby opens up the discourse of faith not only to its counterpart—the discourse of lie, unfaithfulness, and inauthenticity—but also to the overcoming of this fault. Therefore, on the other hand, the performative discourse of faith offers a possibility to establish or reestablish a relation based on the personality of the self. The revealing of the subject and the venturing of a persistently insecure, existential bond, form the twofold core of the meaning of faith as it is developed in Paul and unfolded by Agamben.

However, the penitential performances and their existential establishment of a personal as well as communal bond (despite of its persisting precariousness) represent only one part of Agamben's clarification of the meaning of faith. At the beginning of the Sixth Day of his seminar, Agamben has already started to unfold an aspect of the traditional understanding of πίστις which is even more tied to the juridical and political realms of the foundations of Occidental culture and tradition than the emergence of subjectivity in the Christian practices of the self. I have evaded this foundational topic until now because it not only exceeds the specific religious context of the letters of Paul but also the realm of Christianity as a specific religious tradition. In 2008, Agamben devoted a whole book on the topics he had begun to analyze in his book on Paul, namely *The Sacrament of Language*, which is part of his *Homo Sacer*-project. Although I will, in what follows, mostly stick to Agamben's remarks on the oath with respect to πίστις and faith in the context of his reading of Paul, the elaborations from

---

18 Agamben, *The Time That Remains*, 134.
19 Ibid., 131.

the later book may shed light on his earlier comments and will be taken into account.

b. Modes of "Veridiction" (παρρησία), or: The Sacrament of Language. Agamben's archeological reconstruction of the historical meaning of faith has laid the foundation for many of his later works, which could and should be read in this respect. In fact, his book on Paul seems to mark the starting point for this development.[20] Although these connections cannot be elaborated more closely here, the observation of Agamben's continuous work on this topic may give a first hint to the broad significance of the cultural "institutions" implicated in the semantic field of faith, πίστις, and *fides*. Paul did not invent this semantic field, but he used and transformed it with regard to the specific context of his own message.[21] A closer investigation into the meaning of the traditional cultural institution of faith may elucidate these transformations.

Let us, therefore, follow Agamben's approach to the meaning of faith in the context of the oath. In this respect, *The Time that Remains* and *The Sacrament of Language* comprise identical formulations. I quote from the latter text because it includes both the Greek and the Latin semantics:

> The proximity between faith and oath has not escaped scholars and is attested by the fact that, in Greek, *pistis* is synonymous with *horkos* in expressions of the type *pistin kai horka poieisthai* (to take an oath) or *pista dounai kai lambanein* (to exchange an oath). In Homer oaths are what are *pista* (trustworthy) par excellence. And in the Latin sphere, Ennius, in a verse cited by Cicero, defines *fides* as "an oath of Jove" (*ius iurandum Iovis*). And it is significant that there are attested not only formulas of an oath "by the *pistis* of the gods" but also "by one's *own pistis*"—*kata tes heauton pisteos diomosamenoi* (Dionysius of Halicarnassus, 11.54)—and that, in fact, the "*pistis* of each person" (*idia ekastoi pistis*) counts as the *megistos horkos* (greatest oath; Dionysius of Halicarnassus, 2.75).[22]

Agamben points out that the oath belongs to one of the most archaic areas of the law, which is also called *pré-droit*, prelaw.[23] In *The Sacrament of Language* he shows at great length that the area of *pré-droit* should not be mistaken with a "more archaic" form of law by projecting the characteristics of later political or juridical spheres upon a supposed "primordial sphere." Instead, the "origi-

---

20 Agamben's book on Paul and the juridical aspects of faith (as πίστις or *fides*) can be read as precursor and methodological source for his later works, especially *The Signature of All Things*, the corresponding "archaeological" readings of Occidental history in *The Sacrament of Language* and Agamben, *The Kingdom and the Glory*.
21 Agamben, *The Time That Remains*, 114.
22 Agamben, *The Sacrament of Language*, 25; cf. Agamben, *The Time That Remains*, 113 ff.
23 Agamben, *The Signature of All Things*, 16, with references to Louis Gernet and Paolo Prodi.

nal" meaning of faith and oath should be reconstructed with respect to their own forms of performance prior to their use in later religious and political contexts:

> Prelaw cannot be merely a more "archaic" law, just as what stands before religion as we know it historically is not only a more primitive religion (*mana*); it would, in fact, be advisable to bypass the very terms *religion* and *law* and to try to imagine an *x*. To find the definition of this *x*, we must put forward every possible precaution, practicing a sort of archaeological *epoche* that suspends, at least provisionally, the attribution of predicates with which we are used to defining religion and law.[24]

It should be noted of course, that in this regard Agamben has not yet been as careful in *The Time that Remains* as in his later texts. But the result remains the same: "'Faith' (or trust) is the credit that one enjoys in another, the result of placing our trust in him, having consigned something like a pledge to him that links us in a relation of loyalty."[25] Agamben thereby affirms the research of the French linguist Émile Benveniste on the ancient Indo-European institution called πίστις in Greek and *fides* in Latin, and which he defined as "personal fidelity."

> "the one who holds the *fides* placed in him by a man has this man at his mercy. This is why *fides* becomes almost synonymous with *dicio* ['force,' 'power,' PZ] and *potestas*. In their primitive form, these relations involved a certain reciprocity: placing one's *fides* in somebody secured in return his guarantee and his support. But this very fact underlines the inequality of the conditions. It is authority which is exercised at the same time as protection for somebody who submits to it, in exchange for, and to the extent of, his submission. (Benveniste 1973, 97–98)"[26]

Benveniste's description attests to the importance of the relation established by *fides*. *Fides* institutes a mutual bond by incorporating a hierarchical *and* a reciprocal aspect at the same time. When πίστις means "to have credit" and "to give credit," it thereby expresses "the existence of a relation of trust," which concatenates two poles that nevertheless remain heterogeneous.

In *The Sacrament of Language*, Agamben gives many examples showing that the cultural, juridical and religious practices of the oath can be seen as strategies to bridge a gap inherent to man's relation to the world as well as to other human beings. In this sense, the structure of the oath is unavoidable for the constitution of a social bond and its later institutional representations through *law* and *reli-*

---

24 Agamben, *The Sacrament of Language*, 16 f; cf. Agamben, *The Signature of All Things*, 90.
25 Agamben, *The Time That Remains*, 114.
26 Benveniste quoted in ibid., 115; Agamben, *The Signature of All Things*, 26.

gion.²⁷ Of course, the specific forms and arrangements of oaths may actually vary in many ways in different times, regions and cultures. Therefore, it is only the *linguistic* gesture and not its actual form that is of interest here. But it is this structure of the oath that can be found at the basis of every cultural institution engaged in the establishment or maintenance of society.

Additionally, Agamben points out that the act of taking an oath in itself involves two fundamental consequences for the individual subject as well as for the community addressed by this saying: First of all, the oath is a performative act, in which the subject who takes the oath publicly identifies itself by its utterance and with the help of this utterance. In this sense, the oath can be compared to the performative practices of confession examined by Foucault in early Christianity. The oath performs an act of self-identification and subjectification in the same sense as in the Christian confessions of sin by which the one who confesses reveals who he or she really is. Although the context of the oath is not an act of penance, its connotations are still juridical: Subjectification, in the sense of identifying the self by a speech act of this self, takes place in a public realm and enables corresponding public consequences. The oath performs a *publicatio sui in* the same way as Tertullian interpreted the confessional act.²⁸ However, there is also a second consequence established by the oath. Its structure marks the basis for any social cohabitation as such. Only with reference to subjects identifiable by their utterances, a system of law can be elaborated and a political structure based on juridical decisions can be established, in order to guarantee some sort of continuity, security, and equity for the individual as well as for the community. Agamben's reference to the meaning and use of the term *sacramentum* in Roman law gives a good example for this aspect. Let me summarize this example of judicial performativity in short.²⁹

The oldest Roman form of trial was a procedure called *legis actio sacramenti* ("the bringing forward of the legal oath"). In it, the declarative oath was neither demanded by a sovereign nor by religious obligations, but it was a properly ju-

---

27 For Agamben, the structure found in the oath is fundamentally linked to the development of man as such: "This is the moment to situate the oath archaeologically in its relationship to anthropogenesis. In the course of our investigation, we have often looked to the oath as the historical testimony of the experience of language in which man was constituted as a speaking being" (Agamben, *The Sacrament of Language*, 66).
28 Additionally, one may note here that taking an oath and becoming a subject responsible for oneself does not characterize a realm of sovereignty. Instead, we find ourselves here within the realm of pastoral οἰκονομία to which Agamben has devoted his book on *The Kingdom and the Glory*.
29 Agamben, *The Sacrament of Language*, 60–61.

ridical procedure. At first, each of the two parties affirmed its right with a specific formula. Subsequently, the one who had pronounced the first declaration provokes the other (and also themselves) to the *"sacramentum"* of a certain sum of money. That is to say, the term *sacramentum* designates an act of depositing oneself—in terms of something one owns and to which one is existentially bound. This objectification accompanies the linguistic oath. All of this takes place in a public trial. The case in question is thereby transformed into a speech act in correspondence with existential objectivities (mostly in form of money). Agamben quotes such a case, in which the first party says to the other: "Inasmuch as you have made a claim without right to support it, I challenge you in a deposit of ... ."[30] Following this example, Agamben points out that it was the *sacramentum*, the existential deposit of a certain amount of money as representation of oneself, which marked the central point of the trial and gave the procedure its name. The juridical conflict was transformed into an antagonistic speech act and both parties existentially bound themselves to this speech act via the *sacramentum*. From now on, they were identified—affirmatively or negatively—with their utterances. An act of establishing *fides* had taken place. The role of the judge was in fact limited. After the examination of the case, he declared the *sacramentum justum* and the *sacramentum injustum*, whereby one party got back his money and the other was punished with regard to the false oath given.

It is with regard to this procedure, the *legis actio sacramenti*, that Agamben calls the oath in itself a "sacrament of language." But this is not the only comparison he draws to clarify the performativity of the oath. He also identifies, in the very same context in *The Sacrament of Language*, the taking of an oath with the concept of παρρησία ("truth-telling") to which Foucault has turned his interest in his very last lecture courses before his death:

> This [the oath, PZ] is neither an assertion nor a promise but something that, taking up a Foucauldian term, we can call a "veridiction," which has as the sole criterion of its performative efficacy its relationship to the subject who pronounces it. Assertion and veridiction define, that is to say, the two co-originary aspects of the *logos*. While assertion has an essentially denotative value, meaning that its truth, in the moment of its formulation, is independent of the subject and is measured with logical and objective parameters (conditions of truth, noncontradiction, adequation between words and things), in veridiction the subject constitutes itself and puts itself in play as such by linking itself performatively to the truth of its own affirmation. For this reason the truth and consistency of the oath coincide with its performance.[31]

---

30 Ibid., 60.
31 Ibid., 57.

Here, the structure of the oath becomes a sort of ventured guarantee for the ungraspable and insecure logos. "Truth" is transformed into a performative speech act in the same way it was the case with the *legis actio sacramenti*. This transformation is crucial: Neither Agamben nor Foucault says that the performative speech act as such is true. Rather, what one can call "truth" after the collapse of metaphysical certainties is transformed into a performative speech act. The result of this transformation reveals an interesting background for the discussion of faith in Paul, from which we started: First, by these kinds of speech acts a subject is identified (in the sense that a subjectification takes place), and second, the so-called "truth" gains its power or force from the performative fact that the subject binds him or herself to his or her linguistic utterance. Therefore, the performative assertion as such becomes the truth of the subject. This is also the moment where in *The Sacrament of Language* for Agamben the meaning of πίστις in Paul comes back to mind:

> Here the oath shows its performative proximity with the profession of faith *(homologia,* which in Greek also designates the oath). When Paul, in Romans 10:6–10, defines the "word of faith" *(to rema tēs pisteōs)* not by means of the correspondence between word and reality but by means of the closeness of "lips" and "heart," it is the performative experience of veridiction that he has in mind [...].[32]

But Agamben is also aware that the subtle performativity of speech acts like the oath or the confession is always in danger to be overlooked, ignored or neglected:

> If one pretends to formulate a veridiction as an assertion, an oath as a denotative expression, and (as the Church began to do from the fourth century on by means of conciliar creeds) a profession of faith as a dogma, then the experience of speech splits, and perjury and lie irreducibly spring up. And it is in the attempt to check this split in the experience of language that *law and religion are born*, both of which seek to tie speech to things and to bind, by means of curses and anathemas, speaking subjects to the veritative power of their speech, to their "oath" and to their declaration of faith.[33]

In the same way, the oath is always haunted by the possibility of perjury; in addition, also the confession, the act of faith and the trustfully "given credit" *(fides)* may fail. But beyond that, Agamben elaborates—in the same way as Foucault and many others such as Badiou, Derrida, Levinas or Lyotard do, who have worked on faith, the oath, confession or testimony—nothing less than a *criterion*

---

[32] Ibid., 58.
[33] Ibid., 57; italics by Peter Zeillinger.

for the establishment of *truth* or, more generally put, a structural criterion for the institution of a social bond. And the question of the efficacy of this *linguistically established* bond finally leads back to Agamben's readings of Paul.

The last two quotations from *The Sacrament of Language* not only show that Agamben combines the structure of the oath and the structure of πίστις in Paul; and they do not only show what Agamben means by the birth of law and religion as institutions who try to control the venture of performativity and the risk of perjury by domesticating the structure and the performative bond of the oath by a more and more formalized ritual; they also show that Paul's understanding of πίστις is regarded differently and prior to the institutions of law and religion. Paul's πίστις is not regarded as a *religious term* in the sense of *relegere*.[34] Instead, πίστις is a performative practice in the same way the oath is not merely the cultural form of its ritual, but rather the performative *expression* of a *"structural necessity."* Only by this performance, social institutions may arise.

The final section of the last day of Agamben's seminar on Paul is devoted to the *"performativum fidei,"* the performative aspects of faith according to Paul. He starts with a retrospective question that reassembles all the topics I tried to unfold and contextualize so far: "What is the relation between the *performativum fidei* and the penitential and sacramental performative? [i.e. the early Christian practices of ἐξομολόγησις and the judicial oath, PZ]"[35] Agamben's summary is clear in this respect: "Between the performative of the oath and of penance, the *performativum fidei* defines the originary messianic—that is, Christian—experience of the word."[36] The speech acts of faith, πίστις, *fides,* or ὁμολογεῖν exceed any determinate signification. Instead, they express *and*—at the same time—also perform a relation, that is, they institute a bond between the subject and the addressee of its words. This relation or bond cannot be deduced from a given status of the subject. Therefore, Agamben is right to call it "an expression of the subject's freedom" and links this freedom to Paul's understanding of the messianic in Gal. 2:4: "our freedom which we have in the messiah."[37] He describes these speech acts as "an experience of a pure event of the word," a "revelation," inso-

---

34 Agamben refers in this respect to Cicero, and his description of *religio* as meticulously following the traditions: "'*qui autem omnia quae ad cultum deorum pertinent diligenter retractarent et tamquam relegerent, sunt dicti religiosi ex relegendo.*'" / "'those on the other hand who *carefully reviewed* and so to speak *retraced* all that, which belongs to the cult of the Gods, were called 'religious', from *relegere*' [Agamben quoting Cicero]" (Agamben, *The Sacrament of Language*, 25; emphasis by Peter Zeillinger, translation modified).
35 Agamben, *The Time That Remains*, 134.
36 Ibid.
37 Ibid., 135.

far as they introduce something new into a given context.³⁸ So the performative aspects of πίστις and ὁμολογεῖν designate a creation or (re-)birth, the establishment and performative beginning of a new order of relations—with a subject at the center of these relations, who identifies itself by these relations. The oath and the practices of ἐξομολόγησις show this very clearly. But what must still be clarified is the meaning of the messianic in this context.

4 The Messianic Temporality of (Not Only Christian) Πίστις

Agamben emphasizes the specific surplus of the Christian confessing to the Messiah with regard to the temporality of the messianic message:

> The messianic is the instance, in religion and equally in law, of an exigency of fulfillment which—in putting origin and end in a tension with each other—restores the two halves of prelaw in unison. At this same moment, it shows the impossibility of their ever coinciding.³⁹

Confessing Jesus as the Messiah—or more generally spoken: confessing in a *messianic* way—means to venture an attitude that attests to something as already presently effective whose fulfillment has yet to come. This characteristic is not solely restricted to the realm of (Christian) religion but describes a fundamental structure of any political or social order built upon relations between individuals.

At this point, a wide field of further research can only be indicated: Today's political thinking seems to have overcome the practices of oath, confession or faith. But the so-called "theories of social contract" could only arise—and *had to* be developed—after the practices of oaths and confessions had been politically disavowed in the Middle Ages. At the beginning of *The Sacrament of Language*, Agamben identifies this, with reference to the Italian historian Paolo Prodi, as a "crisis of the oath." Nevertheless, it was the very same structure that afterwards had to be politically re-established, though by other practices. Agamben's reading of the messianic structure of faith in Paul therefore correlates to a reading of the structure of any social or political bond not based on the presupposition of a pre-given and identifiable instance of sovereignty. The crisis of political founda-

---

38 Ibid., 134.
39 Ibid., 135.

tions today may gain profit from a rethinking of the discourse of faith and confession unfolded by Agamben and many other contemporary philosophers, like Badiou, Derrida, Levinas, Butler, or Lyotard. All of them take recourse on a specific form of temporality that Agamben calls—in the context of Paul and early Christianity—*messianic time.*

In the context of the *structure of the messianic,* the tension between the present situation and the attested fulfillment to come is performatively bridged by the speech acts of faith (πίστις, *fides,* ὁμολογία) and its corresponding consequences. Like the oath, they bind the subject to the content of its utterance. From the moment of its confession, its *performativum fidei* or its judicial oath, the subject may not only be identified by its words but has also obliged itself to take the consequences of this act. In the case of πίστις or *fides,* a new foundation has thereby been made for the credibility and further elaboration of public relations resulting in a new form of community. In this respect, the early Christian practices of penance are nothing but practices of re-establishing this social bond after it has become implausible. It is always a certain betrayal of the bond between the present (i.e. present attitudes) and the confessed future that causes the loss of credibility and necessitates a penalty or an act of "penance."

To conclude, let me risk a sort of πίστις or confession here: The structure of the discourse of faith—though based only on an uncertain, that is, *weak messianic force,* as it is found in the work of Benjamin to whom Agamben refers in the final "threshold," his epilogue to his seminar on Paul—at least opens the horizon and gives a first hint for a renewed approach to the history of the Occident and its fundamental juridical, political and religious institutions that may have to be interpreted otherwise than modern theories tend to do. The "archeological" approach of Agamben in continuation of the research of the late Foucault seems promising and historically more accurate in this respect.

References

Agamben, Giorgio. *The Time That Remains: A Commentary on the Letter to the Romans.* Translated by Patricia Dailey. Stanford, CA: Stanford University Press, 2005.
Agamben, Giorgio. *The Signature of All Things: On Method.* Translated by Luca D'Isanto with Kevin Attell. New York: Zone Books, 2009.
Agamben, Giorgio. *The Sacrament of Language: An Archaeology of the Oath.* Translated by Adam Kotsko. Stanford, CA: Stanford University Press, 2011.
Agamben, Giorgio. *The Kingdom and the Glory: For a Theological Genealogy of Economy and Government.* Translated by Lorenzo Chiesa with Matteo Mandarini. Stanford, CA: Stanford University Press, 2011.

Foucault, Michel. "About the Beginning of the Hermeneutic of the Self: Two Lectures at Dartmouth." *Political Theory* 21, no. 2 (1993): 198–227.
Foucault, Michel. "On the Government of the Living." In *Ethics, Subjectivity and Truth. Essential Works of Foucault*, vol. 1, edited by Paul Rabinow, 81–85. New York: The New Press, 1997.
Foucault, Michel. *Wrong-Doing, Truth-Telling: The Function of Avowal in Justice*. Edited by Fabienne Brion and Bernard E. Harcourt. Chicago, IL: University of Chicago Press, 2014.
Raffnsøe, Sverre, Marius Gudmand-Høyer, and Morten Sørensen Thaning, *Foucault: Studienhandbuch*. München: Fink, 2011.
Zeillinger, Peter. "Das christliche 'Pastorat': Elemente einer Relecture der politischen Kultur des Abendlandes im Spätwerk Michel Foucaults." *Geist und Leben* 86, no. 4 (2013): 351–73.

Gert-Jan van der Heiden
On What Remains: Paul's Proclamation of Contingency

Abstract: In this article, it is shown how the senses of crisis, transformation and contingency that mark the modern philosophical interest in Paul can be traced in the philosophical readings of Paul's accounts of time, law and world, and especially Paul's almost nihilistic language concerning the end of time, the universal condemnation of the law, the passing away of the world and the description of himself as the waste of the world. If time, law and world are marked by a crisis and are coming to an end (or are being transformed), two questions arise, which determine the order of this article: (1) What remains of time, law and world in and by this ending? (2) What type of comportment, attitude or ethos allows the believer, according to the philosopher's Paul, to have a sense of or access to what remains of time, law and the world? The second question is a question into the nature and the meaning of the notion of faith or πίστις since it is faith that is the word characterizing this comportment or ethos of the believers. These questions will be addressed in three steps. First, the specific conception of time as a time of urgency or emergency is discussed. Subsequently, it is shown in which sense this account of urgency affects what humans *can do* (or can not do); this will be done in relation to the philosophical discussions of the law in *Romans*. Finally, it is shown what this urgency means for what humans or the world *can be* (or can not be) according to Paul; this will be done in relation to his comments on the form of the world, σχῆμα τοῦ κόσμου, and other τοῦ κόσμου-formulas as used in *1 Corinthians*.

If one would try to pinpoint one shared interest in many of the present-day philosophical readings of Paul, it must be the sense of crisis and transformation proclaimed in his letters. Crisis and transformation go hand in hand with a definite concern for *contingency,* in its various meanings: contingency in the sense of what happens to us or what may befall us, but also contingency in the sense of what is not necessary, that is, what may pass away, and what thus has a transitory nature, and which by consequence implies that it can also not-be or can be otherwise. In this paper, I want to show how these senses of crisis, transformation and contingency mark the Paul that intrigues the philosophers and, in par-

---

This paper is made possible by the Netherlands Organisation for Scientific Research (NWO) and is part of the project, "Overcoming the Faith–Reason Opposition: Pauline Pistis in Contemporary Philosophy" (no. 360–25–120), financed by NWO.

ticular, the way Paul applies these senses to his account of time, law and world. If time, law and world are marked by a crisis, are being transformed and may be characterized as contingent—and these are all claims that will be explicated and argued for in what follows—two questions arise, which determine the order and the focus of my account of the philosophers' Paul in this article. (1) What remains of time, law and world? (2) What type of comportment—and this English word translates the German *Haltung* and may therefore also be understood as *ethos*—allows the believer, according to the philosophers' Paul, to have a sense of as well as an access to what remains of time, law and world?[1] The second question is a question into the nature and the meaning of the notion of faith or πίστις since it is faith that is the word characterizing this comportment or ethos of the believers.

In the course of these analyses, it will become clear, albeit mainly in an implicit way, why Paul is such an important and prolific partner in conversation for present-day philosophers: the way in which he elaborates the senses of crisis and transformation in terms of an explication of what remains (of time, of the law and of the world) resonates with the fundamental concerns for contingency that mark the present-day philosophical inquiry into notions such as event and potentiality.[2]

1 The Sense of an Imminent Ending

Whoever reads Paul's letters will immediately notice that they are charged with a sense of urgency. If we want to understand how and in which way Paul enters the philosophical debate, it may be helpful to first inquire into this sense of urgency. For Paul, the time and the situation in which he and the people whom he addresses as members of his communities find themselves are *critical*.[3] To capture the depth and the scope of these senses of urgency and crisis, an analysis of the conception of time that Paul introduces in order to make the readers of his epistles susceptible to these senses turns out to be highly instructive. The believers of Paul's community and their comportment to their environment are in the

---

[1] In what follows I will drop the addition "of the philosophers," when I speak about Paul as presented by philosophers assuming that it is understood that my analysis is in the first place marked by the present-day philosophical account of Paul.
[2] For an elaborate account of this present-day philosophical interest in contingency through the lens of the concepts of event and potentiality, see Van der Heiden, *Ontology after Ontotheology*, esp. chap. 4–7.
[3] Critchley, *The Faith of the Faithless*, 170.

first place determined by a particular understanding of time from which the senses of urgency and crisis stem.

In line with the work of Agamben on Paul, one could grasp this understanding of time as follows: the time of the present is determined as the time that is marked by two ends or limits; at the beginning of this time, one finds the resurrection of the Christ, that is, an event by which something has begun, and at the (other) end of this time one finds the παρουσία, the second coming of Christ, that is, an event for which the believers are waiting and for which they hope. The time of the present is therefore a time in which something has already begun but has not yet been brought to completion. If one sees resurrection and παρουσία as part of what ought to be seen as *one* event, it makes sense to say that the time of the present is the time of this event in its very happening: on the one hand, it has begun but, on the other hand, it is not assured of its own completion. This is why this time is critical in the sense of κρίνειν, to separate or to discern: it is the time in which an event is being discerned, but this is taking place in a context or a worldly order that is foreign to this event and in which it therefore introduces a difference. The time of the present is therefore an all-determining moment in the world (in the sense of the German *Augenblick* and the Greek καιρός), but it is at the same time a transitory and fleeting moment that is in need of continuous affirmation, determination and perseverance.[4]

The previous paragraph connects crisis, the time of an event, and the attitude of perseverance. Thereby, it gathers the main ingredients of the philosophical interest in Paul. In order to explicate this, let us first deepen this understanding of time more carefully by two Pauline figures of time that are taken up by Agamben and Heidegger, respectively. The first figure of time is found by Agamben in 1 Cor. 7:29 in which Paul speaks of the time grown short. Agamben relates Paul's use of the word καιρός to the other word for time, χρόνος, which represents the normal temporal order of the world.[5] Agamben explicates the relation between καιρός and χρόνος as follows: "*kairos* is not another time, but a contracted and abridged *chronos*, [...], a time remaining."[6] One might say that καιρός

---

4 Let me simply note that, for example, Agamben, Badiou and Heidegger (to mention only these three) all insist in their own way on this complex and ambiguous temporality. For them, it is not only the temporality of a particular (say, Christian) faith but rather offers a framework to understand the experience of the temporality of human life or of the event.

5 The importance of this passage cannot be overstated since it inspired the title of Agamben's book, *The Time That Remains*.

6 Ibid., 69; similarly, and on the same page he writes, "the messianic world is not another world, but the secular world itself, with a slight adjustment, a meager difference."

is nothing but χρόνος turned short and thereby urgent since it is this short time that remains, the only time left to us before time ends.

I'm not interested here in the question of whether Agamben properly interprets the Greek terminology of χρόνος and καιρός in Paul's letters, but rather in the particular insight this distinction aims to convey: χρόνος turned καιρός means that the end of time is transformed into an *imminent* ending and into an emergency of time. If the time of the world is experienced in this way, in its imminent ending, the present time requires a particular attitude to the time of the world we inhabit, namely one that does not experience this world in its permanence but rather in its crisis of passing away, as coming to an end.[7]

Agamben connects this understanding of time to Paul's notion of the παρουσία. It was Heidegger who, long before Agamben, develops the temporality at stake in this latter notion, and he does so in his reading of *1 Thessalonians*.[8] The fulfillment of what has begun with the resurrection is imminent, and what this means can best be seen from Paul's description of the παρουσία. The temporality of the second coming is not determined as a fixed, future point in the time of the world, that is, not as a future present, but is rather determined as that which *can* happen every moment—as Paul notes, the lord will come "as a thief in the night" (1 Thess. 5:2), so fully unexpected and unforeseen. Such an imminent event requires a particular attitude to attune to it. Faith, as Paul names this attitude, refers to a mode of living that is attuned to this imminent possibility by persevering in the expectancy that the παρουσία can happen here and now, at this very moment. One might perhaps say, in a vocabulary reminiscent of Heidegger's, that the proclamation announces first and foremost a distress that is lacking in the normal experience of the time of the world. This world's tendency to forget this distress, this emergency of time, grants faith as attitude or ethos, its particular form: Its goal is to persevere in experiencing this distress so that one is truly prepared for what may come. This means in particular that one experiences the (time of the) world in light of its imminent ending or transformation, that is, in its very contingency.

The temporal structure of time grown short as well as of the παρουσία thus imply two things: first, that it is the finitude or contingency of the world (and its

---

7 For Agamben, this time is indeed the only time we have and are: "Whereas our representation of chronological time, as the time in which we are, separates us from ourselves and transforms us into impotent spectators of ourselves—spectators who look at the time that flies without any time left, continually missing themselves—messianic time, an operational time in which we take hold of and achieve our representations of time, is the time that we ourselves are, and for this very reason, is the only real time, the only time we have" (ibid, 67–68).
8 Heidegger, *Phänomenologie des religiösen Lebens*, 98–105.

time) that is at stake in this proclamation and, second, that this temporal structure is not easily or automatically offered to be experienced, but that we are rather confronted here with an experience that requires perseverance and persistence. One might perhaps also say that the *recognition* or the *understanding* of this contingency depends on an attitude *that perseveres in one basic refusal*, namely the refusal to let oneself be seduced by the rhetoric that understands everything in terms of the present reality and the present order of the world. Heidegger insists on this in his discussion of *1 Thessalonians* when he notes that Paul exactly warns the believers about this: those that are taken away by this rhetoric and "are caught up in what life offers," will be overcome by a sudden ruin because they are not attuned to the possibility of such a sudden breakdown of the world in its present state.[9] It is exactly in this sense, as Heidegger suggests, that Paul compares faith not to some form of drunkenness or enthusiasm, but rather describes faith as "an urging to awaken and to be sober."[10] Hence, by consequence, this proclamation is concerned with a suspension, an ἐποχή, of the world as it is, in its present form—the normal experience of the world is supplemented by the thought "this is not it"—in order to get access to the contingency of this world that is announced in this temporal structure of which Paul speaks, that is, to the world's potentiality of not-being or being-otherwise.

Yet, what does this discovery of contingency imply and how does the aforementioned suspension grant access to it? In what follows—and I will develop here a main line of thought rather than a detailed account of the arguments involved—I will discuss two crucial structures in which this suspension plays a further, fundamental role in Paul's rhetoric and consider what remains after this suspension. These two structures concern what one can (not) do and what one can (not) be, respectively. More in particular, the first structure concerns the issue of the law in relation to *Romans*, while the second concerns the hierarchical structures that determine the order of the world and will be discussed in reference to some of the τοῦ κόσμου-formulas in *1 Corinthians*.

---

9 Ibid., 105; Heidegger, *Phenomenology of Religious Life*, 74. See also Heidegger, *Phänomenologie des religiösen Lebens*, 102–4.
10 Ibid., 105; Heidegger, *Phenomenology of Religious Life*, 74.

2 Suspension of the Law: On What One Can (Not) Do

In *Romans*, if there is one central crisis proclaimed by Paul, it is the crisis of the law, and I will limit myself to some remarks concerning the Jewish law.[11] What is the crisis of this law? In its normal or common application, the law makes particular demands and offers well-formulated norms that prescribe or prohibit something.[12] The law promises the just and good life for everyone who observes these norms. Yet, and this is the core of Paul's famous account of the law as the law of works, this normal functioning of the law is proclaimed to be in a fundamental crisis—a crisis summarized for instance in the following quote: "the very commandment that promised life proved to be death to me" (Rom. 7:10).[13] And the law does not only prove to be death to him, Paul, but rather to everyone (as stated in Rom. 3:9–20). Therefore, as Agamben notes, the law is proclaimed to be "absolutely unobservable."[14] Hence, rather than offering ways to obtain the good life, the law, despite itself, has turned into a universal accusation of everyone, affecting everything.[15]

By becoming a universal accusation, the law's normal aim to offer guidelines that lead to life (the original goal of the law of works) is suspended and the law as the law of works is by the same token deactivated. One might say that in a certain sense Paul is emptying out the law (as law of works) in the following way. The law of works differentiates between those who observe and those who transgress it. Yet, the demands have become so high—or, as Agamben suggests, the demands can no longer be formulated in a clear prescription or prohibition that could be observed—that the law now only differentiates between

---

[11] I'm aware that Paul's usage of the concept of law is more complex than that and refers also to Roman law and natural law, but I will limit myself here to a few remarks concerning Jewish law.
[12] Agamben, *The Time That Remains*, 108.
[13] See Agamben, *Potentialities*, 269; Badiou, *Saint Paul*, 56, 79–82.
[14] Agamben, *The Time That Remains*, 107.
[15] In contemporary philosophy, in the debate concerning Paul's universalism—between e.g. Agamben and Badiou—one might too easily forget that the real universalism does not concern the Christ- or messianic event itself but rather the condemnation by the law, which is truly universal. Yet, this universal rejection has no real nihilistic consequences but rather concerns the transformation of the covenant and is as such the starting point of a remarkable dialectics that starts from the production of a remainder or rest, which becomes the point of application of salvation for Paul.

no one and everyone: "there is no one who is righteous, not even one" (Rom. 3:10), as Paul writes.

Moreover, the Jewish law, as discussed in the context of Rom. 3, does not only distinguish between observance and transgression, but also between Jew and Greek, between the people of God and the nations. The infinite amplification of the demands of the law that empties out the first distinction—between observance and transgression—also suspends the second one between Jew and Greek since, as Paul writes, "all, both Jews and Greeks, are under the power of sin" (Rom. 3:9). One might be tempted to say that if there is a universal moment in Paul's letters, it is to be found *here*, in the suspension of the law as the law of works and as the law that divides Jew and Greek or Jew and non-Jew.

Yet, this twofold suspension of the law is *not* the annihilation of the law as such, nor of the distinctions it makes; and the crisis of the law is not announced for the sake of this crisis itself. Rather, the suspension of the law, as is the case with every ἐποχή, is concerned with something else. *It is concerned with revealing a domain to which the law as the law of works belongs, from which it stems and by which it is made possible, but which the law of works at the same time tends to conceal.* As we will see, when Paul interrogates this preliminary domain, this domain reveals the *contingency* of the law, that is, its non-necessity. I would like to discuss in some more detail two basic (and related) constituents of this contingency or non-necessity of the law. These elements are inspired by Jacob Taubes's reading and are taken up (at least partially) by Agamben.

(1) The first constituent concerns the hermeneutic or interpretative logic that Paul uses in *Romans* when accounting for the position and the role of the law as given by Moses.[16] For Moses, the covenant defines the people of God. (In Taubes's reading, Paul is portrayed as someone whose main adversary is Moses exactly because Paul like Moses is concerned with the question of how to form a people of God). Yet, as Paul insists in *Romans*, this covenant has an earlier beginning in history, namely in the history of Abraham who lived before the Mosaic law. By going back to this earlier beginning of the covenant, Paul reveals the non-coincidence and the non-identity of law and covenant, thus implying that there is a reserve or a residue hidden in the law that is only fully made manifest when the law of works is suspended. The proclamation of the crisis of the law is thus taken up in a particular argumentation or interpretation of the Jewish law in its historical relation to the covenant.[17] Differently put—and this why I use the

---
[16] Taubes, *The Political Theology of Paul*, 49.
[17] Cf. Ricoeur, "Paul apôtre"; Ricoeur problematizes especially Badiou's insistence on mere declaration.

term *suspension* rather than, for instance, destruction or annihilation—by the suspension of the law we are not left with nothing. Rather, something remains; so what remains of the law?

In the famous passages from Rom. 4, Paul describes how Abraham's righteousness or justice is not due to this observance of the law but due to his faith in the divine promise. Similarly, in terms of the covenant, Abraham and his offspring will inherit the earth not through observance of the law but through the promise.[18] Hence the suspension of the law shows that the law itself *is made possible* and goes back to the preliminary domain of *promise* and *faith*. Exactly because the law of works is in a crisis and is deactivated, this preliminary domain can finally overcome its concealment by the law of works and reveal itself as the original value of the covenant. As Agamben suggests, one might connect this interpretative logic employed by Paul to *Galatians* where Paul writes:

> My point is this: the law, which came four hundred thirty years later, does not annul a covenant previously ratified by God, so as to nullify the promise. For if the inheritance comes from the law, it no longer comes from the promise; but God granted it to Abraham through the promise. (Gal. 3:17–19)

Thus, we see what happens in this logic; it discovers the non-identity of covenant and law by interpreting the history of the covenant. Because the promise is found to be older than the law, the law cannot annul the promise. Moreover, by returning to this older, earlier beginning in light of the suspension of the law of works, Paul *rediscovers the possibilities that constitute the very origin of the law and which he needs in light of the law's crisis and its universal condemnation.* Hence, it is the dead-end of the law that allows him to go back to the primary possibilities of the covenant that exceed the particular possibilities that were actualized in the law. Thus, he reinterprets the covenant as well as its *inheritance:* by suspending the law, both covenant and inheritance receive another meaning—other than the one it has in Paul's world but which at the same time, according to Paul, is in fact the older and more basic meaning of the covenant.

Hence, *what remains of the law* in its suspension is its very contingency that opens up the realm of the covenant's original possibilities: the relation between covenant and law is not fixed, permanent or necessary but is rather contingent; its meaning can be otherwise—the keywords are no longer "law of the works" and "observance," but turn out to be "promise" and "faith"—and this possibility that remains of the law, is the very possibility of salvation given the crisis of the

---

18 See Rom. 4:13; cf. also Agamben, *The Time That Remains*, 93.

law. Differently put (if we would like to avoid the term of salvation for now), one might say that it is the very principle of transformation that is discovered here. Faith is thus holding on to the promise that the believer will be reckoned righteous despite the fact that he or she is "already as good as dead" (as is said of Abraham's body in the context of Rom. 4:19) due to the condemnation of the law.

(2) This brings me to the second constituent that the suspension of the law aims to reveal and that is closely connected to the first one. Paul's proclamation depends on one presupposition, or perhaps we should rather say that, at its core, Paul's proclamation is the proclamation of this presupposition, namely that the covenant—and consequently also the people of God—can be transformed or has a definite motility. Taubes identifies this capacity of transformation in terms of the famous πνεῦμα–σάρξ distinction, spirit versus flesh. To illustrate what Paul means by the word πνεῦμα, Taubes refers to Paul's peculiar hermeneutical practice: he does not expel the stories and the books of the Old Testament, as Marcion would have preferred, but he rather offers *allegorical* readings of them. In what I consider to be one of the most intriguing passages of Taubes's book on Paul, he provides a lengthy quote of Nietzsche in which Nietzsche accuses the deep dishonesty at work in the allegorical readings that the history of the Church offers. These readings are dishonest according to Nietzsche because no one offering such a reading would actually believe it. He aims to prove this by a mere rhetorical question: "Has anyone who asserted this ever believed it?" Taubes answers Nietzsche's question: "Yes, Paul the Apostle," and he continues to show the significance of the allegorical readings of the Old Testament one finds in Rom. 9–11.[19] This allegorical reading practice, that something from the past is not simply discarded, but taken up with a different meaning, is a consequence of what Taubes calls the pneumatic logic of Paul: Πνεῦμα is the principle that stands for the capacity of the covenant to be changed and to build up another people, and that stands for the *exception* to the law. In another important passage of Taubes's book, in which once more Nietzsche is the main opponent and which also shows how Paul's pneumatic logic does not only concern the Jewish law but also the laws of the cosmos itself, Taubes introduces this notion of the exception: "And it's a different matter whether one decides, in whatever way, to understand the cosmos as immanent and governed by laws, or whether one thinks the miracle is possible, the exception."[20]

It is clear why this exception is needed in Paul's logic: if all are condemned and if the law can only distinguish between no one and everyone, the question is

---

19 Taubes, *The Political Theology of Paul*, 45.
20 Ibid., 85.

whether there is an exception to the law, that is, whether the condemnation of the law itself can be bracketed, as a kind of second order suspension, leaving room for a remainder or a remnant through which salvation will be possible (Rom. 9:27)—the new people of God is that remainder of the people of God.[21] Πνεῦμα is thus the principle that neither respects the distinctions of the law nor introduces another, independent distinction, but instead displaces the distinctions of the law (whether it concerns the universal condemnation or the delimitation of the people of God) thus producing a remainder, which in turn is the point of application of salvation.

This particular logic that is disclosed in the contemporary readings of Paul also indicates an answer to the question of nihilism that is sometimes raised in relation to Paul and Paul's philosophical interpreters. The nihilism of the law—"no one is righteous"—discloses a human inability; it discloses what humans can *not* do. Yet, this human incapacity or impotentiality is taken up in a narrative that uses this incapacity to disclose the remains or the reserve of the law. This is the strange reversal of the law that also reverses this human incapacity—and this might be the most difficult thing to understand with respect to Paul's pneumatic logic: this human sheer *in*capacity turns out to be or is proclaimed to be a *capacity not to* act in accordance with the law of works. That is to say, it is not simply the capacity to act in opposition to the law in order to take pleasure in sin, or something odd like that—such acting in opposition would be a simple re-acting and thereby a reactivation of the law of works rather than a suspension or deactivation of this law. It is rather the capacity to insist on letting this reserve of the law and this transformation of the covenant manifest itself, that is, to insist on the non-identity of law and covenant, work and promise, letter and spirit. A similar logic that applies here to the law can be discerned in Paul's usage of the τοῦ κόσμου-formulas in *1 Corinthians*, to which I turn now.

3 A World of Waste: On What One Can (Not) Be

The second example of the basic role of deactivation or suspension that leaves a remainder can be found in *1 Corinthians*. The rhetoric of this letter is quite different from that of *Romans*. Rather than the question of the Jewish law, the question

---

21 As Paul writes: "So too at the present time there is a remnant, chosen by grace" (Rom. 11:5). In the logic between the crisis of universal condemnation and the eschatological universal mercy, which Paul unfolds in Rom. 9–11, the present of the work of salvation is left with nothing but the remnant, as Agamben stresses, by which salvation is made possible, see Agamben, *The Time That Remains*, 56–57.

of the present order of the world is at stake. According to Paul, this world has its own fixed distinctions by which it judges what is worthwhile and what is worthless: the wise versus the foolish, the rich versus the poor, the powerful versus the powerless, and ultimately even being versus non-being (in the particular sense of what *is* something in (the eyes of) the world versus what *is nothing* in the world). This particular focus on these dichotomies is clearly visible in some of the τοῦ κόσμου-formulas Paul uses in this letter.[22]

From a present-day philosophical perspective, one does not exaggerate when one states that for the Paul readings of Badiou and Agamben (and with them many others), *1 Corinthians* is a crucial letter.[23] This letter is important because of the political stand it inspires: Paul stands up for and identifies himself with what the world holds in no esteem whatsoever. In Paul's rhetoric, an exemplary example of this gesture may be found in the following passage from the fourth chapter of this letter:

> We are fools for the sake of Christ, but you are wise in Christ. We are weak, but you are strong. You are held in honor, but we in disrepute. To the present hour we are hungry and thirsty, we are poorly clothed and beaten and homeless, and we grow weary from the work of our own hands. When reviled, we bless; when persecuted, we endure; when slandered, we speak kindly. We have become like the rubbish of the world, the dregs of all things, to this very day. (1 Cor. 4:10–13)

In this quote we see how Paul brings the worldly or secular distinctions into play and how he identifies himself with what is base, up to saying that he has become the waste or refuse of the world. Refuse is *what remains of the world* after the world is done with its work and which is of no use to the world whatsoever; it is rather a burden to the world. After all, how to get rid of all this waste and garbage that is piling up in unspeakable masses?

While it may seem that in the context of the distinctions Paul introduces, the refuse should be placed on the side of what is simply nothing, thus reinforcing

---

[22] I'm thinking here of the σχῆματοῦ κόσμου, the form of the world (1 Cor. 7:31), περικαθάρματα τοῦ κόσμου, the refuge or waste of the world (1 Cor. 4:13), σοφίαν τοῦ κόσμου, the the wisdom of the world (1 Cor. 1:20), τὰ μωρὰ τοῦ κόσμου, the the foolish things of the world, and τὰ ἀσθενῆ τοῦ κόσμου, the weak things of the world (both in 1 Cor. 1:27), τὰ ἀγενῆ τοῦ κόσμου, the base things (i.e., what is of no esteem) of the world (1 Cor. 1:28).

[23] For Taubes this is *Romans* and for Heidegger *1 Thessalonians*. Despite the fact that Agamben calls his interpretation of Paul *A Commentary on the Letter to the Romans*, as the subtitle of his book reads, *1 Corinthians* is crucial for him. As Critchley writes, referring to Agamben: "What is at stake is a politics of the remnant, where the off-cuttings of humanity are the basis for a new political articulation" (Critchley, *The Faith of the Faithless*, 159).

the idea that philosophers who embrace this idea will end up with a nihilistic version of Paul, the logic Paul develops in this letter is subtler, perhaps more dialectical (in a non-Hegelian way); in fact, it is comparable to the one he develops in relation to the law. Both the law and the order of the world share one basic, formal feature: they make distinctions—the law between those who observe and those who transgress, and the world between what is something in the world and what is nothing in the world. As we saw in our discussion of the suspension of the law, the crisis of the law results in an emptying out of these distinctions, leaving us with nothing but a division between everyone and no one, except for what remains of the law. Paul's argumentation in *1 Corinthians* follows a similar path, but now in relation to the present form or order of the world.

When Agamben discusses Paul's notion of the refuse of the world—and this passage is also referred to by Heidegger and Badiou—he connects it to Rom. 8:20–22, and it is not difficult to understand why he does so.[24] For Paul, to be mere waste or to be nothing, is not limited to a few unlucky beings alone. Rather, the futility and caducity—the transitory nature exemplified by the words "refuse" and "waste"—apply to all creation: "creation was subjected to futility" (Rom. 8:20), as Paul writes. A similar experience of the transience of the world is at stake in 1 Cor. 7:29–31 where Paul speaks of the passing away of the order of the world, the σχῆμα τοῦ κόσμου. This passing away is revealed by the contraction of time of which I spoke in the first section of this article: the end of the world is brought near by this contraction or, differently put, the effect of time grown short is that all that exists and all that counts as something in the world is understood, dealt with and lived in light of its imminent ending, of its futility—what is, is interpreted as being-waste. Thus, the same fate befalls the order of the world as has befallen the Jewish law due to the crisis Paul proclaims in both cases: if the refuse counts as nothing and if we understand the world in light of its transitory nature, the order of the world that aims to distinguish between what is worthwhile and worthless, between what can prevail and what will go under, ends up distinguishing between nothing and everything since everything is futile and nothing is permanent. In this sense, the present form of the world "is passing away" (1 Cor. 7:31). Paul's proclamation thus reveals the world in its crisis, in light of its own futility and contingency, in light of its own going or running to waste.

In the context of 1 Cor. 7, in between the statements on the time grown short and those on the passing away of the world, we find the famous ὡς μή-passages,

---

24 Agamben, *The Time That Remains*, 40–41. Cf. also Badiou, *Saint Paul*, 56. Heidegger, *Phänomenologie des religiösen Lebens*, 120–21.

to which both Heidegger and Agamben pay significant attention as they describe the ethos required of the believers to attune to what remains of the world. These passages read as follows:

> from now on, let even those who have wives be as though they had none, and those who mourn as though they were not mourning, and those who rejoice as though they were not rejoicing, and those who buy as though they had no possessions, and those who deal with the world as though they had no dealings with it. (1 Cor. 7:29–31)

The crisis of time and world asks for a particular attitude, namely to do the things in the world in such a way that their passing away is taken into account: one should mourn as not mourning, rejoice as not rejoicing, and have dealings with the world as not having dealings with the world. Thus, also in his or her actions, the believer is called upon to persevere in approaching the world as not-being, in light of its passing away. The believer thus lives his or her life in accordance with his or her account of the world: Paul asks for a harmony between λόγος and ἦθος.²⁵ Ὡς μή as enactment of life accomplishes a reserve towards the mode of life prescribed by the order of the world, and in this way ὡς μή allows the space of what remains after the suspension of this order to appear. The attitude of the "as not" is thus not simply nihilistic—it is not the annihilation of all modes of living; rather, it is a mode of being reserved with respect to the given modes of living so that what remains after the suspension of these modes of living can appear. Similarly, the understanding of the world in terms of its non-being or its passing-away should not be mistaken for a nihilistic one: Paul is concerned with the deactivation or suspension of the world's order rather than with its annihilation. Hence, what truly matters here is what remains of the world, the meaning of the waste with which Paul identifies himself.²⁶ To capture what this means, let us turn to a third and final example of the τοῦ κόσμου-formulas in *1 Corinthians*.

What the world considers to be mere waste is once more, as in the case of what remains of the law and what remains of time, the very point of application

---

25 According to Foucault, the harmony of λόγος and βίος would be the heart of Socratic παρρησία, see e.g. Foucault, *Fearless Speech*, 101. We see a similar harmony here in Paul's conception of the world and the attitude to the world that follows from it: they correspond with each other.

26 In relation to the previous section on the law and its universal condemnation, one should perhaps emphasize here that this sense of waste should not (at least not in the first place) be understood in terms of Paul's sense of his own sinfulness. Rather, it concerns his sense of the order of the world in which he appears as nothing.

for salvation. To see this, let me quote an important passage from 1 Cor. 1 that repeats the worldly or secular distinctions that Paul confronts in this letter:

> Has not God made foolish the wisdom of the world? [...] Consider your own call, brothers and sisters: not many of you were wise by human standards, not many were powerful, not many were of noble birth. But God chose what is foolish in the world to shame the wise; God chose what is weak in the world to shame the strong; God chose what is low and despised in the world, things that are not (τὰ μὴ ὄντα), to reduce to nothing things that are (τὰ ὄντα). (1 Cor. 1:20, 26–28)

The recurring phrase of τοῦ κόσμου, "of the world," indicates that we are dealing with the distinctions that are valid in the present form of the world. Yet, Paul proclaims that God puts this order upside down: according to him, God chooses what is foolish, what is weak, what is low and despised and, ultimately, τὰ μὴ ὄντα, what is not, in order "to reduce to nothing" what is, τὰ ὄντα. Note that Paul uses here the verb καταργεῖν to state what is translated here as "reduce to nothing." Agamben, for whom this verb καταργεῖν is the keyword *par excellence* in Paul's letters, emphasizes that this verb does not mean to annihilate or to destroy. Rather than being the opposite of ποιεῖν, καταργεῖν is the opposite of ἐνεργεῖν and thus means to deactivate or render inoperative (or to empty out).[27] Hence, God does not destroy the order of the world, but rather *deactivates* the secular order that is at work in the present; he deactivates the distinctions valid in the world. We have already seen what this deactivation means in relation to the passages from the fourth and the seventh chapter of this letter: the contraction of time places the secular order in light of its imminent end. Yet, this deactivation is not nihilistic since the refuse of the world is not nothing; it is rather the very point of departure or application of salvation and even of the transformation of the world.

The waste of the world can take on this role (of being the point of departure of transformation) because it is exactly this waste that cannot be identified as something in the present order of the world—it is out of tune with this world. Once more, one may find a pneumatic logic at work here that changes the meaning and the value awarded to things in the order of the world: what is considered to be nothing has *an absolute significance* for Paul exactly because it is the point of non-coincidence with the given order. In more down to earth terms, this may be understood as follows: the *weakness* of the believers of which Paul speaks here, their incapacity to fulfill the requirements of the secular order turns into their power because confronted with this secular order of the world, they can

---

27 Agamben, *The Time That Remains*, 96.

only say: we *can not* participate in this order. By this incapacity, inability or weakness they become the very point of departure for the transformation of this order: considered as nothing in the world, they are in the world the very traces of the incapacity of the world to gather everything in its order; they are what remains when the order of the world is suspended.²⁸

4 Final Remarks: The Non-Conformity of What Remains

What remains of time, what remains of the law and what remains of the world is a sense of non-conformity. The time grown short concerns a dimension of time that cannot be conformed to the presupposed permanence of time—that we have plenty of time—or the presupposed permanence of the order of the world. This non-conformity generates a particular sense of time in its urgency and emergency of an upcoming transformation. The suspension of the law discloses the non-conformity to the law of works of the excessive potentialities in the covenant of promise and faith. This non-conformity generates a particular pneumatic hermeneutics, a sense of πνεῦμα or spirit that brings into play the exception to the given order of the law and insists on its transformative capacities. What remains of the world in the passing away of the present form of the world (σχῆμα τοῦ κόσμου τούτου) is often related to Rom. 12:2 in which Paul calls on the members of his community in Rome not to be conformed to the world.²⁹ In each of these contexts, it becomes clear that the ontological dimension of this non-conformity cannot be separated from what one might call its ethical dimension, that is, the dimension of the believers' attitude, comportment or ethos. Whereas the believers are called on not to be conformed and to persist in the incapacity to be integrated in the order of the world, the non-conformity on the ontological level calls forth the idea of contingency and potentiality: what is, can be otherwise.

---

28 Agamben develops this in his short text "On What We Can Not Do," in *Nudities*, 43–45. In light of what he writes there (esp. 45), one might describe the present secular order as an order that separates the weak, the foolish, the poor from what they can do—they alienate them from their own capacities—yet, in doing so, the secular order still leaves room for resistance: "they can still not do," and by this impotentiality they are the refuse of the world that reveals why salvation is needed.
29 See Heidegger, *Phänomenologie des religiösen Lebens*, 119–20; Barth, *Der Römerbrief*, 571, 584.

If the resource or the reserve of this potentiality-for-being-otherwise is found by the philosophers in what seem to be Paul's most nihilistic moments—his writings on the waste of the world, the passing away of the world, the universal condemnation of all, the end of time, and so on—one should not be surprised. From the very beginning of philosophy, in Plato and Aristotle, it has been the question of non-being that paved the way for thinking what-is-other and what-is-in-potential as modes of being. A similar gesture marks the present-day philosophical interest in Paul. The non-being of the world, of time and of human righteousness are taken up by Paul to demonstrate the non-conformity of what remains and to disclose what these remains keep in reserve: as sense of the being of the time, of the world and of the law as what-can-be-otherwise.

References

Agamben, Giorgio. *Potentialities: Collected Essays in Philosophy*. Translated by Daniel Heller-Roazen. Stanford, CA: Stanford University Press, 1999.

Agamben, Giorgio. *The Time That Remains: A Commentary on the Letter to the Romans*. Translated by Patricia Dailey. Stanford, CA: Stanford University Press, 2005.

Agamben, Giorgio. *Nudities*. Translated by David Kishik and Stefan Pedatella. Stanford, CA: Stanford University Press, 2011.

Badiou, Alain. *Saint Paul: The Foundation of Universalism*. Translated by Ray Brassier. Stanford, CA: Stanford University Press, 2003.

Barth, Karl. *Der Römerbrief, Zweite Fassung 1922*. Zürich: Theologischer Verlag Zürich 2010.

Critchley, Simon. *The Faith of the Faithless: Experiments in Political Theology*. London: Verso, 2012.

Foucault, Michel. *Fearless Speech*. Edited by Joseph Pearson. Los Angeles: Semiotext(e), 2001.

Heidegger, Martin. *Phänomenologie des religiösen Lebens*. Edited by Matthias Jung, Thomas Regehly, and Claudius Strube. Frankfurt am Main: Klostermann, 1995.

Heidegger, Martin. *Phenomenology of Religious Life*. Translated by Matthias Fritsch and Jennifer Anna Gosetti-Ferencei. Bloomington, IN: Indiana University Press, 2010.

Ricoeur, Paul. "Paul apôtre. Proclamation et argumentation." *Esprit* 292 (2003): 85–112.

Taubes, Jacob. *The Political Theology of Paul*. Translated by Dana Hollander. Edited by Aleida Assman and Jan Assmann in conjunction with Horst Folkers, Wolf-Daniel Hartwich, and Christoph Schulte. Stanford, CA: Stanford University Press, 2004.

Van der Heiden, Gert-Jan. *Ontology after Ontotheology: Plurality, Event, and Contingency in Contemporary Philosophy*. Pittsburgh, PA: Duquesne University Press, 2014.

Part II. **Paul and Πίστις in the Greco-Roman World**

George van Kooten
Paul's Stoic Onto-Theology and Ethics of Good, Evil and "Indifferents": A Response to Anti-Metaphysical and Nihilistic Readings of Paul in Modern Philosophy

Abstract: This paper discusses the characterization of Paul as an anti-philosopher and messianic nihilist by modern philosophers such as Badiou, Agamben and Taubes. These philosophers mainly focus on passages in Paul's *1 Corinthians*. Whereas they show themselves sensitive to philosophically relevant sections in this letter, the current article challenges their rather far-reaching interpretations. Differently from Badiou, who interprets 1 Cor. 2:1–5 (with its disapproval of "persuasive words of wisdom") as an anti-philosophical passage, this article sees its criticism directed, not against philosophy but against the sophists who championed effective rhetoric instead of truth. Furthermore, in contrast with his interpretation of 1 Cor. 1:26–29 as an anti-onto-theological reflection about "the things that are not" that God preferred over "the things that are," it actually seems that Paul shares the ontology of the Stoics who believe that all things emerge from God and return to God. In contrast with Taubes and Agamben, who see Paul's "nihilism" at work in his statements in 1 Cor. 7:29–31 about performing particular actions "as if not" performing them, this article tries to understand this passage against the background of the Stoic theory of the so-called ἀδιάφορα: the things which are morally indifferent and are located between the absolute good and the absolute wrong. Hence, it is argued, Paul is not nihilistic but just indifferent about particular things (although he does articulate his preferences). He is not anti-philosophical, but actually draws on the philosophical criticism of the sophistic movement. He is not anti-onto-theological either, but is deeply convinced that the whole of reality is grounded in God. Yet, although their interpretation of Paul can be contested, Badiou's, Taubes's and Agamben's sensitivity for identifying philosophically relevant passages in Paul is confirmed by contextualizing them in their ancient philosophical context.

1 Introduction

In the modern interpretation of Paul's writings by philosophers such as Badiou, Taubes, and Agamben, Paul is depicted as an anti-philosopher, a critic of onto-theology, and a Messianic nihilist.[1] The relevant passages are found in Badiou's *Saint Paul: The Foundation of Universalism* (1997), Taubes's *The Political Theology of Paul* (1993), and Agamben's *The Time That Remains* (2000). These studies—originally written in French, German, and Italian, respectively—were all published in an English translation by Stanford University Press well over a decade ago, and have acquired a large readership.[2] In this paper, I will comment the passages in these writings that are most revealing of the author's stance. The philosophers base their interpretation especially on certain sections from Paul's *1 Corinthians*. In my paper, I will examine the relevant texts, comment on them, and refer to certain ancient-philosophical texts, especially Stoic texts, which I judge to warrant further exploration in relation to Paul. First, I discuss Badiou's characterization of Paul as an anti-philosopher, followed by a discussion of his sketch of Paul as a critic of onto-theology; I continue with Taubes's and Agamben's depiction of Paul as a Messianic nihilist and with my suggestion for an alternative interpretation, before coming to my final conclusions.

2 Badiou's Characterization of Paul as an Anti-Philosopher

In the second chapter of his *Saint Paul*, Badiou offers the following quotation of Paul from 1 Cor. 2:1–5:

> When I came to you, brothers and sisters, I did not come proclaiming the mystery of God to you in lofty words or wisdom. For I decided to know nothing among you except Jesus Christ, and him crucified. And I came to you in weakness and in fear and in much trembling. My speech and my proclamation were not with plausible words of wisdom, but

---

1 This article draws on my preparatory article (in Dutch) "Paulus als anti-filosoof en messiaans nihilist?," further developing and expanding its argumentation. I gratefully acknowledge the feedback from my MA-student Tom van Gemeren on a draft of the present paper.
2 Badiou, *Saint Paul*; Taubes, *The Political Theology of Paul*; Agamben, *The Time That Remains*.

with a demonstration of the Spirit and of power, so that your faith might rest not on human wisdom but on the power of God. (1 Cor. 2:1–5)[3]

Badiou takes this passage as the starting point for his interpretation of Paul as an anti-philosopher. By depicting Paul in this way, Badiou does not mean that Paul does not engage in a philosophical discourse, but rather that he enters this debate with the attitude of an anti-philosopher, in the same way that modern anti-philosophers such as Nietzsche, Lacan, and Wittgenstein participate in a philosophical discourse.[4] On the subject of the passage quoted from 1 Cor. 2:1–5, Badiou writes the following:

> We find ourselves here on the second of Paul's major fronts (the first being the conflict with the Judeo-Christians): the contempt in which he holds philosophical wisdom. Basically, what gets him into difficulty in Athens is his antiphilosophy. In 1 Corinthians, we find a clear, albeit indirect, appraisal of these expeditions into philosophical territory by an anti-philosopher: [then follows the quotation of 1 Corinthians 2:1–5, GvK]. The problem lies in knowing how, armed only with the conviction that declares the Christ-event, one is to tackle the Greek intellectual milieu, whose essential category is that of wisdom (*sophia*), and whose instrument is that of rhetorical superiority (*hyperokhē logou*). (...) Paul opposes a show of spirit (*pneuma*, breath) and power (*dunamis*) to the armed wisdom of rhetoric. The wisdom of men is opposed to the power of God. It is thus a question of intervening *ouk en sophiai logou*, "without the wisdom of language." This maxim envelops a radical antiphilosophy.[5]

What is remarkable about this interpretation is that Badiou views Paul as an "anti-philosopher" who crosses over into philosophical territory, with the strategy of intervening "without the wisdom of language." Badiou even speaks of a "radical anti-philosophy." However, Badiou's characterization of Paul's words in 1 Cor. 2:1–5 does not seem correct. Differently from what Badiou assumes, the opponents of Paul in Corinth are not the philosophers, but the so-called sophists who, unlike philosophers, seek their wisdom in rhetorical eloquence. Paul's criticism of these sophists, with their "wisdom of language," is actually similar to the criticism that philosophers express of the sophists.[6] Understood in this way, Paul's strategy is in fact philosophical. Therefore, Badiou's depiction of Paul as an anti-philosopher is rather problematic and seems to re-

---

3 Unless otherwise stated, translations of biblical passages are taken from the New Revised Standard Version (NRSV), and translation of passages of Classical authors from the Loeb Classical Library, all with small adaptations where necessary.
4 Badiou, *Saint Paul*, 58.
5 Ibid., 27–28.
6 Cf. Van Kooten, "Rhetorical Competition."

flect his own strategy to place modern anti-philosophers, including himself, in the context of a long and important tradition. Nevertheless, Badiou is indeed right in surmising that Paul strays into philosophical territory.

3 Badiou's Characterization of Paul as a Critic of Onto-Theology

3.1 Paul's Phrase τὰ μὴ ὄντα in 1 Cor. 2:1–5

Not only does Badiou characterize Paul as an anti-philosopher but also a "critic of onto-theology"; as we shall see, both depictions are coherent from Badiou's perspective. Badiou develops this interpretation of Paul in close connection with the passage from 1 Cor. 2:1–5 already discussed. That is to say, in the fourth chapter of his *Saint Paul*, Badiou returns to the issue of the anti-philosophical Paul and quotes the passage immediately preceding 1 Cor. 2:1–5, 1 Cor. 1:17–29, where Paul contrasts "the wisdom of language" and "the wisdom of the world" with the proclamation of the gospel and "the wisdom of God." This passage ends as follows:

> Consider your own call, brothers and sisters: not many of you were wise by human standards, not many were powerful, not many were of noble birth. But God chose what is foolish in the world to shame the wise; God chose what is weak in the world to shame the strong; God chose what is low (τὰ ἀγενῆ τοῦ κόσμου) and despised (τὰ ἐξουθενημένα) in the world, the things that are not (τὰ μὴ ὄντα), to reduce to nothing the things that are (τὰ ὄντα), so that no one might boast in the presence of God. (1 Cor. 1:26–29)

Before examining Badiou's comments on this passage, I note that the NRSV translation of the phrases "what is low (τὰ ἀγενῆ τοῦ κόσμου) and despised (τὰ ἐξουθενημένα) in the world" (1 Cor. 1:28) is questionable. This also holds for the translation used in Badiou's *Saint Paul* ("God chose what is base and despised in the world"). In fact, the phrase "τὰ ἀγενῆ" can probably best be translated as "the things that are uncreated."[7]; the term "ἀγενής" in this sense of "uncreated" occurs, for instance, in Plato's *Timaeus* (27c) when Timaeus tells Socrates:

---

[7] See LSJ [= Liddell-Scott-Jones, *Greek-English Lexicon*] s.v. ἀγενής I: "unborn, uncreated", and hence s.v. ἀγενής II: "of no family, ignoble."

> ... all men who possess even a small share of good sense call upon God always at the outset of every undertaking, be it small or great; we therefore who are purposing to deliver a discourse concerning the Universe, how it was created or haply is uncreate (ἢ γέγονεν ἢ καὶ ἀγενές ἐστιν), must needs invoke Gods and Goddesses (if so be that we are not utterly demented), praying that all we say may be approved by them in the first place, and secondly by ourselves.[8]

And rather than translating the phrase "τὰ ἐξουθενημένα" as "what is despised," it seems better to translate it as "that which is set at naught."[9] These meanings suit the register in which the immediate continuation of this line is written, that talks of "the things that are not (τὰ μὴ ὄντα)" and "the things that are (τὰ ὄντα)":

> God chose the uncreated things of the cosmos (τὰ ἀγενῆ τοῦ κόσμου) and the things that are set at naught (τὰ ἐξουθενημένα), the things that are not (τὰ μὴ ὄντα), to reduce to nothing the things that are (τὰ ὄντα). (1 Cor. 1:28, translation mine)

I will return to this passage soon to explore the notion of "the things that are not (τὰ μὴ ὄντα)," but I will first present Badiou's commentary on 1 Cor. 2:1–5, which leans heavily on his understanding of the phrases "the things that are not (τὰ μὴ ὄντα)" and "the things that are (τὰ ὄντα)" in 1 Corinthians 1:28.

3.2 Badiou's Interpretation of Paul's τὰ μὴ ὄντα

Badiou's commentary on 1 Cor. 2:1–5 runs as follows:

> From a more ontological viewpoint, it is necessary to maintain that Christian discourse legitimates neither the God of wisdom (because God has chosen the foolish things), nor the God of power (because God has chosen the weak and base things). But what unites these two traditional determinations, and provides the basis for their rejection, is deeper still. Wisdom and power are attributes of God to the extent that they are attributes of being. God is said to be the sovereign intellect, or to govern the world and men's destiny to the precise extent that pure intellect is the supreme point of being specified by a wisdom, and universal power [is] that whose innumerable signs—equally signs of Being as that which is beyond beings—can be distributed or applied to the becoming of men. One must, in Paul's logic, go so far as to say that the Christ-event testifies that God is not the god of Being, is not Being. Paul prescribes an anticipatory critique of what Heidegger calls onto-theology, wherein God is thought as supreme being, and hence as the measure for what being as such is capable of.

---

8 Plato, *Timaeus* 27c.
9 See LSJ s.v. ἐξουθενέω = ἐξουδενόω; and LSJ s.v. ἐξουδενόω, "set at naught."

> The most radical statement in the text we are commenting on is in effect the following: "God has chosen the things that are not [ta mē onta] in order to bring to nought those that are [ta onta]." That the Christ-event causes non beings rather than beings to arise as attesting to God; that it consists in the abolition of what all previous discourses held as existing, or being, gives a measure of the ontological subversion to which Paul's antiphilosophy invites the declarant or militant.
>
> It is through the invention of a language wherein folly, scandal, and weakness supplant knowing reason, order, and power, and wherein non-being is the only legitimizable affirmation of being, that Christian discourse is articulated. In Paul's eyes, this articulation is incompatible with any prospect (and there has been no shortage of them, almost from the time of his death onward) of a "Christian philosophy."[10]

Badiou is certainly correct in his view that the phrases "the things that are not (τὰ μὴ ὄντα)" and "the things that are (τὰ ὄντα)" are to be understood as ontological terminology, and he is right that Paul's use of these terms shows Paul's ontology, his vision on what (really) exists: God is able to let appear the things that are not, and to let disappear the things that are.

However, Badiou's view that Paul's view on "the things that are not (τὰ μὴ ὄντα)" entails an anti-philosophical criticism of ontology, an "ontological subversion" fails to convince. It seems as if Badiou understands Paul's assertion that "God chose what is uncreated (τὰ ἀγενῆ τοῦ κόσμου) and set at naught (τὰ ἐξουθενημένα) in the world, things that are not (τὰ μὴ ὄντα), to reduce to nothing things that are (τὰ ὄντα)" as alluding to a creation from nothing, a "creatio ex nihilo." Yet the final lines of the first chapter of *1 Corinthians*, which Badiou does not quote, indicate that this is not the case. I will discuss these lines in the next section, and open up an alternative, non-nihilistic, Stoic interpretation of Paul's "things that are not (τὰ μὴ ὄντα)."

3.3 An Alternative, Stoic Interpretation of Paul's τὰ μὴ ὄντα

The lines that immediately follow Paul's discussion of "the things that are not (τὰ μὴ ὄντα)" but that Badiou leaves out of consideration continue as follows:

> God chose the uncreated things of the cosmos (τὰ ἀγενῆ τοῦ κόσμου) and the things that are set at naught (τὰ ἐξουθενημένα), the things that are not (τὰ μὴ ὄντα), to reduce to nothing the things that are (τὰ ὄντα), *so that no one might boast in the presence of God from whom (ἐξ αὐτοῦ) you are in Christ Jesus*, who became for us wisdom from God, and righteousness and sanctification and redemption, in order that, as it is written, "Let the one who boasts, boast in the Lord." (1 Cor. 1:28–31)

---

10 Badiou, *Saint Paul*, 46–47.

The prepositional determination "from whom (ἐξ αὐτοῦ) you are in Christ Jesus (ἐξ αὐτοῦ δὲ ὑμεῖς ἐστε ἐν Χριστῷ Ἰησοῦ)" is a very important indication of the nature of Paul's ontology and raises doubts about whether Paul indeed propagates the kind of "ontological subversion" that Badiou deems characteristic of Paul's anti-philosophical criticism of the existing Greek-philosophical onto-theology. The antecedent to which the prepositional determination refers is God. He is conceived of as the one "from whom" human beings derive their existence: The Christians in Corinth are, according to Paul, "from God (ἐκ τοῦ θεοῦ)" (see, for the full phrase, 1 Cor. 11:12), and "in Christ Jesus (ἐν Χριστῷ Ἰησοῦ)." These prepositional determinations are, as Gregory Sterling has demonstrated, examples of the so-called "prepositional metaphysics" current among Greek philosophers.[11] If the entire passage 1 Cor. 1:28–31 is read in an integral way, it emerges that "the uncreated things of the cosmos (τὰ ἀγενῆ τοῦ κόσμου)" and "the things that are not (τὰ μὴ ὄντα)" do not arise from nothing, from an "ontological subversion"; rather they derive their existence from God himself: they arise from God. This view we also encounter elsewhere in Paul's *1 Corinthians*, in chapter eight, in a passage that is simultaneously cosmological and soteriological and again shows Paul's use of prepositional metaphysics:

> ... yet for us there is one God, the Father, from whom (ἐξ οὗ) are all things and unto whom (εἰς αὐτόν) we exist, and one Lord, Jesus Christ, through whom (δι' οὗ) are all things and through whom (δι' αὐτοῦ) we exist. (1 Cor. 8:6)

This passage demonstrates that Paul structures the process in which the cosmos ("all things," τὰ πάντα) and human beings find themselves with the aid of the prepositions "from," "through," and "unto." The statement about the emergence of the cosmos from God is also found later in the same letter, in 1 Cor. 11:12, where Paul states that "all things are from God (τὰ δὲ πάντα ἐκ τοῦ θεοῦ)." And the full process, with its protological, present, and eschatological phases, is also depicted in Paul's *Romans*, in which he concludes a particular hymnic passage in the following way:

> For from him (ἐξ αὐτοῦ) and through him (δι' αὐτοῦ) and unto him (εἰς αὐτὸν) are all things. To him be the glory for ever. Amen. (Rom. 11:36)[12]

---

11 Sterling, "Prepositional Metaphysics in Jewish Wisdom."
12 See also Eph. 3:14–15 about the divine "Father, from whom (ἐξ οὗ) every family in heaven and on earth takes its name." Cf. Van Kooten, "The Divine Father of the Universe."

The structuring of this process that encompasses cosmos and human beings reflects the Stoic view that the ontological reality arises out of God and eventually reverts back to him. According to Diogenes Laertius, for instance, the Stoic Zeno holds that God

> is indestructible and uncreated (ἀγένητος), being the artificer of this orderly arrangement (διακόσμησις), who at stated periods of time absorbs into himself (εἰς ἑαυτὸν) the whole of substance and again creates it from himself (ἐξ ἑαυτοῦ).[13]

Of course, there is a difference between Paul and the Stoics, insofar as the latter are of the opinion that there is not a single final, exclusive, definitive return to God, but an eternally cyclical process of creation from, and return to God.[14] But what this comparison with Stoic thought shows is that Paul's assertion that cosmos and human beings originated "from God" implies that God constitutes the ontological foundation of the reality that emerges from him. Hence, contrary to Badiou's claims, there is no "ontological subversion" in Paul's thought, and therefore also no criticism of contemporary philosophical onto-theology. There is little foundation for Badiou's view that Paul is anti-ontological because he uses the terminology of "the uncreated things of the cosmos (τὰ ἀγενῆ τοῦ κόσμου)," "the things that are set at naught (τὰ ἐξουθενημένα)," and "the things that are not (τὰ μὴ ὄντα)" and contrasts these with "the things that are (τὰ ὄντα)." Rather Paul regards the ontological foundation of "the things that are not (τὰ μὴ ὄντα)" as provided by the fact that they are "from God" (ἐκ τοῦ θεοῦ). If Paul criticizes "the things that are (τὰ ὄντα)," it is not as Badiou believed because of his "anticipatory critique of what Heidegger calls onto-theology, wherein God is thought as supreme being," but in order to challenge the view of those who have forgotten about the emergence of things from God and wrongly believe that the existence of these things is unconnected with their ultimate ontological foundation in God. As Paul says elsewhere, at the beginning of his *Romans*, these people: "exchanged the truth about God for a lie and worshipped and served the creature rather than the Creator (καὶ ἐλάτρευσαν τῇ κτίσει παρὰ τὸν κτίσαντα), who is blessed for ever" (Rom. 1:25). It is actually against this "ontological subversion" that Paul raises his protest. In fact, what Paul points to is the ontological continuity between God and creation; it is creation itself that reflects the divine attributes of power and divinity (Rom. 1:19–20), at least if these

---

13 Diogenes Laertius, *Lives of Eminent Philosophers* 7.137–38 = *SVF* 2.580. *SVF* is an abbreviation of the collection of Stoic fragments in Arnim, *Stoicorum veterum fragmenta*.
14 For a fuller comparison of Paul's eschatology with Greek eschatology, see Van Kooten, "Quaestiones disputatae."

attributes are perceived, not with a limited, incapable mind (Rom. 1:28), but with a renewed, properly functioning mind (Rom. 12:1–2). Nothing is wrong with creation, "the things that are (τὰ ὄντα)," unless their continuity with God, their derivation from God, and their dependence on God go unnoticed and they are wrongly seen as independent, rather than being viewed in a hierarchical ontological perspective in which creation is ontologically grounded in its creator. It is for this reason that Paul emphasizes that "the things that are not (τὰ μὴ ὄντα)," "the uncreated things of the cosmos (τὰ ἀγενῆ τοῦ κόσμου)," to which he likens the marginalized, despised Christians at Corinth, are now generated and created "from God," in the technical Stoic sense of their derivation from God as the ontological foundation of their existence. They did not exist, but now they arise from God. This is not a creation from nothing, but a creation from God.

Elsewhere, in *Romans*, in a passage that features the only other text in his writings where he employs the term "the things that are not (τὰ μὴ ὄντα)," Paul can also express himself in a less technical way, stating that God can be trusted as the God "who gives life to the dead and calls the things that do not exist (τὰ μὴ ὄντα) into existence (ὡς ὄντα)" (Rom. 4:17) or, more literally, "calls the things that do not exist just as existing."[15] Here the imagery is one of "calling into existence," the non-technical version of the emergence of "the things that do not exist (τὰ μὴ ὄντα)" *from* God (ἐκ τοῦ θεοῦ, 1 Cor. 1:28, 30; 11:12). Abraham, Paul asserts, trusted that this God could give him a son despite the "mortification," "the state of death" (νέκρωσις), i.e., the barrenness of Sarah's womb (Rom. 4:19), just as Christians can trust this God because he "raised Jesus our Lord from the dead" (Rom. 4:23–24).

It is this latter event, the resurrection, that Badiou describes as "the Christ-event": "That the Christ-event causes non beings rather than beings to arise as attesting to God; that it consists in the abolition of what all previous discourses held as existing, or being, gives a measure of the ontological subversion to which Paul's antiphilosophy invites the declarant or militant."[16] However, Badiou ignores the fact that according to 1 Cor. 1:28–31 these things that are not are created "from God," rather than "ex nihilo."

This last view, that God generates "the things that not" out of nothing, "*from the things that are not*" (ἐξ οὐκ ὄντων), is a misunderstanding that occurred already early in Christian tradition. The second-century apologist Theophilus of Antioch, for instance, in his writing *Ad Autolycum* contrasts his interpretation

---

15 See LSJ s.v. ὡς Ab I.2, "like as, just as."
16 Badiou, *Saint Paul*, 47.

of what he regards to be the Jewish-Christian view on creation with Greek views on creation. According to Theophilus, "… and God has made the cosmos from things that are not (καὶ τὰ πάντα ὁ θεὸς ἐποίησεν ἐξ οὐκ ὄντων εἰς τὸ εἶναι)."[17]

As Gerhard May has shown in his study on the notion of the creation from nothing, by employing this notion Theophilus criticized Christians such as Hermogenes who had shared the Middle-Platonic conviction that God had created the world out of pre-existing matter.[18] As May indicates, this view that Theophilus criticized seems to have been the standard view among Christians in the second and third centuries AD, until the view of a creation out of nothing took root. Although Christians only came to express it from Theophilus onwards, the view of a creation out of nothing (ἐκ μηδενός / ἐξ οὐδενός; ἐξ οὐκ ὄντος / ἐξ οὐκ ὄντων; ἐκ [τοῦ] μὴ ὄντος / ἐκ μὴ ὄντων) had itself already been the subject of extensive philosophical debate and had occupied pre-Socratic philosophers such as Anaxagoras, Empedocles, Melissus, and Parmenides, as well as subsequent philosophers such as Aristotle, Epicurus, Chrysippus, Plutarch, Sextus Empiricus and others. Aristotle, for instance, engaged with the view of the pre-Socratic philosopher Melissus who maintained that

> … if anything exists it must be eternal, on the ground that it is impossible for anything to come into existence from nothing (ἐκ μηδενός). Whether everything has come into existence or only some things, they are in either case eternal; otherwise they would have come into existence from nothing (ἐξ οὐδενὸς).[19]

Aristotle, however, challenges Melissus' argumentation and reminds his readers of respectable philosophers who did argue that things arose from what did not exist:

> … Melissus has not proved anything by showing that the premise from which he starts is correct, nor any more certain than that concerning which he is arguing. For it may be regarded as more probable that something should arise from nothing (γίνεσθαι ἐκ μὴ ὄντος) than that many things should not exist. In fact, it is very commonly said that things which do not exist do come into existence, and that many things arise from what does not

---

17 Theophilus, *Ad Autolycum* 1.4; cf. 2.4, 2.10, 2.13.
18 See May, *Creatio Ex Nihilo*, 140–47 on Hermogenes, and especially 147: "Theophilus of Antioch, the earliest opponent of Hermogenes, is the first church theologian known to us—and this is certainly no accident—to use unambiguously the substance and the terminology of the doctrine of *creatio ex nihilo*. His manifesto was read by Tertullian and Hippolytus (…). And Tertullian in his broadsheet again delivered a penetrating case for and defence of *creatio ex nihilo*." For the collected fragments and testimonies of Hermogenes, see Chapot, "L'hérésie d'Hermogène."
19 Aristotle, *On Melissus* section 1, 974a2–4.

exist (λέγεταί τε καὶ σφόδρα ὑπὲρ αὐτῶν γίγνεσθαί τε τὰ μὴ ὄντα, καὶ [μὴ] γεγονέναι πολλὰ ἐκ μὴ ὄντων); and this is the opinion not merely of chance persons, but some men with reputations, as philosophers have said it too. So Hesiod says "first of all there was created Chaos, then the broad-bosomed earth, ever the safe foundation of all things, and then Love which belongs to all the Immortals." All the rest of the universe he says grew out of these, but these out of nothing (τὰ δ' ἄλλα φησὶ γενέσθαι <ἐκ τούτων>, ταῦτα δ' ἐξ οὐδενός). (...) So it is clear that some at any rate believe that things come into existence from what does not exist (ὥστε τοῦτο μὲν δῆλον, ὅτι ἐνίοις γε δοκεῖ καὶ ἐξ οὐκ ὄντων ἂν γενέσθαι).[20]

Similarly, Plutarch too finds himself discussing pre-Socratic views on a possible creation from nothing. Counter to a particular interpretation of Empedocles, that of the Epicurean Colotes of Lampsacus, Plutarch maintains that Empedocles refutes the idea of a generation from the non-existent:

Empedocles (...) is controverting a point of fact, generation from the non-existent (Ἐμπεδοκλῆς ... πραγματικῶς διαφέρεσθαι περὶ τῆς ἐξ οὐκ ὄντων γενέσεως) (...). (...) he [i.e., Empedocles] does not abolish generation, but only generation from the non-existent (οὐκ ἀναιρεῖ γένεσιν ἀλλὰ τὴν ἐκ μὴ ὄντος); nor abolish destruction, but only out and out destruction, that is, the destruction that reduces to non-existence (οὐδὲ φθορὰν ἀλλὰ τὴν πάντῃ, τουτέστι τὴν εἰς τὸ μὴ ὂν ἀπολλύουσαν).[21]

This is just a brief glimpse of the discussion of *creatio ex nihilo* in ancient philosophy, but the topic would certainly deserve a full detailed study; this, however, is beyond the scope of the present article.[22] What matters here is, firstly, that by adopting the view of a *creatio ex nihilo*, Christians such as Theophilus did not move beyond ancient philosophy; secondly, that this view was only explicitly adopted by Christians from the second century AD onwards, though in the course of the second and third centuries it became the common Christian view on creation; thirdly, that this view differs profoundly from the Stoic view that sees creation emerging not from nothing but from God himself, as I will shortly confirm by discussing a passage in Philo of Alexandria; and fourthly and finally,

---

20 Ibid., 975a4–17. I here follow the Greek text of Apelt's Teubner edition, which is used in the Loeb Classical Library, rather than Bekker's edition, which is used in the Thesaurus Linguae Graecae.
21 Plutarch, *Reply to Colotes in Defence of the Other Philosophers* 1113C.
22 May, *Creatio Ex Nihilo*, does not discuss the pagan Greco-Roman antecedents of the notion of creation from nothing. For the Jewish and Christian adoption of this notion, see Bockmuehl, "Creatio ex nihilo"; Soskice, "Creatio ex nihilo"; McFarland, *From Nothing*. On Pre-Socratic discussion of the notion (notably with regard to Parmenides, Empedocles and Anaxagoras), see Mourelatos, "Pre-Socratic Origins"; Cornford, "Anaxagoras' Theory of Matter." On Aristotle's view on the issue, see Anagnostopoulos, "Aristotle's Parmenidean Dilemma"; Shields, "The Generation of Form in Aristotle." For Lucretius, see Tatum, "Lucretius."

that there is ample reason to believe that Paul, in the mid-first century AD, employed this Stoic notion of emergence from God, and not the "nihilistic" notion of *creatio ex nihilo*.

I will now highlight the essential difference between Middle-Platonic, Stoic and *ex nihilo* conceptions of creation by commenting on a passage from Philo's *On the Eternity of the Cosmos*. In this treatise Philo, taking sides within a Middle-Platonic debate, avers that the world itself has not been created in time but has existed as God's creation from eternity, so that the world is eternal. In this treatise, he applauds the mid-third century BC Stoic philosopher Boethus of Sidon for abandoning the common Stoic view on the periodic creation and destruction of the cosmos in favor of the conviction that the cosmos is eternal:[23]

> The demonstrations given by the school of Boethus are very convincing and I will proceed to state them. If, they [i.e., Philo's opponents] say, the world is created and destructible (εἰ, φασί, γενητὸς καὶ φθαρτὸς ὁ κόσμος) we shall have *something created out of the non-existent* (ἐκ τοῦ μὴ ὄντος τι γενήσεται) and even the Stoics regard this as quite preposterous.[24]

In Philo's view, even the Stoics would disagree with the notion of a *creatio ex nihilo*. Of course they would, because while believing that the cosmos is generated and involved in a cosmic process, they definitely do not think that the cosmos emerged out of nothing. Instead, they argue that this process takes its starting point in God, from whom everything emerges and unto whom it returns in an eternal movement of διακόσμησις and conflagration. Indeed, as we have seen, the Stoics (despite their strongly processual theology, in which they differ from the static theology of the Platonists) are not of the opinion that the cosmos emerges "from the non-existent (ἐκ τοῦ μὴ ὄντος)." According to the Stoics, the cosmos emerges from God himself. Hence, a *creatio ex nihilo* is opposed to a creation from God, and Paul, too, adheres to the latter view, of a creation from God. The notion of a *creatio ex nihilo* is alien to his thought.

That the antithesis indeed lies between a creation from God as opposed to a creation from nothing is even confirmed by the Nicene Creed from 325 AD, even though this creed is concerned with the christological question of how the generation of the Son must be conceived, and not with the cosmological question of how creation came about. Here too, however, a generation "from God (ἐκ θεοῦ)" is contrasted with a generation "from the things that are not (ἐξ οὐκ ὄντων)." In the body of the creed it is stated with regard to the generation of the divine Son:

---

23 Philo, *On the Eternity of the Cosmos* 76–77.
24 Ibid., 78.

> We believe (…) in (…) the Son of God, generated from the Father, the Only-Begotten, that is from the essence of the Father, God *from God* (θεὸν ἐκ θεοῦ), light from light, true God from true God, begotten, not made, one in essence with the Father …

In the so-called ἀναθήματα with which the creed ends, however, it is asserted:

> However, those who say: (…) that he [i.e., the divine Son] was made *from nothing* (καὶ ὅτι 'ἐξ οὐκ ὄντων ἐγένετο') (…), <such persons> the Catholic Church anathematizes.[25]

Actually, one could even say that precisely the early fourth-century AD Nicene Creed, which crowns the increasing Christian adoption of the notion of *creatio ex nihilo* since the second century AD, marks the official break with the Pauline-Stoic view that the cosmos emerges from God; this view is now reserved for the way the Son is generated. He is generated from God, whereas creation is now separated from God by an ontological rift. The divine Son is generated from God, and creation apparently now takes place from nothing, although mediated by the Son as the one "through whom all things were made, those in heaven and those on earth." The ontological basis of creation now, for the first time, becomes "nihilistic" and probably also voluntaristic and contingent, in the sense of expressing God's will rather than his essence. According to Paul on the other hand creation still displays the very qualities of God himself, his eternal power and divine nature (Rom. 1:20). It is no wonder, then, that the modern interpreters of Paul, unconsciously influenced by the enormous impact of the Nicene Creed on the common perception of Christianity, naturally assume that Paul already believed in the creation from nothing. But nothing is further from the truth, as Paul believed that creation ontologically derived from God himself.

The opposite of a creation or generation "from God (ἐκ θεοῦ)" is a creation or generation "from the non-existent things (ἐξ οὐκ ὄντων)." It is therefore inconceivable that Paul, who uses the phrase "from God" to depict God's creation of the world, could have applied the notion of a *creatio ex nihilo*; the one concept excludes the other *a priori*. It is ironic that the standard Christian view of creation after Paul has become that of a creation out of nothing. Not only does Paul not know this view, he excludes it because he shares the Stoic view that the cosmic reality emerged from God. This is essential for our evaluation of Badiou's thesis of a supposed "ontological subversion" in Paul's thought. The contrary is the case. Paul is not a critic, but an upholder of the classic, Greco-Roman onto-theology.

---

[25] Reference to Denzinger, *Compendium of Creeds*, 125–26.

Badiou's characterization of Paul, on the basis of 1 Cor. 1:28–29, as an anti-philosophical, proto-Heideggerian critic of onto-theology finds a parallel, to a certain extent, in the labelling of Paul as a Messianic nihilist by Taubes and Agamben. They too base their depiction of Paul on an interpretation of *1 Corinthians*, albeit on a different passage, 1 Cor. 7:29–31, which shows Paul's ambiguous evaluation of earthly life. We shall first study this passage and the interpretation that Taubes and Agamben offer, before I offer an alternative reading of this passage.

4 Taubes's and Agamben's Characterization of Paul as a Messianic Nihilist

4.1 Paul's ὡς μή in 1 Cor. 7:29–31

The passage that Taubes and Agamben comment on is derived from the seventh chapter of *1 Corinthians* where Paul advises the Corinthians how they, in their new position as Christians, must relate to their ethnic identity as Jew or non-Jew, their social position as slave or master, and their societal status, as married or unmarried. Paul encourages his Christian readers to remain in the ethnic, social and societal situation in which they found themselves when they were "called" to a new life as Christian. Despite this new mode of life, they best remain in the situation of their "calling":

> ... let each of you lead the life that the Lord has assigned, to which God called you. (...) 20 Let each of you remain in the condition in which you were called. (...) 24 In whatever condition you were called, brothers and sisters, there remain with God. (1 Cor. 7:17, 20, 24)

This advice concerns both the ethnic (1 Cor. 7:18–19), social (1 Cor. 7:21–23) and civic-societal (1 Cor. 7:1, 7–8, 25–40) features of the lives of the converted. The circumcised should not have their circumcision annulled, the uncircumcised should not let themselves be circumcised. Slaves must not be obsessed by their slavery, although if the opportunity presents itself to become free, they are advised to take it. And the unmarried, preferentially, should not bind themselves in marriage, and not let themselves become inundated in terrestrial concerns. These specific advices, which Paul indeed emphatically presents as advices and not as prescriptions (1 Cor. 7:6–7, 12, 25, 35, 40), then broaden out to reflections about the general attitude that a Christian should adopt in the world, and this is the actual passage that Taubes and Agamben quote and comment upon:

I mean, brothers and sisters, the appointed time has grown short; from now on, let even those who have wives (οἱ ἔχοντες γυναῖκας) be as though they had none (ὡς μὴ ἔχοντες), 30 and those who mourn (οἱ κλαίοντες) as though they were not mourning (ὡς μὴ κλαίοντες), and those who rejoice (οἱ χαίροντες) as though they were not rejoicing (ὡς μὴ χαίροντες), and those who buy (οἱ ἀγοράζοντες) as though they had no possessions (ὡς μὴ κατέχοντες), 31 and those who make use of the world (οἱ χρώμενοι τὸν κόσμον[26]) as though they were not consuming it (ὡς μὴ καταχρώμενοι[27]). For the present form of this world (τὸ σχῆμα τοῦ κόσμου τούτου) is passing away. (1 Cor. 7:29–31)

It is especially the repetitive phrase "as if not (ὡς μή)" that Taubes and Agamben focus upon and deem characteristic of the life-style propagated by Paul, a lifestyle that they characterize—as we shall now see—as "Messianic nihilism."

4.2 Taubes's Messianic-Nihilistic and Politically Subversive Interpretation of Paul

Taubes's *The Political Theology of Paul* contains the following two passage about 1 Cor. 7:29–31. In the first passage, Taubes connects 1 Cor. 7:29–31 with the ethical instructions that Paul gives in Rom. 13 after his injunction to obey the Roman State (Rom. 13:1–7), and explains what he regards as Paul's disinterested, world-denying, non-revolutionary yet still subversive and destructive political resignation and quietism as the result of his general "nihilistic" attitude:

> I read this (and now we are talking about [Romans] 13:11 ff.) just like the following passage from 1 Corinthians; I mean the nihilistic passage of the *hōs mē* [1 Cor. 7:29 ff.]: to have as if one didn't have:
>
> The appointed time has grown short [that's how the text begins]. From now on, let even those who have wives be as though they had none [as if they had none, *comme si*], and those who mourn as though they were not mourning, and those who rejoice as though they were not rejoicing, and those who buy as though they had no possessions, and those who deal with the world as though they had no dealings with it. For the present form [the *morphē*] of this world [*tou cosmou*] is passing away. I want you to be free from anxieties.
>
> This means: under this time pressure, if tomorrow the whole palaver, the entire swindle were going to be over—in that case there's no point in any revolution! That's absolutely right, I would give the same advice. Demonstrate obedience to the state authority, pay

---

[26] See LSJ s.v. χράω (B) C. Med. Χρáομαι II "use, make use of."
[27] See LSJ s.v. καταχράομαι II.1 "do what one likes with a person or thing," II.2 "use up, consume", II.3 "misuse, abuse."

taxes, don't do anything bad, don't get involved in conflicts, because otherwise it'll get confused with some revolutionary movement [*Revoluzzer-Bewegung*].[28]

In this passage Taubes characterizes 1 Cor. 7:29–32 as "the nihilistic passage of the *hōs mē*." About twenty pages further on, Taubes returns to his earlier analysis, in the context of his discussion of Walter Benjamin's view of nihilism in support of a worldly politics, and writes:

> I contend that this concept of nihilism, as developed here by [Walter] Benjamin, is the guiding thread also of the *hōs mē* in Corinthians and Romans. The world decays, the *morphē* of this world has passed. Here, the relationship to the world is, as the young Benjamin understands it, world politics as nihilism. And that is something that Nietzsche understood, that behind all this there is a profound nihilism at work, that it is at work as world politics, towards the destruction of the Roman Empire. (…) Here we have a nihilistic view of the world, and concretely of the Roman Empire. And that's something Nietzsche understood.[29]

According to Taubes, Paul's ambiguous world-view of the "as if not" ("*comme si*") is not only nihilistic,[30] but, in its nihilism also politically subversive and destructive. Paul is not only anti-philosophical, in Badiou's sense of the word, but he is also against the political establishment of his time.[31] Just as Badiou compares and connects Paul's view with Heidegger's anti-philosophical criticism of onto-theology and with the views of modern anti-philosophers such as Nietzsche, Lacan, and Wittgenstein, so Taubes compares Paul with philosophers such as Nietzsche and Walter Benjamin. Comparable with this nihilistic stipulation of Paul is also Agamben's interpretation.

---

28 Taubes, *The Political Theology of Paul*, 53–54.
29 Ibid., 72.
30 For a discussion of the best translation of the phrase ὡς μή, as "as if not" or as "as not," see the second section of the epilogue to the current volume.
31 Cf. also the comments by Wolf-Daniel Hartwich, Aleida Assmann and Jan Assmann in their "Afterword" to Taubes's *The Political Theology of Paul:* "… Taubes links Benjamin's order of the profane to the negative political theology of Paul. Taubes sees the closest parallel to Benjamin's 'nihilism as world politics' in Paul and his relation to the world in the mode of 'as though not' (ὡς μή)" (ibid., 134).

4.3 Agamben's Interpretation of Paul's Theology as Messianic Nullification of Reality

Agamben too, in his *The Time That Remains*, devotes much attention to the passage from 1 Cor. 7:29–32. Agamben develops his remarks about this passage in connection with his comments on Paul's notion of "calling (κλῆσις)," which we discussed earlier. The Corinthians are encouraged to remain in the ethnic, social, and societal situation in which they found themselves when "called" to a new life as Christians. Those circumcised should therefore not reverse their circumcision, nor should the uncircumcised have themselves circumcised:

> Was anyone at the time of his call already circumcised? Let him not seek to remove the marks of circumcision. Was anyone at the time of his call uncircumcised? Let him not seek circumcision. Circumcision is nothing, and uncircumcision is nothing; but obeying the commandments of God is everything. Let each of you remain in the condition in which you were called. (1 Cor. 7:18–20)

This "remaining" in what Agamben describes as "the Messianic calling," this "remaining" in a situation of "nothing" (as according to Paul both being circumcised and being uncircumcised mean "nothing") "revokes a condition [i.e., the condition of being (un-)circumcised] and radically puts it into question in the very act of adhering to it."[32] Hence, there is a nullification, "the Messianic nullification" as Agamben calls it subsequently in his commentary on 1 Cor. 7:29–32, in a section that bears the title "Vocation and Revocation":

> This [i.e., the revocation of the condition in which one was called, especially by the patient adherence to this condition] is what Paul says just a bit further on, in a remarkable passage that may be his most rigorous definition of messianic life (1 Cor. 7:29–32) [Here follows the full quotation of 1 Cor. 7:29–32.] (...). *Hōs mē*, 'as not': this is the formula concerning messianic life and is the ultimate meaning of *klēsis*. (...)
> At this point, the *hōs mē* shows itself as a technical term essential to Pauline vocabulary and must be understood in its specificity on both the syntactic-grammatical and semantic levels. (...) The Pauline *hōs mē* seems to be a special type of tensor, for it does not push a concept's semantic field toward that of another concept. Instead, it sets it against itself in the form of the as not: weeping as not weeping [cf. 1 Cor. 7:30]. The messianic tension thus does not tend toward an elsewhere, nor does it exhaust itself in the indifference between one thing and its opposite. The apostle does not say: 'weeping as rejoicing' nor 'weeping as [meaning =] not weeping,' but 'weeping as not weeping.' According to the principle of messianic *klēsis*, one determinate tactical condition is set in relation to itself—the weeping is pushed toward the weeping, the rejoicing toward the rejoicing. In this manner, it revokes the tactical condition and undermines it without altering its form. The

---

32 Agamben, *The Time That Remains*, 23.

Pauline passage on the *hōs mē* may thus conclude with the phrase '*paragei gar to schēma tou kosmou toutou* [for passing away is the figure, the way of being in this world]' (1 Cor. 7:31). In pushing each thing toward itself through the *as not*, the messianic does not simply cancel out this figure, but it makes it pass, it prepares its end. This is not another figure or another world: it is the passing of the figure of this world. (...)

In Paul, the messianic nullification performed by *hōs mē* is completely inherent to *klēsis* and does not happen to it in a second time (...), nor does it add anything to it. In this way, the messianic vocation is a movement of immanence, or, if one prefers, a zone of absolute indiscernibility between immanence and transcendence, between this world and the future world. From this perspective, the passage 1 Corinthians 7:29–32 can be read as though it were implicitly opposed—perhaps even knowingly—to the passage in Ecclesiastes (3:4–8) in which *Qoheleth* clearly separates the times Paul melds together: 'A time to weep, and a time to laugh; a time to mourn, and a time to dance ... a time to seek and a time to lose; a time to keep, and a time to throw away ... a time for war and a time for peace.' Paul defines the messianic condition by simply superimposing, in the *hōs mē*, the times Qoheleth divides.[33]

As this passage shows, Agamben's commentary on the Pauline ὡς μή strongly resembles that of Taubes. Of course, their interpretations also differ, and their individual interpretations can no doubt be explained from the context of their philosophizing, but it seems clear that both Taubes and Agamben read the Pauline ὡς μή as an expression of Paul's nihilism (Taubes) or of his "Messianic nullification" (Agamben). The commentary of both philosophers rests on a very detailed reading of the relevant passage from *1 Corinthians*. What is striking is that they show themselves sensitive to the philosophical potential they detect in Paul's writings but, at the same time, seem unaware of the possible ancient philosophical context of Paul and the resonances of this context in 1 Cor. 7. I will draw attention to this context in the following section and compare the results of this comparison with Taubes's and Agamben's interpretation.

But moving on to this context, I have two remarks about Agamben's reading of 1 Cor. 7:29–32. First, it seems that Agamben's observation that Paul, in his "as if not" passage, contrasts each verb with itself is not entirely correct. Indeed "those who have wives (οἱ ἔχοντες γυναῖκας)" are encouraged to be "as though they had none (ὡς μὴ ἔχοντες)"; "those who mourn (οἱ κλαίοντες) as though they were not mourning (ὡς μὴ κλαίοντες), and those who rejoice (οἱ χαίροντες) as though they were not rejoicing (ὡς μὴ χαίροντες)." Yet the subsequent encouragements that "those who buy (οἱ ἀγοράζοντες)" must be "as though they had no possessions (ὡς μὴ κατέχοντες)," and that "those who make use of the

---

33 Ibid., 23–26. Cf. also ibid., 68, where Agamben discusses the statement "the appointed time has grown short" at the beginning of 1 Cor. 7:29–32 and develops a differentiation between two kinds of time, καιρός time and χρόνος time.

world (οἱ χρώμενοι τὸν κόσμον)" must be "as though they were not consuming it (ὡς μὴ καταχρώμενοι)" show variations that use (slightly) different verbs that do not coincide, and are therefore not directly opposed, but rather seem to indicate differences in attitude: the positively phrased verbs, without negations, indicate actions that can be morally right or wrong, whilst the verbs that are negated refer to actions that are morally insufficient, or even plainly immoral: claiming something as one's indisputable possession to which one will always cling, and the unrestrained consumption of this world that degenerates into plain misuse. These variations indicate that the verbs that are contrasted with one another do not simply coincide, and that Paul is keen to make visible a difference in attitude. I will come back to this in the next section.

Secondly, I also briefly draw attention to the fact that Agamben seems to take Paul's remark that "the form of this cosmos (τὸ σχῆμα τοῦ κόσμου τούτου) is passing away" (1 Cor. 7:31) not in a cosmological sense, but in a metaphorical sense: "for passing away is the figure, the way of being in this world," as he translates this passage. In Agamben's view, Paul's statement concerns "the way of being" in this world. However, in Greek-philosophical texts, philosophers are interested in the form of the physical cosmos. Stoic philosophers such as Zeno, Chrysippus, and Heraclitus, the first century AD author of the *Homeric Problems*, believe that the "form (σχῆμα)" of the cosmos is spherical.[34] And Marcus Aurelius explicitly connects the form, or "plan" of the cosmos with the Stoic periodic movement of the end and regeneration of the cosmos:

> More than this, it [i.e., the Rational Soul] goes about the whole cosmos (ἔτι δὲ περιέρχεται τὸν ὅλον κόσμον) and the void surrounding it and traces its plan (καὶ τὸ σχῆμα αὐτοῦ), and stretches forth into the infinitude of Time, and comprehends the cyclical regeneration of all things.[35]

---

34 See Chrysippus on the spherical form of the cosmos in *SVF* 2.557 (... ἐν τῷ κόσμῳ, σφαιρικῷ τὸ σχῆμα ὄντι ...) and 2.1009 (καλὸς δὲ ὁ κόσμος· δῆλον δὲ ἐκ τοῦ σχήματος καὶ τοῦ χρώματος καὶ τοῦ μεγέθους καὶ τῆς περὶ τὸν κόσμον τῶν ἀστέρων ποικιλίας. σφαιροειδὴς γὰρ ὁ κόσμος, ὃ πάντων σχημάτων πρωτεύει); Heraclitus, *Homeric Problems* (*Quaestiones Homericae / Allegoriae*) 36.4 (Τὸ δὲ σφαιρικὸν ... τοῦ κόσμου σχῆμα ...) and 43.14 (Πρώτη δ' ἀπὸ τούτων τῶν στοιχείων ἀσπὶς ὑπ' αὐτοῦ χαλκεύεται, σφαιροειδὲς ἔχουσα τὸ σχῆμα, δι' οὗ τὸν κόσμον ἡμῖν ἐμφανῶς ἐσήμηνεν); and Diogenes Laertius, *Lives of Eminent Philosophers* 7.1 Zeno 140: "The cosmos, they [i.e., the Stoics] say, is one and finite, having a spherical form (Ἕνα τὸν κόσμον εἶναι καὶ τοῦτον πεπερασμένον, σχῆμ' ἔχοντα σφαιροειδές), such a form being the most suitable for motion, as Posidonius says in the fifth book of his *Physical Discourse* and the disciples of Antipater in their works on the Cosmos."
35 Marcus Aurelius, *Meditations* 11.1.2.

The phrase "τὸ σχῆμα τοῦ κόσμου" also matches the term διακόσμησις, the orderly arrangement of the cosmos, that we found in the description of Stoic physics in the passage from Diogenes Laertius quoted above. Here God is qualified as

> ... the artificer of this orderly arrangement (διακόσμησις), who at stated periods of time absorbs into himself (εἰς ἑαυτὸν) the whole of substance and again creates it from himself (ἐξ ἑαυτοῦ).[36]

Indeed, the σχῆμα τοῦ κόσμου is thus equivalent with the structure and constitution of the cosmos in all its parts as described by Balbus, the Stoic spokesperson in the second book of Cicero's *On the Nature of the Gods*, in a passage in which he argues for God's providential creation and government of the cosmos:

> But if the structure of the world in all its parts is such (*Quodsi omnes mundi partes ita constitutae sunt*) that it could not have been better whether in point of utility or beauty, let us consider whether this is the result of chance, or whether on the contrary the parts of the world are in such a condition that they could not possibly have cohered together if they were not controlled by intelligence and by divine providence.[37]

If "the form of the cosmos (τὸ σχῆμα τοῦ κόσμου)" has this technical cosmological meaning in Greek philosophical texts,[38] there is no reason to suppose that Paul differs from the normal cosmological meaning of this phrase. In point of fact, the statement that "the form of this cosmos is passing away" (1 Cor. 7:31) correctly describes the last phase of the cosmic process that—as we have seen previously—extends, in Paul's Stoic prepositional metaphysics, "from God, through God and *unto God*" (Rom. 11:36). It is "the form of this cosmos" that disappears at the end of the cosmos. What replaces the current cosmos is the convergence of the whole of cosmic reality with God himself: after Christ has submitted the universe to himself, and has subsequently submitted himself, with the entire universe, to God, the phase begins in which God is "all in all" (1 Cor. 15:24–28). Cosmos and human beings no longer exist in their semi-independence from God, but return unto God as the ontological ground of everything: God *is* all in all (1 Cor. 15:28).[39]

---

36 Diogenes Laertius, *Lives of Eminent Philosophers* 7.137–38 = *SVF* 2.580.
37 Cicero, *On the Nature of the Gods* [*De natura deorum*] 2.87.
38 Even a looser reference to the "form" of (cosmic) order still presupposes this cosmological form. See Philostratus of Athens, *The Life of Apollonius of Tyana* (*Vita Apollonii*) 8.7.22–23: "What form, then, does this order take? (καὶ τί τὸ σχῆμα τοῦ κόσμου τοῦδε;)," about the "kind of order dependent on a good man," alongside the cosmic order of God's creation (8.7.22).
39 For this interpretation, and the Stoic meaning of the statement that "God will be all in all", see Van Kooten, *Cosmic Christology*, 103–8.

What is most interesting is that the anonymous pagan Platonic critic of Christianity in Macarius Magnes's *Apocriticus*, who was formerly commonly identified as Porphyry, explicitly finds fault with Paul's use of the phrase "τὸ σχῆμα τοῦ κόσμου τούτου" and criticizes Paul's Stoic processual view from a static Platonic perspective that does not allow for such a dynamic, processual god:

> What does Paul mean by saying that the form of the world passes away? (…) Or how can the form of this world pass away? What is it that passes away, and why does it do so? For if the Creator were to make it pass away He would incur the charge of moving and altering that which was securely founded. Even if He were to change the form into something better, in this again He stands condemned, as not having realised at the time of creation a fitting and suitable form for the world, but having created it incomplete, and lacking the better arrangement. In any case, how is one to know that it is into what is good that the world would change if it came to an end late in time? And what benefit is there in the order of phenomena being changed? And if the condition of the visible world is gloomy and a cause for grief, in this, too, the Creator hears the sound of protest, being reduced to silence by the sound of reasonable charges against Him, in that He contrived the parts of the earth in grievous form, and in violation of the reasonableness of nature, and afterwards repented, and decided to change the whole.[40]

Although the identification of this anonymous critic of Christianity with Porphyry is now widely questioned,[41] the text remains very relevant for its Platonic criticism of Paul's (unrecognized) Stoic views on the cosmos.

We may thus conclude that, whereas Badiou, Taubes and Agamben interpret Paul's thought in a strongly anti-onto-theological and nihilistic way, his views make more sense in a Stoic metaphysical context. This is also the case for a central part of the argumentation of 1 Cor. 7, as we will now see.

4.4 An Alternative Interpretation of Paul's ὡς μή with the Aid of the Stoic Notion of ἀδιάφορα

The argumentation that Paul develops in 1 Cor. 7 displays profound similarities with the Stoic views regarding the so-called ἀδιάφορα, the things that are "indifferent": that is to say things that are neither good nor bad, so that they are, in a

---

40 Anonymous *apud* Macarius Magnes, *Apocriticus* 4.1; translated by T.W. Crafer, 1919, included in the digital "Early Church Fathers – Additional Texts" collection, edited by Roger Pearse, at www.tertullian.org/fathers.
41 See, e.g., the latest edition of Porphyry's fragments in Becker, *Porphyrios*, "Contra Christianos," which excludes all fragments from Macarius, see 103–5. The text is included as fr. 34 in von Harnack's edition (1916).

moral sense, indifferent. According to Diogenes Laertius, the Stoics are of the opinion that

> Of things that are, some (...) are good, some are evil, and some neither good nor evil (that is, morally indifferent). Goods comprise the virtues of prudence, justice, courage, temperance, and the rest; while the opposites of these are evils, namely, folly, injustice, and the rest. Neutral (neither good nor evil, that is) are all those things which neither benefit nor harm a man: such as life, health, pleasure, beauty, strength, wealth, fair fame and noble birth, and their opposites, death, disease, pain, ugliness, weakness, poverty, ignominy, low birth, and the like.[42]

In themselves the ἀδιάφορα are neither good nor bad, but all depends on the way in which these things are used; whether they contribute to moral happiness or to immoral unhappiness depends on their use:

> The term "indifferent" has two meanings: in the first it denotes the things which do not contribute either to happiness or to misery, as wealth, fame, health, strength, and the like; for it is possible to be happy without having these, although, if they are used in a certain way, such use of them tends to happiness or misery.[43]

This is exactly what we encountered earlier in our discussion of Paul's encouragements in 1 Cor. 7:29–32 that "those who buy (οἱ ἀγοράζοντες)" must be "as though they had no possessions (ὡς μὴ κατέχοντες), and those who make use of the world (οἱ χρώμενοι τὸν κόσμον) as though they were not consuming it (ὡς μὴ καταχρώμενοι)." The verbs in these encouragements are not turned against themselves, as Agamben suggests, but show variations that point to a difference in attitude. These examples that Paul gives concern some of the ἀδιάφορα that the Stoics mention, namely "wealth, fame, health, strength, and the like"; and like the Stoics, Paul evaluates these ἀδιάφορα in the light of the way they are used. Being wealthy and able to buy things, for instance, is an ἀδιάφορον and can be seen as morally good (although it is never in itself an absolute good), but only if it does not lead to an attitude of arrogance; usage of this world is an ἀδιάφορον that can be morally good, but is wrong if it leads to exploitation, extortion, and misuse of the cosmos.

Although ἀδιάφορα are in themselves neither good nor wrong, one can have a preference for particular ἀδιάφορα; in this case, the Stoics talk of a προηγμένον

---

[42] Diogenes Laertius, *Lives of Eminent Philosophers* 7.1 Zeno 101–2 = LS 58A. The reference "LS" stands for Long and Sedley, *The Hellenistic Philosophers*, see section 58: "Stoic Ethics—Value and indifference," 58A.
[43] Diogenes Laertius, *Lives of Eminent Philosophers* 7.1.104–15; = LS 58B.

ἀδιάφορον, a "promoted, or advanced ἀδιάφορον" that is still "neither good nor bad,"⁴⁴ "but promoted or advanced above the zero point of indifference."⁴⁵ This is called a "preferential indifference." This notion was not generally accepted among Stoic philosophers. According to Stoics such as Aristo of Chios the notion of a preferential ἀδιάφορον was in contradiction with the principal Stoic insight that only virtues can be good and only vices bad, with the ἀδιάφορα positioned between good and bad as morally indifferent.⁴⁶ According to Aristo an ἀδιάφορον, by definition, can never be preferred, and a ranking of ἀδιάφορα depends solely on circumstances: an ἀδιάφορον is never preferential, but merely circumstantial. Other Stoics such as Chrysippus, however, defended the view that one can have a preference for particular ἀδιάφορα, despite the fact that they, in themselves, are indeed neither good nor bad.⁴⁷ This seems to be exactly the position that Paul takes in his advice in 1 Cor. 7 with regard to the question of whether those who are unmarried should marry or not. What is remarkable, and does not surface in Taubes's and Agamben's interpretations, is that Paul treats getting married or remaining unmarried as ἀδιάφορα but still expresses his personal preference for not marrying: he regards remaining unmarried as a preferential ἀδιάφορον, that is, preferred by him, but acknowledged to be morally indifferent. That being married or unmarried is an ἀδιάφορον for Paul is clear from the following advice:

> Are you bound to a wife? Do not seek to be free. Are you free from a wife? Do not seek a wife. But if you marry, you do not sin, and if a virgin marries, she does not sin. (1 Cor. 7:27–28)

Marrying is not a bad thing, although Paul expresses his preference—his "preferential statement or reason (προηγούμενος λόγος)," the Stoics would say⁴⁸—for not marrying (see 1 Cor. 7:1–2, 7:8–9 and 7:39–40). Perhaps it is Paul's innovation that he includes marriage among the ἀδιάφορα, but his argumentation entirely follows the line of the Stoic ἀδιάφορα theory. And for Paul remaining unmarried is the preferential ἀδιάφορον. The same holds for his view on slavery: whether, as a Christian, one is (in a civic-social respect) free or enslaved is an ἀδιάφορον, although there is a preference, if as a slave one receives the opportu-

---

44 Cf. *SVF* 3.128 = LS 58E.
45 LSJ s.v. προάγω A6.
46 See *SVF* 1.361 = LS 58F; *SVF* 1.351 = LS 58G.
47 See *SVF* 3.137 = LS 58H. Cf. also the defence of Cato in *SVF* 1.365 = LS 58I.
48 See *SVF* 3.128 = LS 58E.

nity to become free, to use this opportunity (1 Cor. 7:21–24). If granted a choice, civic-social freedom is the preferential ἀδιάφορον (1 Cor. 7:21–24).[49]

My suggestion is to read the passage from 1 Cor. 7:29–32, which has been intensively discussed by Taubes and Agamben, within the context of the Stoic ἀδιάφορα.[50] The Pauline ὡς μή, "as if not," indicates that actions such as marrying, mourning, rejoicing, buying, and using the world are essentially ἀδιάφορα: they are in themselves neither good nor bad. Only virtues such as righteousness (δικαιοσύνη; see LS 58A) are good in an absolute sense, and in *1 Corinthians* it is indeed said of Christ Jesus that it is he who "became for us wisdom from God, and righteousness (δικαιοσύνη) and sanctification and redemption" (1 Cor. 1:30). Only vices such as unrighteousness (ἀδικία; see LS 58A and 1 Cor. 13:6) are bad in an absolute sense. That does not mean that because of the status of the above actions as ἀδιάφορα Paul cannot express his personal preference in each case. On the contrary, in line with the Stoic theory of preferential ἀδιάφορα Paul can say that he would wish and prefer that all were as he himself is (1 Cor. 7:7), and that "It is well for a man not to touch a woman" (1 Cor. 7:1; cf. 1 Cor. 7:8). The "preferential reason" that Paul gives for this is that those who are unmarried are without earthly concerns, whereas those who are married need to devote themselves to earthly matters (7:32–33). Even Paul's

---

49 For the Stoic notion of ἀδιάφορα, see also Brennan, *The Stoic Life*, Chapter 8, devoted to "Goods and Indifferents." For Paul's use of Stoic ἀδιάφορα theory, see also the monograph by Jaquette, *Discerning What Counts*; as well as the following papers from his hand: "Paul, Epictetus, and Others on Indifference to Status," "Foundational Convictions," and "Life and Death." See also Deming, "Paul and Indifferent Things." For a strong criticism of a Stoic reading of 1 Cor. 7:29–31, see Schrage, "Die Stellung zur Welt bei Paulus"; and Barclay, "Apocalyptic Allegiance." Barclay's view that "Paul's policy of disinvestment in dealings with 'the world' is only partially similar to the Stoic policy of 'indifference.' The Stoic … treats all external conditions as ἀδιάφορα, matters of no ultimate significance … Paul is not advocating a blanket emotional disinvestment (to preserve the serenity of the inner self)" (ibid., 268–69) does not do full justice to the Stoic theory of indifferents: Stoics are not "indifferent" to reality, in the sense of "uninterested" and "detached"; their point is that the value of "indifferents" is not absolute (either good or evil) but relative, as it depends upon their actual use. For a Stoic reading of 1 Cor. 7, see also Huttunen, *Paul and Epictetus on Law*, 26–36, esp. 31 on 1 Cor. 7:29–31. As Huttunen rightly remarks: "externals are indifferent as such, but their use is not" (ibid., 31). For my interpretation of 1 Cor. 7:21–24 as an encouragement to use the opportunity to set oneself free and as an expression of Paul's view on freedom from slavery as a *preferential* indifference, cf. Harrill, "Paul and Slavery," and Horsley, "Paul and Slavery." Cf. also Neutel, *A Cosmopolitan Ideal*, chap. 3.

50 Cf. Plato, *Laws*, Book 5, 732b–d, but his argument focuses rather on the idea that in all circumstances one should avoid showing extreme joy or sorrow, but should trust that God will balance all blessings and troubles.

statement that being unmarried is "good/noble/honorable" (καλός; 1 Cor. 7:8, cf. 7:1, 26) does not conflict with the Stoic notion of a preferential ἀδιάφορον. After all, Chrysippus too indicates that a preferential ἀδιάφορον can be called "good" (ἀγαθός) in the colloquial sense of the word,[51] even if, strictly speaking, only the virtues are good. Paul takes care to state clearly that he is expressing his personal preference, and not a rule that is derived from Jesus himself (1 Cor. 7:12; cf. 7:6).

Hence the Pauline ὡς μή is not nihilistic at all, despite Taubes's and Agamben's claims to the contrary. Granted, Paul refers to the disappearance of "the form of this cosmos (τὸ σχῆμα τοῦ κόσμου τούτου)" (1 Cor. 7:31), and does so in support of his preference not to marry, as marriage forces one to devote oneself to earthly affairs, which will eventually pass away. Yet despite his preference, Paul's opinion retains the status of an ἀδιάφορον, and his intention seems to be for the Corinthians, regardless of whether they are convinced by his preferential reason, to become aware of the attitudes they adopt towards the things that are ἀδιάφορα. This is exactly the point the Stoic ἀδιάφορα address.

Stoics too develop the same argumentation as Paul, that in the circumstances of particular crises—to use Paul's wording—one should primarily be concerned with "the affairs of the Lord" and not with "the affairs of the world" (1 Cor. 7:32–34), and should maintain "unhindered devotion to the Lord" (1 Cor. 7:35).

Whereas for Paul the imminent end of the cosmos constitutes a crisis (1 Cor. 7:26, 29, 31), a Stoic such as Seneca imagines crises that consist of such situations as "when thrown into prison, or when stranded in some foreign nation, or when delayed on a long voyage, or when cast upon a lonely shore."[52] In such cases, according to Seneca, a philosopher needs to model his life on that of Zeus-Jupiter himself at the moment of the world's conflagration:

> His life will be like that of Jupiter, who, amid the dissolution (!) of the world (*cum resoluto mundo*), when the gods are confounded together and Nature rests for a space from her work, can retire into himself and give himself over to his own thoughts. In some such way as this the sage will act; he will retreat into himself, and live with himself.[53]

Seneca here refers to the same Stoic thought that is essentially also shared by Paul: the cosmos passes away, and what has emerged from God will return unto God. This theocentric approach is relevant in times of crisis. At other mo-

---

51 *SVF* 3.137 = LS 58H.
52 Seneca, *Epistles* 9.16.
53 Ibid., 9.16–17.

ments, however, according to Seneca, in the absence of crisis, the philosopher tries to combine his orientation towards God, and the self-sufficient stability that he derives from it, with his full engagement in the world:

> As long as he is allowed to order his affairs according to his judgment, he is self-sufficient—and marries a wife; he is self-sufficient—and brings up children; he is self-sufficient—and yet could not live if he had to live without the society of man.[54]

Paul differs slightly from this, in that he seems less positive about marriage (1 Cor. 7:1–2, 5, 9, although cf. 7:14).[55] Yet despite this difference, Paul too is of the opinion that a Christian cannot cope without other human beings; the Christian community, with a Stoic imagery, is a communal body in which all Christians participate on equal terms: a communal body that is at the same time the body of Christ himself (1 Cor. 12:12–27; cf. Rom. 12:4–5).[56] Moreover, Paul emphasizes that the social responsibility of Christians extends beyond the Christian community (1 Cor. 10:32–33) and that one must submit oneself to the State, which is established by God (Rom. 13:1–7). And differently from what Taubes asserts, Rom. 13 does not show Paul's political resignation that derives from his general "nihilistic" attitude; that is directed, in a politically subversive manner, against the Roman empire. Rather it is for moral reasons, "because of conscience" as Paul puts it (Rom. 13:5), that one must submit to the Roman State.

In the end, Paul and Seneca seem to express the same tension between God-oriented self-sufficiency on the one hand, and social-societal engagement on the other hand, a tension that we recognize in the Stoic notion of the ἀδιάφορα and the Pauline ὡς μή. This Pauline phrase is even quite similar in wording to the way the Stoic Epictetus applies ἀδιάφορα theory to the figure of Socrates in his time of need. As Epictetus exhorts his readers,

> 159 (…) take Socrates and observe a man who had a wife and little children, but as belonging to another / as foreign / as strange (λάβε Σωκράτη καὶ θέασαι γυναῖκα καὶ παιδία

---

54 Ibid., 9.17.
55 Paul seems to judge less favorably about marriage. It is chiefly "because of cases of sexual immorality," that "each man should have his own wife and each woman her own husband" (1 Cor. 7:2), to quench the fire of desire if one lacks self-control (1 Cor. 7:9; cf. 1 Cor. 7:5). Yet he is also convinced that the believing partner exerts a sanctifying effect on his or her unbelieving partner and children (1 Cor. 7:14). In his negative emphasis, Paul more resembles those movements within Platonism that criticize marriage because it impedes full devotion to philosophy (see Plutarch, *Amatorius* 750C–751B, countered in 751B–754E). However, against this background, the Stoic nature of Paul's view that marriage is morally indifferent, and non-marriage only a preferential ἀδιάφορον, sticks out.
56 Epictetus, *Discourses* 4.1.159, 162. See Lee, *Paul, the Stoics, and the Body of Christ*, chap. 5.

ἔχοντα, ἀλλὰ ὡς ἀλλότρια[v]), who had a country, as far as it was his duty, and in the way in which it was his duty, and friends, and kinsmen, one and all subject to the law and to obedience to the law. (...) 162 (...) Later on, when he had to speak in defence of his life, he did not behave as one who had children, or a wife, did he? (... μή τι ὡς τέκνα ἔχων ἀναστρέφεται, μή τι ὡς γυναῖκα;) Nay, but as one who was alone in the world (ἀλλ᾽ ὡς μόνος).⁵⁷

The Loeb translation translates the clause ἀλλὰ ὡς ἀλλότρια[v] as a verbal clause: "take Socrates and observe a man who had a wife and little children, *but regarded them as not his own*," whereas the clause in fact qualifies how Socrates possessed a wife and children, namely "as belonging to another / as being foreign / as being strange" (LSJ s.v. ἀλλότριος): "... Socrates (...), a man who had a wife and little children, but as belonging to another / as foreign / as strange." This provides a close parallel to Paul's exhortation "... from now on, let even those who have wives be as though they had none (... τὸ λοιπὸν ἵνα καὶ οἱ ἔχοντες γυναῖκας ὡς μὴ ἔχοντες ὦσιν)" (1 Cor. 7:29). This ambiguous attitude, which reflects the ambiguous status of the ἀδιάφορα as neither good nor bad, clearly shows itself in a time of crisis, when Socrates is indicted and needs to speak in defence of his life, and "he did not behave as one who had children, or a wife (... μή τι ὡς τέκνα ἔχων ἀναστρέφεται, μή τι ὡς γυναῖκα)."⁵⁸ This seems to confirm that, contrary to the view of modern philosophers, Paul's "as if not" (ὡς μή) phrase is not nihilistic, but an expression of the ambiguity of the ἀδιάφορα. Only good things should be followed, and only bad things should be avoided, but the indifferent things should be lived with an "as if not" (ὡς μή) attitude. Their preferential value depends on the way in which they are used. Whether they contribute to moral happiness or to immoral unhappiness depends on their use.

5 Concluding Reflections

So where does this evaluation of the modern philosophical interpreters of Paul such as Badiou, Taubes, and Agamben leave us, when Paul is seen from an ancient philosophical perspective?

---

57 I am grateful to my PhD student Birgit van der Lans for bringing this passage to my attention.
58 For the tension between Stoic engagement and detachment, see also Reydams-Schils, *The Roman Stoics*, esp. chap. 1–2. Cf. also Rist, "The Stoic Concept of Detachment," and Engberg-Pedersen, "The Relationship with Others."

First and foremost, such a comparison of Paul with his contemporary philosophers confirms that the modern interpreters are right in their intuition that Paul can be read philosophically. This contextualization of Paul within ancient philosophical discourse shows, independently from the modern interpreters, that Paul does indeed traverse into philosophical territory and engages in an ancient philosophical debate.

At the same time, a few misapprehensions can be corrected from the perspective of the history of ideas. Paul's thinking developed differently than these modern interpreters assumed: Paul is not an anti-philosopher, but presents a philosophical critique of sophistic rhetoric.

Differently from what Badiou claims, Paul's reflections in 1 Cor. 1:26–29 on "the things that are not" (τὰ μὴ ὄντα) and "the things that are" (τὰ ὄντα) do not involve a criticism of onto-theology but are actually compatible with the Stoic view of the emergence of the entire reality from God. Paul is not an anti-metaphysical thinker; he shares much of Stoic metaphysics, and sees creation not as emerging out of nothing, but as emerging from God, existing through God, and eventually returning to God, to the point that God is all in all, and thus sums up the totality of reality in himself. It is exactly this process of temporality that leads him to express his reservation. Because the form of the cosmos is passing away, one should not limit oneself to the present physical reality.

And whereas Taubes characterizes Paul as Messianic-nihilistic, and therefore as politically subversive, and Agamben, in a similar mode, emphasizes Paul's Messianic annihilation of reality, it is in fact more expedient to compare Paul's views with the Stoic theory of "indifferents" (ἀδιάφορα). Paul's exhortation in 1 Cor. 7:29–32 to develop a world-view characterized by the ὡς μή, "as if not," is not nihilistic, but expresses the ambiguity of the ἀδιάφορα, the things that are in themselves neither good nor bad but morally indifferent, and depend on the individual's attitude. In this way, Paul challenges his readers to explore the dialectical tensions between detachment from, and engagement with the world.

So could the modern philosophers be satisfied with this ancient philosophical reading of Paul? I think they largely could, because the basic tenet of what they wish to say can be maintained: the reservation with regard to the present world. This reservation remains, though it is not nihilistic but reflects an awareness of the temporality of the world and the importance of an ethics that challenges one's attitude towards the ἀδιάφορα. Or do the modern philosophers really need their anti-metaphysical critique? Is it essential for them to maintain their anti-metaphysics, even if what they argue for can be adapted to fit within the framework of Stoic metaphysics? It seems that, essentially, the modern philosophers' interpretation of Paul stands to benefit from this ancient contextualization. It would help to overcome the enigma of Paul's alleged Gnosticism, for instance, as discussed in Marin Terpstra's contribution to this volume. Paul then is not opposed to the present cosmic reality in a Gnostic or dualistic mode, but displays an ambiguous, dialectic (and, if I dare say, Hegelian)[59] attitude towards it: its basic metaphysics are not dualistic at all, but regard the whole of reality as a unity that emerges from God, exists through him, and eventually returns to him in a long, extensive process. In Paul's understanding, it is not the physical cosmos that is a problem, but the world view that disconnects creation from its creator, subverts their ontological relationship, and worships the creature rather than the Creator (Rom. 1:25). This world view reduces the world to a social, sophistic universe that develops a "truth-less," rhetorical "wisdom of the world," contrary to the true, comprehensive "wisdom of God" (1 Cor. 1:20–21), and restricts its attention to the current world-phase that is dominated by "the god of this age" (2 Cor. 4:4: ὁ θεὸς τοῦ αἰῶνος τούτου, not: "the god of this world" as the NRSV translation wrongly translates, but: the god of "the current Zeitgeist").

Paul's own outlook is positive concerning the real, "God-grounded" ontological status of the cosmos, his ambivalence only applies to the attitude that one develops towards it: whereas good and bad constitute the opposite poles of morality, it is the things in between, the ἀδιάφορα, the things that are indifferent in themselves, that are morally ambiguous and need to be assessed in light of the use to which they are put in each instance. This is very much the kind of attitude, it seems to me, that we need in an age of ecological crisis: we can use the cosmos, but should not utterly consume and exploit it (1 Cor. 7:31).[60]

---

59 Badiou, Taubes and Agamben seem to loathe these Hegelian dialectics and to be determined not to find them in Paul. Badiou speaks of Paul's "antidialectic" (Badiou, *Saint Paul*, chap. 6). Instead of paying attention to God's finally being "all and all," the eventual identification of God with the cosmos (1 Cor. 15:28), Agamben is interested in "the remnant" rather than in the totality (Agamben, *The Time That Remains*, 55–57), and Taubes explicitly denies that the Pauline Spirit should be understood in a Hegelian way (Taubes, *The Political Theology of Paul*, 41–44). Whereas Badiou seems to reject dialectics altogether in his reading of Paul, Agamben and Taubes seem to develop a non-Hegelian dialectics, see Van der Heiden, "The Dialectics of Paul."
60 For an ecological reading of Paul, see the principle publications from the Exeter "Uses of the Bible in environmental ethics" project: Horrell, Hunt, Southgate, and Stavrakopoulou, *Ecological Hermeneutics*; Horrell, Hunt, and Southgate, *Greening Paul*; Horrell, *The Bible and the Environment*. The text from 1 Cor. 7:31 could be added to the texts that they discuss. If the Stoic theory of indifferents is properly understood, such an understanding, and its application to 1 Cor. 7:2931, helps move the reading of this text away from contributing to a stance of "indifference" to the world—in the sense of its being of no lasting significance—towards the sense of opposing any consuming of the world, without due care for it. This seems to cohere very well with the kinds of themes the Exeter project emphasised in Pauline theology, namely the incorporation of all things into the reconciliation and redemption being accomplished in Christ. (I gratefully

Finally, once the modern philosophers become aware of Paul's engagement in an ancient philosophical discourse, will they turn to their ancient colleagues, rather than to Paul himself? My view is that this awareness will only help them to appreciate Paul more. On the one hand, Paul's engagement with philosophers confirms the relevance of ancient philosophical thought. On the other hand, the real practice of the inclusive Pauline communities that welcomed Jews and Greeks, slaves and free people, men and women (Gal. 3:28) has some added value over the elitist Stoic discourse of the small community of Stoic sages. Paul's communities did not remain in utopian isolation, but were actually founded to express Paul's inclusive and universalist world view.[61] It was the Christian communities that changed Antiquity from within, by involving not just the few, but *all* people in an ethical exercise. The imitation (μίμησις) of Christ was thought to enable people to turn into Christ-like figures themselves (1 Cor. 4:16, 11:1; 1 Thess. 1:6) and to constitute entire communities of sages (Rom. 16:19). The Christian communities offered an alternative to the State without subverting it. Perhaps for these reasons, it does indeed remain relevant to turn to Paul.

References

Agamben, Giorgio. *The Time That Remains: A Commentary on the Letter to the Romans.* Translated by Patricia Dailey. Stanford, CA: Stanford University Press, 2005.

Anagnostopoulos, A.H. "Aristotle's Parmenidean Dilemma." *Archiv für Geschichte der Philosophie* 95 (2013): 245–74.

Badiou, Alain. *Saint Paul: The Foundation of Universalism.* Translated by Ray Brassier. Stanford, CA: Stanford University Press, 2003.

Barclay, John M.G. "Apocalyptic Allegiance and Disinvestment in the World: A Reading of 1 Corinthians 7:25–35." In *Paul and the Apocalyptic Imagination*, edited by Ben C. Blackwell, John K. Goodrich, and Jason Maston, 257–74. Minneapolis, MN: Fortress Press, 2016.

Becker, Matthias. *Porphyrios, "Contra Christianos": Neue Sammlung der Fragmente, Testimonien und Dubia mit Einleitung, Übersetzung und Anmerkungen.* Berlin/Boston: De Gruyter, 2016.

---

acknowledge my discussion of this issue with David Horrell, and have borrowed from his phraseology.) The (form of the) cosmos that is moving towards its end (1 Cor. 7:31) has originally been brought into being through Christ (1 Cor. 8:6) and will eventually be identified with God himself (1 Cor. 15:24–28) when it is freed from the chain of coming-to-be and passing-away (1 Cor. 15:42, 50; cf. Rom. 8:21).

61 Cf. Neutel, *A Cosmopolitan Ideal*, 235–36.

Bockmuehl, M. "Creatio ex nihilo in Palestinian Judaism and Early Christianity." *Scottish Journal of Theology* 65 (2012): 253–70.
Brennan, Tad. *The Stoic Life: Emotions, Duties, and Fate*. Oxford: Oxford University Press, 2005.
Chapot, F. "L'hérésie d'Hermogène: fragments et commentaire." *Recherches augustiniennes et patristiques* 30 (1997): 3–111.
Cornford, F.M. "Anaxagoras' Theory of Matter." *Classical Quarterly* 24 (1930): 14–30 and 83–95.
Deming, W. "Paul and Indifferent Things." In *Paul in the Greco-Roman World: A Handbook*, edited by J. Paul Sampley, 384–403. Harrisburg, PA: Trinity, 2003.
Denzinger, Heinrich. *Compendium of Creeds, Definitions, and Declarations on Matters of Faith and Morals*. Revised and edited by Peter Hünermann, Robert Fastiggi and Anne Englund Nash. San Francisco: Ignatius Press, 2012[43].
Engberg-Pedersen, Troels. "The Relationship with Others: Similarities and Differences Between Paul and Stoicism." *Zeitschrift für die neutestamentliche Wissenschaft und die Kunde der älteren Kirche* 96 (2005): 35–60.
Harrill, J. Albert. "Paul and Slavery: The Problem of 1 Corinthians 7:21." *Biblical Research* 39 (1994): 5–28.
Horrell, David G., Cherryl Hunt, Christopher Southgate, and Francesca Stavrakopoulou, eds. *Ecological Hermeneutics: Biblical, Historical, and Theological Perspectives*. London & New York: T&T Clark, 2010.
Horrell, David G., Cherryl Hunt, and Christopher Southgate, *Greening Paul: Rereading the Apostle in an Age of Ecological Crisis*. Waco, TX: Baylor University Press, 2010.
Horrell, David G. *The Bible and the Environment: Towards a Critical, Ecological Biblical Theology*. London & New York: Equinox, 2010.
Horsley, Richard A. "Paul and Slavery: A Critical Alternative to Recent Readings." *Semeia* 83–84 (1998): 153–200, 182–86.
Huttunen, Niko. *Paul and Epictetus on Law: A Comparison*. London/New York: T&T Clark, 2009.
Jaquette, James L. "Paul, Epictetus, and Others on Indifference to Status." *Catholic Biblical Quarterly* 56 (1994): 68–80.
Jaquette, James L. "Foundational Convictions, Ethical Instruction and Theologising in Paul." *Neotestamentica* 29 (1995): 231–52.
Jaquette, James L. *Discerning What Counts: The Function of the Adiaphora Topos in Paul's Letters*. Atlanta: Scholars Press, 1995.
Jaquette, James L. "Life and Death, Adiaphora, and Paul's Rhetorical Strategies." *Novum Testamentum* 38 (1996): 30–54.
Lee, Michelle V. *Paul, the Stoics, and the Body of Christ*. Cambridge: Cambridge University Press, 2008.
Long, A.A., and D.N. Sedley. *The Hellenistic Philosophers*. 2 vols. Cambridge: Cambridge University Press, 1987–89.
May, Gerhard. *Creatio Ex Nihilo: The Doctrine of "Creation out of Nothing" in Early Christian Thought*. Translated by A.S. Worrall. London/New York: T&T Clark, 2004.
McFarland, Ian A. *From Nothing: A Theology of Creation*. Louisville, KY: Westminster John Knox Press, 2014.

Mourelatos, A.P.D. "Pre-Socratic Origins of the Principle That There Are No Origins from Nothing." *The Journal of Philosophy* 78 (1981): 649–65.
Neutel, Karin B. *A Cosmopolitan Ideal: Paul's Declaration "neither Jew nor Greek, neither Slave nor Free, nor Male and Female" in the Context of First-Century Thought.* London: Bloomsbury, 2015.
Reydams-Schils, Gretchen. *The Roman Stoics: Self, Responsibility, and Affection.* Chicago, IL: The University of Chicago Press, 2005.
Rist, John M. "The Stoic Concept of Detachment." In *The Stoics*, edited by John M. Rist, 259–72. Berkeley: University of California Press, 1978.
Schrage, W. "Die Stellung zur Welt bei Paulus, Epiktet und in der Apokalyptik: Ein Beitrag zu 1 Kor 7:29–31." *Zeitschrift für Theologie und Kirche* 61 (1964): 125–54.
Shields, C.J. "The Generation of Form in Aristotle." *History of Philosophy Quarterly* 7 (1990): 367–90.
Soskice, Janet M. "Creatio ex nihilo: its Jewish and Christian Foundations." In *Creation and the God of Abraham*, edited by David B. Burrell and others, 24–39. Cambridge: Cambridge University Press, 2010.
Sterling, Gregory E. "Prepositional Metaphysics in Jewish Wisdom Speculation and Early Christian Liturgical Texts." *Studia Philonica Annual* 9 (1997): 219–38.
Tatum, W.J. "Lucretius, *De rerum natura*, 1, 199–204." *L'Antiquité classique* 67 (1998): 225–30.
Taubes, Jacob. *The Political Theology of Paul.* Translated by Dana Hollander. Edited by Aleida Assman and Jan Assmann in conjunction with Horst Folkers, Wolf-Daniel Hartwich, and Christoph Schulte. Stanford, CA: Stanford University Press, 2004.
Van der Heiden, Gert-Jan. "The Dialectics of Paul: On Exception, Grace, and Use in Badiou and Agamben." *International Journal of Philosophy and Theology* 77, no. 3 (2016): 171–90.
Van Kooten, George. *Cosmic Christology in Paul and the Pauline School.* Tübingen: Mohr Siebeck, 2003.
Van Kooten, George. "Rhetorical Competition within the Christian Community at Corinth: Paul and the Sophists." In *Cults, Creeds and Identities in the Greek City after the Classical Age*, edited by Richard Alston, Onno M. van Nijf, and Christina G. Williamson, 261–88. Louvain: Peeters, 2013.
Van Kooten, George. "The Divine Father of the Universe from the Presocratics to Celsus: The Greco-Roman Background to the 'Father of All' in Paul's Letter to the Ephesians." In *The Divine Father: Religious and Philosophical Concepts of Divine Parenthood in Antiquity*, edited by Felix Albrecht and Reinhard Feldmeier, 293–323. Leiden/Boston: Brill, 2014.
Van Kooten, George. "Paulus als anti-filosoof en messiaans nihilist? Kanttekeningen vanuit antiekwijsgerig perspectief bij Badious, Taubes' en Agambens interpretatie van Paulus." *Tijdschrift voor Theologie* 54 (2014): 277–94.
Van Kooten, George. "Quaestiones disputatae: How Greek was Paul's Eschatology?" *New Testament Studies* 61 (2015): 239–45.
Von Arnim, H. *Stoicorum veterum fragmenta.* Leipzig: Teubner, 1903–1905.

Teresa Morgan
Narratives of Πίστις in Paul and Deutero-Paul

Abstract: This essay argues that πίστις is an inherently narrative concept and that a narrative analysis of πίστις in *1 Thessalonians, Galatians, Ephesians,* and *1* and *2 Timothy* helps to reveal the subtle variations and, in some cases, evolutions of thinking in early churches about Christ, salvation, and the nature of the new divine-human community on earth. This furthers and elaborates on the author's work in *Roman Faith and Christian Faith*. Analysis of these five letters shows how πίστις language is used to tell stories about the relationship between God and Christ and God, Christ and humanity; about the working of God's mercy, salvation, and the restoration of the faithful to righteousness; about the appointment of apostles to preach the gospel and their relationship with those they preach to; about how the faithful are chosen to accept the apostles' preaching; about how community members should live and relate to one another; about how traditions and writings are authorized as objects and tools of πίστις. This indicates that the use of πίστις language by Paul and his followers cannot be properly understood from the distinction between faith and reason. Rather, in addition to the concern of present-day philosophers with, for instance, the structure of the oath and the particular comportment of the believers to the world, Morgan shows that once one approaches the narratives in which πίστις figures, it becomes clear that πίστις language functions on many different levels. Πίστις is not only a theological notion, but also a term with ethical and ecclesiological connotations, informing the developing structure and life of churches.

In 1982, Richard Hays argued for a narrative interpretation of Gal. 3–4 and, within it, for a particular interpretation of the role of πίστις.[1] One conclusion of his argument which has been widely accepted was that, although the two chapters deploy slightly different Christological formations and seem to take slightly different perspectives on the drama of salvation (one probably Jewish in origin, the other gentile), their narrative structure, and hence their Christology, is essentially the same. Another, more controversial, conclusion was that we should understand πίστις in these chapters as referring not to faith in Christ, but to the faith or faithfulness of Christ towards God. The phrase πίστις Ἰησοῦ Χριστοῦ,

---

[1] Hays, *The Faith of Jesus Christ*, esp. chapters 3–4.

Hays concluded, is best understood in the narrative of salvation as "the faithfulness of 'the one man Jesus Christ' whose act of obedient self-giving on the cross became the means by which 'the promise' of God was fulfilled."[2]

Hays's argument about πίστις made a major contribution to a debate which already had a lengthy history and which has continued with undiminished scholarly enthusiasm ever since.[3] Almost all participants in the debate have continued to argue that πίστις Ἰησοῦ Χριστοῦ must mean either "faith in Christ" or the "faithfulness of Christ" to God.[4] In 2015 I argued that we should understand πίστις Ἰησοῦ Χριστοῦ in *Galatians* and *Romans* as referencing *both* these key meanings of πίστις simultaneously (in a way which was common in Paul's day) and that, in addition, we should understand πίστις Ἰησοῦ Χριστοῦ as referring to *both* of the two-ended relationships in which Christ stands: with God and with humanity. The πίστις of Christ, I argued, should be heard both as the trust of God in Christ and the faithfulness of Christ to God, and as the trust of Christ in human beings and their trust (faith) in him, which between them enable Christ to stand (very much like a mediator at law or in politics) between the parties and reconcile them (bringing human beings into a state of δικαιοσύνη).

Roman Faith and Christian Faith explored the treatment of πίστις across the whole of the New Testament, and one of its aims was to show subtle differences in the ways in which πίστις language was used by different writers, not least to capture their different Christologies. I also aimed to show how very early Christians took πίστις language—ubiquitous in the world to which they belonged—and began to adapt it to the theological, ethical, ecclesiological and eschatological needs of their communities. In that study, I did not emphasize the narrative implications of New Testament writers' treatment of πίστις. All πίστις language, however, is inherently narrative.[5] Relationships of trust or mistrust, the exercise of belief and so on, are inherently socially, psychologically, and spiritually productive: they move individuals and groups on from one state or relationship to another.[6] In this essay, I shall focus specifically on the narrativity of πίστις. Un-

---

2 Ibid., 161. He argued further that the same understanding of πίστις Χριστοῦ and hence Christology underlies *Romans*.
3 See, e.g., Easter, "The *pistis Christou*."
4 The exception is Hooker, "*Pistis Christou*," whose view of πίστις Χριστοῦ is not unlike mine, though arrived at differently.
5 As is *fides* language in Latin.
6 Morgan, *Roman Faith*, 15–21 and chapters 1–3, *passim*, explore common themes in the economics, sociology, and psychology of trust (the core meaning of both πίστις and *fides*) and belief as well as in analyses of πίστις and *fides* in Greek and Roman society, including its social productivity and relationship with hope, mistrust, doubt, fear, and scepticism.

like Hays, I shall not draw on a particular modern theoretical model for analyzing narrative structure, but will take as read what he effectively established, that treatments of πίστις in the New Testament respond well to narrative analysis.⁷ Focusing on Paul and deutero-Paul, in particular on *1 Thessalonians*, *Galatians*, *Ephesians*, and *1* and *2 Timothy*, I shall argue that a narrative analysis of πίστις in these letters helps to reveal the subtle variations and, in some cases, evolutions of thinking in early churches about Christ, salvation, and the nature of the new divine-human community on earth.⁸

1 The Narrative of Πίστις in *1 Thessalonians*

1 Thessalonians is a relatively neglected text in the study of Pauline πίστις—undeservedly so, since it makes extensive use of πίστις language and, in the form in which it has come down to us, may well be the earliest surviving Christian document.⁹ Paul's treatment of πίστις language (which occurs fourteen times in the letter's five short chapters) makes clear the role it plays in his narrative of salvation.

Paul affirms that God is πιστός (1 Thess. 5:24), surely here "faithful." To a Jewish writer or listener this is an obvious echo of the Septuagint, where God is often said to be πιστός.¹⁰ Faithfulness is an intrinsically temporal concept, established over time. In the Septuagint, the faithfulness of God through time is often contrasted with the vacillations of Israel, which is sometimes faithful in return, and sometimes strays and has to be brought back to its right relationship with God.¹¹ For Paul, therefore, referring to God's faithfulness both makes a point about the nature of God now, and underlines Paul's sense of the continuity between past, present and future, the covenant with Israel and the "new covenant in [Christ's] blood."¹² It also implies that the call to the Thessalonians to turn from idols to serve the living and true God (1 Thess. 1:9) is part of God's long-

---

7 Hays, *The Faith of Jesus Christ*, 82–95.
8 Following the widespread view that Paul's authentic letters are *Romans*, *1* and *2 Corinthians*, *Galatians*, *Philippians*, *1 Thessalonians* and *Philemon*.
9 See Morgan, *Roman Faith*, 212–13.
10 Ibid., 196–200. I refer to the LXX rather than the Hebrew Bible throughout on the basis that it was the main scriptural collection of Greek-speaking Christians of Jewish background; on this and on the possible Hebrew background to NT *pistis* language see Morgan, *Roman Faith*, ch. 5, *passim*.
11 Morgan, *Roman Faith*, 200–4.
12 1 Cor. 11:25. Given that *1 Thessalonians* is addressed to gentiles it is no surprise not to find the phrase there.

term plan—God's long-term faithfulness—not the incomprehensible break with tradition which some faithful Jews saw it as being.

God, Paul tells the Thessalonians, called the Thessalonians and chose them (1 Thess. 1:4, 5:24). The faithfulness of God calls forth an answering πίστις from the Thessalonians because they are chosen for salvation (5:9). The language of chosenness too locates the Thessalonians' πίστις in a longer narrative (one which might, in principle, go back to the moment of creation, though Paul does not pursue that idea in this letter). The moment of the Thessalonians' πίστις forms the moment of the forging of a new relationship: a moment in one sense without history, though it will have a future. In another sense, the Thessalonians have always been destined to make this commitment at this time, so their πίστις is part of the long story of God's relationship with humanity.

Paul's periodic references to chosenness, even if they fall short of being a central or fully worked-out dimension of his theology, have always been something of an embarrassment to those churches which have not held a doctrine of predestination.[13] One likely explanation of them is that by claiming that (some or all) gentiles were chosen for salvation through Jesus Christ, Paul sought to graft the gentiles onto the history of Israel, integrating them conceptually into the Jewish history of the new community without denying the uniqueness of that history.[14] To this task πίστις language proved very adaptable. By connecting the long-term faithfulness of God to Israel lexically with the trust/belief which converts put in God and Christ, Paul was able to imply that the latter was connected with the former, even in passages where he does not seek explicitly, for instance, to integrate gentiles by claiming Christ as the true "seed" of Abraham.

God did not, however, call the Thessalonians directly, but through the gospel of Jesus Christ and through Paul, who was "entrusted" (πιστευθῆναι) with the gospel. Paul's being entrusted with the gospel forms part of what I have called a "cascade" of πίστις in his letters: from God, through Christ and sometimes the spirit, through Paul, and in some letters Paul's co-workers, to community members.[15] Paul does not describe other parts of the cascade with πίστις language in *1 Thessalonians*, but elsewhere he does. At 1 Cor. 4:17, for example, Paul calls Timothy "my beloved and πιστός son in the Lord." Timothy will act as Paul's representative, reminding the Corinthians of "my ways in Christ Jesus."[16] Πιστός here is usually, no doubt rightly, taken to mean "faithful," but it also marks that Timothy has been entrusted with representing Paul, and there-

---

13 E.g., Rom. 8:33, 1 Cor. 1:27.
14 Cf. Rom. 11:17–24.
15 Morgan, *Roman Faith*, 216–19.
16 Translations taken from New American Bible, sometimes emended.

fore that Paul trusts him. Community members can trust both: Paul because he has been entrusted with the gospel by God, and Timothy because he has been entrusted with it by Paul, and their preaching will help foster the πίστις of the Corinthians.

The cascade of πίστις mirrors the structure of authority, flowing from God, through Christ, the spirit, apostles and their co-workers to community members, in the new divine-human relationship created by the life, death, and resurrection of Jesus Christ. As such, it stands at the heart not only of Paul's theology but also of his ethics and ecclesiology. It also suggests that however active and urgent Paul's expectation of the second coming—in his early letters or at any point— he also recognizes and accepts that the spreading of the gospel will take time. At no point does he indicate that he expects Christ to reveal himself directly to others as he did to Paul himself (Gal. 1:12, 15–16). Paul expects the gospel to be spread by apostles like himself, travelling through time and place, preaching and demonstrating the power of God and the spirit (for instance, 1 Cor. 2:4–5). *1 Thessalonians*' use of πίστις therefore suggests that Paul does not so much hold a view of the imminence of the second coming in this letter (cf. 1 Thess. 4:15, 5:6) which he later abandons, as that his sense of urgency and his sense of the diachronic nature of his mission are always in tension.

There is no hint in Paul's letters that the πίστις of God is in danger of being weakened by the "cascading" process. It remains as strong as ever through place, time, and divine and human mediation. A need to affirm this may be one reason why, in this letter and elsewhere, Paul, if anything, downplays the active role of human beings in transmitting πίστις. He describes the gospel as having come to the Thessalonians not only with his words, but with power and the holy spirit (1 Thess. 1:5), while his words were not really his at all but the word of God mediated through him which now works in the Thessalonians (2:13–14). Moreover, when the Thessalonians act, as he says they do, as an inspiration to other communities (1:7), it is less by any active effort on their part than because the word of God is "projected out" of them (ἐξήχηται) (1:8).[17]

In *1 Thessalonians* (and arguably elsewhere) community members are not called to practice πίστις towards one another simply as fellow community members.[18] (The difference between πίστις and, for instance, ἀγάπη here is striking: community members are constantly told by Paul, as by Jesus himself and others

---

17 Contrast Paul's view of the law elsewhere (e.g., Gal. 3:24, 4:2, Rom. 3:20, 5:20–21), that over time it did change and, arguably, weaken (beginning as covenant and ending as παιδαγωγός or even "consciousness of sin").
18 Though see below.

in other books of the New Testament, to love one another, but to trust/be faithful, and so on, towards one another only in specific contexts.[19]) They do, however, practice πίστις in their life in community. The Thessalonians seem to have suffered as Christians, receiving the word "in great affliction" (1:6, cf. 3:3), and experiencing something of the same reaction from some Jews as did the churches of Judaea (2:14). Having exercised πίστις initially in the form of trust/belief/faith in God, in the act of turning from idols to serve God (1:8–9), the Thessalonians now practice it in a different sense, that of enduring faithfulness and obedience as they wait for second coming (1:10, 4:16). During this period, it also emerges that human (unlike divine) πίστις can grow or decline. Paul has sent Timothy, he says, to "strengthen and encourage you in your πίστις" (3:2); Paul prays for the ongoing "deficiencies" in the Thessalonians' πίστις be remedied (3:10), and he expresses himself delighted that Timothy has been able to report that, so far, their πίστις is standing strong (3:6–7). Πίστις, therefore, not only bring the Thessalonians into their relationship with God and Christ, but articulates the ongoing narrative of the relationship.

Πίστις emerges in *1 Thessalonians* as integral to every part of the story of the Thessalonians' salvation, conversion, and life in community in expectation of the second coming. Paul plays on the multivalency of πίστις language to carry the theological burden of this narrative and to tie the stages of the story together, so that πίστις is the enduring quality of God which makes God reach out to the Thessalonians in the first place, the means by which Paul is commissioned to preach to them, the means by which the Thessalonians forge their own relationship with God, and the single most important quality by which they live, seek to become better Christians, and await the return of Christ.

Even Paul's interest in the bases (in addition to chosenness) on which the Thessalonians put their trust in God contributes to the narrative structure of πίστις in this letter. The Thessalonians do not have πίστις *purely* because they are chosen and preached to. Paul says that he has worked "hard and blamelessly" for the Thessalonians, like a nurse or a father (2:7–12). There is a hint here that his dedication has made his message more believable. Most importantly, the Thessalonians were persuaded by their own experiences—of Paul (cf. 2:1) and of God's power and the spirit (1:5). Paul emphasizes the role of the Thessalonians' own experience throughout the letter: "You yourselves know, brothers" (2:1); "You are witnesses" (2:10); "As you know" (2:11); "For you yourselves know" (5:2). When the Thessalonians encountered Paul's preaching, together

---

[19] All the New Testament writers stand in sharp contrast here with writers of the LXX, and Greek and Roman writers in general, for whom intra-human trust etc. are central.

with the power and Spirit of God, they had experiences on which they could rely and on which they could build their response. Paul's conviction that there are reasons why the Thessalonians turned from idols to serve God becomes part of his narrative of πίστις.

In *1 Thessalonians*, πίστις is central to Paul's construction of a narrative of God's developing relationship with humanity and how the Thessalonians come into it. It is important to note that this narrative is not the only one that could be created with πίστις at its heart. It is not even the only one that Paul creates, and other New Testament (not to mention later) writers create yet others.

2 Πίστις in *Galatians*

In *Roman Faith and Christian Faith*, I discussed at length the interpretation of Gal. 2:15–21 and the meaning of πίστις Ἰησοῦ Χριστοῦ within it, concluding that πίστις should be understood there (and elsewhere in this letter, *Romans*, and *Philippians*), in keeping with its nature and common use as an action nominal, as simultaneously subjective and objective, and in fact doubly so: as expressing both the subjectivity and the objectivity of πίστις Χριστοῦ in relation to both God and humanity.[20]

In interpreting πίστις Χριστοῦ at Gal. 2:15–21, I argued, we should focus on what Paul has already said about Christ in this letter and says in this passage. Christ "gave himself for our sins that he might rescue us from the present evil age in accord with the will of our God and Father ... ." (1:4), and Christ "has loved me and given himself up" (2:20) for Paul's justification (2:21). Together, these passages show Christ facing two ways. Christ carries out God's will, in accordance with what Paul calls elsewhere his obedience to God.[21] We could paraphrase this by saying that Christ is πιστός towards God, a term which is used in the Septuagint of those who are obedient towards God and of intra-human obedience in other Greek texts. Christ also loves human beings and acts to save

---

[20] Action nominals are nouns derived from verbs which abandon distinctions of transitivity to encompass both active and passive meanings of the verb (e.g., trust/trustworthiness or faith/faithfulness), and in which frequently deploy both meanings simultaneously (see Morgan, *Roman Faith*, 31). On the challenges of handling the multivalency of πίστις language see ibid., 19–22 and *passim*.

[21] Rom. 5:19, Phil. 2:8. On the relationship between πίστις Χριστοῦ and Jesus' faithfulness and obedience in the gospels see, e.g., Bolt, "The faith of Jesus Christ in the synoptic gospels"; Salier, "The obedient son."

them. In the Septuagint (and also in writing about Greek gods[22]), when God is described as loving and saving human beings, he is (as already noted) sometimes called πιστός, and we could describe Christ in the same way here. Christ could therefore be said, in Gal. 1–2, to be πιστός towards God and (like God) towards human beings.[23] We can further infer that God trusts Christ to enact his will, and that it is by putting their trust in him that human beings become δίκαιοι. This passage therefore places Christ at the center of what I have called a nexus of divine-human πίστις: simultaneously faithful and trustworthy towards both God and human beings and trusted by both God and the faithful. It expresses both a vision of the qualities of Christ—his faithfulness, trustworthiness and trustedness by God and humanity which makes his salvific actions possible—and a vision of his unique position between God and humanity.

Hays linked his subjective reading of πίστις Χριστοῦ with his narrative reading of Gal. 3–4, and a narrative aspect is clearly also embedded in my reading of πίστις in Gal. 1–2. Christ's unique relationship with God and humanity enables his salvific actions, which in turn enable the faithful to become δίκαιος. At the same time, occurrences of πίστις in these chapters are not purely narrative, but appear in passages of highly compressed argument (one reason why they have engendered so much debate). When Paul says that a person is justified not ἐξ ἔργων νόμου but διὰ πίστεως Χριστοῦ (Gal. 2:16), his choice of prepositions makes clear that he is thinking primarily in terms of logical rather than diachronic consequentiality. (Ἐκ can carry a diachronic meaning but usually only does so with terms for time, such as ἐξ οὗ χρόνου or ἐκ παλαιοῦ. In the phrase ἐξ ἔργων νόμου it surely bears its instrumental meaning: people are made righteous by means of/through the law. Διὰ with the genitive can refer to duration, the interval between points in time, or successive intervals, but none of these makes sense here, while the causal meaning, in which πίστις is the agent of righteousness, makes perfect sense and coheres with the use of ἐκ.) When Paul describes himself as living only insofar as he is ἐν πίστει of the Son of God (2:20), whether we understand his use of ἐν as instrumental, locative or participatory, it points (admittedly rather obliquely) to a structural description of a relationship and a state rather than a narrative one of events or experiences. Alongside Paul's narrative understanding of πίστις, we can conclude, runs another, which uses πίστις language to express Paul's sense of the new structure of the divine-human relationship and the place of Christ in it.

---

22 Morgan, *Roman Faith*, 128–37.
23 The πίστις of Christ may also act as an example to others, adding a further narrative aspect to his work: see e.g. Morgan, "Not the Whole Story?"

Πίστις language is also central to Gal. 3. Here again interpretation is complex and, having discussed the passage at length elsewhere, I only summarize my arguments here.²⁴ The relationship with God into which Paul understands the faithful as entering is that of the "children of Abraham" (3:7), a phrase which is obviously intended to put gentiles on an equal footing with Jews and integrate the whole community into the narrative history of Israel. No-one, however, enters that community simply by putting their trust in God as Abraham did; Abraham's children are those who are ἐκ πίστεως (3:7).²⁵

Δικαιοσύνη, Paul indicated in the previous chapter, comes through the πίστις of Christ to God and to human beings, and human beings put their trust in God through Christ (and his actions). Ἐκ πίστεως and, a little later, διὰ τῆς πίστεως (3:12, 14) echo 2:16 where, as we have seen, πίστις is conceived in terms more structural than narrative. In Gal. 3, Paul's argument is partly structural and partly narrative: Abraham put his trust in God as was reckoned δίκαιος; gentiles are reckoned δίκαιος, and hence children of Abraham, by putting their trust in God and Christ. They are able to do because of the πίστις of Christ.²⁶ Paul recognizes, however, that for a contemporary gentile to put her trust in God through the πίστις of Christ does not automatically connect her with Abraham or make her part of Israel (even if the proclamation of the resurrection and the Lordship of Christ were not being rejected by many Jews). Paul responds to this by arguing that Christ alone is Abraham's "seed," through which God fulfils his promise to Abraham. This, he claims, is why scripture foretells Christ and why those who believe in Christ are blessed along with Abraham.

Paul then argues that keeping the law of Moses is not necessary for those who follow Christ. The law long postdates Abraham (3:18). It does not necessarily follow from πίστις between God and humanity (3:12) nor necessarily lead to human δικαιοσύνη (3:11). It may, indeed, be a curse (3:10), or at best a παιδαγωγός or interim custodian (3:23–25). Without plumbing the deep waters of Paul's views on the law here, we can say with some confidence that Paul is claiming that while the law was in operation, it was intrinsic to Israel's relationship with God, but that now Christ has ransomed human beings from sin, it is no longer intrinsic to God's relationship with all of Abraham's descendants.

---

24 Morgan, *Roman Faith*, 274–77.
25 On whether ἐκ πίστεως and διὰ πίστεως mean the same thing see e.g. Stowers "*Ek pisteōs and dia tēs pisteōs* in Romans 3.30"; Campbell, "Romans III as the key."
26 Paul's rendition of Hab. 2:4 here as "the δίκαιος will live by πίστις" avoids both the Hebrew Bible's specification that the *pistis* is the just man's and the Septuagint's that it is God's, allowing it to be multivalent.

The complexities of Paul's argument about νόμος and πίστις are formidable, probably not fully resolvable, and probably inevitable given that he is addressing diverse audiences.[27] His understanding of πίστις in this passage, however, is not in itself over-complicated. As in Gal. 2, it is the nexus of trust "through" or "out of" which human beings are made δίκαιος, which becomes universally accessible and effective because of the πίστις of God in Christ towards humanity, the πίστις of Christ towards God and humanity, the saving action of Christ which grows out of that πίστις, and the πίστις of human beings towards God and Christ.

Hays rightly observed that Gal. 3 and 4 take slightly different perspectives on the drama of salvation. We can go further and say that the narrative of πίστις throughout Gal. 2–4 operates rather differently for Jews and gentiles. For Jews, Abraham's trusting in God led to his righteousness and his descendants' becoming a great nation and receiving the law. The law has been the Jews' παιδαγωγός until now, when it is superseded by πίστις towards Jesus Christ. For Jews, therefore, the whole of history since Abraham has been an expression of πίστις and a preparation for πίστις Ἰησοῦ Χριστοῦ and is part of Paul's narrative of salvation. For gentiles, exercising πίστις towards Jesus Christ makes them children of Abraham without any need to have participated in Israelite history or to have kept the law. Gentiles circumvent most of Israelite history: for them, time is concertina'd to create a new, compressed story of salvation. One might go further, and suggest that the concept of παιδαγωγία implies that the Jews needed preparation and training for salvation by Jesus Christ in a way that gentiles did not, but Paul surely does not intend this inference. He wants to explain why the law has been essential to Israel even though it is not essential for gentile Christians because, as a Jew, he is interested in the history of Israel's relationship with God. He is not here (or, on the whole, elsewhere) interested in the gentiles' past relationship with God *per se* or in explaining how it relates to their capacity for salvation now.[28] (Given that the differences behind it were doubtless one cause of ongoing tensions between Jews and gentiles in Christian churches, it is perhaps surprising that Paul's differential history of Jewish and gentile salvation does not receive more attention or generate more explicit debate in later texts.)

Elsewhere in *Galatians*, the narrative aspect of the divine-human πίστις relationship receives somewhat mixed treatment. In the first appearance of πίστις in this letter, for example, Paul tells the Galatians how, during his early years as a

---

27 Also, no doubt, because he did not start with one conviction and develop the others out of it, but started with at least two, developed another in answer to his opponents, and then needed to reconcile them.

28 Though he is capable of making claims about the gentile past for other purposes, e.g. Rom. 1:18–32.

missionary, he was not personally known to the churches of Judaea. "[T]hey only kept hearing that 'the one who once was persecuting us is now preaching τὴν πίστιν which he once tried to destroy (ὁ διώκων ἡμᾶς ποτε νῦν εὐαγγελίζεται τὴν πίστιν ἥν ποτε ἐπόρθει),' and they glorified God because of me." (1:23–24)

Ἡ πίστις here is sometimes read as a synonym for τὸ εὐαγγέλιον, parallel to 1 Cor. 15:1: "Now I am reminding you, brothers, of the gospel I preached to you … ." Ἡ πίστις would then refer to the content of Paul's call to potential converts to put their trust in God and be freed from their sins in preparation for the end time, with its embedded narrative about Jesus Christ. This reading has its attractions, but it presumes a significant shift in the meaning of πίστις from a relationship of trust to the content of the kerygma, of a kind which, I argue at length in *Roman Faith*, we should not take for granted.[29]

The basic meanings of πίστις, such as "trust" or "belief" are not obviously appropriate here either: they only make sense if one assumes, for instance, that "trust" is a shorthand for "the message of trust which I [Paul] preach," which is simply another way of referring to the content of the kerygma. Among the other common meanings of πίστις, "argument" or "proof" could act as the object of εὐαγγελίζομαι but do not make much sense in the context of Paul's self-understanding here (he is proclaiming what he sees as a truth, not an argument). I have argued for another interpretation, suggested by Paul's use of πορθεῖν. Πορθεῖν (an unusual variant of πέρθειν) is normally used of ravaging or destroying places (such as towns) or communities. Paul has just used it himself in this sense, at Gal. 1:13, of his persecution of the "assembly of God."[30] Πορθεῖν would be an odd word to use of disputing a viewpoint or the content of a proclamation, but it could be used of destroying a relationship. Paul's reference to τὴν πίστιν ἥν ποτε ἐπόρθει (1:23) could therefore refer to an attempt to destroy the trust, in the sense of "the relationship of trust" (or even "the bond of trust") between God, Christ and Christ's followers. The latter part of 1:23 could then be translated: "the one who was persecuting us is now proclaiming the relationship of trust [between God and human beings] which he once tried to destroy." Paul's narrative of salvation is, of course, in the background of any reference to this relationship, as it is of any reference to πίστις, but much more distantly than if Paul were referring to the content of the kerygma; primarily, this is a reference to the structure rather than the story of divine-human πίστις.

---

29 E.g., Morgan, *Roman Faith*, 265–67, cf. 3–4.
30 Cf. Acts 9:21.

Paul returns to πίστις in what looks like a similar sense at the end of this letter, when he exhorts the Galatians "while we have the opportunity, let us do good to all, but especially to τοὺς οἰκείους τῆς πίστεως" (6:10). To translate this phrase "members of the household of trust" does not make sense. To translate it, as it is sometimes translated, as "members of the household of *the* faith," assumes a large evolution of meaning in πίστις and still makes doubtful sense, since one cannot be an οἰκεῖος, for instance, of a set of doctrines, or even the combination of a set of doctrines and an attitude or orientation of the mind and heart. One can, however, without difficulty be an οἰκεῖος of a community formed by a relationship (such as the relationship of trust between God, Christ, and the faithful). To translate this phrase "fellow members of the relationship" or "the bond of trust" does not presuppose a major evolution in the meaning of πίστις and makes good sense in context. We might press the evolution of the term a little further and suggest that ἡ πίστις here means "the community of trust." 6:10 would then run: "While we have the opportunity, let us do good to all, but especially to fellow members of the relationship/community of trust [which exists between God, Christ and faithful human beings]."[31] This again is a primarily reference to Paul's understanding of the divine-human structure of πίστις rather than to its narrative. If, though, we hear echoing through this chapter the list of the fruits of the spirit given by Paul only a few verses earlier, we might speculate that here, as in *1 Thessalonians*, Paul imagines community members practicing πίστις as part of the ongoing narrative of their spiritual life (cf. 6:1), while they await the "due time" when they will reap their reward (6:9).

Ultimately, Paul's understanding of the narrative and structure of divine-human πίστις are always entwined: the one creates and sustains the other, so it is unsurprising that he refers to both within a single letter. The narrative aspect of πίστις in these passages, however, speaks to one of the most significant aspects of πίστις language in Paul's writings—and the New Testament—as a whole: the way it characterizes, not just the salvific relationship and action that take place between God, Christ, and humanity, but the structure of communities that arise from that action and relationship and the relationships between members of those communities. Πίστις in Paul, and throughout the New Testament, is not only theological, but ethical and ecclesiological. The narrative of πίστις continues to develop out of the drama of salvation and through the structure of divine-human πίστις to describe the developing relationships be-

---

[31] This interpretation need not read counter-intuitively to modern Christians, since "the relationship of trust between God, Christ and the faithful" captures an important aspect of the modern faith, if not, for most, the whole of it.

tween the saved and the nature of the communities in which they live and await the second coming.

Even the bond or community of πίστις, though in principle it is more a structural than a narrative concept, is subject to evolution through time and therefore has a narrative dimension.[32] In different passages and different letters, Paul can talk of communities being formed and sustained by the Spirit, by Paul, by other apostles, by Paul's co-workers, and by local community leaders. These are surely not alternatives, but indicate the increasing complexity and hierarchy of churches which accompanied their growth and development through time. One of Paul's periodic concerns, as already noted, is to emphasize that this increasing complexity does not diminish the power of πίστις which cascades from God, through Paul and other apostles, to these communities. The quality and relationship of πίστις which brings about δικαιοσύνη continues to operate undimmed among the saved as their churches grow and become more complex.

One passage in *Galatians* which may testify to this is 5:22–23, where, as already noted, Paul includes πίστις among the fruits of the spirit. It is hard to be sure what kind of πίστις Paul has in mind here. If he has adapted a Hellenistic virtue list, for example, as some have suggested, he may be referring straightforwardly to intra-human trust or good faith of the kind that is commonly invoked in the Septuagint and many other Greek texts.[33] I have argued, however, that πίστις is so strongly marked in Paul as a quality of the divine-human relationship that he is more likely to be referring here to the particular πίστις which God places in apostles and apostles in their co-workers. This would bring Paul's understanding of πίστις here into line with his treatment of it at 1 Cor. 12:9, where πίστις, like wisdom, healing, or prophecy, is a particular gift of the spirit given to some community members, not all.[34] On this interpretation, πίστις as a fruit of the spirit is equally a theological, ethical and ecclesiological quality, informing the developing structure and life of churches.

---

[32] At Gal. 1:6–9 (cf. 5:7) Paul is worried that the gospel he preached to the Galatians is being "perverted" by others, and hence, presumably, that the Galatians' πίστις can degrade through time (as the Thessalonians' apparently could), but he does not connect his concern explicitly with πίστις language. The idea of a "cascade" of πίστις, with its diachronic aspect, is at best a minor theme in Galatians. Paul does not in this letter describe himself as entrusted with the gospel, nor as a faithful slave or steward, nor a co-worker as πιστός, though the cascade is hinted at when he describes himself a "divine messenger" to the Galatians (4:14), and the Galatians as his children (4:19) and pupils (6:6).
[33] So, e.g., Martyn, *Theological Issues in the Letters of Paul*, 532–33.
[34] Morgan, *Roman Faith*, 277–78.

3 Πίστις in *Ephesians*

Ephesians is the letter whose ascription to Paul is most hotly debated, and even those who regard it as pseudepigraphical recognize that much of its argument and language, including its πίστις language, remain very close to Paul's. Πίστις plays a particularly significant role in Eph. 2–3, in which the author outlines his understanding of God's plan of salvation and its implications for the Ephesians.

The Ephesians, says [Paul], were "dead in your transgressions and sins" (2:1) until God, "who is rich in mercy, because of the great love he had for us ... brought us to life with Christ," and raised us to heaven (2:4–6). God did this "that in ages to come he might show the immeasurable riches of his grace in his kindness to us in Christ Jesus. For by grace you have been saved διὰ πίστεως, and this is not your doing, it is the gift of God; it is not from works, so no one may boast (τῇ γὰρ χάριτί ἐστε σεσῳσμένοι διὰ πίστεως· καὶ τοῦτο οὐκ ἐξ ὑμῶν, θεοῦ τὸ δῶρον· οὐκ ἐξ ἔργων, ἵνα μή τις καυχήσηται)" (2:7–9).

It is not self-evident whose πίστις is involved here. The emphasis of the passage is on the narrative of God's grace through Christ towards sinful human beings, so it could be Christ's πίστις towards God or, following *Galatians* and *Romans*, the doubly reciprocal πίστις between God and Christ and Christ and humanity. Alternatively, the author could be implying that God saved the Ephesians by grace, through Christ, and that the Ephesians responded with πίστις, though, since their πίστις is a gift from God, they cannot take credit for it.[35] It is also possible that the author is being deliberately ambiguous, to indicate the activity of πίστις in every part of the story of salvation. Whichever model we follow, however, it seems clear that the author is thinking here of salvation in narrative terms very similar to Paul's in *Galatians*, and of πίστις as integral to it.

In Eph. 3 the author uses πίστις to tie Paul's ministry into his account of salvation. He describes (3:7–12) how Paul was granted the grace of ministry to the gentiles so that the wisdom of God might be revealed to the world. This was in accordance with God's purpose, accomplished in Christ Jesus, in whom we have "boldness of speech and confidence of access διὰ τῆς πίστεως αὐτοῦ." (3:12) This is often taken as meaning "through [human] faith in Christ," but, as Paul Foster has pointed out, grammatically and in context it is more likely to refer to the πίστις of Christ himself.[36] Either way (or both), the narrative of salvation through

---

[35] See ibid., 308–11.
[36] Foster, "The first contribution to the *pistis Christou* debate"; cf. Foster, "*Pistis Christou* terminology." This fits well with what the author has said so far: not only in Eph. 2:1–6 but also in

πίστις continues and acquires an ecclesiological dimension with Paul's mission and the creation of the Ephesian church.

Towards the end of this chapter, [Paul] describes himself as kneeling before the Father to ask that the Ephesians may be strengthened with power through God's spirit (3:16), "and that Christ may dwell in your hearts διὰ τῆς πίστεως; that you, rooted and grounded in love, may have strength to ... know the love of Christ that surpasses knowledge (γνῶναί τε τὴν ὑπερβάλλουσαν τῆς γνώσεως ἀγάπην τοῦ Χριστοῦ), so that you may be filled with all the fullness of God." (3:17–19) The emphasis here is on qualities which come from God and/or Christ. The spirit comes from God explicitly, while the love in which the Ephesians are "rooted and grounded" cannot be their own because (logically and elsewhere in the New Testament) one is rooted in, or grounded on, something other than oneself.[37] This love may be both God's and Christ's, since verse 19 speaks of the "love of Christ." The "love of Christ" in this verse, as the object of γινώσκειν, must, in the first instance, be the love that comes from Christ,[38] but since it also surpasses knowledge which must be ours (Christ's knowledge presumably being unsurpassable), the author may have in mind that the Ephesians should respond to love that comes from Christ with love of their own. If so, then the "economy" of love here is very like that of πίστις in the previous chapter and in *Galatians* (and *Romans* and Phil. 3), and the economy of πίστις may be understood as operating in the same way here too.[39]

Since love is the attitude and relationship which, more than any other, community members are urged by Paul and [Paul] to practice towards one another, we might take this comparison further and suggest that the author of this letter also wants community members to practice πίστις towards another. Even in passages where πίστις is most clearly marked as human, however, it seems, as in Paul's letters, to be directed primarily at God and Christ rather than fellow community members. At 4:5 and 4:13, for example, πίστις features in the argument (4:1–16) that the community should be unified in practice as it is in principle.

Chapter 1, where the adoption of οἱ πιστοί by God comes through Christ (1:5), redemption comes through Christ's blood (1:7), and οἱ πιστοί are raised up to heaven by God with Christ (2:5).
37 Cf. Rom. 15:20, 1 Cor. 3:10,12, Col. 1:23.
38 I do not know of an instance (in κοινή or literary Greek) of γινώσκειν being used of experiencing an emotion, as English-speakers talk e. g. of "knowing grief." Elsewhere in this letter, the author talks of God's love for Christ (Eph. 1:6) and us (1:4, 2:4), Christ's love for the Ephesians (5:2, 6:24) and the *ecclesia* (5:25, cf. 4:15), community members' love for one another (1:15, 4:2, 5:2, 6:23), and husbands' love for wives (5:25, 28, 33), but not directly of community members' love for God or Christ.
39 On this use of the term "economy" see Morgan, *Roman Faith*, 142, 217.

There is "one Lord, one πίστις, one baptism; one God and Father" (4:5).[40] The focus here is on what the community holds in common, so πίστις is likely to be a human quality, but we should surely read it, with baptism, as an expression of commitment to God and Christ. At 4:13, πίστις is paired with knowledge (ἐπίγνωσις) of the Son of God as something to which every community member aspires: "[Christ] gave some as apostles, others as prophets ... to equip the holy ones for the work of ministry, for building up the body of Christ, until we all attain to the unity of πίστις and of knowledge of the Son of God ..." (4:11–13). Grammatically, the πίστις phrase presents as "πίστις of the Son of God," but the genitive of the Son of God follows ἐπίγνωσις; since the unity of πίστις is something community members can hope to attain and appears to be parallel to ἐπίγνωσις, this must refer to trust in the Son of God. Though the narrative of πίστις continues from conversion to life in community, therefore, it does not, here, seem to be practiced by community members towards one another, but to unite the faithful in ongoing πίστις towards God and Christ.

Πίστις towards Christ has also been identified at 1:13 and 1:15:

> (11) In whom [Christ], we were also chosen, destined (ἐκληρώθημεν προορισθέντες) in accord with the purposes of the One who accomplishes all things according to the intention of his will, (12) so that we might exist for the praise of his glory, we who first hoped in Christ (ἐν τῷ Χριστῷ). (13a) In whom (Ἐν ᾧ) you also, who have heard the word of truth, the gospel of your salvation, (13b) in whom/which (ἐν ᾧ) you have trusted/believed (πιστεύσαντες), were sealed with the promised holy spirit, (14) which is the first instalment of our inheritance toward redemption as God's possession, to the praise of his glory. (15) Therefore I, too, hearing of your πίστις in the Lord Jesus (τὴν καθ' ὑμᾶς πίστιν ἐν τῷ κυρίῳ Ἰησοῦ) and of your love for all the holy ones, do not cease giving thanks for you...' (1:11–15)

At verse 13b, the second ἐν ᾧ is often taken to refer to trusting "in Christ," following verses 11–13a where ἐν and ἐν ᾧ refer repeatedly to Christ. This makes for a rather roundabout sentence, so it may be preferable to understand ἐν ᾧ at 13b as referring to trusting/believing in the gospel. (The author may want to emphasize either that people can trust the preaching they hear because the preacher is trustworthy, or that they can trust its content, for the same reason. Both ideas have Pauline roots and a narrative aspect: the first alludes to the content of the kerygma, the second also to the contribution of πίστις to the development of communities.) At verse 15, πίστιν ἐν τῷ κυρίῳ Ἰησοῦ follows five occurrences

---

40 Some commentators (e. g., Best, *A Critical and Exegetical Commentary on Ephesians*, 268–69; cf. Lincoln, *Ephesians*, 240) see this as the content of "faith" or of a baptismal confession, but this implies an evolution in meaning beyond what is necessary to make sense of the passage, so should be resisted (see Morgan, *Roman Faith*, 3–4).

of ἐν Χριστῷ in the previous eight verses (1:7, 10, 11, 12, 13) in the strong and (opaque but) distinctively Pauline meaning of "in Christ." It is therefore tempting to hear "πίστις in the Lord Jesus" as meaning "πίστις, in the Lord Jesus," but given that the author has shifted from speaking of "Christ" to "the Lord Jesus," this phrase may bear its everyday meaning of "trust in the Lord Jesus."

The most striking aspect of this passage is the connection which the author makes between πίστις, being "in Christ," and pre-election. 1:11 echoes 1:3–5:

> Blessed be the God and father of our Lord Jesus Christ, who has blessed us ἐν Χριστῷ with every spiritual blessing in the heavens, as he chose us in him [Christ] (ἐξελέξατο ἡμᾶς ἐν αὐτῷ), before the foundation of the world, to be holy and without blemish before him [God]. In love he destined us for adoption (υἱοθεσίαν) to himself through Jesus Christ, in accord with the favour of his will ....

It is not self-evident here whether [Paul] is talking about himself in the plural or about all community members. The link καὶ ὑμεῖς at 1:13 hints at the former but κἀγώ at 1:15 suggests the latter. The likely hymnic origin of some of these verses, however, together with their echoes of the language of Rom. 8, where Paul is talking in the first-person plural about the whole community, make it most likely that the author is talking about all community members.[41] Community members are adopted through (the salvific action of) Christ—they become God's children after the crucifixion and resurrection—but they are *chosen* long before that, "in Christ." Exactly where being "in Christ" fits in the sequence of events is not clear, but it precedes the foundation of the world and may be another way of describing pre-election itself. Either way, the πίστις of human beings, in Jesus and probably in the gospel, is not so much an act of trust which brings people, from the human side, into a relationship with God, as an expression and confirmation of their chosenness and pre-election.

This story of salvation is significantly different from what Hays identified as either the Jewish or the gentile narrative of *Galatians*. The law plays almost no part in it (apart from a glancing reference to its being abolished by Christ at Eph. 2:15), and descent from Abraham none at all. Instead, this letter picks up occasional suggestions by Paul (notably in *1 Thessalonians*) that certain people are chosen to hear and receive the gospel before it is preached to them.[42] In a sense, here as in *1 Thessalonians*, we can see the story of pre-election as anti-nar-

---

41 See, e. g., Muddiman, *Ephesians*, ad loc.
42 Though it moves beyond Paul's understanding of being "in Christ" as a consequence of πίστις. Paul also talks of pre-election (e. g., 1 Thess. 1:4) and *pistis* occasionally comes into proximity with being ἐν Χριστῷ (1 Cor. 4:17, Gal. 2:16–17, 5:6, cf. 2 Cor. 13:5), but Paul does not connect πίστις, pre-election and being ἐν Χριστῷ as this passage does.

rative: no long process of history has led the Ephesians to this moment. At the same time, as in *1 Thessalonians*, there are signs that the author does think of the Ephesians' conversion as the culmination of a historical process. He refers to God's will, for instance, as "a plan for the fullness of times" (1:10), and even though the Ephesians have been destined for conversion, they can only be saved through πίστις after Christ has died and been raised (for instance, 2:5–10). The crucifixion and resurrection, however, seem to be the only part of history that matters. The history of salvation has been dramatically compressed to consist of pre-election, creation, the death and resurrection of Christ, and adoption.

Πίστις in this letter comes from both God and Christ (6:23), is mediated by Paul, and calls out an answering πίστις from the Ephesians. In this respect, its narrative is closely related to that of *1 Thessalonians*, *Galatians*, and other Pauline letters. The Ephesians' πίστις has led to their being "sealed" with the Holy Spirit. The narrative of salvation which began before the foundation of the world, is not yet complete.

Despite the reference to the Ephesians being strengthened with power through the spirit at 3:16, we may note in passing that this letter has little to say about πίστις as a quality which helps the community through times of trial. The extended image of the armor of light, however, (6:10–17) does exhort them to "stand firm against the tactics of the devil," and πίστις plays a role in this action. At 6:16, it has become a shield with which to "quench all the flaming arrows of the evil one."

4 Πίστις in *1* and *2 Timothy*

The author of *1* and *2 Timothy* also treats πίστις primarily as a relationship between God and the faithful and Christ and the faithful. I have argued that he adopts Paul's understanding of πίστις Χριστοῦ, in *Galatians* and elsewhere, as the doubly reciprocal πίστις of Christ towards God and humanity and that of God and humanity towards Christ which enables the new covenant.[43] In addition, he develops further Paul's narrative of πίστις as the quality and action which articulates the relationship between apostles and community members and between community members. In these letters, the narrative of πίστις is strongly ethical and ecclesiological.[44]

---

[43] Morgan, *Roman Faith*, 318–19.
[44] Ibid., 237, 318–24, 329–30.

God is not explicitly called πιστός in either letter, but Christ is said to remain πιστός at 2 Tim. 2:13. Occurring as it does at the climax of a series of acclamations about Christ's relationship with the saved, this verse invites us to take it as an affirmation of Christ's πίστις towards human beings. This and the previous verse, however, run: "If we deny him he will deny us. If we are unfaithful he remains faithful, for he cannot deny himself." For Christ to "deny himself" surely refers to his denying his role in salvation (which the writer affirmed at 1:9–10), so verse 13 may also refer to Christ's faithfulness to God. If so, the writer may be drawing on Paul's model (thought not on much of his language) of salvation in Gal. 2 and Rom. 3.

2 Tim. 3:10–16 offers some support for this view. [Paul] is praising Timothy for his πίστις (3:10) and other qualities under persecution and exhorting him to hold fast to the teaching he has learned from the apostle and from the (Jewish) scriptures, which give him "wisdom for salvation through πίστις ἐν Χριστῷ Ἰησοῦ" (3:14–15). Like the author of *Ephesians*, the author of *2 Timothy* understands the faithful as saved by God's plan and the grace given to them before the beginning of time ἐν Χριστῷ Ἰησοῦ (1:9). Being "in Christ" there (leaving aside for present purposes what that much-debated phrase means) is something given to Christ's followers, not achieved by them. This suggests that πίστις τῆς ἐν Χριστῷ Ἰησοῦ at 3:15 too is something achieved by Christ. In this passage, therefore, πίστις is practiced both by Christ and by those who are "in Christ."

1 Timothy also follows Paul's example in using πίστις language to connect the theological narrative of salvation with the story of the developing ecclesia. At 1:12, [Paul] is grateful to Christ for considering him πιστός and appointing him to his ministry. He has already called Timothy his "loyal child in πίστις" (1:4), leaving open whether πίστις here is [Paul]'s and/or Timothy's πίστις towards God or Timothy's πίστις towards [Paul], or all three. Πίστις towards Christ gives [Paul] authority among the faithful: he is πιστός towards them and they have πίστις towards him. At 2:7, the author has just affirmed that Christ gave himself as a ransom for all. He continues, "For this I was appointed preacher and apostle … teacher of the gentiles ἐν πίστει καὶ ἀληθείᾳ." Both πίστις and ἀλήθεια may refer both to [Paul]'s relationship of trust and trustworthiness with God and his truthful or reliable witness on God's behalf.[45] At 2 Tim. 3:10 [Paul] says, "You have followed my teaching, way of life, purpose, πίστις, patience, love, endurance, persecutions, and sufferings, such as happened to me in Antioch, Iconium, and Lystra … ." Here [Paul]'s πίστις (towards God, the faithful, or both) gives Timothy a reason to follow him and perhaps also a model to

---

45 Ibid., 209–10, 286 n. 90.

imitate. In all these passages, the πίστις of God and Christ calls out an answering πίστις in the apostle which encourages πίστις among the faithful, spreading the news of God's plan (cf. 1 Tim. 1:4) and at the same time creating a hierarchy in the emerging ecclesia.

1 Timothy, like Paul's letters, refers several times to followers of Christ as πιστοί.[46] More unusually, the author refers three times to the πίστις of female community members. At 2:15, the author says that women "will be saved through child-bearing, if they persist in πίστις and love and holiness with prudence." At 3:11, he insists that women must be "dignified, not backbiting, sober, πιστάς in everything." The inclusion of virtues directed at God and fellow community members leaves open whether the πίστις of women here is directed towards God or human beings. Comparing these passages with 1 Tim. 6:2, however, may indicate that the πίστις of women is meant to be directed towards God. At 6:2 the author says, "Those [slaves] who have masters who are πιστούς must not be disrespectful towards them because they are brothers, but must give better service, because those benefiting from their work are πιστοί ... ." The parallel made between masters as πιστοί and as ἀδελφοί of Christian slaves makes clear that their πίστις here is not everyday, intra-human πίστις but their πίστις towards God. In Greek literature in general, it is commonplace to refer to the πίστις of masters towards slaves and slaves towards masters, but the author does not take the opportunity to commend that kind of πίστις here.[47] Rather, he makes the point that relationships between community members are conditioned by those members' relationship of πίστις with God and Christ. Though the parallel between this passage and 2:15 and 3:11 is not exact (because in the former it is the πίστις of the dominant partner in the relationship that is specified, in the latter, that of the subaltern), it is suggestive. It implies that *1 Timothy* understands certain behaviors as appropriate for certain community members, such as women and slaves, *as* women or slaves. If so, this is the first time that gendered behavior, or behavior specific to one's social station, has been explicitly linked by a Christian writer with πίστις and the first time that a Christian writer has suggested that πίστις towards God may express itself in different ways in community members of differing status.[48] In *1* and *2 Timothy*, the use of πίστις language to describe the structure of the community of the faithful, and the narrative of how the πίστις of God is played out in the post-res-

---

[46] 1 Tim. 4:10, 5:8, 5:16, 6:2; non-members may be called ἄπιστοι at 1 Tim. 5:8, cf. 1:13 (on these terms see Morgan, *Roman Faith*, 234–41).
[47] Morgan, *Roman Faith*, 51–55.
[48] As is common elsewhere in Greek (and Roman) society: see Morgan, *Roman Faith*, 39–65.

urrection world, takes a further step, giving a distinctively Christian theological justification to certain human social structures and activities.

Within these structures, πίστις is also a quality and praxis that must be maintained through time. At 1 Tim. 5:8 the author warns that anyone who does not take care of family members has "broken the πίστις" (using a word, ἀρνέομαι, often used of the breaking of treaties). At 6:10–12 he condemns those who wander away from πίστις for love of money (cf. 6:21). At 2 Tim. 4:7 Paul claims of himself that "I have competed well; I have finished the race; I have kept the faith." The importance of the ongoing narrative of πίστις throughout the life of the faithful, whether in quiet times, under persecution (2 Tim. 3:1–9), or through internal dissentions (2 Tim. 2:14–19) is clear.

In one other respect 1 and 2 Timothy (and other deutero-Pauline letters) take Paul's narrative of πίστις a step further. They emphasize the trustworthiness of the teachings—the λόγοι—Timothy and his community have received, as opposed to the trustworthiness of Paul and the other apostles as direct witnesses of the saving actions of Christ. I have argued that this emphasis is particularly appropriate to a moment in time when communities are moving further from direct contact with those who knew Jesus in life, and are having to rely more on second- and third-hand testimonies, oral and, increasingly, written.[49] Every time the author uses the phrase πιστός ὁ λόγος, for example (for instance, 1 Tim. 1:15, 3:1, 4:9, 2 Tim. 2:11), he puts an affirmation of the reliability of tradition into the mouth of Paul himself. By this means he encourages his community to accept that soon (if not already) they must rely on indirect and written accounts of the life, death, and resurrection of Jesus Christ, and that these can sustain their πίστις through their lifetimes as effectively as direct contact with an apostle. The narrative of πίστις here begins another chapter: one which will become centrally important to churches in later centuries. The πίστις which flows undiluted from God, through Christ and the spirit, through the apostles and their co-workers, is now being understood as flowing, still undiluted, through the traditions passed down through communities, and, increasingly and decisively, in writing.

5 Conclusion

Πίστις, I noted at the beginning of this essay, is an intrinsically narrative concept: inescapably hopeful, forward-looking, and socially productive. In the writings of Paul and his followers the narrative of πίστις takes a number of different

---

49 Morgan, *Roman Faith*, 314, 341, 346.

forms which are more or less important for different writers (and, perhaps, communities). Πίστις language is used to tell stories about the relationship between God and Christ and God, Christ and humanity; about the working of God's mercy, salvation, and the restoration of the faithful to righteousness; about the appointment of apostles to preach the gospel and their relationship with those they preach to; about how the faithful are chosen to accept the apostles' preaching about the different but connected historical trajectories by which Jews and gentiles gain access to grace; about how community members should live and relate to one another; about how traditions and writings are authorized as objects and tools of πίστις. It is hard to conceive of any other lexical family in Greek that could have captured all these stories and bound them together into one grand, complex, (more or less) integrated system of thought and practice. Together with that of the other writers of the New Testament, Paul's and his followers' use of πίστις language integrated theology, ethics, ecclesiology and eschatology inextricably in early Christian thinking. In the process, it ensured that πίστις, *fides*, and their translations into manifold later languages would become and remain central to every form of Christianity.

References

Best, Ernest. *A Critical and Exegetical Commentary on Ephesians*. Edinburgh: T&T Clark, 1998.
Bolt, P. "The faith of Jesus Christ in the synoptic gospels." In *The Faith of Jesus Christ: Exegetical, Biblical, and Theological Studies*, edited by Michael F. Bird and Preston M. Sprinkle, 209–22. Milton Keynes: Paternoster, 2010.
Campbell, W. "Romans III as the key to the structure and thought of Romans." In *The Romans Debate*, edited by Karl P. Donfried, rev. ed., 251–64. Peabody, MA: Hendrickson, 1991.
Easter, M. C. "The *pistis Christou* debate: main arguments and responses in summary." *Currents in Biblical Research* 9 (2010): 33–47.
Foster, Paul. "The first contribution to the *pistis Christou* debate: a study of Ephesians 3:12." *Journal for the Study of the New Testament* 24 (2002): 75–96.
Foster, Paul. "*Pistis Christou* terminology in Philippians and Ephesians." In *The Faith of Jesus Christ: Exegetical, Biblical, and Theological Studies*, edited by Michael F. Bird and Preston M. Sprinkle, 91–110. Milton Keynes: Paternoster, 2010.
Hays, Richard B. *The Faith of Jesus Christ: The Narrative Substructure of Galatians 3:1–4:11*. Grand Rapids, MI: Eerdmans, 2002.
Hooker, Morna. "*Pistis Christou*: Faith in Christ or the Faith of Christ: A New Testament Analysis." *New Testament Studies* 35 (1989): 321–42.
Lincoln, Andrew. *Ephesians*. Dallas: World Books, 1990.
Martyn, J. Louis. *Theological Issues in the Letters of Paul*. Edinburgh: T&T Clark, 1997.
Morgan, Teresa. *Roman Faith and Christian Faith*. Oxford: Oxford University Press, 2015.

Morgan, Teresa. "Not the Whole Story? Moralizing Biography and *Imitatio Christi*." In *Fame and Infamy: Essays on Characterization in Greek and Roman Biography and History*, edited by Rhiannon Ash *et al.*, 353–66. Oxford: Oxford University Press, 2015.

Muddiman, John. *Ephesians*. London: Continuum, 2001.

Salier, W. "The obedient son: the 'faithfulness' of Christ in the fourth gospel." In *The Faith of Jesus Christ: Exegetical, Biblical, and Theological Studies,* edited by Michael F. Bird and Preston M. Sprinkle, 223–38. Milton Keynes: Paternoster, 2010.

Stowers, Stanley Kent. "*Ek pisteōs* and *dia tēs pisteōs* in Romans 3.30." *Journal of Biblical Literature* 108 (1989): 665–74.

Françoise Frazier
Returning to "Religious" Πίστις: Platonism and Piety in Plutarch and Neoplatonism

Abstract: This essay extends the discussion on the meaning and importance of πίστις language in the ancient world by discussing how Plutarch's successors use this language and by comparing the use of πίστις in Neoplatonism and Plutarch. This essay continues previous studies on "religious" πίστις in Plutarch, which show that for Plutarch πίστις does not yet indicate "suprarational faith," that his use of the word still remains close to Plato's, and that for all Middle-Platonists πίστις remains at the level of δόξα. For the comparison between Neoplatonism and Plutarch, two aspects need to be taken into account. As far as the intellectual and doctrinal aspect (i.e., Platonism) is concerned, the case of Plotinus emerges as particularly illuminating: Πίστις does not mean "suprarational faith" in the *Enneads* either. Πίστις appears, with πιστεύειν, in the ascension of the soul, which may be compared to the philosophical approach of the Intelligible in Plutarch. Whereas Plotinus thinks the soul can join the Intelligible because the One has replaced it as an unattainable Absolute, for Plutarch contemplation is still impossible here below. As a consequence, the second, existential aspect—piety—brings into play another Neoplatonist: not Plotinus, for whom philosophy and piety are one and the same, but rather his disciple Porphyry and, after him, Iamblichus and Proclus, who trace a spiritual itinerary through the triad (or the tetrad) πίστις, ἔρως, ἀλήθεια (and ἐλπίς). By following this line of thought, Frazier reinterprets important themes and imageries that are used throughout the history of Platonism and thus situates Plutarch more precisely in this movement.

For modern readers, the translation of the Greek word πίστις as "faith" can be misleading, especially in a religious context, due to the connotations the word has acquired from centuries of Christianity—connotations, that is, that were unknown in pagan philosophy. But, already in Greek, πίστις and πιστεύειν had a large range of meanings. We must first get a clear idea of them before examining their uses in context. Pierre Chantraine's *Etymological Dictionary*,[1] for example,

---

[1] Chantraine, *Dictionnaire étymologique de la langue grecque*, s.v. πείθομαι, 868–69, esp. 869: "Le système πείθομαι, ἐπιθόμην, πέποιθα issu d'une base **beidh-* présente un aspect archaïque et trouve un correspondant dans le lat. *fido*. Les mots de cette famille expriment originellement la notion de 'confiance, fidélité', cf. Benveniste, *Institutions indo-européennes* 1, 115, avec divers-

indicates that the Greek word and its cognates have the basic sense of "*persuader* de toutes les façons"—which denotes a rather intellectual process; moreover, it derives from an Indo-European root involving "confiance, fidélité"—trust, fidelity—which belongs to the ethical domain. Two axes appear immediately, which I will roughly label "Platonism" for the intellectual, doctrinal aspect and "Piety" for the, so to speak, existential one. Furthermore, πίστις does not only apply to different *domains*, but may also indicate things of different *natures:* in the sense of "belief," it is a kind of opinion, often opposed to knowledge; in the sense of "confidence," it is rather a state of the soul, a πάθος, which may be associated with self-assurance (θάρσος) or hope; in the sense of "loyalty," it is a virtue, which depends on justice, and last, but not least, in the "Pauline sense," it is a theological virtue.

This complex notion has already provided me with material for two studies devoted to "religious πίστις" in Plutarch. In the first of these papers,[2] I have reconsidered the possible emergence of a suprarational faith, expressed through the word πίστις, by examining not only the Plutarchan religious contexts which have inspired Daniel Babut to formulate this hypothesis,[3] but also the passages in Plato's works that he has read as foreshadowing this new sense. For my second paper,[4] Philippe Hoffmann suggested that I could focus on all the passages containing πίστις in Plutarch and, beyond that, in all the preserved fragments of Middle-Platonism. As I first examined Plato, then the Middle-Platonists, I thought that I could now consider Neoplatonists and resume the questioning by comparing Plutarch to his successors. Indeed, the presence and meaning of πίστις in Neoplatonism might help us to understand its absence in Plutarch, might assist in unveiling some lasting themes or images, and, finally, might help to highlight the interpretation specific to each philosopher. As far as I am concerned, this hypothesis seems well worth testing.

On this basis, in keeping with the Research Project "Overcoming the Faith-Reason Opposition," I will briefly sum up my refutation of the hypothesis that a new notion of suprarational faith is apparent in Plutarch. I do so in order to firmly establish, as a starting point, the idea that πίστις in Plutarch, as in

---

es implications juridiques; ce sens est apparent dans les termes les plus archaïques, comme πιστός de *bhidh- to et πίστις nom d'action en *-ti-, avec un vocalisme zéro, qui pourrait être dû à l'analogie avec πιστός."

2 Frazier, "Philosophie et religion dans la pensée de Plutarque."
3 Babut, "Du scepticisme au dépassement de la raison."
4 See my "Les emplois de πίστις chez les médioplatoniciens," paper presented at the meeting *Conviction, croyance, foi: Pistis et fides de Platon aux Pères*, organized by C. Grellard, Ph. Hoffmann and L. Lavaud, Paris, May 31–June 2, 2012.

other Middle-Platonists, stays at the level of δόξα. We can then consider the higher levels of Reality, which play an increasingly important part in Neoplatonism. In fact, after Plotinus, the existence of a Neoplatonic faith is a commonplace, but the case of Plotinus is trickier,[5] and I became increasingly aware how illuminating it would be to study him in depth and then to compare his conception of the ascension of the soul to the philosophical approach to the Intelligible in Plutarch. Finally, I will turn to the existential aspect. In this regard, we will see that after Plotinus πίστις is to be found in the triad "love, truth, faith" (ἔρως, ἀλήθεια, πίστις), which is often supplemented by hope (ἐλπίς), to delineate a spiritual itinerary: what can be found in Plutarch that might hint at some connection with the Divine in this world? This will be the last point that is considered.

1 Status Quaestionis: Πίστις, Tradition and the "Δόξα Level"

The role that Plutarch gave to neo-academic skepticism in his own Platonism has proved a greatly debated question among historians of philosophy in the last ten years. In his research on this theme, Daniel Babut asserts that there emerges a new concept of πίστις, a "fideistic" one, and does so by making reference to *one* "famous text" (in Babut's terms) of *Amatorius,* while rejecting other references in a footnote:[6]

> Pemptides, he said,[7] it is, I believe, a grave and dangerous matter that you are broaching; or rather, you are altogether violating our inviolable belief in the gods (τὰ ἀκίνητα κινεῖν τῆς περὶ θεῶν δόξης ἣν ἔχομεν), when you demand an account and proof (λόγον ἀπαιτῶν καὶ ἀπόδειξιν) of each of them. Our ancient traditional faith (ἡ πάτριος καὶ παλαιὰ πίστις) is good enough. It is impossible to assert or discover evidence more palpable (τεκμήριον ἐναργέστερον) than this faith (ἧς),
>
> Whatever subtle twist's (τὸ σοφὸν) invented by keen wit. (Euripides, *Bacchae* 203)

---

[5] On Plotinus' faith, see Rist, *Plotinus*, 231–46.
[6] Actually, he refers to another footnote in Babut, *Plutarque et le stoïcisme*, 515 n. 5, which listed Plutarch, *De Pythiae oraculis* 402E, *De Iside et Osiride* 359F, *De sera numinis vindicta* 560D (πιστεύοντες), *Non posse suaviter vivi secundum Epicurum* 1101C, *Caius Marcius Coriolanus* 38.3 and 38.4 (ἀπιστίῃ , quotation from Heraclitus) and *Aratus* 43, 4. This is quite a variety of texts.
[7] Plutarch is referred to in the third person as his son is the narrator.

This faith is a basis, as it were, a common foundation of religion (πρὸς εὐσέβειαν); if confidence and settled usage (τὸ βέβαιον αὐτῆς καὶ νενομισμένον) are disturbed or shaken at a single point, the whole edifice is enfeebled and discredited (ἐπισφαλὴς καὶ ὕποπτος).[8]

Against this hypothesis, a reconsideration of all texts containing possible references to a "religious πίστις" has shown that no opposition between faith and reason, such as we, modern people, conceive it, is to be found in them. For the λόγος mentioned is not the reason of the philosopher, but the overly subtle reasoning of a sophist, a bad use of reason which has nothing to do with the good philosophical one. Nor is πίστις used as a self-sufficient notion, "*the* faith" as such. Rather, in all texts, Plutarch qualifies the term, speaking of the *ancient* πίστις of our fathers or of *ancestral* beliefs, and he often associates it with tradition or customary practices (νενομισμένα). Consequently, the point at stake is not the opposition between faith and reason, but the relation of the philosopher to tradition and, especially, to religious tradition. Daniel Babut himself devoted a monograph to this topic, and, with reference to Plato concluded:

> The Olympians no doubt belong to Platonic theology, but amongst other manifestations of the divine, and probably in one of the lower regions. Logically, *to such an intermediate position on the ontological map corresponds a similarly intermediate level of cognition – that of* πίστις *versus* ἀλήθεια [*Timaeus* 29c2–3]. One could also say that, as the gods of tradition are the reflection, on a lower plane, of the absolute Divine, so also the uncertainty involved responds, in some way, to the difficulty of perceiving the Supreme Principle, the Idea of the Good. This way, the apparent inconsistency of Plato's attitude to popular religion disappears. *The use of tradition does not in any way imply a subordination of philosophy to religion,* but rather the most appropriate means to comply with the objective evidence of a religious issue. No matter what may have been said [Wilamowitz], there is no conflict between reason and faith, since both retain their value, only on different levels.[9]

This conclusion still holds true for Plutarch, who, in his *De Iside*, clearly asserts the preeminence of philosophy and specifies the role that is to be played by tradition in this advice to Clea:

> If, then, you listen to the stories about the gods in this way, accepting them from those who interpret the story *reverently and philosophically* (ὁσίως καὶ φιλοσόφως), and if you always perform and observe *the established rites of worship* (τῶν ἱερῶν τὰ νενομισμένα), and believe that no sacrifice you can offer, no deed that you may do will be more likely to find

---

[8] Plutarch, *Amatorius* 756B. Unless otherwise noted, all translations are taken from the Loeb Classical Library. For the sake of convenience, I have retained the various translations of πίστις, and have only indicated the Greek word in brackets.
[9] Translated by Suzan Sierksma-Agteres from Babut, *La religion des philosophes grecs*, 94–95; references in brackets and italics are mine.

favour with the gods than *your true opinion about them* (τοῦ δ' ἀληθῆ δόξαν ἔχειν περὶ θεῶν), you may avoid superstition which is no less an evil than atheism.¹⁰

Such an attitude towards religious tradition actually continues up to and includes Plotinus.¹¹ For example, at the end of his treatise "On the immortality of the soul" (*Enneads* 4.7) he comments that after "what needed to be said to those who required proof" (πρὸς τοὺς ἀποδείξεως δεομένους) has been said, references to traditional rites, needed by "those who require confidence supported by the evidence of the senses" (πρὸς τοὺς δεομένους πίστεως αἰσθήσει κεκρατημένης) can be given.¹² Only post-Plotinian Neoplatonists consider truth and tradition, reason and authority, as one and the same thing and take historical tradition to be the standard of the truth.¹³

In his study, Daniel Babut refers to a famous passage from Plato's *Timaeus* and speaks of "*an intermediate position on the ontological map corresponds a similarly intermediate level of cognition—that of πίστις versus ἀλήθεια*" whereas Plutarch's *De Iside* insisted on true *opinion*. The specialized dictionaries¹⁴ confirm that the philosophical uses of πίστις are at the level of δόξα, and list two major senses: "belief," with references to Plato,¹⁵ and "proof" or better "what instills belief," which is a sense that particularly interested Aristotle.¹⁶ A third sense is also to be found in a Hellenistic collection of rather Stoic and Aristotelian definitions (falsely) attributed to Andronicus of Rhodes: "πίστις is the assent to (what is) known as true."¹⁷ The assent and credibility given to sensation and which are seen as constituting the bases of knowledge are major themes in the Hellenistic polemics surrounding knowledge and continue to be debated in Middle Platonism: πίστις as confidence of the knower or credibility of the

---

10 Plutarch, *De Iside et Osiride* 355C–D, translation of F.C. Babbitt slightly altered.
11 See also Plato, *Phaedrus* 230a1–3, Aristotle, fr. 44 Rose [= Plutarch, *Consolatio ad Apollonium* 215B–C], Plutarch, *De sera numinis vindicta* 560C8–D2.
12 Plotinus, *Enneads* 4.7.15.
13 Hadot, *Qu'est-ce que la philosophie antique*, 235–36.
14 Peters, *Greek Philosophical Terms*, s.v. πίστις; Urmson, *The Greek Philosophical Vocabulary*, s.v. πίστις.
15 Plato, *Timaeus* 29c2–3 and *Republic* 509d ff. See also *Timaeus* 37b3 about δόξαι καὶ πίστεις βέβαιοι καὶ ἀληθεῖς.
16 E.g. Aristotle, *Posterior Analytics* 90b14 (ἱκανὴ δὲ πίστις καὶ ἐκ τῆς ἐπαγωγῆς) or *Rhetoric* 1355b35 (τῶν δὲ πίστεων αἱ μὲν ἄτεχνοί εἰσιν αἱ δ' ἔντεχνοι).
17 Pseudo-Andronicus of Rhodes, *On Emotions*, 2.8.3: ἡ ὡς ἀληθεῖ τῷ γνωσθέντι συγκατάθεσις; this kind of definition inspired also Basil, *Prologue* 8 (*De Fide*, vol. 31, 677): "Πίστις is the assent without any discrimination (συγκατάθεσις ἀδιάκριτος) to things heard in full confidence in the truth (ἐν πληροφορίᾳ τῆς ἀληθείας) of what has been announced by the grace of God."

thing known plays an important part in these controversies. Such a notion of πίστις has nothing to do with πίστις as a Platonic δόξα that is inferior to knowledge. Nor does it denote a suprarational faith. Instead, it accounts for the fact that the human mind needs to have something firm upon which it can base its assent. This can be put in Aristotelian terms:

> Again every *opinion* (ἔτι πάσῃ μὲν δόξῃ) is accompanied by *belief* (πίστις), belief (πίστει) by *conviction* (τὸ πεπεῖσθαι), and conviction (πειθοῖ) by *rational discourse* (λόγος).[18]

Staying at the level of δόξα, Plutarch uses the notion of πίστις in the sense of confidence, conviction or belief. Before considering how he deals with the higher levels of reality, it is necessary first to take a closer look at Neoplatonic philosophy.

2 "Platonism": Πίστις and the Higher Levels of Reality

The most comprehensive summary of ancient and new (*viz.* Neoplatonist) definitions of πίστις is found in Proclus' treatise *On the Theology of Plato*. He starts with a very clear definition of what is evidently a suprarational πίστις, though it is rather different from modern faith:

> It is, in short, the faith (πίστις) of the Gods, which *ineffably unites* all the genera of the Gods, of dæmons, and of happy souls *to the good* (ἡ πρὸς τὸ ἀγαθὸν ἀρρήτως ἑνίζουσα). [...] For such a faith (πίστις) ... *is more ancient than the gnostic energy* (πρεσβύτερόν ἐστι τῆς γνωστικῆς ἐνεργείας).[19]

He then strictly distinguishes it from three possible conceptions of πίστις: first from the πίστις "which is conversant with the wandering about sensibles" (τῇ περὶ τὰ αἰσθητὰ πλάνῃ), namely, Plato's πίστις of the Divided Line; second, from the Stoic "belief in common conceptions" (τῇ τῶν κοινῶν καλουμένων ἐννοιῶν); and, finally, from the "intellectual energy" (τὴν κατὰ νοῦν ἐνέργειαν). The explanation he gives for this third form leads us to the heart of Neoplatonism and deserves to be quoted:

---

18 Aristotle, *De Anima* 428a22–24.
19 Proclus, *On the Theology of Plato*, 1.25 (p. 110, ll. 6–8 and 12–14 ff. Saffrey-Westerink), translation by Thomas Taylor, accessed July 15, 2016, https://archive.org/details/ProclusOnTheTheologyOfPlato-ElectronicEdition (my italics).

For intellectual energy is multiform, and is separated from the object of intellection through difference; and in short, it is intellectual motion about the intelligible. But it is necessary that divine faith (πίστις) should be *uniform and quiet* (ἑνοειδῆ καὶ ἤρεμον), *being perfectly established in the port of goodness* (ἐν τῷ τῆς ἀγαθότητος ὅρμῳ τελείως ἱδρυνθεῖσαν).²⁰

This "Proclian πίστις" can conveniently be used as a kind of endpoint for Neoplatonism with regard to this matter, but it is too far from Plutarch to even warrant comparison with him. Indeed, it only sheds light on the gap between Middle Platonism and Neoplatonism.

Plotinus' case is different, however, since the Proclian πίστις does not exist in his work either: as in Middle Platonism, most of his uses of πίστις address Hellenistic problematics, but πίστις, and, more often, πιστεύειν,²¹ also appears in relation to the effort of the soul to ascend, which characterizes Plotinus' philosophy. His conception is highlighted, for example, in his treatise "On the Good or the One" (*Enneads* 6.9): Plotinus states that the One, "(as) Plato says,²² cannot be spoken or written,"²³ and continues as follows:

> but we speak and write impelling towards it and *wakening from reasonings to the vision of it* (ἀνεγείροντες ἐκ τῶν λόγων ἐπὶ τὴν θέαν), as if showing the way to someone who wants to have a view of something. For teaching goes *as far as the road and travelling* (μέχρι τῆς ὁδοῦ καὶ τῆς πορείας)²⁴, but the vision is the task (ἔργον) of someone who has already resolved to see.²⁵

This first distinction between the road and travelling—something in progress— and the final vision—an immediate experience expressed elsewhere in terms of contact—may be refined yet further. In fact, there are two possible ways for the soul to join the purest part of itself, which Plotinus suggests a little later:

> If then someone is not yet there but is outside because of these impediments, or *through lack of a reasoning to guide him and give him assurance about the One* (δι' ἔνδειαν τοῦ παιδαγωγοῦντος λόγου καὶ πίστιν περὶ αὐτοῦ παρεχομένου), let him blame himself for those hindrances and try to depart from all things and be alone, but as for what *he disbelieves*

---

20 Proclus, *On the Theology of Plato*, 1.25 (p. 111, ll. 5–7 ff. Saffrey-Westerink).
21 This use of the verb deserves to be pointed out because it immediately suggests a certain activity of the soul in its ascension.
22 Plato, *Epistles* 7, 351c.
23 In other words, it is beyond reason and unattainable by means of the discursive approach. See Plotinus, *Enneads* 6.9.4, 12.
24 This hints at Plato, *Republic* 532e3.
25 Plotinus, *Enneads* 6.9.4, 12–15, my italics.

> *because he is deficient in his reasoning* (ἃ δὲ ἐν τοῖς λόγοις ἀπιστεῖ ἐλλείπων), let him consider (διανοείσθω) the following.[26]

I put in italics those claims that concern the outer way, which involves teaching and learning and fails because of the deficiency in λόγοις; in this context πίστις does play a part and indicates something firm that supports the quest at its beginning.

With regard to the other, inner way, Plotinus here speaks only of certain "hindrances," which are specified in "On the immortality of the soul" (*Enneads* 4.7):

> But when one considers the nature of any particular thing one must *concentrate on its pure form* (εἰς τὸ καθαρὸν αὐτοῦ ἀφορῶντα), since what is added is always a hindrance to the knowledge of that to which it has been added [cf. *Phaedrus* 65a10]. Consider it by stripping [cf. *Republic* VII 534b9], or rather *let the man* who has stripped *look at himself* (ἑαυτὸν ἰδέτω) and *he will believe* (πιστεύσει) himself to be immortal, when he will have looked (ὅταν θεάσηται) at himself as he has come (γεγενημένον) in the intelligible and the pure.[27]

The inner way is the road of asceticism and requires that the soul strip itself of its passions, and, more generally, of all that distorts and conceals the "pure form" of everything. If this has been accomplished by the soul, then the man who has seen its true nature *"will believe* himself to be immortal." Expressed in the future tense, πίστις here appears as the result of the contemplation, or, rather, it is not πίστις as such that manifests itself, but πίστις *in something:* the firm belief that the nature of the soul is immortal. We are no longer at rest in the Intelligible since it is possible to assert a judgment.[28] Thus, we see that πιστεύειν also plays a part *after* the ascension.

But what happens *during* the ascension of the soul? Plotinus gives us a glimpse of this spiritual experience at the beginning of "On the descent of the soul into bodies" (*Enneads* 4.8), the first nine lines of which form a single sentence in Greek, which sets a kind of challenge for the modern translator. Therefore, Armstrong has chosen to cut it into segments. I begin with the translation of the last two lines, which finally introduce the theme:

---

26 Ibid. 6.9.4, 31–36.
27 Ibid. 4.7.10, 27–32, translation slightly altered, references in brackets are mine.
28 See also ibid., 5.3.17 ("On the knowing hypostases and that which is beyond"), 25–32: Plotinus asserts that reasoning (συλλογίζεσθαι) is impossible before contemplation has ceased and then explains it by πιστεύειν (to believe) and νομίζειν (to think) on the same level: "One must believe one has seen when the soul suddenly takes light: for this is from him and he is it; we must think that he is present when ... he comes and brings light to us."

Then after that rest in the divine, when I have come down from Intellect to discursive reasoning (εἰς λογισμὸν ἐκ νοῦ καταβάς), I am puzzled how I ever came down...[29]

This "rest in the divine" has been described in the previous seven lines with nine participles, not all of which are on the same level: some of these are coordinated, but some are not and consequently explain a specific aspect of the action expressed by the participle that precedes them; some are used in the present tense, involving some duration, some in the aorist tense denoting punctual, pure action—an important aspect in an ecstatic vision. It seems almost impossible to render this accurately in English,[30] and Armstrong has chosen to translate all participles on the same level (using the conjunction "and" or a comma), and in the same tense (the present perfect):

> Often I have woken up (ἐγειρόμενος) out of the body to myself and have entered (καὶ γινόμενος) into myself, going out from all other things; I have seen (ὁρῶν) a beauty wonderfully great *and felt assurance* (καὶ πιστεύσας) that then most of all I belonged to the better part; I have actually lived (ἐνεργήσας) the best life and come to identity (καὶ εἰς ταὐτὸν γεγενημένος) with the divine; and set firm (καὶ ἱδρυθεὶς) in it I have come (ἐλθὼν) to that supreme actuality, setting (ἱδρύσας) myself above all else in the realm of Intellect.[31]

I do not intend, nor am I able, to give a better translation, but I will try to reconsider the beginning of the description until the verb πιστεύειν occurs and examine the way it is used in order to clarify the role that is played by πίστις in the vision. We first meet two coordinated present participles, whose literal translation would read: "waking up (ἐγειρόμενος, meaning 'when I wake up') out of the body to myself and becoming (καὶ γινόμενος, 'and become') outside the other things and within myself." The following two, which are not coordinated to the previous ones, explain what "becoming within oneself" means: it involves both a vision (ὁρῶν) and a feeling of certainty (πιστεύσας), but whereas the first participle is in the present tense and refers to a vision that is lasting ("seeing a beauty wonderfully great"), Plotinus uses the second one in aorist tense. Why this sudden change in the tenses? Aorist tense may indicate the precise moment when the soul reaches the realm of Intellect, something like "and feeling *suddenly* confident," or "*suddenly* experiencing assurance (πιστεύσας) that then..." But as a timeless, not durative tense, it is also in keeping with the ineffable and time-

---

[29] Plotinus, *Enneads* 4.8.1, 8–9.
[30] Hadot tries to render them in French, though he does so without maintaining the exact relations between them—with the exception of the last one ("*en* m'étant établi"), all the participles are merely juxtaposed. Hadot, "L'union de l'âme," 14.
[31] Plotinus, *Enneads* 4.8.1, 1–7.

less experience which Plotinus tries to describe, and it thus evokes a certain immediacy. In transferring the confidence, which is easy to conceive when it is felt *at the beginning* of the contemplation or *after* the contemplation, to the moment of contemplation itself, Plotinus suggests a kind of immediate intellectual apperception or, rather, a feeling, a πάθος of the soul, which accompanies the apperception by the νοῦς. The following participles, not coordinated to the previous ones, in turn explain this feeling of assurance.[32] They are less interesting for our analysis, the point of which is the presence of a certain form of πίστις during the contemplation.

This presence seems to be confirmed by another description of the rest of the soul in the unity in "On Nature and Contemplation and the One" (*Enneads* 3.8). Plotinus asserts that πίστις and θεωρία are proportionate to one another, so to speak, and involve evidence, quietness and unity.[33] But although πίστις here is somehow related to unity, it is still far from the Proclian πίστις. It lies closer to the confidence, the assent, whose importance was underlined by Aristotle and the Hellenistic schools. What changes here is that it does not go with opinion, but with contemplation.

Thus πίστις, as evidenced by these texts, may be felt before, during and after contemplation. But this contemplation, "the union of the soul with divine Intellect," in Pierre Hadot's terms,[34] is possible because Plotinus conceives of an upper unattainable level above and beyond the Intelligible. The One has, so to speak, replaced the Intelligible as the Absolute. This is not so for Plutarch. To put it in Plotinian (and Platonic) terms, Plutarch knows the way indicated by philosophy, but joining the Intelligible is impossible for him as long as our souls are encompassed by bodies and emotions.[35] The philosophical way is the better one indeed. Thus, in *De Iside*, the treatise to which I have already referred with regard to the pre-eminence of philosophy, Plutarch explains how philosophy deals with religious customs:

> ... for that one rationality (ἑνὸς λόγου) which keeps all these things in order (κοσμοῦντος) and the one Providence which watches over them and the ancillary powers that are set over all, there have arisen among different peoples, in accordance with their customs (κατὰ νόμους), different honours and appellations. Thus men make use of *consecrated symbols*

---

[32] The aorist tense is no more problematic here, because the participles depend from πιστεύσας and are used in the same tense, as usually.
[33] Plotinus, *Enneads* 3.8.6, 14–17: "In proportion as the confidence is clearer (ὅσῳ ἐναργεστέρα ἡ πίστις), the contemplation is quieter (ἡσυχαιτέρα), in that it unifies (εἰς ἓν ἄγει) more, and what knows, in so far as it knows ... comes into unity with what it knows."
[34] Hadot, "L'union de l'âme."
[35] Plutarch, *De Iside et Osiride* 382F–83A.

(συμβόλοις καθιερωμένοις) [...] *in guiding the intelligence toward things divine* (ἐπὶ τὰ θεῖα τὴν νόησιν ὁδηγοῦντες), though not without a certain hazard (οὐκ ἀκινδύνως). For some go completely astray and become engulfed in superstition; and others, while they fly from superstition as from a quagmire, on the other hand unwittingly fall, as it were, over a precipice into atheism. Wherefore in the study of these matters it is especially necessary that we adopt, *as our guide in these mysteries* (μυσταγωγόν) *the reasoning that comes from philosophy* (λόγον ἐκ φιλοσοφίας), and *consider reverently* (ὁσίως διανοεῖσθαι) each one of the things that are said and done.[36]

As the sensibles give an image of and possibly an access to the intelligibles, human rituals may be used as symbols that "guide the intelligence towards things divine." But, as sensible, they may fascinate the soul and make it forget the upper world. Their guidance, then, is hazardous and may lead to two possible abysses, atheism or superstition. The only true guide is the philosophical λόγος. More accurately, philosophy is like a "mystic guide," and, keeping with the same imagery, Plutarch then refers to its completion, the τέλος, as an ἐποπτεία, that is the highest grade of mysteries:

Plato [*Symposium* 210a] and Aristotle call this part of philosophy *the epoptic or mystic part*, inasmuch as those who have passed beyond these conjectural and confused matters of all sorts (τὰ δοξαστὰ καὶ μικτὰ καὶ παντοδαπὰ ταῦτα) by means of Reason (τῷ λόγῳ) proceed by leaps and bounds to that primary, simple, and immaterial principle; and when they have *somehow* attained contact (θιγόντες) with the pure truth abiding about it, *they think* (νομίζουσι) that they have the whole of philosophy completely (ἐντελῆ τέλος), *as it were,* within their grasp.[37]

Although he here evokes the possibility of "attaining contact" with the truth, Plutarch already introduces many qualifications (in italics) before more strictly delimiting what is possible for the souls to attain:

[T]here is no association (μετουσία) with this god [*sc.* Osiris] except in so far as they may attain to *a dim vision of his presence by means of the apperception which philosophy affords* (ὀνείρατος ἀμαυροῦ θιγεῖν νοήσει διὰ φιλοσοφίας). But when these souls are set free and migrate into the realm of the invisible and the unseen, the dispassionate and pure, then this god becomes *their leader* (ἡγεμών) and king, since it is on him that they are bound to be dependent in their insatiate contemplation and yearning (θεωμέναις ἀπλήστως καὶ ποθούσαις) for that beauty which is for men unutterable and indescribable.[38]

---

36 Ibid. 377F3–78B1.
37 Ibid. 382D6–E2.
38 Ibid. 382F3–83A5, reference in brackets is mine.

Thus, in this life, Reality can only be suggested by images, such as the mystical terminology[39] or the *Phaedrus*' imagery, from which Plutarch borrows the image of God as the leader and guide of the souls, which follow him "in their insatiate contemplation."

Here we find one of the few mentions of contemplation in Plutarch. For contemplation belongs to a totally free νοῦς and can be achieved only after death. There is no "inner way," contrary to what Plotinus thinks, because νοῦς—even the νοῦς of each of us—is rather external in Plutarch's view. For example, he has the demonic guide explain in the myth of *De Genio* that

> [t]he part carried submerged in the body is called the soul, whereas the part left free from corruption is called by the multitude the understanding (νοῦν), *who take it to be within themselves*, as they take reflected objects to be in the mirrors that reflect them; but those who conceive the matter rightly call it *a daemon, as being external*.[40]

Moreover, neither in this myth nor in the myth of *De sera* can either of the heroes, Timarchos and Thespesios, who are not dead, see the higher levels beyond the lunar area, "for the cable of (their) soul gives no further upward play, [...] being made fast to the body."[41] This suggests the impossibility of joining the Intelligible and, consequently, the necessity as well as the limits of philosophy.

Furthermore, for Plotinus philosophizing is a solitary quest,[42] whereas for Plutarch, as for Plato, it is first and foremost a cooperative quest, a searching together. Hence, Plutarch retains the literary genre of the dialogue, especially in his discussions of religious matters. In such instances πίστις (meant as "confidence in something") often appears in the context of opening admonitions: for example, "the πίστις in providence" may be destroyed by the slowness of divine justice,[43] or "the so-called deteriorated style of Apollo militates against the πίστις in the oracle."[44] This confidence undoubtedly has more to do with the common conception of God, which is supplemented by a Platonic trust in God's goodness, than with suprarational faith. It sets out the basic premises of any discussion about the Divine, which is identified with the Platonic Supreme Being. In other words, if we wish to continue the comparison with Plotinus,

---

39 See Riedweg, *Mysterienterminologie*.
40 Plutarch, *De genio Socratis* 591E5–9.
41 Plutarch, *De sera numinis vindicta* 566D1–3.
42 Significantly Porphyry chose to make the Enneads end with the invitation to escape in solitude to the solitary—a rewriting of Plato's *Theaetetus* 176b.
43 Plutarch, *De sera numinis vindicta* 549B, "belief" in LCL.
44 Plutarch, *De Pythiae oraculis* 492B, "confidence" in LCL.

we could say that Plutarchan πίστις stays at the first Plotinian level. This would also be right with regard to the ethical field. In relation to the virtue of piety (εὐσέβεια), πίστις appears along with cautiousness (εὐλάβεια): the pious man has to find the balance between πιστεύειν everything, that is, superstitious credulity, and ἀπιστεύειν everything, that is atheistic incredulity.[45] Here too πίστις and πιστεύειν are located at a rather low level.

3 Piety Hic et Nunc: Concerning the Tetrad "Faith, Truth, Love, Hope" (πίστις, ἀλήθεια, ἔρως, ἐλπίς)

The comparison with Plotinus will also provide an illuminating starting point for the analysis of the existential aspect of πίστις. Whereas in the foregoing discussion the possibility of joining the intelligible was present in Plotinus' work and absent in that of Plutarch, the opposite is the case here as the "existential elements" are only to be found in Plutarch's work. For one who chooses a purely contemplative life, philosophy and piety cannot be dealt with separately. This is certainly the case for Plotinus, who, according to Porphyry's biography, considered philosophy and life to be one and the same thing. However important a role philosophy played in his life, Plutarch did not choose such a contemplative life. Instead he lived a practical one or, rather, what was called a mixed way of life —one which combined politics, civic life and philosophy. To delineate his piety, we then have to look rather at Plotinus' successors, who have used either the tetrad "love, truth, faith and hope" (πίστις, ἀλήθεια, ἔρως, ἐλπίς)[46] or the triad "love, truth, faith,"[47] which, according to Philippe Hoffmann, "donne forme chez les hommes et en particulier dans le 'je' du philosophe, à une manifestation de *religion personnelle, qui s'exprime dans l'étude et la prière.*"[48] As was also the case previously, Proclus serves as a convenient end point for this theme, which we can use as a point of comparison. In his commentary on Plato's *Timaeus* 27b–c, when Socrates has invited Critias to speak "after duly calling

---

45 Plutarch, *Camillus* 6.6; see also *Alexander* 75.2 or *De sera numinis vindicta* 549E6.
46 It is probably the original form. See Hoffmann, "*Erôs, Alètheia, Pistis* ... et *Elpis*," 265: "Triade ou tétrade? Une tétrade assurément, ayant originellement une structure [3+1] qui a sans doute facilité la modification, dans le sens *triadique*." I am deeply indebted to the extensive analysis provided in this brilliant article.
47 The order varies according to the authors.
48 Hoffmann, "La triade chaldaïque," 489 (my italics).

upon the Gods," he underlines that "prayer is no small part of the whole ascent of the soul" and goes on to elaborate a number of pieces of advice, the purpose of which are just to direct a movement analogous to the Plotinian "escaping in solitude to the solitary":

> It is also necessary to observe a stable order in the performance of divine works; to exert those virtues which purify and elevate the soul from generation, *together with faith, truth and love*; to preserve this triad and *hope of good* (ἐλπίδα τῶν ἀγαθῶν), this immutable reception of divine light, and segregation from every other pursuit, that thus becoming alone, we may associate with solitary deity (ἵνα μόνος τις τῷ θεῷ μόνῳ συνῇ) and not endeavour to conjoin ourselves with multitude to *The One*.[49]

According to the Proclian definition of faith as a unifying element, Philippe Hoffmann has convincingly argued that here the triad is arranged in descending order: the impulse is given by love, as in Plato, the soul then reaches the truth and, finally, unites itself with the Henads through faith.[50] As Iamblichus has already done, he inverts the hierarchy established by Plotinus' pupil Porphyry, who delineates a very precise itinerary in *Ad Marcellam:*

> Let four principles in particular be firmly held with regard to God: faith, truth, love, hope. For it is necessary *to have faith* (πιστεῦσαι) that *conversion toward God is the only salvation* (ὅτι μόνη σωτηρία ἡ πρὸς τὸν θεὸν ἐπιστροφή); *and for the faithful* (καὶ πιστεύσαντα)[51] to be as eager as possible to know the truth about Him; and for the knower (καὶ γνόντα) to love the one who is known; and for the lover (ἐρασθέντα δὲ) to nourish his soul *throughout life on good hopes*. For by good hopes the good prevail over the wicked.[52]

Good hopes are the last step and constitute a sustainable result which will endure for the rest of one's life. Πίστις, on the other hand, is thought to mark the first step, as Plotinus also maintained. Nevertheless, what Porphyry means by πίστις is more particular to him, though it also has an undeniable Platonic flavor. Πίστις gives the assurance needed for one's turning towards God (ἐπιστροφή): the Greek word immediately reminds us of Plato's famous Allegory

---

49 Proclus, *In Timaeum*, 1.212, 20–25. Translation by Thomas Taylor (https://archive.org/details/ProcluscommentaryOnTheTimaeusOfPlato, accessed July 15, 2016.
50 Hoffmann, *Erôs, Alètheia*, 300 and n. 130, comparing Proclus' and Iamblichus' conception of the prayer (Iamblichus, *On the Mysteries* V 26: "(the prayer) brings to perfection good hope and the faith in the light"); on Iamblichus, see ibid., 287–95.
51 The stress that Porphyry places on the ongoing activity of the soul by using verbal forms somewhat fades in the English translation, where nouns replace participles.
52 Porphyry, *Ad Marcellam*, 24.377–82. Translation taken from Porphyry, *Porphyry the Philosopher.*

of the Cave, which has remained important for Platonists of every epoch, including Plutarch himself.

Plutarch also uses the same theme, but more often in a negative way, namely, he warns against all that can make one turn away from God. The opposed actions of Sun and Love in *Amatorius* give a good example of his thought in this regard:[53]

> The sun *turns our attention* (ἀποστρέφει τὴν διάνοιαν) from intelligibles to sensibles, bewitching us by the charm and brilliance of vision, and *convincing* (ἀναπείθων) us that truth and everything else is to be found in the sun, or in the realm of sun, and not in any other place.[54]

And the result of that "bad persuasion," which makes of Sun something of a sophist or a wizard, will be that

> the soul is *persuaded* (πειθομένη) that beauty and value exist nowhere but here, unless it secures divine, chaste Love to be its physician [cf. *Phaedrus* 252b], *its saviour* (σωτῆρος), *its guide* (ἀγωγός). […] Love conducts it *to the Plain of Truth* [cf. *Phaedrus* 248b] where Beauty, concentrated and pure and genuine, has her home. When we long to embrace and have intercourse with her after our separation, it is Love who graciously appears to lift us out of the depths and escort us upward, *like a mystic guide beside us at our initiation* (οἷον ἐν τελετῇ παρέστη μυσταγωγός).[55]

Against Sun's harmful action, Love is presented by means of the imagery from the *Phaedrus* as our physician, who leads us to the Plain of Truth, as our savior also—as with Porphyry, who found salvation in conversion—and our guide, or rather our mystic guide, as was philosophy in *De Iside*.

In *De Pythiae*, Theon ends his discourse by condemning those who "go away" presumptuously "after pronouncing judgement against the god, but not against us nor against themselves for being unable *by reasoning* (τῷ λογισμῷ) to attain to a comprehension of the god's purpose."[56] Conversely, we must turn our attention to all the things that make us feel the presence of God. Plutarch, who was a Priest of Delphi, has Theon suggest that the revival of the sanctuary could not "have been brought about if a god were not *present here* to lend divine inspiration to his oracle."[57] Moreover, he compares it to an ancient, mirac-

---

53 See also Plutarch, *De E apud Delphos* 393C ff.; *De Pythiae oraculis* 400A ff.
54 Plutarch, *Amatorius* 764E2–6.
55 Ibid. 764F6–65A6.
56 Plutarch, *De Pythiae oraculis* 409D4–7.
57 Ibid. 409C5–7.

ulous flow of milk at Galaxium and asserts that in Delphi "for us the god grants *clearer, stronger, and plainer evidence* (λαμπρότερα καὶ κρείττονα καὶ σαφέστερα σημεῖα) than this by bringing about after a drought, so to speak, of earlier desolation and poverty, affluence, splendour, and honour."[58] This evidence makes the detractors of the oracle, those who have turned away, yet more blind and guilty. It may also remind us of the symbolic value that Plutarch ascribes to the cult and rites, the interpretation of which is another way of turning us towards God. Finally, they can even make us feel a divine presence.

If the revival of Delphi is an exceptional event, then the same kind of experience is more often present at festivals, and it is then accompanied by feelings like hope—one of the four elements of the tetrad—or by joy or cheerfulness (χάρα). Two beautiful texts highlight this theme. Significantly, the first of these belongs to the polemical treatise *Non posse suaviter vivi secundum Epicurum* and deals with the pleasures of which Epicurus' followers are deprived by adhering to a purely sensual life. Of these lost superior pleasures, the highest are related to God. In suppressing bad feelings such as fear and superstition, Epicurus thereby also suppresses "the element of *cheerful hope, of exultant joy* (τὸ εὔελπι καὶ περιχαρές), and whether in prayer or in thanksgiving of ascribing every furtherance of felicity to the gods." This high value, Plutarch goes on,

> is proved by the strongest kind of evidence (δῆλον δὲ τεκμηρίοις τοῖς μεγίστοις): no visit delights (εὐφραίνουσιν)[59] us more than a visit to a temple; no occasion than a holy day; no act or spectacle than what we see and what we do ourselves in matters that involve the gods.[60]

Thus, civic worship and ceremonies, which we earlier saw as symbols to be interpreted by philosophical λόγος, are now provided as evidence of the delight and sweetness we all feel "wherever we believe and conceive most firmly that the god is present."[61] And Plutarch resumes and expands the description of the state of the souls once more:

> When *they believe that their thoughts come closest to God* (τοῦ θείου τῇ ἐπινοίᾳ ψαύειν[62] δοκῶσι) as they do him honour and reverence, it brings pleasure and sweetness of a far

---

58 Ibid. 409B7–9.
59 The verb itself suggests a more spiritual pleasure; the name of the Grace Euphrosyne derives from the same root.
60 Plutarch, *Non posse suaviter vivi secundum Epicurum* 1101E1–4.
61 Ibid. 1101E8–9.
62 Another verb indicating a kind of contact.

superior kind. Of this a man gets nothing if he has given up the providence.⁶³ For it is not the abundance of wine or the roast meats that *cheer the heart* (τὸ εὐφραῖνόν ἐστιν) at festivals, but *good hope* (ἐλπὶς ἀγαθὴ) and *the belief in the benign presence of the god* (δόξα τοῦ παρεῖναι τὸν θεὸν εὐμενῆ) and his gracious acceptance of what is done.⁶⁴

In speaking of festivals here and the sanctuary of Delphi before, we have so far been dealing with real worship and places. In the last text, taken from the parenetic treatise *De tranquillitate animi* (περὶ εὐθυμίας, which would be translated more accurately by *On Cheerfulness* than by *On Tranquility of Mind*), these realities are used as metaphors, and these metaphors are extended to include the whole sensible world:⁶⁵

> For the universe is *a most holy temple and most worthy of a god* (ἱερὸν ἁγιώτατον καὶ θεοπρεπέστατον); into it man is introduced through birth *as a spectator* (θεατής), not of handmade or immovable images, but of those sensible representations of intelligibles (αἰσθητὰ μιμήματα νοητῶν) that the divine mind, says Plato [cf. *Timaeus* 92c: εἰκὼν τοῦ νοητοῦ θεὸς αἰσθητός], has revealed.⁶⁶

The spectacle thus revealed to man may be read as a substitute for the impossible contemplation, which means a rest in the Intelligible. These sensible beauties invite him to turn to their models, but they also inspire in him feelings of religious cheerfulness, which may anticipate the moment of rest. Plutarch continues the metaphor:

> Since life is *a most perfect initiation* into these things *and a ritual celebration* of them (μύησιν ὄντα καὶ τελετήν), it should be full of tranquillity and joy (εὐθυμίας καὶ γήθους), [...] (but) by spending the greater part of life in lamentation and heaviness of heart and painful cares men shame *the festivals with which the god supplies us and in which he initiates us* (ἃς ὁ θεὸς ἡμῖν ἑορτὰς χορηγεῖ καὶ μυσταγωγεῖ).⁶⁷

Consequently, the right and pious attitude should be to

> accept a word of admonition⁶⁸ by following which they would acquiesce in the present without fault-finding, remember the past with thankfulness, and meet the future without

---

63 As do the Epicureans: another way of turning away from God.
64 Plutarch, *Non posse suaviter vivi secundum Epicurum* 1102A4–B1.
65 Plutarch is not the inventor of this image. The whole passage is commented on in Hirsch-Luipold, *Plutarchs Denken*, 171–73 ("Die Welt als Tempel und Hinweis auf das Göttliche").
66 Plutarch, *De tranquillitate animi* 477C7–10.
67 Ibid. 477D3–4 and 477D10–E2.
68 The treatise which this passage concludes is actually an admonitory one.

fear or suspicion, *with their hopes cheerful and bright* (ἵλεω τὴν ἐλπίδα καὶ φαιδρὰν ἔχοντες).⁶⁹

Again, keeping bright and good hopes for one's entire life is another way of acknowledging the ceaseless and benign presence of God and Providence in the world. This text may be considered as the crowning achievement of the mystic imagery, and also a kind of reinterpretation of Plato's idea in the *Timaeus* that the contemplation of the world, of the planets, has inspired mathematics and philosophy.⁷⁰

Having reached such a height, we cannot but stop. I think that, according to our initial hypothesis, the comparison with the Neoplatonists has highlighted Plutarch's own way of thinking and living the relation between man and god and emphasized what Platonism and piety meant for him. Moreover, the present paper leads us to reconsider the starting point of my series of studies, namely, Daniel Babut's hypothesis that an apparent verbal continuity sometimes conceals real philosophical differences. Although in my view this is erroneous when it is applied to Plato and Plutarch, it has proven to be very fruitful when applied to Plutarch and Plotinus. It serves the very purpose for which Babut articulated it: providing a better understanding of Plutarch's place in the history of Platonism. Finally, beyond this historical interest and beyond Plutarch himself, it seems to me fascinating that the same Platonic themes and images are reinterpreted by Plotinus and inserted into a new system of thought.

References

Babut, Daniel. *Plutarque et le stoïcisme*. Paris: Presses Universitaires de France, 1969.
Babut, Daniel. *La religion des philosophes grecs*. Paris: Presses Universitaires de France, 1974.
Babut, Daniel. "Du scepticisme au dépassement de la raison: Philosophie et foi religieuse chez Plutarque." In *Parerga: Choix d'articles de D. Babut (1974–1994)*, 549–81. Lyon: Maison de l'Orient Méditerranéen, 1994.
Chantraine, Pierre. *Dictionnaire étymologique de la langue grecque: Histoire des mots*. Revised by Jean Taillardat, Olivier Masson, and Jean-Louis Perpillou. Paris: Klincksieck, 2009.
Frazier, Françoise. "Philosophie et religion dans la pensée de Plutarque: Quelques réflexions autour des emplois du mot πίστις." *Études platoniciennes* 5 (2008): 41–61.

---

69 Plutarch, *De tranquillitate animi* 477F1–5.
70 Plato, *Timaeus* 47b–c.

Hadot, Pierre. "L'union de l'âme avec l'intellect divin dans l'expérience mystique plotinienne." In *Proclus et son influence*, edited by Gilbert Boss and Gerhard Seel, 3–27. Zurich: Ed. du Grand Midi, 1987.

Hadot, Pierre. *Qu'est-ce que la philosophie antique*. Paris: Gallimard, 1995.

Hirsch-Luipold, Rainer. *Plutarchs Denken in Bildern*. Tübingen: Mohr Siebeck, 2002.

Hoffmann, Philippe. "La triade chaldaïque, ἔρως, ἀλήθεια, πίστις: De Proclus à Simplicius." In *Proclus et la théologie platonicienne*, edited by Alain-Philippe Segonds and Carlos Steel, 459–89. Leuven/Paris: Leuven University Press/Les Belles Lettres, 2000.

Hoffmann, Philippe. "*Erôs, Alètheia, Pistis* ... et *Elpis:* Tétrade chaldaïque, triade néoplatonicienne (OC 46 des Places, p. 26 Kroll)." In *Die Chaldaeischen Orakel: Kontext – Interpretation – Rezeption*, edited by Helmut Seng and Michel Tardieu, 255–324. Heidelberg: Winter, 2011.

Peters, Francis E. *Greek Philosophical Terms: A Historical Lexicon*. New York: New York University Press, 1967.

Suzan Sierksma-Agteres
The Metahistory of Δίκη and Πίστις: A Greco-Roman Reading of Paul's "Justification by Faith" Axiom

Abstract: The message of the apostle Paul that "all are now justified through faith" has resulted in diverse interpretations over the centuries. Questions have been raised concerning the negative evaluation of the *law*, the importance of *works*, and the nature of *faith* in Paul's letters. The traditional Lutheran interpretation, which focuses on the individual sinner being declared righteous for free, has been heavily challenged by the so-called New Perspective that emphasizes the universal application of this justice. Philosopher Alain Badiou has recently chipped in by labeling Paul "an antiphilosophical theoretician of universality." This article contributes to the debate by viewing "justification by faith," or rather δικ- and πιστ-language, against Greco-Roman discourses, concepts and semantics of the time. It will be shown that precisely Paul's philosophical contemporaries offer proof for such a universalistic agenda. Greco-Roman "metahistorical," grand narratives show a widespread belief in an initial golden age of divine rule, followed by a period of retreat of virtues and moral decline, and sometimes including utopian, universalistic visions of a return of the days of faith and justice. A similar metahistorical discourse can be discerned in *Romans*, where Paul announces the renewed disclosure of divine justice against the background of the gentiles' collective godforsakenness and unrighteousness. At the same time, semantic research confirms the proximity of justice and faith as virtues of high regard in Greco-Roman sources. This ethical approach to justice is further developed by the platonic concept of an internal law, identified as a divinely given "mind" or "measure." In *Romans*, these findings resonate with the moral reform of the mind according to the "measure of faith." Hence, Pauline justice is argued to be deeply universal, ethical and participational in nature.

1 Introduction: "Justification by Faith" and Its Interpretations[1]

As one of the contributors to the revival of Paul's letters in contemporary philosophy, Alain Badiou is known for his particular interest in Pauline universalism: "For Paul," so Badiou claims, "the truth event repudiates philosophical Truth … Paul is an antiphilosophical theoretician of universality."[2] Paul's conceptions of justice and faith and their cognates are also explained by him in this light. Badiou's Paul is the one "who identifies his faith only in being affected by the collapse of customary and communitarian differences."[3] The connection between faith and justice is offered by the concept of hope, yet not hope in a future judgment that would again bring separation.[4] Instead, for Paul, "it is of utmost importance to declare that I am justified only insofar as everyone is."[5] By framing Paul in this manner as his founding hero of universalism, Badiou not only addressed a metaphysical conception from a creative angle, yet also advertently or inadvertently picked up on a major contested issue in Pauline scholarship. In the vocabulary of the field of New Testament Studies, the issue pertains to the doctrine of "justification by faith," or, in broader terms, to the question what Paul's good news was all about, and what it was formulated against.

In the traditional, particularly Lutheran interpretation, what is at stake for Paul is the salvation of the individual, a sinful person who is declared righteous in the eyes of God based on nothing more or less than his or her faith in Christ. Consequently, in this view, Paul is arguing against legalism, that is, justification based on "works of the law," as supposedly propagated by the Judaism of his days. In light of this collection of articles, it is interesting to point out that such an interpretation appeals not only to broad strands of Protestantism, but also to existentialist philosophy in that this act or "leap" of faith is located in the individual subject. The objections voiced in New Testament Scholarship against this traditional, Lutheran interpretation can be summarized as directed at the following three aspects.

Law: undeserved or universal justice? Firstly, they are directed against the anachronism of a widespread existence of such a form of legalism in the Judaism

---

[1] Part of the research presented in this article also appeared in Dutch: Sierksma-Agteres, "(N)iets nieuws onder de zon."
[2] Badiou, *Saint Paul*, 108.
[3] Ibid., 102.
[4] Ibid., 93, cf. 95.
[5] Ibid., 96.

of Paul's days. The so-called New Perspective argues that Paul did not oppose a Jewish attempt to earn salvation through the law, but a Jewish exclusivism or ethnocentrism with an appeal to the law.⁶

Works: vindicative or ethical justice? Secondly and somewhat adversely, they are directed against the supposed absence of justification based on works in Paul or the New Testament. According to the Lutheran view, Gods justice vindicates the sinner for free, disregarding his unrighteousness. By contrast, recent contributors to the debate highlight the inseparability of ethics and justification in first-century Judaism and Christianity with a renewed fervor.⁷

Faith: anthropological or participational justice? Thirdly, criticisms are directed against the so-called "anthropological" understanding of justification as something procured by the faith of each individual in Christ.⁸ Instead, the (in)famous phrase that people are justified διὰ πίστεως Ἰησοῦ Χριστοῦ (Rom. 3:22) can also be taken to mean "by the faithfulness of Jesus Christ."⁹ Hence, πίστις is construed as a historical intervention of God in order to reach out to all ethnicities, genders and social positions, enabling them to participate in faithfulness by becoming Christ-like.¹⁰

It is not my main aim in this paper, however, to merely summarize the main currents in research on Paul's justification by faith axiom. Instead, having done so briefly, I hope to contribute to the debate by adding the proof of Greco-Roman semantics, concepts and discourses pertaining to justice and faith. Even though the amount of exegetical scholarly work on these issues reaches enormous proportions, relatively little has been unearthed in this particular material. On the contrary, Paul's Jewishness and Hellenism are often played off against one another in the context of this discussion.¹¹ By contrast, I hold that both on the level of participation in similar discourses, and on the level of shared semantics, Paul and his pagan contemporaries had a lot in common. Based on the sources I discuss in this article, Paul's δικ- and πιστ- language will be shown to belong to

---

6 Main proponents of this view include E. P. Sanders, J. D. G. Dunn and N. T. Wright.
7 E.g., Vanlandingham, *Judgment and Justification*.
8 Cf. for an extreme example of this position Rudolf Bultmann, *Glauben und Verstehen*, 102: "Die entscheidende Geschichte ist nicht die Weltgeschichte, die Geschichte Israels und der anderen Völker, sondern die Geschichte, die jeder Einzelne selbst erfährt."
9 This shibboleth in Pauline studies, the Πίστις Χριστοῦ debate, cannot be further addressed here, but see for my own approach: Sierksma-Agteres, "Imitation in Faith."
10 For a survey of scholarly interpretations that argue for this interpretation, see Heliso, *Pistis and the Righteous One*, 19–26.
11 E.g., Dunn and Suggate, *The Justice of God*, 31; Coutsoumpos, "Paul's Attitude towards the Law," 45–46; Gonzalez, "Pauline Universalism," 69; Seifrid, "Paul's Use of Righteousness Language," 45, 52.

a larger, "metahistorical" narrative, rendering it universal, ethical, and participational in nature.

2 Greco-Roman Metahistorical Discourses and the Semantics of Δίκη and Πίστις

Before we turn to the sources, a short note on the concept of "metahistory" is due. I use the term metahistory to denote a conception of past, present and future that supersedes the description of "ordinary" or "objective" historical events. It encompasses the collective memory of myths of origin, ancestral traditions and glorious or inglorious ages in the past, interpretations of the present in light of these stories, and visions and expectations of the future. These grand narratives function as cultural identity markers in creating a self-understanding of a community, including its important values, *mores* and beliefs.

In this article, my methodology is to combine findings that are based on Greco-Roman metahistorical narratives (sections 2.1 and 2.2) with a TLG/LLT-based linguistic, semantic approach to δίκη, πίστις, and cognates (section 2.3, with more diachronic conceptual explorations in section 2.4).[12]

2.1 Greco-Roman Protologies: The Golden Age of Gods and Virtues and Their Retreat from Earth

In most Greco-Roman accounts of the earliest history of humanity, the very first phase was a good and prosperous one, in which the gods themselves were involved and intimately known. According to Dio of Prusa, "these earlier men were not living dispersed far away from the divine being or beyond his borders apart by themselves, but had … grown up in his company and had remained close to him in every way."[13]

This initial phase is described by Dio in cognitive and universal terms. The knowledge of the gods was common "to the Greeks and Barbarians alike," innate in "every creature endowed with reason (ἐν παντὶ τῷ λογικῷ)."[14] "How, then,

---

12 TLG is an abbreviation of *Thesaurus Linguae Graecae* and LLT of *Library of Latin Texts*.
13 Dio Chrysostom, *De dei cognitione* (Oratio 12) 28. The translations of Greco-Roman texts have been taken from the editions of the Loeb Classical Library, and biblical translations from the NRSVA, both where necessary with minor revisions of my own.
14 Dio Chrysostom, *De dei cognitione* (Oratio 12) 27.

could they have remained ignorant (ἀγνῶτες) and conceived no inkling of him who had sowed and planted and was now preserving and nourishing them (...)?" he exhorts.[15] In Latin literature, we could refer to the fifteenth satire of Juvenal, where he states that at the beginning of the world (*mundi principio*) the creator gave life (*animae*) to the animals, but also a mind to humans (*nobis animum quoque*) so that civilization could develop out of solidarity or "combined confidence" (*conlata fiducia*).[16]

If specific gods are linked to such protological accounts, often either Cronos (Saturn) or Zeus (Jupiter) is named. For our present purposes, it is interesting how often this divine age is described in terms of justice. The poet Hesiod speaks of a law of justice, given to the human race by Cronos' son.[17] But also in times closer to Paul's, Cronos and his son are remembered as kings in the ancient days of justice, like in this suggestion of Plutarch in answer to the question why the temple of Saturn is the place to store records of contracts:

> Is it because the opinion and tradition prevailed that when Saturn was king there was no greed or injustice among men, but good faith and justice (οὐκ εἶναι πλεονεξίαν ἐν ἀνθρώποις οὐδ' ἀδικίαν Κρόνου βασιλεύοντος, ἀλλὰ πίστιν καὶ δικαιοσύνην)?[18]

In particular, πίστις and δικαιοσύνη, the very terms under consideration in this article, are mentioned as characteristic virtues of Saturn's rule, with πίστις used here in the sense of the fundamental societal virtue of mutual trust, or *bona fide*. According to Ovid, Saturn's golden age was a time in which everyone "without a law, of its own will, kept faith and did the right (*sponte sua, sine lege fidem rectumque colebat*)."[19]

It was, however, also a common diagnosis that after this golden age of divine rule degeneration set in. The fortune of the first period of human history often functions as a set-off to the bemoaned present state of affairs. "But now there is greater harmony among snakes," Juvenal laments.[20] Dio of Prusa speaks of the earliest and most ancient men who were *not* dozed or indifferent towards the gods, implying a later decline.[21]

---

15 Dio Chrysostom, *De dei cognitione* (Oratio 12) 29.
16 Juvenal, *Satirae* 15.147–158. See on Juvenal and Lucretius' accounts of the dawn of civilisation Konstan, *Pity Transformed*, 122–23.
17 Hesiod, *Opera et dies* 276–280.
18 Plutarch, *Quaestiones romanae et graecae* 275A (42).
19 Ovid, *Metamorphoses* 1.90.
20 Juvenal, *Satirae* 15.159.
21 Dio Chrysostom, *De dei cognitione* (Oratio 12) 27.

This degeneration narrative is often pictured as a retreat of gods and personified virtues from the earth.²² In Hesiod it is an hypostasized Αἰδώς, that is, shame following from an evil deed, together with Νέμεσις, that is, retribution as a form of social control, abandoning mankind, marking the worst stage ever in humanity's evolution.²³ In the *Phaenomena* of the poet Aratus—whose work the apostle Paul quotes according to the author of *Acts*²⁴—this role is played by the constellation Virgin, who is there identified as Ἀστραῖα (the goddess of innocence), also known as Δίκη (the goddess of judgment). She stood by humanity in the golden age, lingered to warn men throughout the silver age, but left for the sky when the vile Race of Bronze arose.²⁵ We even have a similar scheme of events whereby it is the goddess Πίστις herself leaving, together with Σωφροσύνη and the Graces: the poet Theognis of Megara describes how upon this departure righteous oaths were no longer trustworthy (πιστός) and piety towards the gods disappeared.²⁶

Closer to Paul's time, Catullus also speaks of the somewhat unclear chicken-and-egg connection that when justice was "chased away from the minds of men," the gods also "averted their righteous mind."²⁷ Ovid mentions the flight of modesty, truth and faith in the iron age (*omne nefas: fugere pudor verumque fidesque*).²⁸ The common theme across these and even more similar narratives, is that the absence of piety or of the gods themselves is closely linked to the disappearance of the virtues of justice and faithfulness from the earth.²⁹

2.2 Greco-Roman Eschatologies: Return of the Golden Age and Utopian Universalism

These pessimistic "decline of civilization" narratives were not all these or other Greek and Roman authors had in store. More hopeful stories have also been

---

22 In Hellenistic-Jewish material, we have similar accounts of a personified Wisdom leaving: cf. 1 *Enoch* 42.2, 44.5; *4 Ezra* 5.10; Philo, *Quaestiones et solutiones in Genesin* 2.40.
23 Hesiod, *Opera et dies* 174–201.
24 Acts 17:28b, quoting Aratus, *Phaenomena* 5. Aratus's poetry was much translated from at least the first century onwards. See Wallace-Hadrill, "The Golden Age and Sin in Augustan Ideology," 20, n. 7.
25 Aratus, *Phaenomena* 96–136, esp. 133–136.
26 Theognis, *Fragment* 1.1135–42.
27 Catullus, *Carmina* 64.397–408, esp. 397–398, 405–406.
28 Ovid, *Metamorphoses* 1.129.
29 Cf. also Horace, *Carmina* 1.35.21; Pseudo-Seneca, *Octavia* 429–434; Silius Italicus, *Punica* 2.494–506.

handed down to us telling tales of a return of the earliest golden age set either in the past, present, or future. And here as well, we see the fascinating combination of the virtues of piety, justice and faithfulness recurring throughout different sources.

One well attested setting of such a prosperous period in the early Roman history is the reign of Numa, the second kind of Rome, famous for his religious laws. In his biography of Numa, Plutarch states that the Romans in these days "made no statues in bodily form for them [i.e. the gods], convinced that it was impious to liken higher things to lower, and that it was impossible to apprehend Deity except by the intellect."[30] Furthermore, Cicero ascribes to Numa that he "implanted in them a love for peace and tranquility, which enable justice and good faith to flourish most easily (*quibus facillime iustitia et fides convalescit*) ... ."[31] *Iustitia* and *fides* are paired here as the outcome of a peaceful reign.

A more elaborate account, focusing on justice (δικαιοσύνη) and temperance (σωφροσύνη), but especially emphasizing the importance of πίστις to Numa's kingship, is given by the Greek historian Dionysius of Halicarnassus. He credits Numa with bringing the State "to frugality and moderation (εὐτέλειαν καὶ σωφροσύνην)" in a new, innovative way. He felt that contracts without witnesses rest purely on "the faith of the parties involved," therefore:

> ... he thought it incumbent on him to make this faith the chief object of his care and to render it worthy of divine worship. ... And in truth the result was bound to be that this attitude of good faith and constancy (ἦθος πιστὸν καὶ βέβαιον) on the part of the State toward all men would in the course of time render the behaviour of the individual citizens similar. ... Such regulations, devised by Numa at that time to encourage moderation and enforce justice (σωφροσύνης τε παρακλητικὰ καὶ δικαιοσύνης ἀναγκαστήρια), rendered the Roman State more orderly than the best regulated household.[32]

In this rich description of a glorious Roman past, the part played by πίστις is connected to the human virtue of keeping agreements, a virtue vital for living in a righteous community. The golden age of Numa functioned for the Romans as an identity marker on the border of mythology and history, in which justice, moderation and faith(fulness) were valued most emphatically.

---

30 Plutarch, *Numa* 8.8. Cf. the historian Varro, who praises this phase of Rome's religious development, up until the reign of Tarquinius Priscus, as purer than the present day, while accusing the people who introduced divine images of diminishing reference and introducing error. See Augustine, *De Civitate Dei* 4.31, 7.5.
31 Cicero, *De republica* 2.26.
32 Dionysius of Halicarnassus, *Antiquitates romanae* 2.75.1–4.

With Numa, however, we are still talking about the Roman past, even though his reign could be considered a return of the earliest glory of humanity. Can we also find traces of a more eschatological discourse in which the ancient days of justice and faith are re-enacted in the present or expected to return? And what should such a return look like?[33]

Such eschatological Greco-Roman narratives appear for the first time in the reign of August. In his fourth *Eclogue*, Virgil explicitly refers to the return of the reign of Saturn in the present: "Now is come the last age of Cumaean song; the great line of the centuries begins anew. Now the Virgin returns, the reign of Saturn returns (*iam redit et Virgo, redeunt Saturnia regna*); now a new generation descends from heaven on high."[34] The Virgin Vergil speaks of is the same Δίκη the poet Aratus described as the goddess who had left the earth after the silver age. The same theme of a return of this golden age is picked up again in the Aeneid.[35] Virgil's colleague and friend at the Augustan court, Horace, describes the present 'new age' in the same glorious vain, and counts Fides among the returnees:

> Now Good Faith, Peace, and Honour, along with old-fashioned Modesty and Virtue, who has been so long neglected, venture to return (*iam Fides et Pax et Honos Pudorque priscus et neglecta redire Virtus audit*), and blessed Plenty with her full horn is seen by all.[36]

The "return of the virtues" *topos* recurs in Flavian literature, not long after the probable death of Paul. In the tragedy *Octavia*, the character Seneca is reminiscing the days of Saturn, when Iustitia and Fides reigned, but also predicts that those days may soon return:

> (...) we are now approaching that final day which will crush this sacrilegious race beneath the collapsing sky. That will allow a reborn and better cosmos to bring forth once again a new progeny, such as it bore in youth when Saturn held the throne of heaven. In those days that virgin goddess of great power, Justice, descended with holy Faithfulness from heaven, and ruled the human race mildly on earth (*tunc illa virgo, numinis magni dea, Iustitia, caelo missa cum sancta Fide, terra regebat mitis humanum genus*). The nations knew no wars, no

---

33 See on this theme of the return of a golden age Neutel, *Cosmopolitan Ideal*, esp. 42–66.
34 Vergil, *Eclogae* 4.4–7. According to Wallace-Hadrill, this return of the golden age was an innovation inspired by Isaiah, via the Jewish eschatology in book 3 of the Sibylline Oracles: Wallace-Hadrill, *Golden Age*, 21.
35 Vergil, *Aeneid* 4.791–794, cf. 1.292–293: "Then wars shall cease and savage ages soften; hoary Faith (*cana Fides*) and Vesta, Quirinus with his brother Remus, shall give laws."
36 Horace, *Carmen Saeculare* 57–60.

grim trumpet's blare, no weapons, nor the practice of surrounding cities with walls; travel was open to all, everything was held in common *(communis usus omnium rerum fuit)* (...)³⁷

Again, the overall condition of humanity is one of faithlessness. To cure this illness, Justice and Faith are paired as hypostasized virtues that once descended and will again descend upon the earth, effecting peace, wall-less cities and communal property. The entrance of the divine duo of Justitia and Fides is remarkable, for anyone who is familiar with Paul's version of this metahistorical narrative.

The idea of a nations-transcending community without walls and private property was not uncommon in antiquity. Similar future oriented, utopian visions can be discerned in genres that are more explicitly philosophical in nature. At the end of his enormous wall inscription, the Epicurean Diogenes of Oenoanda wrote his vision that "then truly the life of the gods will pass to human beings; for all things will be full of justice and mutual love, and there will be no need of fortifications or laws and all the things which we contrive on account of one another."³⁸ In his description of Alexander the Great's rule, Plutarch claims that Alexander did not follow Aristotle in distinguishing between Greeks and Barbarians,but rather the Stoic Zeno, who's ideal *Republic* is summarized by Plutarch with these words:

> ... that all people should not live differentiated by their respective rules of justice into separate cities and communities, but that we should consider them to be of one community and one polity, and that we should have a common life and an order common to us all ... .³⁹

Both schools, Epicureans and Stoics, seem to envision a community in which laws and justice are differently configured: either justice and love are so ubiquitous that there is no need for laws at all, or one type of universal justice will be applicable to all, to Greeks and Barbarians alike. Notwithstanding the idealized nature of these accounts, they function as a feasible Greco-Roman background for understanding Paul's treatment of the theme of justice.

---

37 Pseudo-Seneca, *Octavia* 391–403.
38 Diogenes of Oenoanda, *Fragment* 56.
39 Plutarch, *De Alexandri magni fortuna aut virtute* 329A–B.

2.3 Being Just and Trustworthy as Ethical Directives of the Soul and of Society

Now that we have seen how δίκη and πίστις are taken up in the macro-perspective of what I have called "metahistory," it is good to learn more about the possible and probable meanings of the lexemes. By looking into the co-occurrence of words formed from the lemma's δικ- and πιστ-, that is either nouns, adjectives or verbs, making use of the proximity search option of the TLG, we learn a great deal about the contexts, or semantic fields, in which these notions are used together. The predominant usage of these words, in non-Jewish and non-Christian texts around the time of Paul (100 BC – 200 AD), as we could have already guessed from the previous sections, occurs in the context of virtues of high regard.

In his oration *On Distrust*, Dio of Prusa remarks "It would indeed be a blessing if, just as one becomes successively a lad, a stripling, a youth, and an old man by the passing of time, one might also in the same way become wise and just and trustworthy (καὶ φρόνιμον οὕτως καὶ δίκαιον καὶ πιστόν)."[40] Diodorus Siculus designates δικαιοσύνη and πίστις as the virtues of a good, accountable steward of a city-state.[41] One of the spokespersons in Plutarch's *Discourse on Love* grants "masculine virtues," including the pair πίστις and δικαιοσύνη, even to women.[42] Epictetus also repeatedly names πίστις and δικαιοσύνη, often in combination with αἰδώς (moral respect), as the virtues in which a person must excel.[43] The close paring of a δικ- and πιστ- lexeme in all these cases, sometimes accompanied by a third or fourth term that denotes a virtue, is remarkable. This phenomenon is not restricted to Greek usages; the Latin equivalents of *fid-* and *ius-* often appear as mutually reinforcing as well, for instance in several passages from Cicero.[44]

The conception of πίστις as a virtue, or even as identity marker, is closely connected to the feasibility of justice on a broader societal scale.[45] Cicero notes that "the disappearance of piety towards the gods will entail the disap-

---

40 Dio Chrysostom, *De diffidentia* (Oratio 74) 10.
41 Diodorus Siculus, *Bibliotheca historica* 11.66: "Micythus (...) rendered so honest an accounting that all present were filled with admiration of both his justice and good faith (...)."
42 Plutarch, *Amatorius* 769B, cf. also *Aemilius Paullus* 2.6.
43 Epictetus, *Enchiridion* 24.4 – 5; *Diatribae* 2.4.1 – 4, 2.22.29 – 30, 3.14.13 – 14.
44 Cf. Cicero, *De republica* 1.2, 2.61, 3.8, 3.27; *De officiis* 1.23, 26; *De oratore* 2.343 – 44.
45 Strecker, "Fides – Pistis – Glaube," 231: "Die *fides* fungierte in der antiken Welt offenbar über einen weiten Zeitraum hinweg und zumal um 1. Jh. n.Chr. innerhalb wie außerhalb Roms als eine Art *identity marker* römischer Kultur und Herrschaft."

pearance of *fides* and social union among men as well, and of justice itself, the queen of all the virtues."⁴⁶ Epictetus argues that if the personal virtue of πίστις fails, so will neighborly feeling, friendship and the city-state.⁴⁷

The preponderant usage of the δικ- and πιστ- lexemes in the realm of virtue ethics appears to be a relatively late semantic development. Originally, especially the noun δίκη and adjective δίκαιος were related to proper external behavior, to the maintenance of reciprocal relations of right.⁴⁸ According to Eric Havelock, the coinage of the noun δικαιοσύνη and its employment by Plato as righteousness in the full, ethical sense marked the emergence of two contrasting semantic fields:

> ... a conception of propriety based on the maintenance of reciprocal rights and requiring also the right of redress and hence of punishment as the mechanism of enforcement on the one hand – and on the other a more ambitious, generous, and ultimately inward-looking conception which we can conveniently identify as "morality" in the largest sense, or "righteousness."⁴⁹

The disclosure of this more moral and internal meaning in the fifth century BC did not so much lead to a contrast between inner, personal virtue and external, societal justice. Rather, both in the personal and the societal sphere, it was conceived in this more ambitious, ethical manner, intimately linked to σωφροσύνη.⁵⁰

2.4 The Internal Redefinition of Law as "Mind" and "Measure" in Plato's *Laws*

When thinking about just, faithful rulership, a just, faithful society and just, faithful persons, it is hard to avoid considering the place and meaning of law. Yet, as we just saw in Stoic and Epicurean accounts, the relationship of justice and the law is not unproblematic. Looking ahead, the same obviously counts for Paul. But before we come to that, it is helpful to discuss one particular concept developed by his pagan contemporaries that addresses precisely this tension: the concept of an internal or divine law in Platonism, which can be conceived of as an allegorized version of the Golden Age narrative.

---

46 Cicero, *De natura deorum* 1.3.
47 Epictetus, *Diatribae* 2.4.2–3. Cf. Epictetus, *Enchiridion* 24.4–5.
48 Havelock, "Dikaiosune," 51.
49 Ibid., 68.
50 Larson, "The Platonic Synonyms."

Plato's ethical usage of δίκη and cognates also colored his thought on laws and constitutions. In his *Laws*, the actual laws of a city-state are presented as only second best in achieving a virtuous life, for they are incapable of rendering the same results as an internal good nature would.[51] Therefore, laws should be explained by the lawgiver and understood by the citizens, just like the better doctor explains to his patients why he offers the treatment he offers by means of persuasion (*Laws* 720d: μετὰ πειθοῦς), and awaits their consent. The ideal law is conceived of as speaking to the part of human beings that is rational, by means of persuasion.

With this element of persuasion, we arrive at the concept of an internal law. For according to the Athenian, the law should not remain an external means that persuades the νοῦς from without. He refers to the golden age of Cronos, in which mankind was justly ruled by a higher order of demigods instead of by fickle humans who are themselves ruled by arrogance (ὕβρις) and, again, injustice (ἀδικία, *Laws* 713d). The moral and present application of the story, the stranger explains, is that:

> ... we ought by every means to imitate (μιμεῖσθαι) the life of the age of Cronos, as tradition paints it, and both in private and public life, order both our homes and our States (τάς τ' οἰκήσεις καὶ τὰς πόλεις) in obedience to the immortal element within us, giving to reason's ordering the name of "law" (τὴν τοῦ νοῦ διανομὴν ἐπονομάζοντας νόμον).[52]

I have already elaborated on the significance of referring to a golden age in the previous sections, but this passage also shows how, for Plato, the mind is the immortal element that functions as law to be obeyed. This equation is strengthened by the word-play between νοῦς (mind), διανομή (ordering) and νόμος (law).[53] The mind is presented as the internal law of the individual, and the laws of a city-state are to be modeled accordingly.[54]

In later strands of Platonism, this concept of an internal law, guided by the philosophers of old, is still in circulation. Plutarch rebuts the Epicurean argument that without law chaos will rule, by stating that:

> ... if someone takes away the laws, but leaves us with the teachings of Parmenides, Socrates, Heracleitus and Plato, we shall be very far from devouring one another and living the life of wild beasts; for we shall fear all that is shameful and shall honour justice (τιμήσομεν

---

51 Plato, *Laws* 875c–d.
52 Plato, *Laws* 713e–714a.
53 The etymological connection is explicitly presumed in Plato, *Laws* 957c.
54 Aristotle also connects law and reason, and is reluctant to grant too much power to laws in making people virtuous: Aristotle, *Ethica Nicomachea* 1180–81.

δικαιοσύνην) for its intrinsic worth, holding that in the gods we have good governors and in the daemons protectors of our lives, accounting all "the gold on earth and under it a poor exchange for virtue,"[55] and doing freely at the bidding of our reason (διὰ τὸν λόγον), as Xenocrates says, what we now do perforce at the command of the law (διὰ τὸν νόμον).[56]

The loose reference to the age of divine rule and the explicit quotation of the *Laws* confirm the familiarity with this Platonic concept of internal law, here equated with *logos*, in later centuries.

In the *Laws*, besides reinterpreting the law internally in terms of intellect, the Athenian uses a second concept that is of particular interest for understanding Paul's language, namely "measure" (μέτρον). In his address to the citizens of Magnesia, the people are summoned to with God follow Justice (*Laws* 716a). The next question he focusses on is how one can follow in God's footsteps:

> What conduct, then, is dear to God and in his steps (ἀκόλουθος θεῷ)? One kind of conduct, expressed in one ancient phrase, namely, that "like is dear to like" when it is moderate (ὅτι τῷ μὲν ὁμοίῳ τὸ ὅμοιον ὄντι μετρίῳ φίλον ἂν εἴη) … In our eyes God will be "the measure of all things" (πάντων χρημάτων μέτρον) in the highest degree—a degree much higher than is any "man" they talk of. He, then, that is to become dear to such an one must needs become, so far as he possibly can, of a like character; and, according to the present argument, he amongst us that is temperate is dear to God (ὁ μὲν σώφρων ἡμῶν θεῷ φίλος), since he is like him, while he that is not temperate is unlike and at enmity,—as is also he who is unjust (καὶ ὁ[57] ἄδικος), and so likewise with the rest, by parity of reasoning.[58]

This particular wording offers the solution to how Plato envisions the realization of virtue and justice. To live virtuously or justly is to live according to the measure of all things, namely God, and to live like God, means living with temperance (σώφρων) and with measure or moderation (μετρίῳ).

With this central notion, Plato elaborates on the influential topos that also recurs throughout his other works[59] and that goes by the name of ὁμοίωσις θεῷ, "becoming like God."[60] In the *Theaetetus*, this process of imitation is explicitly linked to God's righteousness.[61] As we will see in the following section, Paul

---

55 See Plato, *Laws* 728a4–5.
56 Plutarch, *Adversus Colotem* 1124D–E.
57 The article ὁ is added by Ritter; Schanz brackets καὶ ἄδικος.
58 Plato, *Laws* 716c–d.
59 The main classical *loci* are Plato, *Theaetetus* 176b–c, *Republic* 611d–e, and *Timaeus* 41d–47c.
60 On this particular passage and the ὁμοίωσις θεῷ motive, see Erler, "Epicurus as Deus Mortalis," 165: "Here the traditional concept is enriched by the introduction of the notion of measure (…)."
61 Plato, *Theaetetus* 176c.

employs very similar concepts in describing how faith and justice are to be understood and enacted by his audience.

3 Paul's Metahistorical Discourse and his Semantics of Δίκη and Πίστις

It is my contention in this section that the discourse-level narratives and the semantic and conceptual developments we described shed new light on Paul's use of δίκη, πίστις and their cognates. In this article, I have chosen to speak mainly about Paul's thought as expressed in his letter to the Romans.

3.1 Rom. 1—Paul's Historical Protology: God's Retreat, Debased Minds and Moral Degradation

In the beginning of the letter, Paul starts his first main argument by describing the utter unrighteousness of both Greek—or in this case perhaps rather "Roman"—and Jew in the eyes of God (Rom. 1:18–3:20). The first part of this argument (Rom. 1:18–32) has often anachronistically or dogmatically been interpreted as Paul's either aptly striking or awfully exaggerated depiction of the *condition humaine,* and understood as referring back to the fall of Adam and Eve.[62] An obvious problem with this interpretation, however, is that Paul does not actually refer to Adam here. It is my contention that if we look at it from the perspective of the "decline of the virtues" narratives we discussed, Paul's story perfectly fits this more historical, Greco-Roman genre. Hence, instead of voicing anthropological and timeless concerns about the sinful human nature of all individuals since creation, Paul seems to be presenting a collective and historical analysis, a metahistorical narrative, of the condition of the gentiles as one of initial cognitive harmony with God followed by a gradual religious and moral decline.[63] I will look at some aspects of the text to further substantiate this point.

---

[62] See, e.g., Hooker, "Adam in Romans I"; Bryan, *A Preface to Romans,* 78; Bell, *No One Seeks for God,* 26.
[63] This has also been convincingly argued by Stanley Kent Stowers in *A Rereading of Romans,* 85–100. Rather than claiming one or more specific parallels to Paul's account, Stowers speaks of "broadly shared cultural knowledge manifested in particular narratives" (ibid., 90). Although I agree with Stowers here, based on the actual golden age stories discussed above, I think more can be said about the specific manner in which Paul makes use of these narratives, yet also reconfigures them. Cf. also Van Kooten, *Paul's Anthropology in Context,* 343–56.

Paul starts off with a statement that implies an initial familiarity with God: "Ever since the creation of the world (ἀπὸ κτίσεως κόσμου) his eternal power and divine nature, invisible though they are, have been understood and seen (νοούμενα καθορᾶται) through the things he has made." This first phase of humanity Paul describes, in which knowledge of God was readily available, reminds us of the innate knowledge Dio of Prusa ascribes to the first humans who lived near the gods. Both authors describe these events in a historiographical-collective manner, yet both also offer anthropological reflections relevant to the present on the basis of this historical analysis. For Dio, the result is a positive innate knowledge of the gods in all humans, for Paul, a foolishness regarding the divine combined with moral deprivation common to all pagans in general, resulting in their inexcusability.

Another aspect that stands out is that both the initial harmonious phase, and the subsequent degeneration is described in cognitive terms: ἀλήθεια, γνωστός, νοέω, γιγνώσκω, διαλογισμός, σοφοί, δοκιμάζω, ἐπίγνωσις, νοῦς, ἐπιγιγνώσκω, and their opposites: ματαιόω, ἀσύνετος, μωραίνω, ψεῦδος, ἀδόκιμος. As we saw in for instance Plato, Dio of Prusa, Juvenal and Plutarch, a close connection with the divine was always conceived of as an intellectual affair. People are considered fools for worshipping mere images, because, like in the Numa-narratives, gods are supposed to be perceived by the intellect. In these Greco-Roman sources, however, the rational connection between gods and men is usually not heavily problematized or can be easily restored. Adversely, Paul reveals the underlying problem of the estrangement to God and the rise of immorality as one of an intellectual nature by pinpointing the mind as the location where something went fundamentally wrong. All pagans, Greeks and barbarians, wise and foolish, collectively suffer from a similar condition: a debased νοῦς, leading to free reign of the lower functions of the soul.[64] And, as we shall see, according to Rom. 12, it is in this precise spot where salvation must take hold in order for all people to be able to worship "logically" and think "temperately" again.

One final interesting convergence between Paul's narrative and many similar Greco-Roman discourses is that God, the gods, or the virtues essentially leave humanity to let it stew in its own grease.[65] In Rom. 1, Paul uses the same verb up to three times, to illustrate this point: God gave them over (παρέδωκεν, Rom. 1:24, 26, 28) to their lusts, passions and debased minds. It is against all this ἀδικία

---

64 There is a wordplay between the cause—"they did not acknowledge (οὐκ ἐδοκίμασαν)"—and the result of a debased (ἀδόκιμος) mind, just as with the verb "they exchanged (μετήλλαξαν)" in vv. Rom. 1:25 and 26. See Bryan, *Romans*, 80.
65 A similar motive can also be found in Deut. 32:20.

(Rom. 1:18, 29), this injustice or unrighteousness, that the righteousness of God is now, in the present, revealed anew (Rom. 1:17–18). In other words, God himself returns to the face of the earth.

3.2 Rom. 3—Paul's Realized Eschatology: The Return of Justice and Faith to the Whole World

In light of the diagnosis of unrighteousness and godforsakenness from the past up to the present age, painted in the darkest of colors, it is hard to overestimate the climactic effect of Paul's good news, proclaimed in full in Rom. 3:21ff:

> But now, irrespective of law, the righteousness of God has been disclosed (δικαιοσύνη θεοῦ πεφανέρωται), and is attested by the law and the prophets, the righteousness of God through the faithfulness of Jesus Christ (δικαιοσύνη δὲ θεοῦ διὰ πίστεως Ἰησοῦ Χριστοῦ) for all who have faith (εἰς πάντας τοὺς πιστεύοντας), for there is no distinction ....

On the level of discourse and grand narratives, we can understand this new disclosure of righteousness from a Greco-Roman perspective as the return of God, the return of the main virtues of justice and faith, and the return of the initial golden age. That this involves the beginning of a new age is apparent from Paul's emphasis on the now (Rom. 3:21: νυνὶ δὲ) and the present time (3:26: ἐν τῷ νῦν καιρῷ). Paul announces a new, eschatological age of divine righteousness that seems to break into the present evil age, yet also seems to exist alongside it.[66] The δικαιοσύνη in question has been revealed, but is yet to be appropriated by faith.[67]

This quoted passage from *Romans* in which δικαιοσύνη is said to be disclosed bears remarkable similarity to a passage from the letter to the Galatians, in which it is πίστις, which was supposed to come and to be revealed (3:21), and has now come (3:25), all this so that we would be made righteous based on faith (-fulness) (3:24: ἵνα ἐκ πίστεως δικαιωθῶμεν). This "coming of πίστις" makes a traditional, anthropological interpretation of πίστις as the faith-act of an individual less likely, and at the same time supports my submission that Paul thought of the Christ-event as the metahistorical comeback of justice and faith.[68] In this same passage, the law is presented as disciplinarian (παιδαγωγός). This makes

---

[66] Cf. "do not conform to this age" (Rom. 12:2), as discussed below.
[67] Cf. Gal. 5:5.
[68] A similar point is made by Campbell, yet without mentioning any non-biblical parallels. See Campbell, *Quest*, 195.

perfect sense if we take the platonic relationship between written, external law and divine, internal law into account. Now that, with Christ, faith has come, the external law can be internalised.

Returning to the passage under discussion, Rom. 3:21–31, it is clear that this disclosure of δικαιοσύνη rests on πίστις here as well. The two present a perfectly common combination to the Romans, for they belong closely together in the semantic fields of both personal and societal virtues. More particularly, Paul holds that the life and death of Jesus Christ attest to his faithfulness to God, a faithfulness that was no longer humanly attainable in the present, godforsaken age. By resurrecting and thus vindicating Christ, God again makes his justice available to all who follow in Christ's footsteps by being faithful and trusting God, and in doing so he passes over the sins of the past age (3:25), summed up by Paul in Rom. 1:29–30. Since this return of justice happens on a divine, cosmic scale, I understand the sins and salvation described here not as the forgiveness of each individual, but as an equally collective, historical measure, opening up the possibility of a righteous life to each and every one by a trusting participation in Christ's faithfulness.[69]

Now as for the further specification of this justice, Paul expresses this in terms of something "outside the law (Rom. 3:21: χωρὶς νόμου)," as a "lack of distinction (3:22: οὐ γάρ ἐστιν διαστολή)," and as pertaining to Jew and Greek alike (3:29–30). Just like in the ideal, eschatological community of Diogenes of Oenoanda, full justice does not require laws based on divisions between people. And like Plutarch's Alexander the Great, who, following Zeno, did not distinguish between Greek and Barbarian, but built one community with one law, Paul also proposes one common "law of πίστις" (3:27). In light of these utopian, universalistic tendencies in Paul's Greco-Roman *Umwelt*, it seems more probable that Paul was, as the New Perspective argues, indeed arguing against Jewish— and Gentile[70]—ethnocentrism. His universalism did not merely concern the *scope*, but also the *content* of his message.[71] As Badiou comments on Rom. 3:27–39: "The One is that which inscribes no difference in the subjects to which it addresses itself. The One is only insofar as it is for all: such is the maxim of universality when it has its root in the event."[72]

---

69 I understand the active and passive uses of *pistis* to be closely connected and most instances in the Pauline letters as purposefully ambiguous. See Downing. "Ambiguity, Ancient Semantics, and Faith."
70 See Van Kooten, "Broadening the New Perspective on Paul."
71 *Contra* Gathercole, "Justified by Faith, Justified by His Blood," 155–56.
72 Badiou, *Saint Paul*, 76.

3.3 Rom. 12—Paul's Ethical Program: Renewed Minds, Temperance, and the Internal Measure of Faithfulness

One final passage in *Romans* that is not so much a classical "justification by faith" *locus*, does appear in a different light based on the discussed findings. In what has become the twelfth chapter, Paul calls upon his audience:

> ... to present your bodies as a living sacrifice, holy and acceptable to God, which is your logical worship (τὴν λογικὴν λατρείαν ὑμῶν). Do not be conformed to this age (μὴ συσχηματίζεσθε τῷ αἰῶνι τούτῳ), but be transformed by the renewing of your minds (μεταμορφοῦσθε τῇ ἀνακαινώσει τοῦ νοός), so that you may discern what is the will of God— what is good and acceptable and perfect. For by the grace given to me I say to everyone among you not to think more highly than you ought to think, but to think of each with moderation (μὴ ὑπερφρονεῖν παρ' ὃ δεῖ φρονεῖν, ἀλλὰ φρονεῖν εἰς τὸ σωφρονεῖν ἑκάστῳ), according to the measure of faith (μέτρον πίστεως) that God has assigned.[73]

Even though this section is mostly viewed as merely a hortatory, paraenetic, or practical section in the otherwise overly theological and theoretical epistle, I would argue that Rom. 12:1–3 is a pivotal Pauline self-description and key element in his overall message. The "justification by faith" axiom that has so often been deemed central to Paul's theology cannot be dissociated from this program of inner, ethical reform.

Concretely, Paul speaks of this reform in terms of a non-conformance to this age (αἰών), a renewal of the mind (νοῦς), a discernment (τὸ δοκιμάζειν) of God's will, temperate or prudent thinking (σωφρονεῖν), and thinking according to the measure of faith(fulness) (μέτρον πίστεως). A few things stand out, looking at this terminology in light of the sources I discussed.

First, just as in Rom. 1:18–32, Paul is thinking in terms of historical ages, and he perceives the present age in general in a negative light. His addressees are called upon not to conform (μὴ συσχηματίζεσθε) to this age. This somewhat pessimistic "metahistorical framing" is confirmed by other Pauline expressions that contain similar σχῆμα-language, like 1 Cor. 7:31: "For the present form of this world (τὸ σχῆμα τοῦ κόσμου τούτου) is passing away."

Second, the terminology is again highly rational or "reasonable." Like Plato's focus on the inner law, Paul refers to the νοῦς as the location of renewal. The overarching program Paul has in mind is that of a "logical" service to God. The wordplay with the cognitive verbs φρονεῖν (thinking), ὑπερφρονεῖν

---

[73] Rom. 12:1–3. I adapted the NRSVA-translation, and the punctuation in the Greek text, making ἑκάστῳ refer to the object of the right way of thinking, instead of to the recipient of specific measures of faith. Cf. Johnson, *Contested Issues in Christian Origins*, 265.

(thinking arrogantly, despising) and σωφρονεῖν (thinking thoughtfully, with temperance) is not at all commonplace in extant sources, so it shows Paul's creative application of these modes of thinking.[74]

Third, the combination of the terms mind (νοῦς), temperance (σωφροσύνη) and measure (μέτρον), places this passage in the context of the philosophical discussions of justice and the law. Since Plato, σωφροσύνη is semantically closely linked to δικαιοσύνη and living according to "measure" means living in accordance with God. Even though Paul is not explicitly referring to the law or to justice in this passage, and whereas he need not have been familiar with specific works of Plato or his followers, the semantic field involved relates to the question of how people can be made to live a just life and what external or internal means can be of assistance in this process.

Fourth, if we compare Paul's answer to Plato's, some interesting parallels and differences stand out. A striking convergence is the link between God, a divine measure, and the mind as the part of the human soul that should conform to this measure. As such, both statements can be regarded as responses to the sophists' position of man being the "measure of all things."[75] Hence, even though the measure is meant to function as an inner law, it comes from an external, objective, and divine source. A difference between the aim or scope of Plato and of Paul, however, is that Plato addressed a philosophical elite, whereas Paul is addressing a congregation made up of all social and cognitive strata.[76]

4 Conclusion: Πίστις as Appropriation of Universal, Ethical and Participational Justice

In this paper, I hope to have demonstrated that Paul's language on "justification by faith" is part of a larger metahistorical narrative according to which he perceived and explained the importance of the Christ event. It is Paul's main message that God has chosen this moment, this αἰών, to disclose his righteousness by reintroducing faithfulness embodied in Christ. This was necessary, because righteousness and faithfulness were absent from the world ever since the primor-

---

74 Some of the scarce exceptions include Aeschylus, *Persae* 818–31; Maximus of Tyre, *Dissertationes* 18.1; Euripides, *Oedipus*, fragment 543, 545.
75 As famously phrased by Protagoras: "Of all things the measure is man (μέτρον ἐστὶν ἄνθρωπος), of those that are, that/how they are, and of those that are not, that/how they are not," recorded by Sextus Empiricus, *Adversus mathematicos* 7.60.
76 Cf. Plato, *Theaetetus* 176b.

dial age of humanity, leading to idolatrous religion, dysfunctional minds and moral deprivation. The present is the time where the righteousness, that will be fully enacted in the near future, can already be appropriated through πίστις by all followers of Christ. This appropriation is effective in the individual, who is enabled to live righteously and ethically according to the divine measure of faith(fullness), but also in the community, which is enabled to enact righteousness by incorporating Jew and Greek, by overcoming differences.

This interpretation holds the following consequences for the different positions present in the scholarly discourse on "justification by faith," that I briefly outlined in the introduction.

Law: undeserved or universal justice? Especially the Greco-Roman utopian texts that combine an ideal society with a boundary-breaking outlook suggest that the "works of the law" that Paul opposes are indeed those that promote ethnocentrism or exclusivism. Paul's justice stretches out to the nations and is as such essentially universally configured.

Works: vindicative or ethical justice? The semantic closeness of δικ- and πιστ-language in the time of Paul and their main occurrence in the semantic field of virtues speaks for the importance of actual moral deeds in justification. Being faithful implies being just and therefore justifiable. Consequently, the "works" Paul argues against could be conceived of as deeds that serve only to show off external (self-)righteousness. For Paul, "works" cannot be restricted to external behavior but need to be the outcome of a renewed mind, or differently put, an imitation of the divine measure of faith, personified in Christ. This conclusion need not be at odds with the previous one: critique of external righteousness and ethnocentrism could easily coincide in a world in which the ethnic boast was a moral boast of collective self-righteousness.

Faith: anthropological or participational justice? The Greco-Roman narratives on the withdrawal and return of Δίκη and Πίστις fit perfectly with the historical setting of the initial retreat and renewed revelation of divine justice and faith as presented by Paul. Thus, "justification by faith" is not an a-temporal, individual salvific affair, but rather a historical-eschatological and communal salvific project initialized by the disclosure of God's righteousness and the coming of πίστις. Finally, the ὁμοίωσις θεῷ motive, that is an internal appropriation of the divine law and virtues, offers a philosophical background to the understanding of transformation according to Christ's faithfulness.

There is one question left unanswered: How should we evaluate Badiou's characterization of Paul as the "antiphilosophical theoretician of universality" from the methodological perspective of this study? As for his interpretation of universalism, to a large extent this is endorsed by the New Perspective emphasis on Paul's overcoming of ethnic (and social, gender) differences, and supported by our Greco-Roman sources. However, Pauline universalism seems to be of a structural, ahistorical nature in Badiou's analysis, whereas the convergence with Greco-Roman golden age narratives places Paul's universalism in a metahistorical light, proceeding not only from one "event" but from an understanding of the world's history as divided in ages.

As for Badiou's depiction of Paul as an anti-philosopher, the many parallels with ancient philosophical sources on the level of semantics, concepts and discourses suggest its inadequacy. Nevertheless, Paul's address to *all* and his "not-so-theoretical" utopian social experiment of including these *all* in one community—not only different ethnicities, but also the wise, philosophical elite and the foolish, ignorant plebeians—sets him apart from most philosophical schools of his day. I imagine him smiling as centuries later another branded anti-philosopher labels his project "Platonism for the people."

References

Badiou, Alain. *Saint Paul: The Foundation of Universalism*. Translated by Ray Brassier. Stanford, CA: Stanford University Press, 2003.
Bell, Richard H. *No One Seeks for God: An Exegetical and Theological Study of Romans 1.18–3.20*. Tübingen: Mohr Siebeck, 1998.
Bryan, Christopher. *A Preface to Romans: Notes on the Epistle in Its Literary and Cultural Setting*. Oxford: University Press, 2000.
Bultmann, Rudolf. *Glauben und Verstehen: Gesammelte Aufsätze*. Vol. 3. Tübingen: Mohr Siebeck, 1984.
Campbell, Douglas A. *The Quest for Paul's Gospel: A Suggested Strategy*. London: T&T Clark, 2005.
Coutsoumpos, Panayotis. "Paul's Attitude towards the Law." In *Paul: Jew, Greek, and Roman*, edited by Stanley E. Porter, 39–50. Leiden: Brill, 2008.
Downing, F. Gerald. "Ambiguity, Ancient Semantics, and Faith." *New Testament Studies* 56 (2010): 139–62.
Dunn, James D. G., and Alan M. Suggate. *The Justice of God: A Fresh Look at the Old Doctrine of Justification by Faith*. Grand Rapids, MI: Eerdmans, 1994.
Erler, Michael. "Epicurus as Deus Mortalis: Homoiosis Theoi and Epicurean Self-Cultivation." In *Traditions of Theology: Studies in Hellenistic Theology, Its Background and Aftermath*, edited by Dorothea Frede and André Laks, 159–81. Leiden: Brill, 2002.
Gathercole, Simon J. "Justified by Faith, Justified by His Blood: The Evidence of Rom 3.21–4.25." In *The Paradoxes of Paul*, vol. 2 of *Justification and Variegated Nomism*, edited by D. A. Carson, Peter Thomas O'Brien, and Mark A. Seifrid, 147–84. Tübingen: Mohr Siebeck, 2004.
Gonzalez, Eliezer. "Pauline Universalism: Anachronism or Reality?" *Journal of Asia Adventist Seminary* 14 (2011): 65–77.
Havelock, Eric A. "Dikaiosune: An Essay in Greek Intellectual History." *Phoenix* 23 (1969): 49–70.

Heliso, Desta. *Pistis and the Righteous One: A Study of Romans 1:17 against the Background of Scripture and Second Temple Jewish Literature*. Tübingen: Mohr Siebeck, 2007.

Hooker, M. D. "Adam in Romans I." *New Testament Studies* 6 (1960): 300–3.

Johnson, L. T. *Contested Issues in Christian Origins and the New Testament: Collected Essays*. Leiden: Brill, 2013.

Konstan, David. *Pity Transformed*. London: Duckworth, 2001.

Larson, Curtis W. R. "The Platonic Synonyms, ΔΙΚΑΙΟΣΥΝΗ and ΣΩΦΡΟΣΥΝΗ." *The American Journal of Philology* 72 (1951): 395–414.

Neutel, Karin B. *A Cosmopolitan Ideal: Paul's Declaration "Neither Jew Nor Greek, Neither Slave Nor Free, Nor Male and Female" in the Context of First-Century Thought*. New York: Bloomsbury, 2015.

Seifrid, Mark A. "Paul's Use of Righteousness Language Against Its Hellenistic Background." In *The Paradoxes of Paul*, vol. 2 of *Justification and Variegated Nomism*, edited by D. A. Carson, Peter Thomas O'Brien, and Mark A. Seifrid, 39–74. Tübingen: Mohr Siebeck, 2004.

Sierksma-Agteres, Suzan J. M. "(N)iets nieuws onder de zon. Klassieke Oorsprongsnarratieven in de Romeinenbrief." *Radix* 41 (2015): 325–38.

Sierksma-Agteres, Suzan J. M. "Imitation in Faith: Enacting Paul's Ambiguous Pistis Christou Formulations on a Greco-Roman Stage." *International Journal of Philosophy and Theology* 77, no. 3 (2016): 119–53.

Stowers, Stanley Kent. *A Rereading of Romans: Justice, Jews, and Gentiles*. New Haven, CT: Yale University Press, 1994.

Strecker, Christian. "Fides – Pistis – Glaube: Kontexte und Konturen einer Theologie der 'Annahme' bei Paulus," In *Lutherische Und Neue Paulusperspektive*, edited by Michael Bachmann and Johannes Woyke, 223–50. Tübingen: Mohr Siebeck, 2005.

Van Kooten, George H. *Paul's Anthropology in Context: The Image of God, Assimilation to God, and Tripartite Man in Ancient Judaism, Ancient Philosophy and Early Christianity*. Tübingen: Mohr Siebeck, 2008.

Van Kooten, George H. "Broadening the New Perspective on Paul." In *Abraham, the Nations, and the Hagarites*, edited by Martin Goodman, George H. van Kooten, and Jacques van Ruiten, 319–44. Leiden: Brill, 2010.

Vanlandingham, Chris. *Judgment and Justification in Early Judaism and the Apostle Paul*. Peabody, MA: Hendrickson, 2006.

Wallace-Hadrill, Andrew. "The Golden Age and Sin in Augustan Ideology." *Past and Present* 95 (1982): 19–36.

Anders Klostergaard Petersen
Paul's Use of Πίστις/Πιστεύειν as Epitome of Axial Age Religion

Abstract: This essay goes back to an old debate that has harassed the study of Biblical studies, classics, and the history of religion, that is, the Judaism Hellenism discussion. Despite the influential book by Martin Hengel, *Judentum und Hellenismus*, which undermines the binary understanding of the relationship between Judaism and Hellenism, much of this debate lingers on in different repercussions of the binary scheme in which the gain of the one is understood to imply the loss of the other. Yet, the relationship between Judaism and Hellenism should be conceptualized in terms of a Venn diagram in which the different entities analytically attributed to either Judaism or Hellenism be seen as deeply entangled with each other. This essay targets this debate by focusing on the question of Paul's use of πίστις and πιστεύειν, which has also come to play a prevalent role in current scholarship. More in particular, this essay localizes this question in the context of cultural evolution with a special focus on the transition from archaic to axial age types of religiosity. Needless to say, this is a moot theoretical perspective which has not been applied to the field of late Second Temple Judaism before, but much can be gained – both at a theoretical, methodological, and empirical level – by endorsing such an approach.

Dating back to antiquity and with Tertullian as a particularly prominent paragon of the scheme, there is a time-honored tradition for inserting a robust caesura between philosophy and religion. In the prevalent understanding of the relationship they are seen as categorically different discourses representing respectively reason and irrationality, human thinking over and against divine revelation. Frequently they are understood as radically different, but also as internally opposing realms of thinking: "What indeed has Athens to do with Jerusalem? What concord is there between the Academy and the Church?"[1]

At the same time as Tertullian rejected philosophy, his dichotomous cleavage of philosophy and religion into contradictory phenomena emerged involuntarily self-ironic. For simultaneous with his disavowal of philosophy as incongruent with Christianity, Tertullian embraced the very tradition which he superficially repudiated. This ambivalence permeates much of his work. His fer-

---
1 Tertullian, *De praescriptione haereticorum* 7:9–13. Translation taken from Roberts and Donaldson, eds., *Writings of the Fathers down to AD 325*, Vol. III.

vent rejection of Greek παιδεία—elegantly formulated in a rhetorical and popular philosophical mould which exploited the same tradition that was being denigrated—may be a particular instantiation of the philosophy-religion dualism with a special bearing on specific contestations within parts of the North African Christ-movement of the late second century. Yet, Tertullian was drawing on older traditions (cf. 1 Cor. 1:18–2:5), just as his view in the subsequent history of reception became an epitome for the incompatibility between religion and philosophy. The formulations, therefore, have a legacy with a considerably longer history that is particularly germane to my essay: What has Paul's use of πίστις to do with Platonism and more so with the fundamental epistemology of Hellenistic transcendent forms of philosophy?

Although an increasing number of scholars are prepared to abandon the contrast between philosophy and religion with regard to the ancient world in the dichotomous form of Tertullian's uncompromising formulation, the impacts of the distinction linger on. In 2014, I attended a conference organized by Troels Engberg-Pedersen, *From Stoicism to Platonism? On a Possibly Asymmetrical Relationship of the Two Philosophical Schools in the Period 100 BCE-100 CE*.[2] Leading scholars from around the world the majority of whom came from classics and ancient philosophy were present. I do not think that they will resent if I say that my contributions to the discussions in which I advocated in favor of a close relationship between philosophy and religion in the ancient world with a few exceptions were met with skepticism. I hold this to be not only indicative of the continued predominance of the philosophy-religion dualism but also illustrative of a general way of thinking among classicists and philosophers working on ancient philosophy with regard to conceptualizing the relationship between the two discourses.

It may, of course, be that this manner of understanding the problem is inherent to these disciplines, but my impression is that despite recent attempts to emancipate scholarship from the more dichotomous conceptions of the connections between philosophy and religion in the ancient world, this type of thinking also permeates wide currents in the study of late Second Temple Judaism (early Christ-religion included). The reluctance to acknowledge the proximity of philosophy and religion is perhaps even more prominent when the dualism is applied to the relationship between ancient philosophy and formative Christ-religion,

---

[2] Program available at: http://www.google.dk/url?sa=t&rct=j&q=&esrc=s&source=web&cd=1&ved=0CCEQFjAA&url=http%3 A%2F%2Fpure.au.dk%2Fportal%2Ffiles%2F79657435%2FProgrammeFinal_2_.docx&ei=WSY-VeriEYGdsAG8nIC4Cw&usg=AFQjCNEfsLxt82 AOccB-i2d9N_vlk8EgPQ&sig2=OBhi-ZV9qW-H7PCovrxnfg&bvm=bv.91665533,d.bGg. Accessed September 1, 2015.

presumably because early Christian texts have often been held to constitute the dire contrast to philosophical discourse. After all, what has the vivid imagery of Rom. 8 to do with Epictetus' *Discourses?* Or what has Paul's depictions of heavenly journeys and mystical experiences to do with Plato's *Dialogues?* Ostensibly, there is a world of difference between the discourse traditionally conceived of as being engaged in breaking free from a religious frame of reference by introducing dialogic, reasoning form of thinking and a discourse permeated by mythology.

Two other time-honored scholarly trajectories are closely related to this field of problems and are similarly loaded by ideological baggage. The one is the so-called μῦθος-λόγος debate which is a discussion confined to transformations of classical Greek religion according to which the transition from mythical to philosophical types of discourse represented a decisive and irreversible break with previous thinking.[3] The other current, more directly related to the philosophy-religion discussion in the context of Second Temple Judaism, is the age-old Hellenism-Judaism debate.[4] Within this line of thinking, Palestinian forms of Judaism frequently come out as the epitome of (true) Judaism, whereas Hellenistic versions are considered less Jewish because of their inclusion of elements considered foreign to Judaism. The same holds true for manifestations of early Christ-religion. Whereas in a Jewish context Palestinian versions of Judaism are often conceived to represent the most genuine forms of Judaism, in a Christian context, conversely, Hellenistic types of Judaism are assigned the role of constituting the springboard for the emergence of formative Christ-religion. For the same reason, they are frequently understood to embody the truest forms of Judaism, whereas Palestinian ones are attributed a less flattering role, susceptible to negative value judgements. More than posing the question of the relationship between Paul and πίστις or πιστεύειν, my essay also touches upon these two strands of discussion, since they are by virtue of scholarly history intrinsically related to the former.

To move the debate forward I shall introduce a perspective which to a majority of scholars still appears controversial, namely cultural evolution. Rather than conducting a narrow discussion of the role of πίστις and πιστεύειν in Paul, I shall place the debate in this wider context. The discussion may occasionally appear distant from the topic of πίστις and πιστεύειν, but it is crucial to com-

---

[3] For a critical assessment of this line of thinking, see Lloyd, *Being, Humanity & Understanding*, 77–78; Most, "From Λόγος to Mythos," 31–36, 47; and Petersen and van Kooten, *Religio-Philosophical Discourses in the Mediterranean World*.
[4] See Meeks, "Judaism, Hellenism, and the Birth of Christianity," 23–27; Martin, "Paul and the Judaism/Hellenism Dichotomy," 58–61; and Alexander, "Hellenism and Hellenization as Problematic Historiographical Categories," 63–72.

prehend the wider philosophical and theoretical ramifications of it in order to follow the argument, since I hold Paul's use of πίστις and πιστεύειν to be quintessential in a basic epistemology permeating a variety of religious manifestations from the sixth century BCE and onwards, that is, those of an axial age type.

1 Cultural Evolution as Context for the Discussion of Πίστις and Πιστεύειν in Paul

For a long period of time cultural evolutionary approaches were neglected in the humanities and social sciences due to their contentious nature. Evolutionary reasoning had its heyday from the Enlightenment to around 1920, when the experience of World War One made it intellectually impossible to uphold a form of thinking that had turned Western culture into the apex of civilization and Christianity into the zenith of the history of religion. Although there was a horrendous political aftermath of this thinking with the rise of extreme right-wing political movements of the 1930s, it is fair to say that in leading intellectual circles this type of reasoning came to a halt around 1920. Retrospectively, however, we may have thrown the baby out with the bathwater. There were elements in this thinking from which we can benefit considerably when applying it to our present discussion. To do that, it is pivotal to specify the manner according to which this perspective may be resumed.

Contrary to previous forms of cultural evolutionary thinking, I do not discuss it in light of truth or ethics, but in relation to aesthetics only, that is, pertaining to the question of higher or lesser degrees of cultural complexity. Nobody in the current debate propagates evolution in a manner that implies the superiority of one cultural entity over and against another with respect to the true or the good. In that sense, the contemporary debate does not revitalize the former discussion. But it would be naïve and scholarly unsatisfactory were we no longer willing to make distinctions between different forms of culture in terms of complexity. The emergence of philosophical discourse with the pre-Socratic philosophers, for instance, marked the introduction of a type of thinking which compared to previous forms of religion was more complex due to the fact that it built upon the previous thinking without which it would have been unthinkable. Similarly, the appearance of various types of Judaism subsequent to more archaic forms of Israelite religion was unconceivable without the existence of the former ones which they in a simultaneous process partly presupposed, partly polemicized against. This is what is meant by aesthetic complexity in the context of cultural evolution.

Additionally, ongoing and vibrant research in cognitive science has made it inevitable for the humanities and social sciences to reflect anew upon the relationship between nature and culture. According to Merlin Donald the evolution of human consciousness and, thereby, culture may be divided into three stages— with both onto- and phylogenetic bearing—which allows for gradual transitions to have occurred between four phases. The first decisive change took place, when our bipedal but apelike ancestors acquired the ability to communicate via voluntary motor acts, that is, the transition from episodic to mimetic culture around 3 million years ago. The next significant change occurred with the emergence of mythic culture approximately 500.000 years ago, when predecessors of homo sapiens sapiens obtained the first provisional abilities to communicate by means of linguistic signs. The final crucial evolutionary transition emerged with the appearance of early theoretic or symbolic culture around 40.000 years ago which enhanced the possibilities of external memory storage considerably.[5] This has been a process of increasing acceleration that has not yet come to an end as the internet vividly documents. There is, however, an important addendum to this. A fundamental tenet of Donald's theory which constitutes the foundation for Robert Bellah's work on cultural evolution is the insight that modern mind represents a hybrid structure. It is built from vestiges of earlier biological stages as well as new external symbolic memory devices that have radically altered its organization. This has given rise to Bellah's tenet with regard to cultural evolution: "Nothing is ever lost," that is, nothing decisive is ever lost.[6]

Bellah's and Donald's assumption, with which I concur, implies that all human culture should be conceived of in relation to and built upon older biological and cultural layers. Implied in their view is also the fact that cultural evolution is not of a peremptory, irreversible character. Things may by virtue of being built on older cultural strata be rolled back, just as the cultural evolutionary development envisaged by Bellah is based on the Durkheimian idea that symbolic culture can only persist by means of the underlying biological and cultural layers. But what has this to do with Paul's use of πίστις and πιστεύειν?

A good deal. If one locates the discussion in the wider context of the emergence of axial age culture much of the difference between the Greco-Roman world and Judaism fades away in the sense that the question cannot be reduced to a difference between Hellenism and Judaism, that is, that πίστις/πιστεύειν belongs to Paul's Jewish world in contrast to other elements to be assigned to his

---

[5] Donald, *A Mind So Rare*, 260–62.
[6] Bellah, "What Is Axial about the Axial Age?," 72; Schneider, "Nothing Is Ever Lost." Cf. Joas, *Was ist die Achsenzeit*, 19–20, 59–60.

purportedly Greco-Roman context. His use of πίστις/πιστεύειν should not be embedded in "a zero sum contest in which every gain for Hellenism be understood as a loss for Judaism or vice-versa."[7] The developments in ancient Greece and Israel may advantageously be seen as embedded in larger and more comprehensive cultural processes of transition that occurred in a number of Eurasian cultures from the sixth century BCE and in subsequent centuries from China and India to the Near Oriental world with ancient Israel as a particularly prominent example to ancient Greece. In China, the change was personified by renouncers and thinkers like Laotse (whether a historical figure or not, the traditions ascribed to him are historical), Confucius and later Mencius and Xunzi. In India, the development was embodied by Gautama Siddharta, the Buddha to be, and the subsequent tripartite emergence of the grand Indian religious trajectories, Hinduism, Buddhism, and Jainism; in Israel by the prophets and in particular by Job and Ecclesiastes, and in Greece by the pre-Socratic philosophers and subsequently by Socrates and Plato and the later philosophical schools. Obviously, the development was not of intellectual character only.

As Jared Diamond has argued, there were good reasons why this development occurred in this area and during this period. Natural presuppositions contributed to social processes like enhanced population density and complimentarily increased levels of urbanization which in their turn were conducive to increased social stratification, novel types of political organization, scientific inventions, and better exploitation of natural resources which simultaneously and reciprocally gave rise to new forms of thinking.[8] Although the specific intellectual manifestations in the various Eurasian cultures were individually conspicuously different, there were also noticeable similarities. They all testify to important transitions in terms of thinking with respect to previous forms of religion which obviously continued, but at the same time were extended by the new types of discourses which led to continuous positive and negative interchanges between them. In this manner, the question of the relationship between Hellen-

---

[7] "We avoid the notion of a zero-sum contest in which every gain for Hellenism was a loss for Judaism or vice-versa. The prevailing culture of the Mediterranean could hardly be ignored or dismissed. But adaptation to it need not require compromise of Jewish precepts or practices … . Ambiguity adheres to the term 'Hellenism' itself. No pure strain of Greek culture, whatever that might be even in principle, confronted the Jews of Palestine or the Diaspora. Transplanted Greek communities mingled with ancient Phoenician traditions on the Levantine coast, with powerful Egyptian elements in Alexandria, with enduring Mesopotamian institutions in Babylon, and with a complex mixture of societies in Asia Minor. The Greek culture with which Jews came into contact comprised a mongrel entity—or rather entities with a different blend in each location of the Mediterranean" (Gruen, *Heritage and Hellenism*, xiv).

[8] Diamond, *Guns, Germs, and Steel*, 132–42, 157–75, 361–70.

ism and Judaism cannot be confined to the Western part of the Mediterranean basin and Israel only. We need to locate it in the wider context of axial age types of religion.[9] Thereby, the time-honored dualism between Hellenism and Judaism disappears, since discourses of the two cultures of an axial age type may preferably be understood as alternative forms of cultural-evolutionary development within the context of Eurasian religion. Similarly, the λόγος-μῦθος debate cannot be confined to a Greek context only. It has striking parallels in the other Eurasian cultures under scrutiny. Five points characterize the transition from archaic to axial age forms of religion.[10]

First, the latter exemplifies the emergence of thinking about thinking. Contrary to previous forms of religion, axial age religions are characterized by increasing self-reflexivity frequently expressed in second-order concepts and by the ability to understand one's own thinking and practice from an ostensibly external perspective. Second, this form of self-reflexivity amounting to a foundational epistemology is often voiced in spatial categories whereby differences between opposing views become projected onto a vertical axis manifested as a contrast between the heavenly over and against the earthly perspective. The dualistic spatial staging is occasionally projected onto an axis of depth, whereby the contrast becomes extended to a difference between interiority and exteriority, soul and body, corresponding to the distinction between heaven and earth. Sometimes the ascription of values to these two axes is correlated with a horizontal, temporal axis where the difference is instantiated as a contrast between past and present. This may take several forms such as the difference between a negative past versus a positive present and vice-versa, but it may also—as in 2 Cor. 3—manifest itself as the difference between a negative past and a positive present (Christ-adherents) which simultaneously corresponds to a positively ascribed true past (the Abraham tradition) predating the negatively assigned past

---

9 Throughout most of history culture and religion have been identical or overlapping entities. It is only since Enlightenment that the two have increasingly moved apart whereby it has become possible to distinguish between them; and even this development pertains predominantly to the Western part of the world. Obviously, it was possible in the ancient world to differentiate between different degrees of sacredness, wherefore we have the distinction between sacred and profane. Yet, the notion of secularity is unthinkable prior to Enlightenment traditions at the earliest. Phenomena such as theatre, sport, digestion, toilet visits, etc., were to greater or lesser degrees in the ancient world all part of that which we from an *ethic* perspective designate religion in as much as religious aspects were involved such as prayers, purity rules, etc.
10 See Bellah, "Religious Evolution," 366–68; "What Is Axial," 74–81; and *Religion in Human Evolution*, 265–82. See also Eisenstadt, "Introduction: The Axial Age Breakthroughs—Their Characteristics and Origins"; and Elkana, "The Emergence of Second-order Thinking in Classical Greece," 63–64.

(the Moses tradition).[11] Third, the transition is commonly characterized by the development towards heno- or monotheism, that is, a reduction of the divine pantheon of archaic types of religion. Fourth, axial age religions are typified by strong awareness of the existence of rivalling world-views that in terms of thinking need to be denigrated to substantiate one's own truth. Fifth, these religions are distinguished from archaic ones by the call to the adherents to emulate the godhead to such an extent that they transcend the ontological differentiation between divine and human. Thereby, subscribers to the world-view are transformed into the same material as the deity and in some cases even held to be translocated to the divine abode.[12]

Let me underscore that I do not attempt to conceal differences between the admittedly very different cultural manifestations involved; but I do argue that behind these differences there is a number of prominent similarities which are most plausibly explained in terms of convergent evolution. Since the early Christ-movement in terms of origin is considerably later than the emergence of the first axial age forms of culture, it is obvious to see it as an extension or democratization of axiality to wider population segments, whereby it also presupposes the first axial transition.[13] There were other types of late Second Temple Judaism not only in the Diaspora but also in the land of Israel that testifies to the influence of axial age thinking; but the early Christ-movement is a particularly noticeable example. The Pauline letters patently show this. The pervasive apocalyptic world-view permeating Paul's thinking is of a conspicuously Jewish nature, but this manner of conceptualizing the world simultaneously exemplifies striking similarities with the basic epistemology of Platonism and subsequent forms of Hellenistic transcendent philosophy as demonstrated by Henrik Tronier.[14]

Contrary to traditional ways of discussing the relationship, we need not surmise a historical connection in which Platonism came to exert direct influence on Paul. The theoretical framework endorsed here, I suggest, is superior to such a strong causal-historical model which is confronted with difficulties of substantiating any direct Platonic influence on Paul. The argument is that the two cultural manifestations may advantageously be understood to exemplify convergent cultural evolution, that is, the view that comparable cultural develop-

---

11 Petersen, "The Use of Historiography in Paul," 71–76, 89.
12 Petersen, "Attaining Divine Perfection," 23–34.
13 Hence Nietzsche's acidic remark: "denn Christentum ist Platonismus fürs 'Volk.'" (Nietzsche, *Jenseits von Gut und Böse*, 156.) If one can dispense with Nietzsche's resentments to Christianity I think there is more than a kernel of truth in his statement.
14 Tronier, "The Corinthian Correspondence," 167–69, 195–96.

ments are likely to occur if certain social and basic biological presuppositions are present. In this sense, both may be considered different manifestations of axial age thinking. The same holds true for many of the resemblances existing between Paul and Stoicism which have been highlighted by Engberg-Pedersen.[15] But rather than seeing Paul as a Jewish pursuer of Stoicism which Engberg-Pedersen comes close to do, I find it—similar to the previous example—more plausible to account for the similarities which demonstrably exist in terms of convergent evolution. This does not exclude a direct takeover of particular motifs and specific ideas which had become stock elements of popular philosophy and wider cultural circles. The point, however, is that in relation to the foundational epistemology of the philosophical currents we need not assume a direct takeover in terms of influence of the philosophical trajectories on the semantic system of early Christ-religion which would be genealogically difficult to substantiate. The convergent evolution perspective is also advantageous due to the fact that it simultaneously enables us to acknowledge similarities and to retain obvious differences between the phenomena compared.

2 Πίστις/Πιστεύειν in Paul

One of the most moot and interesting questions during recent decades of Pauline scholarship is the problem of how to interpret and translate Paul's use of πίστις, especially as it occurs in the context of his πίστις Χριστοῦ-formulations.[16] I find the subjective interpretation of the genitive not only congruent with Paul's overall understanding of the Christ-story but also historically more plausible both in the context of the ancient world in general as socially organized on the basis of contractual relationships and in view of the Greek and Latin semantic fields of πιστ- and *fides*. In light of Paul's foundational world-view, the translation of πίστις Χριστοῦ/Ἰησοῦ as the steadfastness, commitment or faithfulness of Christ/Jesus is right to the point. Translations verging on modern ideas about "belief in" or "faith in" are in my view dubious by their anachronistic nature presupposing as they do a later and stronger propositional concept of belief.

---

15 Engberg-Pedersen, *Paul and the Stoics*; Engberg-Pedersen, *Cosmology and the Self in the Apostle Paul*.
16 For excellent overviews of the debate, see Bird and Sprinkle, *The Faith of Jesus Christ*. For a persuasive and comprehensive argument for the understanding of πίστις Χριστοῦ as Christ's faithfulness or trustworthiness, see Morgan, *Roman Faith*, which extends the debate to include the Latin cognate *fides*. Morgan's book has been crucial for my own change of mind to subscribe to the subjective interpretation of the genitive. See my forthcoming review article of the book.

As I have argued in previous works, Paul's world-view is undergirded by a foundational narrative according to which Christ is understood to have paid remedy for the deficiencies of humanity by surrendering himself as a propitiatory sacrifice to God. Obviously, this world-view is differently expressed in the different letters, just as there is a likely development in Paul's thinking from the early to the later letters. That said, however, there is also an astonishing continuity in terms of the basic semantic universe which I here due to constraints of space allow myself to present in highly convoluted form. Ever since Adam's trespass, humanity has been disloyal to God who, therefore, is entirely justified to feel offended.[17] The story initially presupposes an asymmetrical relationship between two parts, the offender and the offended, contractual lord and servant. To pay remedy for the committed offence and, thereby, to reestablish the relationship between the two parties involved an act of propitiation is required. Narratively the cross functions as the point at which Christ's steadfastness and commitment to God's vocation is expressed. Simultaneously, Christ's propitiation is embedded in an act of reconciliation with respect to God as offended part. As compensation for Christ's faithful and substituting sacrifice, God effectuates the reconciliation virtually accessible in God's endowment of Christ with a particular vocation, but actualized in his death on the cross and finalized or realized in God's resurrection of Christ to eternal life.[18] Parallel to Christ but located at a level not ascribed the same collective, universal and substitutive implications as Christ's semiotic program, individual Christ-adherents are contractually enjoined to imitate Christ's trustworthiness in their own lives. By emulating Christ in a manner compliant with Paul's social-moral injunctions, Christ-adherents actualize Christ-behavior in conduct. At the end of days, they will be judged on the basis of their deeds. Crucial in this regard is the fact that Christ-adherents are not held to be on their own in this endeavor. In baptism, they have been bestowed with the spirit which endows them with the modal competences that enable

---

17 There is a certain resemblance between this view and the argument of Hays, *The Faith of Jesus Christ*, but contrary to Hays my reasoning is founded on semiotic formal analysis of the texts which in my view imbues the interpretation with a higher degree of plausibility and the possibility for others to question it at both the theoretical, methodological, and empirical level. The crucial difference between the two approaches rests on the fact that Hays' interpretation to a great extent depends on a theological structure that is applied to the analysis of the text rather than being conducted from third-order level. My view is strongly influenced by the work of my former teacher Davidsen, "The Structural Typology of Adam and Christ."
18 In Greimas' semiotics the terms virtualization, actualization, and realization designate specific stages pertaining to a contractual relationship and each determined by a particular pair of respective endo- and exotactic modalities, see Greimas and Courtés, *Sémiotique*, 9–10, 244–47, 306, 420–21.

them to actualize the life in Christ which ultimately will lead them to the final realization at the time of their resurrection to eternal life.

Admittedly, this vastly condensed summary of Paul's narratively conceptualized semantic universe may echo an Augustinian-Anselmian trajectory of interpretation of Christian universal history. Yet, despite recent attempts to criticize such readings of Paul on the ground that they constitute anachronistic reverberations of an influential interpretative trajectory in subsequent Christian history of reception,[19] I think the understanding holds true as a historically plausible rendering of Paul's semantic system. From this perspective, the subjective reading of πίστις Χριστοῦ resonates very well with the narratively conceptualized semantic system. That said, however, one should not ignore two crucial issues that speak against this reading among which only the first has really received extensive attention in scholarship.

First, Stanley Porter and Andrew Pitts as well as Barry Matlock have emphasized how the subjective interpretation of the genitive is confronted with severe linguistic arguments which none the less cannot ultimately decide the issue. Yet, it makes the burden of proof harder on those who champion the subjective genitive reading.[20] Second, it is not altogether easy to combine the subjective genitive interpretation with Paul's active use of the verb πιστεύειν, since the latter seemingly favors a cognitive emphasis placed on the lexeme which makes it more difficult to assign a different understanding of πίστις in the context of the πίστις Χριστοῦ formulations.[21] It appears counter-intuitive were Paul to use πίστις in juxtaposition with Christ in a manner noticeably different from his active use of the verb in which he undoubtedly places weight on the cognitive aspect, that is, acknowledging Christ as the decisive agent of God in God's renewed dealings with the world and Christ-adherents.

Although these two reasons which I cannot elaborate on here are important I ultimately do not find them decisive for dispensing with the subjective genitive interpretation and corollary understanding of other uses of the πιστ-lexeme. Even if one imputes an important cognitive aspect to Paul's use of πιστεύειν which I think is unavoidable it is *de facto* implied by renderings like to "entrust," "rely on," or "invest trust in," even in cases like 1 Cor. 15:11; 2 Cor. 4:13; Rom. 6:8; 10:9. Trust also implies a cognitive aspect pertaining to the acknowledgement of

---

19 Most outspoken in Stowers, *A Re-reading of Romans*, 2–16, 326–27.
20 Porter and Pitts, "Πίστις with a Preposition and Genitive Modifier," 53; Matlock, "Saving Faith," 88–89.
21 This problem is only superficially dealt with in Morgan, *Roman Faith*. It is noticeable that her discussion of πιστεύειν does not feature largely in the chapters relevant to Paul, cf. ibid., 212–306. See, however, ibid., 227.

the one in whom one invests trust. As Teresa Morgan in her recent book has been keen to point out one should be careful not to play emotional, propositional and relational aspects of the semantic field of πιστ- out against each other, since Paul's use of the lexeme is characterized by elasticity. Ultimately, I have been persuaded by Morgan and others who advocate not only the subjective interpretation of the πίστις Χριστοῦ expressions but also place decisive weight on the relational understanding of the πιστ-lexeme whereby it should be translated primarily in terms of faithfulness and trust. Needless to say, there is far more to discuss in this regard, but I shall take leave of the narrow debate of the semantics of πίστις by resuming the question of how it fits into the larger cultural evolutionary framework of axial age religion. Contrary to Morgan, I place more emphasis on the cognitive dimension of πίστις, but I do it in a different manner from the traditional objective rendering of the genitive as "faith in Christ."

3 Πίστις, Plato, and Paul as Axial Age Phenomena

As indicated I favor an interpretation by which Paul's use of the semantic field appears coherent. That I do not think is the case with the objective understanding. For the sake of argument, I shall focus on 2 Cor. 5:7, but then leave the πίστις debate only to return briefly to it in the conclusion. In 2 Cor. 5:7, Paul is engaged in a heated argument that serves to win his intended audience for his understanding. As a token of Paul's and his fellow-workers' high ethos, Paul claims in 2 Cor. 5:5 (verse 5b) that God has endowed them with the spirit as a pledge. Therefore, they can always be of full confidence (θαρροῦντες) despite their acknowledgement of the fact that at home in the body they are exiled from God. The acceptance of this is counterweighted by the fact that Christ-adherents are guided by complete God-trust and not by sight: διὰ πίστεως γὰρ περιπατοῦμεν, οὐ διὰ εἴδους (2 Cor. 5:7). The statement has an unmistakably Platonic ring to it. As long as one is in this world, true relationship to the heavenly realm is only accessible by means of a particular cognitive activity, that is, πίστις. At this point, some may reasonably object why I have recourse to Plato rather than a later strand of philosophy or philosopher contemporaneous with Paul. The criticism is legitimate, but the idea is that the basic epistemology underlying Paul's thinking is ultimately one that may be seen blatantly clearly in the context of Platonic philosophy as an epitome of axial age religion.

In the famous parable of the Cave in the opening of book seven of the *Republic* (the parable is given in 514a–17a and the interpretation in 517b–21b), Plato recounts how a group of people since their childhood have been captivated in an underground cave. The cave is located at considerable distance from the opening to the outside light. The persons have their necks and legs chained, so that their bodies are entirely locked and, therefore, they can only look straight ahead towards the end of the cave. Behind the prisoners, a fire is burning and between the fire and the prisoners there is a path with a small wall dividing the one from the other. At the other side of the wall, people are carrying different objects sticking up over the edge of the wall. The objects are statues of people, different animals made in stone, wood and other materials. The prisoners can only see the shadows from the objects projected onto the back wall of the cave perceiving it as reality. At one point in time, a prisoner succeeds in liberating himself from the cave. He becomes seriously confused when he is confronted with the fact that what he previously understood to constitute reality in reality constitutes a charade of shadows only. Although he is inclined to return to his previous existence as a captive, the former prisoner is forced to continue his ascent upwards the precipitous slope towards the opening of the cave where at long last he comes to see the sun. Although the radiance of the sun hurts his eyes he will ultimately understand the deceit of his previous existence and feel pity for his former co-prisoners. Yet, in his attempt to convey his new insight to his fellow prisoners he will be met by opposition and ridicule. In the end, Plato in the figure of Socrates has Socrates explain to Glaucon that it is beneficial to the city that the true philosopher devotes himself to enlighten those citizens who have not yet come to see the light. True education does not consist in the transmission of knowledge but in turning the soul away from the visible to the rational world. Although philosophers do not have the inclination to lead cities they should be forced to head them (*Republic* 521b7–10).

Despite his criticism of myth, it is noticeable that when Plato unfolds the basis of his epistemology he often has recourse to mythical narrative. In his similarly famous parable of the nature of the souls in *Phaedrus* 246a–49c5, Socrates among other things recounts how the souls of the philosophers ascend to the abode of the gods. Souls are like the united powers of the charioteer and a winged double span of horses of which the one horse is beautiful, good, and of noble race, whereas the other is the opposite. To steer the horse span, therefore, is an arduous and difficult task (246a6–b4). Souls equipped with wings wander around the heaven paying heed to everything without soul. When the soul is perfect and has its wings intact, it hovers in the air and governs the world. When souls lose their wings, they descend until they can cleave on to something whereby they come to inhabit and transform into earthly form (σῶμα γήϊνον λαβοῦσα) (246c3 f.). Contrary to all other human souls, the soul of the philosopher is particular in virtue of the fact that it is endowed with wings. In as much as it masters the ability, the philosopher's soul remains in the recollection (ἀεί ἐστιν μνήμη) of those things that make a god divine (πρὸς οἷσπερ ὁ θεὸς ὢν θεῖός ἐστι) (249c5f.). The man able to use his recollection correctly shall always be initiated in the perfect mysteries (τελέους ἀεὶ τελετὰς τελούμενος), and he alone shall become truly perfect (τέλεος). He removes himself from the occupations of commoners and moves towards the divine. Among the masses, he shall be conceived as mad (παρακινῶν). That he is possessed by a god (ἐνθουσιάζων) is concealed to them (249c7–d3).

Similar to the parable of the Cave, the philosopher of *Phaedrus* is depicted as one who has attained particular insight which brings him into proximity with the divine. Parallel notions of the philosopher permeate Plato's writings. The philosopher is called to transmit his insight into the divine world to the people despite the opposition he will be confronted with. More than anybody else, the philosopher is characterized by his close relationship to the soul which constitutes that element as we have seen in the *Phaedrus* which brings the philosopher into contact with the divine realm (cf. *Phaedo* 78b–84b). Contrary to archaic types of religion aimed to retain the ontological difference between humans and deities, men and gods (which is the whole *raison d'être* of archaic temple architecture), the philosopher incarnates a form of religion which not only transcends the boundaries of this world but also espouses a strong skepticism over and against this world. The philosopher is the one who has truly emancipated himself from the fetters of this world whereby he has embarked on a process of continuous divinization as it is famously expressed in *Theaetetus* 176a–b (cf. *Timaeus* 90a–d).[22] The philosopher is ontologically on a par with the divine, wherefore he is capable of granting the true insight of the world to his adherents. This is more related to Paul and his use of πίστις than we are wont to think.[23]

Paul's basic thinking reverberate the same type of epistemology characteristic of Platonic philosophy and subsequent post-Aristotelian forms of transcendent philosophy in general: a fact quintessentially seen in 2 Cor. 5:7. If we return to the five points initially highlighted as particularly characteristic of axial age

---

[22] Cf. Petersen, "Attaining Perfection," 28–30.
[23] I am indebted to Tronier who initially opened my eyes for seeing the relationship between the basic epistemological scheme of Platonism and apocalypticism. Tronier, however, leaves it open how one could possibly account for this connection. This is the point at which I introduce the cultural evolutionary reflections. The argument I endorse is that both should be conceived of as not only parallel manifestations of the transition from archaic to axial age types of religiosity but also that they both operate predominantly at the vertical axis of thought. See Tronier, "Corinthian Correspondence."

forms of religion, it is easy to see how Paul's religion corresponds with regard to almost all five elements to the axial age type.

First, although his letters do not pay witness to the element of self-reflexivity *per se* in the form of second-order concepts or are expressed in more evolved forms of abstract language as found in contemporary forms of philosophy,[24] it would be presumptuous to deny this element from his thinking. Certainly, his letters exemplify an aspect of self-reflexivity, and the more so if we take it also to include the ability to relate to one's own thinking and practice from an ostensibly externally situated perspective. 1 Cor. 1:18–2:16 speak for itself in this regard, but it is not unique in Paul as the congruent discussion in 2 Cor. 3 documents. In fact, the more one comes to acknowledge this aspect the easier it is to see how Paul instantiates a heavenly yardstick by which everything in this world is measured. It may of course be objected that such an installment of an extra-terrestrial view is characteristic of religion in general. There is some truth to this with respect to archaic forms of religion as well, but it certainly does not pertain to indigenous peoples' religion. And even in the archaic context, we do not find the more abstract formulations of it, verging on second-order language, as one does in Paul, nor does it testify to the robust caesura inserted between this and the other world. In the axial age perspective, the blessings of the other world like abundant progeny, old age, plentiful harvests, and so on, come to be seen as negative values serving to prolong the sufferings of this age over and against true being to be found only in the other world and on earth only in those instances which correlate with the other world.

Second, we also see in Paul how the self-reflexivity in the context of axial types of religion amounts to a foundational epistemology formulated in spatial categories. Differences between opposing views are projected unto a vertical scale and instantiated as a contrast between the heavenly over and against the earthly view. The projection of the dualism is also transferred to an axis of depth whereby the difference takes the form of a contrast between interiority and exteriority, soul and body. In Paul, the ascription of values to these two axes is correlated with a horizontal, temporal scale as, for instance, in 2 Cor. 3 where the opposition becomes one between past and present with the addendum of a positively ascribed true past pre-dating the negatively assigned past.

Third, the transition from archaic to axial age forms of religion is also characterized by the development towards heno- or monotheism. The noticeable reduction of the divine pantheon of archaic types of religion is clearly seen in the context of formative Christ-religion. Paul does not renounce the existence of

---

24 See Petersen, "Paul as Platonist," in preparation.

other culturally postulated superhuman agents (see for instance 1 Cor. 8:6), but his letters bear ample evidence to a conspicuous emphasis placed on God as the only true god of the universe.

Fourth, axial age forms of religion are typified by strong awareness of the existence of rivalling world-views that in terms of thinking need to be denigrated to substantiate the truth of one's own world-view. This point hardly needs elaboration with respect to Paul. The opening two chapters of *Romans*, for instance, make it abundantly clear that Paul acknowledges the existence of other world-views, but they have to be rhetorically vilified in order for Christ-religion to appear as the only true rendition of the true world. The point is not only pertinent with respect to external out-groups. It also pertains to internal debates against opposing forms of Christ-religion within the in-group. *Galatians* and *Philippians* bear ample witness to the fact that Paul sees himself confronted with rivalling forms of Christ-religion not least promulgated by the Jerusalem community and represented by Peter, John and James, which similarly have to be disparaged.

Fifth, in compliance with axial age forms of religion there is in Paul a strong inculcation on the adherents to emulate the godhead to such an extent that the adherents eventually move beyond the ontological differentiation separating divine and human in order to become god-like and, thereby, be transformed into the same material as the deity. In Paul, Christ-adherents shall even ultimately be transferred to the abode of the godhead.

4 Conclusion

Superficially, my essay has not been particularly focused on the πίστις/πιστεύειν debate. Yet, I argue that this discussion could benefit considerably from being located in the wider examination of cultural evolution in general and the transition from archaic to axial age types of religion in particular. In terms of scholarly history, the discussion of Paul's use of the lexeme πιστ- has been deeply interwoven with the Judaism-Hellenism debate and the philosophy-religion discussion. To disentangle the debate from these perceptual filters, I advocate that we situate the study in the broader context of axial age types of religion. Thereby, we may move beyond the narrower geographical area of Judaism/Hellenism to the wider Eurasian world and break up the time-honored dichotomous mold of casting the discussion in terms of either philosophy or religion in favor of a "both" "and."

Ostensibly, there is a world of difference between Paul's use of the semantic field of πιστ- and philosophical discourses. When viewed through the lens of axial age types of religion, however, Paul's thinking and his use of the πιστ-lexeme comes out as compliant with the same foundational epistemology as subscribed to by contemporary transcendent forms of philosophy. Paul's particular religion is focused on Christ who in virtue of his faithfulness to God's vocation has become God's power and wisdom (cf. 1 Cor. 1:24), whereby Christ is assigned a role similar to that ascribed to wisdom in contemporary forms of philosophy by those who invest trust in him. Ultimately, Athens and Jerusalem, πίστις and σοφία, may have more to do with each other than we are wont to think; but it takes a cultural evolutionary lens to realize it.

References

Alexander, Philip S. "Hellenism and Hellenization as Problematic Historiographical Categories." In *Paul Beyond the Judaism/Hellenism Divide*, edited by Troels Engberg-Pedersen, 63–80. Louisville, KY: Westminster John Knox Press, 2001.

Bellah, Robert N. "Religious Evolution." *American Sociological Review* 29, no. 3 (1964): 358–74.

Bellah, Robert N. "What Is Axial about the Axial Age?" *European Journal of Sociology* 46, no. 1 (2005): 69–89.

Bellah, Robert N. *Religion in Human Evolution: From the Paleolithic to the Axial Age*. Cambridge, MA: Harvard University Press, 2011.

Bird, Michael F., and Preston M. Sprinkle, eds. *The Faith of Jesus Christ: Exegetical, Biblical, and Theological Studies*. Peabody, MA: Hendrickson 2009.

Davidsen, Ole. "The Structural Typology of Adam and Christ: Some Modal-semiotic Comments on the Basic Narrative of the Letter to the Romans." In *The New Testament and Hellenistic Judaism*, edited by Søren Giversen and Peder Borgen, 244–62. Aarhus: Aarhus University Press 1995.

Diamond, Jared. *Guns, Germs, and Steel: A Short History of Everybody for the last 13,000 Years*. New York: Vintage, 1997.

Donald, Merlin. *A Mind So Rare: The Evolution of Human Consciousness*. New York, Norton & Company 2001.

Elkana, Yehuda. "The Emergence of Second-order Thinking in Classical Greece." In *The Origins and Diversity of Axial Age Civilizations*, edited by Shmuel N. Eisenstadt, 40–64. Albany, NY: State University of New York Press, 1985.

Engberg-Pedersen, Troels. *Paul and the Stoics*. Edinburgh: T&T Clark, 2000.

Engberg-Pedersen, Troels. *Cosmology and the Self in the Apostle Paul: The Material Spirit*. Oxford: Oxford University Press, 2010.

Eisenstadt, Shmuel N. "Introduction: The Axial Age Breakthroughs—Their Characteristics and Origins." In *The Origins and Diversity of Axial Age Civilizations*, edited by Shmuel N. Eisenstadt, 9–25. Albany, NY: State University of New York Press, 1985.

Greimas, Algirdas Julien, and Joseph Courtés. *Sémiotique: Dictionnaire rasisonné de la théorie du langage*. Paris: Hachette, 1993.

Gruen, Erich, *Heritage and Hellenism: The Reinvention of Jewish Tradition*. Berkeley, CA: UCL Press, 1998.

Hays, Richard B. *The Faith of Jesus Christ: The Narrative Substructure of Galatians 3:1–4:11.* Chico, CA: Scholars Press, 1983.
Joas, Hans. *Was ist die Achsenzeit? Eine wissenschaftliche Debatte als Diskurs über Transzendenz.* Basel: Schwabe Verlag, 2014.
Lloyd, Geoffrey E. R. *Being, Humanity & Understanding: Studies in Ancient and Modern Societies.* Oxford: Oxford University Press, 2012.
Martin, Dale B. "Paul and the Judaism/Hellenism Dichotomy: Toward a Social History of the Question." In *Paul Beyond the Judaism/Hellenism Divide*, edited by Troels Engberg-Pedersen, 29–61. Louisville, KY: Westminster John Knox Press, 2001.
Matlock, R. Bryan. "Saving Faith: The Rhetoric and Semantics of πίστις in Paul." In *The Faith of Jesus Christ: Exegetical, Biblical, and Theological Studies*, edited by Michael F. Bird and Preston M. Sprinkle, 73–89. Peabody, MA: Hendrickson, 2009.
Meeks, Wayne A. "Judaism, Hellenism, and the Birth of Christianity." In *Paul Beyond the Judaism/Hellenism Divide*, edited by Troels Engberg-Pedersen, 17–27. Louisville, KY: Westminster John Knox Press, 2001.
Morgan, Teresa. *Roman Faith and Christian Faith: Pistis and Fides in the Early Roman Empire and Early Churches.* Oxford: Oxford University Press, 2015.
Most, Glenn W. "From Logos to Mythos." In *From Myth to Reason? Studies in the Development of Greek Thought*, edited by Richard Buxton, 25–47. Oxford: Oxford University Press, 1999.
Nietzsche, Friedrich. *Jenseits von Gut und Böse. Friedrich Nietzsche Werke in Vier Bänden. Band IV.* Salzburg: Verlag das Bergland-Buch, 1985.
Petersen, Anders Klostergaard. "Attaining Divine Perfection through Different Forms of Imitation." *Numen* 60, no. 1 (2013): 7–38.
Petersen, Anders Klostergaard. "The Use of Historiography in Paul: A Case-Study of the Instrumentalisation of the Past in the Context of Late Second Temple Judaism." In *History and Religion: Narrating a Religious Past*, edited by Bernd-Christian Otto, Susanne Rau, and Jörg Rüpke, 63–92. Berlin/New York: De Gruyter, 2015.
Petersen, Anders Klostergaard, and George van Kooten, eds. *Religio-Philosophical Discourses in the Ancient World: From Plato, through Jesus, to Late Antiquity.* Ancient Philosophy and Religion, vol. 1. Leiden/Boston: Brill, 2017.
Porter, Stanley K., and Andrew W. Pitts. "Πίστις with a Preposition and Genitive Modifier: Lexical, Semantic, and Syntactic Considerations in the πίστις Χριστοῦ Discussion." In *The Faith of Jesus Christ: Exegetical, Biblical, and Theological Studies*, edited Michael F. Bird and Preston M. Sprinkle, 33–53. Peabody, MA: Hendrickson, 2009.
Roberts, Alexander, and James Donaldson, eds. *The Writings of the Fathers down to AD 325: Ante-Nicene Fathers. Vol. III. Tertullian I.II.III.* Peabody, MA: Hendrickson Publishers, 1995.
Schneider, Nathan. "Nothing Is Ever Lost: An Interview with Robert Bellah," *The Immanent Frame: Secularism, Religion, and the Public Sphere.* Accessed August, 2015. http://blogs.ssrc.org/tif/2011/09/14/nothing-is-ever-lost/.
Stowers, Stanley K. *A Re-reading of Romans: Justice, Jews, and Gentiles.* New Haven, CT: Yale University Press, 1994.
Tronier, Henrik. "The Corinthian Correspondence between Philosophical Idealism and Apocalypticism." In *Paul beyond the Judaism/Hellenism Divide*, edited by Troels Engberg-Pedersen, 165–96. Louisville, KY: Westminster John Knox Press, 2001.

Part III. **The Political Theologies of Paul**

Marin Terpstra
The Management of Distinctions: Jacob Taubes on Paul's Political Theology

Abstract: Is it justified to depict Paul's letters as an example of political theology, as Taubes did in his Heidelberg lectures on *Romans* in 1987? The justification lies in the fact that as a founder of non-Jewish "Christian" communities Paul has to act as a politician. But he was a politician of a special kind, one who pretended to be called by God (or Christ) to be a spiritual leader with the task to establish a new people. To clarify this point, the author focuses on the way Paul manages distinctions (between Jews and non-Jews, between followers of Christ and those who stick to the world as it is, and so on) and on the impact of his theology on these distinctions. This impact relates to the intensification of distinctions. The extreme consequence of this is the distinction between friend and enemy. This possible consequence connects Taubes's reflections with Carl Schmitt's use of the term "political theology." It turns out that Paul's political theology cannot be taken in the sense Roman intellectuals already used the term (state cult), but points in another direction, a "Messianic" subversion of "the state." The author ends his paper with a comment on what Taubes called the "Gnostic temptation" hidden in this reversed political theology.

Some people do have a life after they die. Unfortunately, they do not have anything to say about their own fate in this afterlife. Their fate and identity is in the hands of those that tell and retell stories about those that walked the earth and left traces of their existence and above all, their actions. These stories have a life of their own. Of course, those that tell these stories or write them down are often sincere in their attempt to do justice to the person they talk about. Nevertheless, even this kind of stories differ from each other and may even become quite conflicting. After this introduction, it must be clear that I am not going to talk about Paul, but will give a comment on some of these stories. It is not Paul but these stories that have shaped our world view. One of these stories is put forward by Jacob Taubes (born in 1923), a philosopher who is as closely connected to non-orthodox Jewish thought as he also is to non-conformist and anti-capitalist movements.[1]

The lectures on Paul, delivered shortly before he died in 1987, are a kind of personal testament, but they nevertheless have a significance that goes beyond

---

[1] For a short but elucidating portrait see Muller, "Reisender in Ideen."

that.² My aim in this paper is to pick out a single theme from these lectures, one which in my view has not gotten very much attention. This theme is the management of distinctions in a situation of regime change, a situation that is at hand when one, like Paul, tries to found a community or a people on the basis of a new covenant with God. As Taubes makes explicit in the second part of his lectures ("Effects. Paul and Modernity: Transfigurations of the Messianic"), Paul's texts show an ambivalence that is still part of contemporary philosophy because of formulations that could be read in a Gnostic way. For Taubes, Paul is not the founding father of the Christian Church, but a Jew confronted with a Messiah that tended to break away from the Jewish tradition, but was part of this tradition too. The ambivalence of founding new communities of faith in Christ is connected to the first attempt, in the second century, to establish an orthodox Christian Church, an attempt greatly inspired by Paul's interventions. This attempt was made by a Gnostic "heretic," Marcion, who was then excluded from the Christian community. This orthodoxy wanted to free itself completely from the Jewish inheritance, and therefore accepted only the Gospels and the letters of Paul as its foundation. The formula of this break with Israel is the rejection of the Creator-God and the God of the Moses's Laws, and the sole affirmation of the Savior-God, the Father of the Messiah. The believers hope for liberation from this evil world, its political and religious order, and its worldly wisdom. If we take away the weird mythology connected to this fundamentally new theological scheme, a mythology that constitutes one variety from the range of Gnostic world views, we can register something very familiar to the modern ear. Indeed, what we encounter may suggest that we are here at the birthplace of the very idea of modernity: the endeavor to overcome the past radically, by way of a total rupture, and to move in the direction of a new and better world.

Taubes chose the following title for his lectures: "On the Political Theology of Paul: From Polis to Ecclesia (for advanced students only)."³ The theme of regime change is clearly present in this title, as is the reason for the concept of political theology. In this case, a community inspired by a "theology" announcing the appearance of the Messiah (or the Messianic) in history is set against the established political order. My aim in this text will be to elaborate on the plausibility of such a reading of Paul. The first question is: can we read Paul as a political thinker? The second question is: while it is obvious that Paul is a theologian (he talks about God), how can we say that his theology is connected

---

2 Taubes, *Die politische Theologie des Paulus*.
3 Ibid., 145/117. When quoting from the translation, the second page number refers to the translation and the first one to the original.

to the political? The third question arises because the concept of political theology is, at least for Taubes, derived from Schmitt's famous or notorious essay entitled "Politische Theologie," which was published in 1922.[4] Thus, the question that arises is: how are Taubes's lectures related to Schmitt's essay? This question is relevant because of the confrontation they had concerning Paul—a confrontation between a German lawyer who became part of the Nazi regime and a Jewish philosopher who sympathized with the 1968 student revolts. Is this reference to Schmitt justified if we want to tell the story of Paul? I will show that the confrontation between Schmitt and Taubes rests on the idea of the intensification of a distinction as the connection between the political and the theological. This point will lead us finally to a short reflection on the "Gnostic temptation" that lies hidden in the problematic.

Before elaborating on these questions, let me first summarize the main point. For Taubes, the current meaning of Paul concerns the fate of the Jews in European history, that is, in Christian history. The revelation of Christ can be seen to have the following consequence: Jews become the enemies of God (Rom. 11:25; see also 1 Thess. 2:15–16). Taubes's argument with Schmitt focused on this theme in Paul. For Schmitt, all distinctions in the political world finally merge into only one distinction, that between friend and enemy.[5] So, the phrase "enemies of God" is a genuinely political one. Marcion is the Christian theologian who proposed a sharp distinction between the Jews and the followers of Christ, between the first and the second covenant, between the Creator-God of the Torah and the Savior-God of the New Testament. The revival of Marcionism within liberal currents in Protestantism in the nineteenth and early twentieth century, which claimed that we can do without this authoritarian God of the Old Testament, signifies for Taubes the cultural climate in which anti-Judaism and anti-Semitism could develop.[6] Taubes's distrust of liberalism in general has to do with his diagnosis that the liberal cultural climate in Germany did not prevent it to become the site of the Holocaust. Whatever one may think of this impudent assertion, this context makes clear that the core of the problem

---

4 The third essay in Schmitt, *Political Theology*.
5 Schmitt, *The Concept of the Political*.
6 Taubes, *Die Politische Theologie des Paulus*, 78 ff./55 ff., comments on the impact of an influential book on Marcion, published in 1921, by the German liberal theologian Adolf von Harnack (see his *Marcion*). The theme of Gnosticism and modernity was debated since Blumenberg's *Die Legitimität der Neuzeit* by a group called "Hermeneutics and Poetics," in which Taubes also participated. Seminars by members of this group led to the publication of three volumes on political theology, Gnosis and politics, and theocracy, which were edited by Taubes under the title *Religionstheorie und Politische Theologie*.

is the way people deal with distinctions. That is the dramatic background of Taubes's attempt to show (1) that the popular anti-Semitism fostered within the Roman Catholic Church in connection to Paul is ill-founded, (2) that Paul remained a Jew in his thought and reasoning, and tried to prevent a total breach between followers of Christ and those Jews that rejected Christ, and (3) that Paul did not established a church but was the founder of communities based on love, not hate.[7] This should be enough of an overview to understand the subsequent sections of this paper, which deal with Paul's politics (1), his political theology (2), the relation between Taubes and Schmitt (3), and the "Gnostic temptation" (4).

1 Paul's Politics

Distinctions are the stuff the human world is made of. Paul is fully aware of what it means to establish communities of people distinguishing themselves from other people by particular principles, that is, distinctions. The core of his letters presents his attempts to manage these communities from a distance. This obvious fact may lead to a reading of Paul's letters in which the text is seen as part of a political praxis and as an articulation of the agonistic relations between different social groups (Jews, Jewish Christians, non-Jewish Christians, pagan Romans and so on). For me, Paul's letters are not diaries or other textual forms of expressing personal experiences; nor are they primarily philosophical or theological treatises. Above all, the letters are constitutional texts, more like the *Federal Papers* or the *Communist Manifesto*, than *The Confessions*—Augustine's or Rousseau's—or a phenomenology of religion *à la* Heidegger. Of course, in Paul's letters we find, to varying degrees, traces of ancient philosophical debates, religious movements from the time and personal experiences. We can read Paul's letters intertextually or as the thinking through of a Messianic experience. Jacob Taubes, however, more than other contemporary readers like Alain Badiou and Giorgio Agamben, was aware of the fact that the texts have a strategic and tactical meaning in the *polemical* context of the formation of early Christianity. Paul was not only a self-appointed apostle, preaching the message of Christ to non-Jews, that is, not a "legitimate" member of the peer group of those that lived with Jesus of Nazareth. He also had to fight for the maintenance of the communities he had founded against internal and external threats. The message of Paul is for us not only part of the history of ideas, but also part of a project of

---

[7] Explicitly in Taubes, *Die Politische Theologie des Paulus*, 72ff./51ff.

transmission: materializing words ("the truth") into a stable community ("the body of Christ").[8] His letters are full of implicit and explicit references to the conflicts inherent to such a project. This means that in these letters Paul's main concern is the *identity* of these communities (1 Cor. 1:10ff.), the faith that holds them together (Rom. 1:11ff.) and the way they have to guard themselves against disintegration (2 Cor. 12:20; Rom. 16:17ff.). This is what I will call the management of distinctions.

To understand the politics of Paul, it is therefore necessary to clarify what is meant by distinctions.[9]

(i) The identity of everything is a based on a distinction. A is A because it is distinguished from not-A and because not-A encompasses other things: A is A because it is not B, C and so on. Addressing the followers of Jesus Christ always means at the same time affirming that there are those who are not followers and that among those there are Jews and Romans (or Greeks).[10] Or if we talk about universalism, we must suppose that there is also non-universalism and that within that there is ethnicism, nationalism and so forth.

(ii) Distinctions will repeat themselves within one or both sides of the distinction. If we distinguish God from not-God, for example the world, then in the world there are things that refer to God and things that are contrary to God. The human mind is divided into ψυχή (oriented to the world) and πνεῦμα (directed to God). If we distinguish the followers of Christ from Jews, then we can distinguish within the side of the followers of Christ between those who resemble the Jews and those who do not resemble the Jews (i.e., circumcised or not).

(iii) This multiplication of distinctions can be further elaborated by combining distinctions, by replacing one distinction with another, by eliminating distinctions, or by arranging distinctions in a different way. Hence, the followers of Christ can be associated with light, the good, love, liberation, knowledge, the new, weakness, purity, whereas the unbelievers can be associated with darkness, evil, law, slavery, worldly wisdom, the old, power and impurity. The human world is a complex of distinctions that assemble to create identities. It also creates order and disorder. This makes clear what a political reading of Paul implies: understanding the use of philosophical

---

8 Debray, *Transmettre*.
9 Especially useful for me was Baecker, *Form und Formen der Kommunikation*; this approach derives from sociological systems theory as put forward in Luhmann, *Social Systems*.
10 A thorough study of Paul's letters from this perspective would require a book-length study; I apologize for merely giving some examples familiar to those who already know Paul's letters without entering into exegetic details.

and religious topics as attempts to separate the group of the faithful from those that are outside, those that will be doomed, destroyed or lost, those that cannot be trusted or should be kept at a distance, and so on.[11] Paul's letters are full of these kinds of distinctions.

(iv) A further step has to be taken in order to grasp the full meaning of this political hermeneutics. It will turn out to be a crucial one. Distinctions can be cognitive, communicative and institutional. All distinctions are cognitive: we cannot think without distinctions. Not all distinctions are communicative, but only those people actually talk about. Institutional distinctions are distinctions that function as frames of communication and thought: they determine what is included and excluded in human interaction. If followers of Christ *as* followers of Christ talk to Jews, that is, if people belonging to one group or social system talk to people belonging to another group or social system, then the distinction is institutional. The important thing here is: how decisive, strict, strong or established is the institutional distinction? Does it exclude communication or even thoughts that use other distinctions? For example, orthodoxy means that one belongs to this group on the condition that one accepts this particular distinction, such as that between the old and the new covenant. Institutional distinctions can function less rigidly: there can be tolerance of people discussing certain distinctions. Communication and thought are potentially subversive for institutional distinctions: if thought and talk about an institutional distinction is allowed, its authority is put in question. If people have very different ideas about the distinction between followers of Christ and Jews, and discuss them openly, the institutional distinction between these groups becomes fluid. Everyone who carefully reads the letters of Paul (e.g., Rom. 14) knows that he is principally concerned with this problem: how can this group of people be stabilized, what distinctions are crucial, what distinctions are secondary, how to deal with people who give different interpretations of a distinction or make other distinctions, and so on. In Paul's letters, we witness the transformation of the distinction between followers of Christ and non-followers of Christ *internal* to the Jewish community, which is itself distinguished from the Gentiles or Greeks, to the distinction between followers of Christ and non-followers of Christ in which the distinction between Jews and Gentiles/Greeks becomes secondary on both sides of

---

11 A theoretical justification of this political reading can be found in Kondylis, *Macht und Entscheidung*.

the distinction or is eliminated.¹² Although Paul aims to address all human beings, his political calculations are based on the assumption that many people will not adhere. Political praxis dealing with distinctions on an institutional and communicative level, therefore, cannot be universal.¹³

(v) Finally, distinctions have logical and polemical consequences. With regard to their logical consequences, we are interested in the consistency of all the basic distinctions made. In thought or even in communication, this should not be a problem, but in the human world logical consequence leads to rigid social systems, and it may therefore have severe polemical consequences. Here one has to decide which distinctions really matter and which distinctions can be taken less rigorously. Marcion can be seen as a Christian theologian who wanted to make theology more consistent.¹⁴ One cannot accept that the God who created and governs this world is the same God that liberates man from this evil world (Gal. 1:4). It is contradictory to assume that God wants to free us from the world he himself created. So, we must get rid of the God of this world and rely exclusively on the message of the Savior-God. This is logically consequent. It also has polemical consequences, such as the expulsion of the Jews from the Christian world or even the intellectual and finally physical annihilation of the Jews, as Jacob Taubes and others have suggested.

To summarize, politics is about managing distinctions: who belongs to our society, on what conditions, within what institutional frames and so on? To manage distinctions properly, decisions must be made, and the consequences of these decisions must be taken care of. That is what political action is about. At the same time, institutional distinctions are always challenged. People propose other distinctions, conceive of a different possible society and so on. In this respect, what Paul is doing in his letters is political in a very simple and elementary way. The greatest part of his texts poses no real problems to interpretation if

---

12 A variation can be found in Agamben, *The Time That Remains*, 47 ff., where emphasis is placed on the fact that whatever distinctions one makes there will be a "remnant" that does not fit.
13 Badiou's attempts to show that the elimination of the distinction between "Jews" and "Greeks" marks the opening of a new way of political thought that foreshadows Marx's universalistic idea of the emancipation of humans from all social determinations and therefore all social and political inequality. This is unconvincing because the distinction between "Jews" and "Greeks" is merely *subordinated to a new distinction*, hence becoming obsolete. See Badiou, *Saint Paul*.
14 This is a central claim in Blumenberg's account of the problem (*Legitimität der Neuzeit*, 141 ff.) that is basic for Taubes's reflection on Paul.

one takes the management of distinctions in order to establish social cohesion to be the essence of politics. The real problem or enigma lies in the theological part that is connected to this management of distinctions.

2 Paul's Political Theology

A modern, sociological concept of contingency looks like this: draw a distinction and see how it works. Social systems emerge as more or less complex networks of stabilized distinctions that have proved themselves to be successful frames of human communication. At the same time, we more or less accept that other distinctions are possible. Society could and, indeed, shall be different. This also applies to our modern concept of liberal and democratic politics, which is based on the acceptance that in the realm of thought and public discourse alternative distinctions can be brought in. It can be claimed, for example, that the distinction between ecological responsibility and irresponsibility is more important than the distinction between economic growth and shrinkage or vice versa. Political theology comes in when a distinction is not a contingent starting point of an evolution that fails or succeeds, and is not an issue in public debate, but a truth that is already there, enclosed in a theo-cosmic order or revealed by the plain decision of a deity that demands obedience and loyalty.

Paul's political theology is not that of the Romans (*theologia civilis* or πολιτική). For them, political theology is the theology of statesmen, distinguished from the theology of poets and that of philosophers.[15] The Romans recognized that one could talk in different ways about the gods (or the one god). Political theology is part of the state cult of Rome, ritual practices that are an integrated ingredient of political life. For the Romans, the gods were partners in the city and in the world, with whom one has to cooperate, and who demand respect and honoring (*pietas*).[16] The gods are part of the vicissitudes of history: one has to have them on one's side if one wants to succeed. The political order should also be loyal to the ancestors and the founders of the city, and therefore respect their religion. The intellectual elite of Rome, like that of Athens, might also dedicate itself to the philosophical way of life, that is to natural theology which they claimed to be the mimetic representation of original religion.[17] Philosophical life makes man a member of a new and different πόλις or *civitas*.

---

15 Lieberg, "The Theologia Tripertita."
16 Scheid, *Religion et piété à Rome*.
17 See also Van Kooten, "Pagan and Jewish Monotheism according to Varro, Plutarch and St Paul."

Christianity, as Nietzsche formulated it, is "Platonism for the people," and in this sense a continuation of dual citizenship.[18] Although it may be justifiable to read in Paul's letters the traces of philosophical debates, a political hermeneutics of his texts shows that Paul's political theology is more in line with that of the Jews: it is theocratic, not anthropocratic (Rom. 9:16). The philosophers lived as men of flesh and bone in earthly cities as well as in the cosmic or ideal city that has a divine glamour: the city they dreamed and talked about. Paul is talking about a city that is founded by God. Theocracy, as Flavius Josephus says in his *Contra Apionem* (early second century), is a fourth kind of political order, not ruled by one person, an elite or the many, but by God and those who represent God in this world, the priests.[19] Between the God that created the world and rules it, and its subjects, there exists a more or less complex hierarchy of mediators. As a subject, man is dependent on these mediators (Rom. 10). The question therefore is: who are the true mediators of God's rule in this world and what do these mediators tell us about God's will?[20]

The God of Paul is an absolute ruler who demands complete loyalty. We should bear in mind that there is not a sharp line separating gods from sacral kings, or sacral kings from gods; the theo-political language is the same.[21] Sometimes this language is militant (for example, 2 Cor. 10:3–4, 11:13–15). Its focus then is on foundation, sovereignty and hierarchy. Those who are not loyal and obedient will be defeated or even destroyed. The theocratic regime leads to a particular political psychology. Paul depicts himself as a former fanatic Jew who tried to be strict in following God's laws (Gal. 1:13f, 6:17; cf. Philem. 3:5–6), but he seems to have despaired about his fate and that of all people (Rom. 3:10ff.). The enigma of his theology is not only that until now God accepted transgression, but that in fact no man ever succeeded in living according to the laws completely. We see in this a very rigid use of the distinction loyal versus disloyal to God (law-abiding or transgressing the law), with the result that all people are categorized on the wrong side of the distinction. The first covenant failed, concludes Paul (Rom. 11:7). The good news of Christ, as a son of God the primary mediator between God and his subjects, is that God is not merciless but wants to give humankind a second chance. I will not dwell on the complex question of the law in the thought of Paul. What matters is the difference be-

---

18 Nietzsche, "Forword," in *Beyond Good and Evil*. See especially Van Kooten, "Philosophical Criticism of Genealogical Claims and Stoic Depoliticization of Politics."
19 Cancik, "Theokratie und Priesterschaft."
20 Metaphors like this can be found in *Hebrews*, which is not a letter written by Paul but can be seen to be written in his spirit: Heb. 3:1, 4:14, 5:1f., 6:16, 7:2–3, 12:9.
21 See Oakley, *Kingship*.

tween the Roman political theology, in which honoring the gods is part of the consolidation of political power in the Roman Empire, and the theocratic political theology, in which the sole question is what and who represents God in this world. The distinction between God and world divides the world itself. For theocracy, the founding distinctions of the social world of humans are not manmade, but are revealed in one way or another. Paul sees himself as the messenger (merely a slave, not separable from the source of his message) of *a change of divine regime* announced by the Son of God, who says that the covenant between God and his people, the Jews, is no longer valid and that a new covenant is established (Rom. 2:17ff.). This new covenant is already at work after Christ's resurrection and will be effectuated fully as soon as Christ returns from heaven to establish a new kingdom. In the meantime, the task that has been set is to save as many people as possible and to prepare them to be members of the mystical body of Christ. We know that this idea "in the meantime," the time between the resurrection of Christ and his second coming, is a key concept in the contemporary discussion of Paul. This is only a consequence of what is the core of the message: a change of regime in God's rule of the world or even a change in the kind of God that rules. Because of this theocratic core of Paul's political practice, it is justifiable to talk about Paul's political theology. This can mean more than one thing, however.

3 Taubes and Schmitt: Intensification of a Distinction

Taubes and Schmitt do not disagree about the idea that "political theology" is an appropriate approach in the history of political ideas. Nor do they disagree that Paul's political discourse is about absolute loyalty to God or that politics as the management of distinctions is ultimately based on the concept of sovereignty. Sovereignty is the key concept in Schmitt's essay on political theology. It refers to the authority who makes the decisions that establish political order, that is, the normative foundation of a given society or people. Sovereign is the authority which decides in the state of exception, a state in which the normative order of society is in crisis.[22] In this situation, only one thing counts: who is friend, who is

---

[22] See the first essay in Schmitt, *Political Theology*. Agamben is right in saying that in this state of exception the law, that is, the normality of a society, is unobservable and unformulable, and that it therefore opens a perspective beyond the law, which he calls the "Messianic." Unfortunately, he does not elaborate on the connection between the twofold perspective that opens

enemy? The basic decision concerns who is for us and who is against us—supposing there is a "we" that can pose such a question. The point is that this "we" must be established first, and it can only be established by making a distinction. In Paul's case, we are simply told that such a decision has been made by God, that this decision was revealed by Jesus Christ, and that Paul was summoned to spread this revelation among mankind.

The key problem of political theology, therefore, is the intensification of a distinction. The final logical and polemical consequences of a distinction appear when the distinction becomes a matter of life and death for those who adhere to it—whether "life and death" is taken literally or metaphorically. It is the existential meaning of a distinction that forces the adherents to view their adversaries as enemies.[23] But the intensification of a distinction can take on many forms. Extreme dualism can lead to war between groups, or it can lead to attempts of eliminating the other side of the distinction; it can also lead to Puritanism, isolation or withdrawal from all contact with the other side of the distinction. It is clear that in Paul's letters the violent forms are left to God: he will destroy. Paul himself struggles with the degree of intensification that is needed to manage and maintain the communities he has founded. Political theology is about the way people have to deal with the distinctions revealed by the highest authority. Nevertheless, there are different political theologies.

As I have said, Schmitt and Taubes agree about the central idea of the intensification of distinctions, but they disagree about the forms this can take. For Schmitt, as a scholar of constitutional law, the emphasis is on distinctions at an institutional level, the foundations of the political order of a given group or people. Like conservative officials of the Roman Catholic Church, Schmitt saw radicalized Christianity (liberation theology for example) as a danger to the established order. His position is often compared to that of Dostoyevsky's Grand Inquisitor. For Taubes, it seems, distinctions have weight on a cognitive and a communicative level. He defends the spiritual against the secular realm, although he fully acknowledges the fact that in our world political intensification is what counts. Both read Paul's letters as constitutional texts, but they disagree about the kind of community that is established by Paul.[24]

---

up as soon as institutional distinctions collapse: concentration camps in which "everything becomes possible" (after civil rights are abolished) or a community based on love, not law (after the law is "fulfilled"). See Agamben, *The Time That Remains*, 104 ff.

23 Schmitt, *The Concept of the Political*, 26: "The distinction of friend and enemy denotes the utmost degree of intensity of a union or separation, of an association or dissociation."
24 The opposition at stake is, I think, well formulated in Georgi, "Gott auf den Kopf stellen."

One important issue is how we relate Rom. 13 to the announcement of the collapse of this world and its powers. In the opening verses of Rom. 13, Paul affirms that the world as it is, with its ruling powers, its hierarchy and its wisdom, is the work of God. The political theology of Paul is the theology of subjects who will always remain subjected and should therefore conform to whatever rules are in place. The real question is who really rules. Along these lines, the development of the "Christian" communities into a church that became a spiritual power within a political order was seen by many Christian thinkers as the fulfillment of God's promise. The Roman Empire was part of God's plan of salvation. This made a Christian political theology look more and more like the Roman political theology.[25] One could even imagine that from this point of view the παρουσία should be postponed until the church succeeded in gathering all people within its borders, except those stubborn sinners who remained loyal to the antichrist. Christianity thus lost its subversive potential, at least until the Final Judgement. In gross terms, this is the theological stance of Carl Schmitt: Paul is the founding father of the Roman Catholic Church, and our loyalty should be with this spiritual power.

For Taubes, as a Jewish thinker, the church's move to eliminate the Mosaic inheritance by appropriating it within its own system (as the prehistory and announcement of Christ's rule) is unacceptable. For him, this is not even a point of discussion. His argument against Schmitt is focused on the reading of Paul. Taubes gives a more apocalyptic interpretation of the same passage (Rom. 13): because the world is at the point of collapsing and being replaced by a new world, why bother about this world? Revolting against this world is a waste of precious time, as is worrying about one's earthly concerns.[26] This interpretation is only possible when the God that established power in this world is of no importance and if this God is, in the last analysis, not the God that will free us from the sufferings of this world and its political order. The only thing that interests Taubes in Paul's writings is his struggle between the ultimate consequence of Christ's message of salvation and his bond with the people to whom he belongs. The logical consequence of God's decision is that the Jews that do not recognize Christ are enemies and will be defeated. According to Taubes, Paul resists this consequence. Who are we to judge the Jews? Let God decide. Perhaps, though Paul claims he knows for certain, God has a plan that will save the Jews in

---

25 This interpretation, connected to Eusebius of Caesarea, was still defended more or less by Carl Schmitt in 1970 in his answer to Erik Peterson's thesis that Christianity is incompatible with political theology: *Political Theology II*.
26 Taubes, *Die Politische Theologie des Paulus*, 58/40 f.

the end. Indeed, Paul's mission to spread Christ's message to non-Jews is part of this plan: making the Jews jealous and thereby seducing them to join the group.[27]

4 The "Gnostic Temptation"

I hope that the foregoing sections have sufficiently clarified the reasons for understanding Paul's letters as examples of political theology. Whether these reasons are convincing or not is left for the reader to decide. In addition, I want to say something about the significance of all this for contemporary political philosophy and its dealing with Paul. I am not a philologist, a historian of ideas or a sociologist, so my interest is not to understand Paul's letters intertextually or as interventions imbedded in a particular socio-historical setting. My aim in this paper has been to show that the concept of political theology relates to a problem that can be summarized with reference to three concepts: distinctions, contingency and loyalty. (1) Distinctions are involved in the constitution of identity, but also in the processes of the change or dissolution of identity. (2) Contingency means that a distinction can always be challenged, that another distinction can be drawn, that a distinction can be taken in a less strict way, and so on. This relates distinctions to the question of the exception: "The question is whether you think the exception is possible ..."[28] (3) The question of loyalty or disloyalty arises when distinctions and their contingency take a social, institutional or political form.

The intervention of the divine in the shape of a revelation, incarnation or related manifestation, that is, the appearance of the "theological" in the domain of mental operations, communication and social institutions, introduces a new distinction in this complex field. It is not just a matter of constituting, maintaining or undermining worldly powers. A new dimension is configured, one which Benjamin called "göttliche Gewalt" ("divine violence") in his "Zur Kritik der Gewalt."[29] At least, if we view the divine as something which is not "of this world," but nevertheless can be present "in this world," the conjunction of dis-

---

27 For more details about the argument between Taubes and Schmitt see my article "God's Love for His Enemies."
28 Taubes, *Die Politische Theologie des Paulus*, 118/85. For further explanation of this aspect of Taubes's thought see Terpstra and de Wit, "'No spiritual investment in the world as it is.'"
29 "if mythic violence is law making, divine violence is law-destroying ... if mythic violence brings at once guilt and retribution, divine violence only expiates ..." (Benjamin, "Critique of Violence," 249).

tinctions, contingency and loyalty turns a new chapter. This chapter is especially connected to Jewish and Christian articulations of the conjunction, of which Paul is a major example. Here we find the different notions of eschatology, apocalypticism, messianism and Gnosticism. In divergent ways, they all point to the establishment of a new distinction (a new community or way of life) that is not seen as merely something people think or talk about, but neither is it something which already takes an institutional or political form. It certainly is something social: people gather in the name of this new distinction. Of interest for political philosophy is the meaning of this "in-between": what actually exists between an established power (as far as power can be established) and possibilities which have not taken shape institutionally and politically—or even cosmologically. This "in-between" can take the form of longing or waiting for changes that will come (eschatology), of expecting the destruction of the world as it is now (apocalypticism) or of being aware of that which shall liberate us or even has already liberated us from the world as it is (messianism).

In a conversation on partisans and militants in revolutionary processes, in this case the regime change led by Mao Tse-Tung in post-war China, Carl Schmitt makes an interesting remark on Christianity which shows why Jacob Taubes could see in his "enemy" also a thinker akin to his own thought. This is what Schmitt says:

> These events, however, remind me of the history of Christianity, which started with the total repudiation of the world of that time, the Roman Empire, and with a total calling into question of the world, and soon organized itself on Roman soil, in the catacombs, hidden beneath the earth, literally underground. [...] And what happened with this total repudiation in the end? After Constantine it became a religion of the state and in the end became a centralized organization with an infallible bishop in Rome [...].[30]

This comparison between Christianity and militant Marxism is of interest because some of the prominent writers on Paul these days have a connection to militant Marxism.[31] Paul has become something of an icon for contemporary leftwing political thinkers looking for an idea of revolution or regime change that can avert the disastrous totalitarian regimes in which previous communist experiments have ended. Here we find another parallel: the "new prophets" Weber foresaw as a possible answer to the total transformation of Christian (prot-

---

30 Schickel, *Gespräche mit Carl Schmitt*, 26; my translation.
31 Badiou compares Paul with Lenin (Badiou, *Saint Paul*, 2), in Badiou's and Agamben's book the allusion to the "human emancipation" in Marx's *Zur Judenfrage* (1843) is present as a shadow. Unfortunately, I cannot elaborate on this here.

estant) culture in the "iron cages" of capitalist society,[32] a protest of the remains of Christianity against its integration into the world as it is. This is the problem of "the Messianic." Agamben is a clear example of this attempt at a total liberation of philosophy and politics from the past. The sharp, intensified distinction between, on the one hand, the disaster of ethical thought that stretches from the ancient world to contemporary sociology and, on the other, "the coming philosophy" reminds us of the kind of "cultural Marcionism" typical of modernity (Brague).[33] Marcionism means the withdrawal from the old world, the expectation of a new world that is not the restitution of an original state, and the rejection of reforms, which presuppose that something in the existing world is good. The preceding section might shed some light on this debate by showing that there are a wide variety of possible solutions to the problem of the intensification of distinctions.

The "Gnostic temptation" can be described as the intensification of the distinction between the divine ("the other world") and the world ("this world", "the world as it is") which affects all other distinctions.[34] The radical withdrawal from the world expresses that the "logic" of this world, or the ἄρχόντες ruling this world, is a realm totally different from everything that has to do with true life. Taubes himself tried to resist this temptation, as he claims Paul did too, but it is a constant force of attraction. He refers to himself as an "apocalyptic," whose main commitment was to defend the distinction between secular and spiritual power, which he sees as "absolutely necessary" for preventing Western thought from suffocating. Against Schmitt's "totalitarian temptation" with its stress on the need for a strict defense of the political distinction between friend and enemy, Taubes pleads for the mind to remain resistant to any apology for the world: no spiritual investment in the world as it is.[35] What I called the "in-between" is, I think, a plausible interpretation of this distinction between the mind that is free from the world (πνεῦμα) and the mind that is invested in the world (ψυχή); it names a space needed simply for calculating the best way to

---

32 See Taubes, "Einleitung."
33 See for example Agamben, *Opus Dei*. "Cultural Marcionism" is a term coined by Brague, and it fits well with a thinker who views the whole philosophical tradition and Western civilization to be catastrophic and aberrant, one for whom the only hope is the "coming philosophy." See Brague, *Eccentric Culture*, 57, 111, and 180 ff.
34 In a preparatory text for the conference on "Gnostics and Politics" (1980) Taubes (in collaboration with Wolfgang Hübener) makes clear that he sees the socio-historical study of the "Gnostic temptation" as the central issue. See Kopp-Oberstebrink, Palzhoff, and Treml, *Jacob Taubes-Carl Schmitt*, 227.
35 Taubes, *Die Politische Theologie des Paulus*, 139/103; the origin of this phrase, in English and italics in the original German text, is unclear.

live in this world. To give in to the "Gnostic temptation" is to give up on the attempt to save the space for this "in-between."

The core of what I have been trying to say concerns our attitude towards distinctions that are intensified in the form of institutions or even in ontologies grounding society as a whole. There is thus a "totalitarian temptation" that one should resist without giving in to the "Gnostic temptation." Paul's letters can provide a fascinating example of an attempt to deal with this problem. Taubes is especially interested in the way Paul explains the distinction between law and love, connecting it to a merciless and a merciful God. Mercy and love point to the same thing: the possibility that a distinction is postponed, an exception is granted or even an annihilation made possible. This is the "apocalyptic": everything that is established can be declared null and void. Taubes's illustration is the Jewish feast of Yom Kippur insofar as it imitates God's power to forgive.[36] There are no absolute distinctions, because the mind is always free to think of other possibilities, and so people will always be willing to put these possibilities into practice.

References

Agamben, Giorgio. *The Time That Remains: A Commentary on the Letter to the Romans*. Translated by Patricia Dailey. Stanford, CA: Stanford University Press, 2005.
Agamben, Giorgio. *Opus Dei: An Archaeology of Duty*. Translated by Adam Kotsko. Stanford, CA: Stanford University Press, 2013.
Badiou, Alain. *Saint Paul. La fondation de l'universalisme*. Paris: Presses Universitaires de France, 1997.
Baecker, Dirk. *Form und Formen der Kommunikation*. Frankfurt am Main: Suhrkamp, 2005.
Benjamin, Walter. "Critique of Violence." In *Selected Writings, Volume 1, 1913–1926*, edited by Marcus Bullock and Michael W. Jennings, 236–52. Cambridge, MA: Harvard University Press, 1996.
Blumenberg, Hans. *Die Legitimität der Neuzeit*. Frankfurt am Main: Suhrkamp, 1966.
Brague, Rémi. *Eccentric Culture. A Theory of Western Civilization*. Translated by Samuel Lester. South Bend, IN: St. Augustine's Press, 2002.
Cancik, Hubert. "Theokratie und Priesterschaft. Die mosaische Verfassung bei Flavius Josephus, c. Apionem 2, 157–198." In *Religionstheorie und Politische Theologie. Band 3. Theokratie*, edited by Jacob Taubes, 65–77. Munich: Wilhelm Fink Verlag/Verlag Ferdinand Schöningh, 1987.
Debray, Régis. *Transmettre*. Paris: Editions Odile Jacobs, 1997). Translated by Eric Rauth as *Transmitting Culture* (New York: Columbia University Press, 2004).

---

36 Ibid., 43 ff./28 ff.

Georgi, Dieter. "Gott auf den Kopf stellen: Überlegungen zu Tendenz und Kontext des Theokratiegedankens in paulinischer Praxis und Theologie." In *Religionstheorie und Politische Theologie. Band 3. Theokratie*, edited by Jacob Taubes, 148–205. Munich: Wilhelm Fink Verlag/Verlag Ferdinand Schöningh, 1987.

Harnack, Adolf von. *Marcion. Das Evangelium vom fremden Gott. Eine Monographie zur Geschichte der Grundlegung der katholischen Kirche*. Darmstadt: Wissenschaftliche Buchgesellschaft, 1996.

Kondylis, Panajotis. *Macht und Entscheidung. Die Herausbildung der Weltbilder und die Wertfrage*. Stuttgart: Klett-Cotta, 1984.

Kooten, George van. "Pagan and Jewish Monotheism according to Varro, Plutarch and St Paul: The Aniconic, Monotheistic Beginnings of Rome's Pagan Cult—Romans 1.19–25 in a Roman Context." In *Dead Sea Scrolls and Other Early Jewish Studies in Honour of Florentino García Martínez*, edited by Anthony Hilhorst, Émile Puech, Eibert Tigchelaar, 633–51. Leiden: Brill, 2007.

Kooten, George van. "Philosophical Criticism of Genealogical Claims and Stoic Depoliticization of Politics: Graeco-Roman Strategies in Paul's Allegorical Interpretation of Hagar and Sarah (Gal 4:21–31)." In *Abraham, the Nations, and the Hagarites: Jewish, Christian, and Islamic Perspectives on Kinship with Abraham*, edited by Martin Goodman, George van Kooten, Jacques van Ruiten, 361–85. Leiden: Brill, 2010.

Kopp-Oberstebrink, Herbert, Thorsten Palzhoff, and Martin Treml, eds., *Jacob Taubes-Carl Schmitt. Briefwechsel*. München: Wilhelm Fink, 2012.

Lieberg, Godo. "The Theologia Tripertita as an Intellectual Model in Antiquity." *Journal of Indo-European Studies Monograph Series* 4 (1984): 91–115.

Luhmann, Niklas. *Social Systems*. Translated by John Bednarz and Dirk Baecker. Stanford, CA: Stanford University Press, 1995.

Muller, Jerry. "Reisender in Ideen: Jacob Taubes zwischen New York, Jerusalem, Berlin und Paris." In *"Ich staune, dass Sie in dieser Luft atmen können." Jüdische Intellektuelle in Deutschland nach 1945*, edited by Monika Boll and Raphael Gross, 40–61. Frankfurt am Main: Fischer Taschenbuch Verlag, 2013.

Nietzsche, Friedrich. *Beyond Good and Evil*. The Complete Works of Friedrich Nietzsche. Volume 8. Translated, with an afterword, by Adrian Del Caro. New York: De Gruyter, 1980.

Oakley, Francis. *Kingship. The Politics of Enchantment*. Malden/Oxford/Victoria: Blackwell, 2006.

Scheid, John. *Religion et piété à Rome*. Paris: Albin Michel, 2001.

Schickel, Joachim, ed. *Gespräche mit Carl Schmitt*. Berlin: Merve Verlag, 1993.

Schmitt, Carl. *Political Theology. Four Chapters on the Concept of Sovereignty*. Translated and introduced by George Schwab. Chicago, IL: The University of Chicago Press, 1985.

Schmitt, Carl. *The Concept of the Political*. Translated by George Schwab. Chicago, IL: The University of Chicago Press, 2007.

Schmitt, Carl. *Political Theology II. The Myth of the Closure of any Political Theology*. Translated by Michael Hoelzl and Graham Ward. Cambridge: Polity Press, 2008.

Taubes, Jacob, ed. *Religionstheorie und Politische Theologie. Band 1. Der Fürst dieser Welt: Carl Schmitt und die Folgen*, Munich: Ferdinand Schöningh/Wilhelm Fink Verlag, 1983.

Taubes, Jacob, ed. *Religionstheorie und Politische Theologie. Band 2. Gnosis und Politik*. Munich: Wilhelm Fink Verlag, 1984.

Taubes, Jacob, ed. *Religionstheorie und Politische Theologie. Band 3. Theokratie*, Munich: Ferdinand Schöningh/Wilhelm Fink Verlag, 1987.
Taubes, Jacob. "Einleitung. Das stählerne Gehäuse und der Exodus daraus oder der Streit um Marcion, einst und heute." In *Religionstheorie und Politische Theologie. Band 2. Gnosis und Politik*, edited by Jacob Taubes, 9–15. Munich: Wilhelm Fink Verlag, 1984.
Taubes, Jacob. *Die Politische Theologie des Paulus. Vorträge, gehalten an den Forschungsstätte der evangelischen Studiengemeinschaft in Heidelberg, 23.–27. Februar 1987*. Edited by Aleida and Jan Assmann in conjunction with Horst Folkers, Wolf-Daniel Hartwich, and Christoph Schulte. munich: Wilhelm Fink Verlag, 1993. Translated by Dana Hollander as *The Political Theology of Paul*. Stanford, CA: Stanford University Press, 2004.
Terpstra, Marin, and Theo de Wit, "'No spiritual investment in the world as it is.' On the negative political theology of Jacob Taubes." In *Flight of the Gods. Philosophical Perspectives on Negative Theology*, edited by Laurens ten Kate and Ilse Bulhof, 320–53. New York: Fordham University Press, 2000.
Terpstra, Marin. "God's love for his enemies. Jacob Taubes's conversation with Carl Schmitt on Paul." *Bijdragen. International Journal in Philosophy and Theology* 70 (2009): 185–206.

Carl Raschke
Paul as Political Theologian: How the "New Perspective" Is Reshaping Philosophical and Theological Discourse

Abstract: This essay explores how the so-called "New Perspective on Paul," focusing on the Jewish context of the apostle's writings and exemplified in the Biblical scholarship of N.T. Wright and others has profound implications for contemporary "political theology." It considers carefully an important book by Theodore Jennings entitled *Outlaw Justice* and compares his approach to key contemporary European philosophical ventures in recent decades that aim to reinterpret Paul and Jewish eschatology in political terms. The essay argues that the central term δικαιοσύνη in Pauline "soteriology" is also a fundamental concept for the ancient theory of the πόλις. Whereas in the *Republic* Plato sought to explicate the integral relationship between ψυχή and the well-ordered πόλις in accordance with the notion of δικαιοσύνη, so Paul follows a comparable trajectory in setting forth the theme of participation "in Christ" as an "existential" as well as a socio-normative project. It is this unique, tensive relationship between the two meanings of the word δικαιοσύνη (both "ethical" and "political") that not only makes Paul intelligible in a whole new way within his own historical setting, but also recontextualizes him as an important figure for political thinking down through the ages. We can thus begin to reconceive Paul's *Romans* especially not only as an ongoing polemic against Judaism and paganism, but as a "radical political theology" that confronts and critiques the apparatus of the imperial state itself.

The standard average Protestant, evangelical, or Reformed Christian reading of Paul makes him into a huckster of cheap grace. Especially in America, but increasingly among the expanding new Christian communities of what has been termed the "global south," one routinely is exposed to sermons on *Romans*, songs by Christian performers, or some plug for a new church or ministry that invokes the Reformation-revivalist message that salvation is all about personal surrender to Jesus, while accepting his lavish love as shown on the Cross. This formula is so familiar, many Christians unconsciously assume that it is what Paul in *Romans* and elsewhere is actually saying.

At the same time, in the past decade a widening, but motley circle of Biblical scholars (for instance, N. T. Wright, E. P. Sanders, and David Brondos) have systematically challenged the Reformation reading, which they see as inextricably tied up with late Medieval philosophy and hermeneutics and which, by dint of their historical staying power, have fatefully blinded us to, as Wright himself has put it, "what Paul really said."¹ The alternative reading of Paul's method and messages has clearly not crystallized around any single strategy of interpretation. But the generalized impact of these readings, affecting not only Protestants, but Catholics and Orthodox academics as well, has conjured up a label for them that connotes more their dissenting and revisionist character than their formulation of any emergent hermeneutics of the New Testament—the so-called "New Perspective on Paul."

But what if something altogether different than classical atonement doctrine or even the New Perspectives, which have tended to fall within the ambit of meticulous textual analysis minus theological posturing—might be going on in Paul? What if Romans amounted to more of what we understand nowadays as a radical "political theology" centered on a vision of universal justice than a therapeutic sop for the lonely and the lost, as it has become in our present culture of Christian spiritual consumerism?

Scholars for some time have noted the curious way in which Paul throughout *Romans* deploys the word δικαιοσύνη, normally translated as "righteousness." But in both the ancient and Hellenistic Greek milieu δικαιοσύνη had more the force of "justice" in both the sense of morally normative social relations and the person virtue of habitually behaving "justly" toward others. It is the same word that constitutes the centerpiece of Plato's deliberations about both the just soul and just government in *The Republic*. In Aristotle, δικαιοσύνη is the binding force that holds competing wills and interests together in the πόλις.

So could *Romans* really be a tract in political theory rather than a view of religion or a soteriology, as we are accustomed to construing it? In his recently published book *Outlaw Justice*, Theodore Jennings makes exactly this kind of case.² Following Jacques Derrida's well-known distinction between "law" and "justice," the latter of which he describes as *undeconstructible*, Jennings sees Paul's much-touted "dialectic" in *Romans* as tantamount to a Hellenistic "deconstructivist" gambit. "While agreeing with the tradition of political thought that the basic issue has to do with justice, Paul deviates from the tradition by offering a fundamental critique of the supposition that justice is to be achieved through a legal structuring of society," Jennings writes.³ Justice instead is "messianic." The familiar Pauline and Reformation refrain that Christ-followers are "justified," or

---

1 See Wright, *Paul*. See also Yinger, *The New Perspective on Paul*. See Sanders, *Paul, the Law, and the Jewish People*; and *Jesus and Judaism*. See Brondos, *Paul on the Cross*.
2 Jennings, *Outlaw Justice*.
3 Ibid., 3.

made just, through faith has nothing to do with a "forensic" mutation of "God declaring people to be just who are manifestly not just," but of the establishment on earth of real justice by means of the transformative resurrection power of the risen Jesus.[4]

The "justice" present in the eschatological community that is "in Christ" is the kind of just order only the messiah can establish. It is not established through "law," that is, νόμος (Paul's locution in *Romans* is the standard Hellenistic term for the broader legal and juridical framework of social obligations and not simply for the Jewish *Torah*), but through "faith," or πίστις—a kind of revelatory intuition of the new Christ-community, or κοινή, in which "justice" or δικαιοσύνη reigns. In the Christ community political justice, social justice, and *divine* justice are all one and the same. Christian eschatological justice, therefore, completely inverts law-based justice, on which both Roman and subsequent Western society are founded.

Jennings argues convincingly that the rhetoric of Rom. 2 is not aimed singularly at the decadent morality and cultic excesses of pagan society, but primarily at a social order that privileges narcissistic preoccupations over interpersonal responsibility, that is founded on ruthless self-aggrandizement at the expense of relationality. It discerns the "liveliness" of a new way of being as "the messianic takes form" in those "societies somehow lodged within the old and increasingly hostile institutional orders of the world."[5]

In his famous essay "Force of Law," on which Jennings depends for much of his interpretation of Paul, Derrida calls justice not a state of relationships between two parties (that is, giving everyone their "due"), as it was for Plato and the Greeks in general, but a "performative force." If God is just, as even the agnostic Thomas Jefferson thought, then does that mean God is the the ultimate performative force? *The force of God*, then, is what we call justice in a Christian sense. Christian justice would also imply that we rely on this force in relation to the other. Justice itself is always surprising. Consider Jesus' parable of the Good Samaritan. All the characters in the story do what they were supposed, or expected, to do according to the νόμος. But Jesus, as both social outcast (like the hated Samaritan) and as a theological *outlier* ("unlike," as the Gospel tells us, the scribes and Pharisees) exercises the performative force of justice that ultimately ensues in the crucifixion.

---

4 Ibid., 62.
5 Ibid., 177.

In doing justice, divine justice, Jesus deconstructs everything about well-ordered human relationships that systems of "justice" (that is, law) have put in place for ages.

In theological language, we can say that by going to the cross as a "criminal" under the highest, rational system of justice that the world at the time had devised—that is, Roman law—Jesus deconstructed the justice system and established justice and righteousness once and for all. We like to think of Jesus as a rebel against the system. But, actually, he *corrected* and *perfected* the system, as we find Jesus saying "unless your justice (δικαιοσύνη) exceeds that of the scribes and Pharisees, you will never enter the kingdom of heaven."[6] It is this "excess" of justice over what is deconstructible that makes justice undeconstructible. Derrida also says that "deconstruction is justice." What he means that justice is also the *force of deconstruction.* We do not merely deconstruct. *Deconstruction happens*, like the Holy Spirit, to us and through us. It happens because of the force of deconstruction that is in all texts, that is "at work" in every work, including the work that is us and in us. We can, therefore, understand the Christian community, or the church *as embodied theodicy.* The church is the outworking of God's universal justice. God's universal justice is not the same as giving everyone their due, but about establishing right relationships and exhibiting justice through the permanence, force, and sustainability of those relationships.

One of the major failures of Christian thought—or at least American Christian thought—in the last fifty years or so has to do with its seeming inability to comprehend the meaning of the term "justice" and its epochal implications for the Christian church. Its clutch has always remained stuck in flitting back and forth between the idea of δικαιοσύνη as either personal "righteousness," or the impersonal and "distributive" modality of social justice. One does not need to distinguish between personal and social justice any more than one can distinguish between pregnant and very pregnant. Whoever is "just," according to Scripture, does justice. Whoever is "saved" does justice in the way the prophets described it—at the gate, in the marketplace, not just in the voting booth or by working two days a week at a homeless shelter. Especially in Plato's routine use of the expression in *The Republic*, as was common throughout the ancient world, the "act" of justice is virtually indistinguishable from the moral character of the agent, thus prompting some relatively recent translators of what has become Western civilization's founding text in political philosophy to render δικαιοσύνη merely as "morality."

---

6 Matth. 5:20.

Jennings is quite thorough in his recasting of Paul as a theoretician of a new "outlaw justice," as he dubs it. As exponents of this new kind of justice, Jennings insists, "we do not play by the rules of the older order" that is, as Paul says in *1 Corinthians* "passing away" (παράγει).⁷ The word παράγει also applies to what the ancients called the αἰών, the *saeculum*, the secular. Justice cannot be found in the secular. That is why Plato's theory of devolutionary cycles of the *polis* has to be taken seriously. The justice of the *saeculum* is always a work as a work of deconstruction, an ephemeral text of discursive positionings and re-positionings, which ultimately disintegrates. Only "in Christ," the justice of eschatological interpersonal relationality, the undeconstructible Christ *community* that is also a universalized "ecumenity," can justice be found. "More law, less justice," Cicero wrote. But the messiah is he who fulfills every kind of law and manifests justice in the fullness of time, and of all human relationships.

In the messianic moment the religious, the ethical, the judicial, and the temporal all converge. Derrida's own introduction of the political question—a question that becomes an all-consuming *political-theological* question in the latter third of his career—during a presentation he gave at a conference at Cornell University in 1989 entitled "Force of Law: The Mystical Foundations of Authority" frames the Pauline project once and for all in such a way.⁸ Messianic justice, which for Derrida does not necessarily require a messiah ("messianism without a messiah") is "undeconstructible," because its fulfillment is not teleological—that is, the ultimate apparition of some immanent aim, or the fructification of some tendency—but eschatological. The eschatological consummation of the historical *force of justice*, as we find it in Pauline thought, is also the unveiling of the meaning of what was "deconstructed" at certain previous moments in history, moments which can be considered "crisis" moments, in the sense that the "judging" (κρίνειν—human as well as divine) of how historical and broader human affairs are represented in our epistemologies and political philosophies now makes itself plain.

But this "final judgment" ultimately manifests itself as what Paul calls παρουσία, or Christ's "coming," a term he borrows from the official state visit of the emperor or some very high Roman official to a provincial municipality. The παρουσία is the climactic elucidation of what heretofore was a perplexing "secret" or "mystery" (μυστήριον), which for Paul encompasses both the first historical appearance of Christ in the world as Jesus of Nazareth, who bears the messianic secret, *and* the hidden messiah's imminent "coming" when everything

---

7 1 Cor. 7:31.
8 Derrida, "Force of Law," 190–228.

behind God's semiological screen will be eminently disclosed. Paul himself was given (by God) the meaning of this messianic secret on the road to Damascus. Such a "vision" (ὀπτασία) is always tied to a profounder "revelation" (ἀποκάλυψις) in Paul's mind.[9] The former grounds the apostle's own authority to expound in a manner today we would term "theological" on the latter, consisting in the exhaustive elaboration of the secret as an historical unfolding of the meaning of the original "crisis," which was Jesus' crucifixion and resurrection.

Yet the παρουσία, or eschatological expectation, also belongs fatefully to our proper understanding of the deeper "crisis," which goes beyond the inaugural event itself, a crisis that pervades the entire structure of signification controlling the contemporary *schema* of thought, including all cultural forms, social formations, political institutions, and patterns of interpretation. The so-called "last judgment" is the world-shaking crisis of this self-consciously, taken-for-granted order of signification. It is "messianic justice" as the universal, albeit *critical*, realization that the "rulership of God" (βασιλεία τοῦ θεοῦ) has been perverted into an *unjust* system of both cognitive and intersubjective relations, and that it must now be, and now is, upended or *inverted* in order to transform the present order where "thy kingdom come" is indistinguishable from "thy will be done." Eschatology must become ontology, and vice versa. God's creation is in Derridean language a work, or *oeuvre*, that is "undergoing deconstruction." It is in transit from initial to climactic *judgment,* enroute to its "critical" moment that at the same time constitutes a "world crisis."

In "Force of Law" Derrida points to this crisis as the dissymmetry of law and justice, which comes close to an edgier, more "political" reading of the Pauline dysfunctionality of the relationship between "law" (νόμος) and "gospel" (εὐαγγέλιον). In Paul, the disconnection derives from the manner in which such an εὐαγγέλιον, (one way of rendering the term as it was actually understood in the ancient world is some kind of "startling news flash" referencing an event, that is, the resurrection), changes radically our understanding of our current, and perhaps, future situation in the world as well as the larger order of meaning within which that understanding is embedded.

The "news" of September 11, 2001 consists in such a contemporary example. It calls into question the grand range of associations for the familiar term νόμος, which applies to both Jews and Gentiles alike. For Gentiles νόμος was the general "order of things," not only political but also cosmic, which the victories of Rome had putatively established once and for all. For the Jews, it lay in the "fence" surrounding the Torah, which Yahweh had revealed to his people as

---

[9] Cf. Eph. 3:2, 2 Cor. 12:1.

the very meaning of exceptional peoplehood, both their responsibility and their destiny. But, for Paul as the founder of the church as we know it, the resurrection event can only be coded as an εὐαγγέλιον that announces God's final victory over the false schemas, or versions of νόμος, for both Romanism and Pharasaic Judaism. It is true justice (δικαιοσύνη) that deconstructs once and for all the false implications of justice implicit in the various connotations of *nomos*.

Justice, for Derrida, is always an "excess" over law. Unlike νόμος, it is never "calculable," but incalculable.[10] Justice is a "performative" that has already been "enacted," yet at the same time it "remains to come, it remains by *coming*."[11] Justice is a singularity that, as Derrida, continues to "haunt" the present and to impinge from the future. It amounts to what he calls an "apparition of the inapparent." Its original indication consists in an event for which the ultimate significance is always "not yet" manifest. In that sense it brings the structures of contemporary experience and everyday understanding into constant crisis, putting them in Derridean language *sous rature*, "under erasure." It is both event and advent. It emerges out of the complex threadings and shadings of spatial and temporal experience, and is both recognizable and locatable as a certain significant happening, a "something that has happened" that is not yet at all clear in its great ramifications. It becomes the nodal point, the convergence, the concrescence of many hidden impulses and tendencies. It is literally a *tour de force*. From that perspective whatever situation it "came out of" it is still in the process of "becoming." What it is on its way to manifesting (*devenir*) is still incessantly, "to come" (*avenir*).

In his Derridean take on Paul, Jennings challenges what he terms "the traditional tendency to overemphasize the Christological concentration in Paul's argument." Paul's soteriology, especially as it comes to be instantiated in *Romans*, should not be read, as the Reformation account would have it, so much in terms of a "shared" righteousness (δικαιοσύνη) that should be construed in some quasi-sacramental fashion as the *unio mystica* of redeemed and redeemer—the moment Luther understood in his theology of Cross as "imputed righteousness" via "justification (δικαίωσις) by faith alone"—as with consideration of what Derrida himself reckons as a form of radical responsiveness and a sense of "infinite" responsibility, which the one who has undergone the total change of perspective (μετάνοια) accompanying the believer's appropriation of the true and deeper meaning of the justice-founding event.

---

10 Derrida, "Force of Law," 257.
11 Ibid., 256.

> The agent of promise and of salvation is God throughout. The object of faithfulness and of obedience throughout is God, not Christ—who is, rather the exemplar of obedience and faithfulness. What is at stake in the resurrection of the messiah is the focalizing on the messianic proclamation of God that, for Paul, has been present in the word spoken (by God) to Abraham and the word spoken to Israel through the prophets.[12]

The παρουσία of the "word spoken" and God's "crediting" of righteousness/-justice becomes apparent from a provisional standpoint as a virtue of the faithful one. "Abraham [responded in faith] to God, and it was credited to him as δικαιοσύνη."[13] We must remember that in the ancient world δικαιοσύνη routinely had its own dual conjugation, especially in the manner we find elaborated in Plato's *Republic*. In order to establish what the meaning of δικαιοσύνη is for the political community (πολιτεία), the interlocutors of the dialogue must first secure its definition with respect to how it functions in patterns of personal behavior, and vice-versa. The entire text of the *Republic* from the anxious discourse of the aged Cephalus about life after death at the opening of the work to the telling of myth of Er ponders the profound interchangeability of the two seemingly antithetical poles in the connotative range of the word "justice."

Paul would seem to take this dual conjugation for granted. However, in an age when the only πόλις standing is not the integral and well-ordered community Plato envisaged, but the Roman empire, the conjugation itself is now radically transmuted and thoroughly deconstructed. The Stoics as apologists for the idea of *Romanitas* had fantasized the new *polis* as a κοσμόπολις, as a world πολιτεία, in which Caesar's "genius" signified the meaning of the specific virtues of the empire's citizenry. But the brutality of Rome and the disintegration of all forms of integral community through the strategy of governing by exploitation and intimidation compelled a new way of conjugating Plato's notion of justice, which is exactly what Paul is doing when he talks about the βασιλεία τοῦ θεοῦ as "Christ's body," the empire to come. The empire to come has already been triumphally founded through the decisive victory that was Jesus' resurrection, his victory over death, the "last enemy." Throughout 1 and 2 Corinthians Paul constantly employs the language of Roman military triumph to characterize, if only "metaphorically," to characterize the ultimate *res gestae* that is the messiah's resurrection. Just as the Roman conqueror in bringing the "benefits" of imperial rule establishes δικαιοσύνη, so does Christ in not succumbing to crucifixion and death. Jesus' "heroic" resistance to the attempt at existential nihilation and humiliation, which execution on the cross represented as a sentence

---

12 Jennings, *Outlaw Justice*, 160.
13 Rom. 4:3, NIV.

imposed by Roman authorities on those who were presumed to have incorrigibly rejected the blessings of Roman rule and authority, implied in the minds of the earliest Christians that God through his suffering servant had triumphed over all the erstwhile "visible" and "invisible" would-be sovereigns of the *saeculum* itself, the "rulers of this age," including Caesar. This triumph constituted a radical inversion of everything associated with political sovereignty. In fact, it was the de-politicization of the political for the sake of the sovereign power, which is God, that grounds all politics itself.

Toward the end of his relatively late work *Rogues*, Derrida makes the tantalizing suggestion that the real distinction between "Athens and Jerusalem" as the fulcrum of any ongoing political theology rests on fundamental differences in how one comes to conjugate the Greek word λόγος itself. "Although the majestic sovereignty of the idea of the Good is not the law (νόμος)," he writes, "it would be easy … to link its necessity to the Platonic thought of the πόλις or the πολιτεία. One could argue … that all these great rationalisms are, in every sense of the term, rationalisms of the state."[14] In other words, the "sovereignty of reason" can be decoded as the transcendental signifier that embodies what the Romans revered as *auctoritas*, which by the time of empire required its own god-like substantiation in the personality of Caesar. Every sovereign authority has its own inaugural instance, its moment of enthronement, which Derrida in "Force of Law" ascribes to an original and violent event in which the victor vanquishes his recalcitrant foes, what Walter Benjamin—cited lavishly and approvingly by Derrida—termed the moment of "justice-founding violence" (*rechtsetzende Gewalt*).

It is a theme Derrida explores consistently in many of his early works, reaching back as far as his essay "Violence and Metaphysics," a meditation on Levinas and, in effect, the true meaning of ethics, the disjunction between the Platonic good as the supreme ordering of the life of man as ζῷον πολιτικόν, or "rational animal," and the infinite responsibility that surpasses all moral valuation when one encounters the face of the other.[15] The "violence" of metaphysics implies the violence of the political order itself, what Benjamin dubs "justice-preserving violence" (*rechterhaltende Gewalt*), the second of these two alternating variables in the continuum of the maintenance of sovereign power and its performances. But the "overcoming" of metaphysics in the founding event of divine justice, which is the dual spectrum of the crucifixion and resurrection, corresponds at the same time to a decisive upending of the very political order that of necessity must be established and maintained by violence. The violence is instead inflicted, per-

---

14 Derrida, *Rogues*, 139.
15 See Derrida, *Writing and Difference*, 164.

haps as an iteration of *rechterhaltende Gewalt,* upon the founder of the true kingdom himself, who "like a sheep led to the slaughter" takes the injustice of the existing order upon himself in order to crystallize the hitherto inchoate elements of a genuine, *universal justice.*

As the philosopher Badiou puts it so elegantly, "Paul's project is to show that a universal logic of salvation cannot be reconciled with any law, be it one that ties thought to the cosmos, or one that fixes the effect of an exceptional election."[16] Furthermore, this kind of "logic" is what Badiou dubs the "discourse of the Son," one which is embedded in the memory of something that constitutes a "pure singularity" (in Paul's case the thing that happened on the road to Damascus), grounding the very possibility of a universal enunciation of truth in a unique subjective confluence of subjective factors, generating a set of what will eventually become "theological" propositions, which paradoxically only the one who experienced the event can proclaim. There is no room for any kind of mediation in this "logic," which binds irrevocably the singular to the universal, as Kierkegaard insisted in his treatment of Abraham obeying the command to sacrifice Isaac.

But this distinctive and incomparable linkage of subject to a force that seizes it and propels it beyond the possibility of mediation (when, as described in *Fear and Trembling,* the singular appears as "higher" than the universal itself), the force that *compels* faithfulness, cannot necessarily be called "religious," as it was for Kierkegaard, in any sense of the word. On the contrary, it is the dramatic disruption of the mediated structure of discursive signs in the strictly singular event, which for Paul is ultimately not his own strange, interior confrontation with the risen Jesus but his understanding of the resurrection itself, that unveils, "apocalyptically," the political meaning of what has, and will for all time, transpire. "Christ is *a coming* [*une venue*]; he is what interrupts the previous regime of discourses. Christ is, in himself and for himself, *what happens to us.*"[17] Moreover, "through the event we enter into filial equality. For Paul, one is either a slave or a son."[18] The "universal truth" that the resurrection portends is a vast new egalitarian *politeia* in which the *rechterhaltende Gewalt* of the universal state has been pre-empted and rendered pointless once and for all. "For Paul, the event...is pure beginning."[19] It inaugurates what might be termed the new "empire of love" in which politics demands an infinite regard for the other.

---

16 Badiou, *Saint Paul,* 42.
17 Ibid., 48.
18 Ibid., 49.
19 Ibid.

In *Rogues* Derrida construes this new form of universal justice as "unconditional hospitality," which he also associates with divine amnesty, with the greatest gift of God, that is, forgiveness. "The incalculable unconditionality of hospitality, of the gift or of forgiveness, exceeds the calculation of conditions, just as justice exceeds law, the juridical, and the political. Justice can never be reduced to ... calculative reason."[20] There is neither retribution nor *distribution* in the free gift derived from the act of forgiveness, which renders "incalculable" justice eschatological justice, the justice Derrida in *Specters of Marx* terms "impossible" and "undeconstructible."

Paul can be considered a "political theologian" because he interprets soteriology as inseparable from a kind of social and moral anthropology, as intimately bound up with a "new being" that is neither transcendental nor psychological, but relational and communal. "Salvation" turns on the free gift inscribed in God's decision to intervene and humble himself during the very time—the "reign of Caesar Augustus"—which Rome's admirers understood as the empire's triumphal moment, as the political fulfillment of humanity's age-old longing for peace and justice, when δικαιοσύνη became truly the "immanent frame," as Charles Taylor would put it, the secular *schema* of the world as a whole.[21]

The "founding" of the new global order of justice is the resurrection itself, which aside from its plausibility as an empirical datum of history, or its subjective value as a "spiritual" reference point for the conduct of each believer's own private life, has world-shaking political ramifications. For Derrida, who as a profoundly Jewish thinker does not treat the resurrection per se, this meaning can be implied within his own immanent frame of the messianic. It is the "deep specter" that haunts every expectation of a "democracy to come"; it permeates even the frame which Derrida names in *Specters of Marx as* the "new Internationale," the recurrent "visible in the invisible" of the relentless historical movement to gift humankind the experience of infinite hospitality.[22] For Badiou, speaking as a purely secular Maoist ex-Catholic, the resurrection on the other hand is the evident controlling factor because it overshadows everything, especially the collective political impulse toward what he terms "the becoming of a truth." Badiou says in *Logic of Worlds:* "Resurrection is itself ... singularized by its truth-content. Resurrection brings to light the egalitarian invariants of every sequence."[23]

---

20 Derrida, *Rogues*, 149.
21 See Taylor, *A Secular Age*.
22 See Derrida, *Specters of Marx*.
23 Badiou, *Saint Paul*, 76.

It is a hefty trek from the simple sort of hermeneutical revisionism we find in the "New Perspectives on Paul" cohorts to the Marxist and radically democratic *revolutionism* we must contend with in Badiou and to a somewhat lesser extent in Derrida and his fellow post-structuralists. But both trends underscore the longer-term importance of, and instances of fascination with, Paul as we leave behind seventeenth century European Christendom and cross over into the shifting and indeterminate frontiers of a global *ecumene*, where we discover unmistakable signs not only of divine kingdom, but also of "empire". What would such an "empire," which in Paul's language employs so many of the familiar tropes of Roman imperial sovereignty but then does headstands with them by assigning them to the persona of a tortured and humiliated political criminal, look like? The question is ultimately unanswerable because its radical "political" content like the specific, religio-historically colored, messianic vision out of which it emerges and fatefully explodes remains indeterminable within the circuit of signifiers that normally make intelligible what is available for a given age. The political image writ large—what Claude Lefort has termed *la politique* as opposed to *le politique*, the plural form of the French word meaning "politics" as usual—can no longer be boiled down to such familiar binary constructs as "kingship" versus "democracy," autocracy versus autonomy, the body politic versus the "king's body," and so forth.[24] The New Testament trope of the "kingdom of God" becomes at once both an immanent and transcendental juxtaposition of all seemingly dialectical opposites within a singularity of generative power—Badiou's "eventfulness"—that enunciates simultaneously the content of the spiritual, religious, ethical, and political altogether. Hence there is far more to Paul's notorious "Christ mysticism" than meets the eye.

> So in Christ Jesus you are all children of God through faith, for all of you who were baptized into Christ have clothed yourselves with Christ. There is neither Jew nor Gentile, neither slave nor free, nor is there male and female, for you are all one in Christ Jesus. If you belong to Christ, then you are Abraham's seed, and heirs according to the promise. (Gal. 3:28)

The "oneness" of Christ Jesus is far less like the Pythagorean, and much more like Badiou's One that inhabits dynamically and temporally the play of material forces as well as the infinite ensemble of putatively disconnected subjective human interventions that constitute what we call "history." It is all about a strange—again, "eventful"—potentiality that is far afield of Aristotle's δύναμις.

---

24 See Lefort, "The Permanence of the Theo-Political?"

It is the παντοκράτωρ of that even more strange empire we can call the GloboChrist.[25]

References

Badiou, Alain. *Saint Paul: The Foundation of Universalism*. Translated by Ray Brassier. Stanford, CA: Stanford University Press, 2003.
Brondos, David. *Paul on the Cross: Reconstructing the Apostle's Story of Redemption*. Minneapolis, MN: Fortress Press, 2006.
Derrida, Jacques. *Writing and Difference*. Translated by Alan Bass. Chicago: University of Chicago Press, 1978.
Derrida, Jacques. *Specters of Marx: The State of the Debt, the Work of Mourning, and the New Internationale*. Translated by Peggy Kamuf. New York: Routledge, 1994.
Derrida, Jacques. "Force of Law: The 'Mystical Foundation of Authority.'" In *Jacques Derrida: Acts of Religion*, edited by Gil Andijar, 190–228. New York: Routledge, 2002.
Derrida, Jacques. *Rogues: Two Essays on Reason*. Translated by Pascale Anne Brault and Michael Naas. Stanford, CA: Stanford University Press, 2005.
Jennings, Theodore. *Outlaw Justice: The Messianic Politics of Paul*. Stanford, CA: Stanford University Press, 2013.
Lefort, Claude. "The Permanence of the Theo-Political?" In *Political Theologies: Public Religions in a Post-Secular World*, edited by Hent de Vries and Lawrence Sullivan, 148–87. New York: Fordham University Press, 2006.
Raschke, Carl. *GloboChrist: The Great Commission Takes a Postmodern Turn*. Grand Rapids, MI: Baker Academic, 2008.
Sanders, E.P. *Paul, the Law, and the Jewish People*. Minneapolis, MN: Fortress Press, 1983.
Sanders, E.P. *Jesus and Judaism*. Minneapolis, MN: Fortress Press, 1985.
Taylor, Charles. *A Secular Age*. Cambridge, MA: Harvard University Press, 2009.

---

25 See Raschke, *GloboChrist*.

Holger Zaborowski
Church, Commonwealth, and Toleration: John Locke as a Reader of Paul

Abstract: Paul is not only a source of inspiration for the left-wing, post-modern accounts of politics and political theology, as can be found in thinkers as diverse as Agamben, Badiou, Taubes, and Žižek, but also an important source of inspiration for modernity, in particular for modern political liberalism with John Locke as one of its fathers. This essay explores this by interpreting Locke and more specifically his *Letter Concerning Toleration*. It is shown that biblical passages often illustrate the context of Locke's argumentation and that Locke aims to do justice to biblical teachings from a philosophical point of view. Locke's account of the difference between Church and commonwealth, in particular, may be understood in light of the Pauline heritage. Locke's definition of the church and of the commonwealth, as defined in the *Letter Concerning Toleration*, shows striking parallels to the views of Paul as Locke understands them. As with other authors, one can, of course, suggest that he reads his own political philosophy into Paul's letters, and more specifically *Romans*. However, this essay argues that Locke was in fact truly inspired by Paul. The author concludes his essay with a question concerning the necessity of a political theology for liberalism today.

1 Ancient, Modern, Postmodern? Paul and Philosophy

Recent years have seen an increasing interest in Paul from the side of philosophers who call themselves or are, more or less properly, called "post-modern." These thinkers are critical of many of the key assumptions of modernity and read Paul as a subversive and radical thinker of difference *avant la lettre*. Paul, so they emphasize, introduced the difference that being a Christian makes, spoke of a radical transformation of the self, and discovered a new, kairological concept of time and an eschatological and event-focused idea of history. There is no doubt that this reading of Paul by scholars such as Taubes, Badiou, Žižek, Agamben and others, has been inspired by Karl Barth's famous commentary on Paul's *Romans*, one of the founding documents of twentieth-century dialectical theology, and by Heidegger's phenomenology, in some cases particularly by his phenomenological lecture course about Paul letters and the phenomenology of religious life.¹ Behind these two thinkers, equally critical of modernity, stands Kierkegaard, another both Pauline and anti-modern thinker, as well as Nietzsche who was as fervently anti-Pauline as he was himself, in the very rigor and radicality of his writings, a true follower of Paul. Given their intellectual background, these post-modern writers use Paul to criticize and to bypass modernity. The apostle of the gentiles appears in their accounts not only pre-, but almost decidedly anti-modern—the anti-dote to modernity and its intrinsic failures, suggesting an utterly un-modern and, therefore, untimely understanding of God, humanity, and world and thus a useful tool to enter a new, truly post-modern age.

Another approach to Paul from the side of philosophers and historians of ideas situates his writings in the context of Hellenistic philosophy. Paul, then, belongs to the wider movement of ancient philosophy (which does, of course, not contradict the idea that he can only properly be understood in the context of Jewish theology). Once again, there is the idea of a stark contrast between Paul's thought, understood as embedded in the world of ancient philosophy, and modernity many principles of which contradict fundamental presuppositions of ancient philosophy and, therefore, also of Pauline thought.

Yet, Paul's relation to modernity or, to be more precise, modernity's relation to him seems to be more complex than these two readings of the apostle and his letters suggest. Paul is not simply the non- or even anti-modern thinker. There is a more positive relation of his thought to modernity that tends to be overlooked and forgotten. Nietzsche, who accused Paul of betraying Christ and of inventing Christianity, was well aware of the positive relation between Pauline thought and modernity. In *The Antichrist*, Nietzsche writes of Paul the following—and with no doubt implicitly alludes to Kant's moral philosophy and his postulate of the immortality of the soul:

> With the rabbinical impudence that characterizes everything about him, Paul put his interpretation, the *perversion* of an interpretation into a logical form: "*if* Christ did not rise from the dead, then our faith is in vain."—And in one fell swoop, the evangel becomes the most contemptible of all unfulfillable promises, the *outrageous* doctrine of personal immortality ... Paul himself still taught it as a *reward!* ...²

---

1 Taubes, *The Political Theology of Paul*; Badiou, *Saint Paul*; Žižek, *The Puppet and the Dwarf*; Žižek and Milbank, *The Monstrosity of Christ*; Agamben, *The Time That Remains*; Barth, *The Epistle to the Romans*; Heidegger, *The Phenomenology of Religious Life*. For general discussions of philosophical readings of Paul see particularly Frick, *Paul in the Grip of the Philosophers*; Blanton and de Vries, *Paul and the Philosophers*; Strecker and Valentin, *Paulus unter den Philosophen*; Caputo and Martín Alcoff, *St. Paul among the Philosophers*.
2 Nietzsche, *The Anti-Christ*, 38 [§ 41].

Nietzsche knew well the significance of the Lutheran reformation, and thus of the Pauline tradition, for the development of modern philosophy. From a Nietzschean perspective, one can read particularly modern German philosophy as a series of comments on, and interpretations of Paul. This reading, as I would like to maintain, is by no means an outrageous statement. Quite the contrary is the case. Nietzsche, it is plausible to argue, is right in drawing attention to the Pauline features of modernity. For there is no way of understanding modernity without taking the influence of Paul into account. More often than not, it is an implicit or even hidden influence, open only to archeological explorations. Many thinkers may not even have been aware of the fact that Paul looked over their shoulders while they explored new paths of thought. In other cases, historians of ideas have not been sufficiently sensitive to discover the Pauline dimension of modern thought. There is, therefore, not only Paul, the ancient, or Paul, the post-modern, but also Paul, the modern (and, for this reason, one could also speak of a Pauline modernity or, at least, Pauline dimensions of modernity).

Particularly modern liberal political philosophy, I would to argue, has been influenced by Paul or Pauline ideas. And Paul, all important differences notwithstanding, can also be read as a proto-liberal thinker of sorts, particularly if one takes the separation of politics and religion, of the worldly and the spiritual, as well as the autonomy of what is called the secular as key elements of liberal doctrine. This is undoubtedly a controversial claim for political liberalism that is, particularly in its contemporary shape, more often than not intrinsically linked to an emancipation from religion in general and from Christianity in particular. In the following, a close reading of Locke's political thought and its development and implications will explain and justify this claim.

2 John Locke, a Pauline Thinker?

It is well known that Locke, commonly held to be the founding father of political liberalism, took a deep interest in Christianity, too, and examined its "reasonableness" from a philosophical standpoint. In his mature political and epistemological works, Locke, at least so he claimed, proceeded as a philosopher, using reason alone, and did not argue theologically if by this one means any kind of indispensable reference to Christianity in general or to biblical texts or the Christian theological or ecclesial tradition in particular. This is why in these texts he neither cited the Old nor the New Testament nor any other authoritative theological source for justificatory purposes strictly speaking. There are, furthermore, only a few references to these sources in his writings. Locke, however, argued theologically if by this one refers to an essential foundation of Locke's thought, that is, the existence of God as a truth of natural reason. For example, God is according to Locke's account not only the reason why human beings can be considered equal, but also the source of any kind of government of human beings over other human beings. At the beginning of the *Second Treatise*, he argues, "that therefore God hath certainly appointed government to restrain the partiality and violence of men."[3] Not only at the beginning of the *Second Treatise*, Locke makes several references to God. He also famously denied toleration to atheists in his *Letter Concerning Toleration* because, as he argued, "[p]romises, covenants, and oaths, which are the bonds of human society, can have no hold upon an atheist. The taking away of God, thought but even in thought, dissolves all."[4] Belief in God seemed to him absolutely fundamental for the existence of human society.

However, as recent research into the foundations and implications of Locke's philosophy has shown, his relation to Christianity is considerably more complex than this first account suggests. Locke was so well versed in the Bible that biblical texts, not forgetting Paul's letters, stand in the background of many of his ideas. At least their genesis, so it seems, cannot properly be understood without taking the Bible, too, into account.[5] Jeremy Waldron has rightly spoken if the "Christian Foundations of John Locke's Political thought," as runs the subtitle of his important book *God, Locke, and Equality*. There is, therefore, and more specifically, also a Pauline foundation of Locke's thought. It is this very foundation that I would like to examine in this essay by focusing in particular on the *Letter Concerning Toleration*.

---

3 Locke, *The Second Treatise*, 105. In the third chapter, Locke argues that "Where there is no judge on earth, the appeal lies to God in heaven" (ibid., 109).
4 Locke, *A Letter Concerning Toleration*, 246.
5 For the significance of Paul for Locke's political thought see also Dunn, *The Political Thought of John Locke*, 99–100 ("Jesus Christ [and Saint Paul] may not appear in person in the text of the Two Treatises but their presence can hardly be missed when we come upon the normative creaturely equality of all men in virtue of their shared species membership. ... Far from being extrinsic, the theology was the sole possible significant locus for equality. Here indeed it was true that the medium was the message."); Waldron, *God, Locke, and Equality*, 12–13, 188, 215 (here, Waldron emphasizes the background role of Jesus and Paul for Locke's Two Treatises of Government). Locke, to be sure, was also aware of the limits of relating to Paul, as rightly stressed by Waldron: "We have no monopoly on the sensitivity of meaning to context. Locke and his contemporaries were not much less sophisticated, hermeneutically, than we are. They knew there were issues of anachronism and incommensurability in relating their political thinking to that of Paul, for example, or Aristotle" (ibid., 9). For Locke's reading of Scripture see also Wainwright, introduction, 2ff.

Before I turn to this important text in the history of political ideas, I would like to draw brief attention to Locke's early *First* and *Second Tracts on Government* (1660 and c. 1662), written after the restoration of the monarchy in 1660. These two texts are often overlooked in discussions of his thought, not only because they were not published until the 1960s, but also because Locke later criticized and abandoned the views that he held in them.⁶ In the *Two Tracts*, Locke shows himself as a moderate restoration thinker and determines his own position in the preface as standing between authority and liberty. He confesses both that "there is no one [that] can have a greater respect and veneration for authority than I," and that "I have no less of liberty without which a man shall find himself less happy than a beast."⁷ In the following, he joins an ongoing debate, concerning particularly the rights of Puritans and their views of a "purer" kind of worship and belief, and focuses on the question as to what extent the legislative political power of the civil magistrate extends to religious rituals or beliefs for which there were no divine regulations and that were, therefore, considered not necessary for salvation and "indifferent." His answer to this question is that, even though he considers freedom in religious practices important, civil authority can nonetheless impose rules with respect to "indifferent things" for the sake of preserving order and tradition in society.⁸ This is why Locke presupposes at least the citizens' passive obedience with respect to the magistrate's decisions regarding indifferent things. Therefore, he does not yet propose the wider concept of religious liberty that he defends in the *Letter Concerning Toleration*. According to this early view, the individual's religious liberty is much more limited than he will later allow for.

What is striking in this context, however, is the extent to which Locke refers to Christ himself, to the Bible, and to Paul's letters in the *Two Tracts*. This is with no doubt an important difference to his later work. The reason for this difference presumable lies in the both political and ecclesiological character and in the historical context of these texts. Locke certainly finds making references both to reason and to Scripture as a widely-accepted authority helpful and necessary. In de-

---

6 See Locke, *Scritti editi e inediti sulla tolleranza*; Locke, *Two Tracts on Government*.
7 Locke, *First Tract on Government*, 7.
8 Cf. "I have not therefore the same apprehensions of liberty that I find some have or can think the benefits of it to consist in a liberty for men at pleasure to adopt themselves children of God, and from thence assume a title to inheritance here and proclaim themselves heirs of the world; not a liberty for ambition to pull down well-framed institutions, that out of its ruins they may build themselves fortunes; not a liberty to be Christians so as not to be subjects; not such a liberty as is like to engage us in perpetual dissension and disorder" (ibid., 8).

fense of his view he provides the following definition of the "two senses only" of Christian liberty:

> One is that Christ frees his subjects from the dominion and slavery of the devil. The other is that he removed from the necks of the Jews that grim yoke of the ceremonial law which, as the Apostle Peter observes [Acts 15], neither they nor their fathers could support ... .[9]

Based on biblical teaching, as he reads it, he proposes a decidedly non-political interpretation of Christian liberty.

In the context of these remarks about Christian liberty, properly understood, Locke also discusses the relation between Christianity and politics in a manner that, indeed, anticipates his later thought. But unlike in his later works, he now explicitly justifies the separation between politics and Christianity with respect to biblical teaching. The "New Testament," as he points out,

> nowhere makes any mention of the controlling or limiting of the magistrate's authority since no precept appointed for the civil magistrate appears either in the Gospel or in the Epistels. In truth it is for the most part silent as to government and civil power, or rather Christ himself ... seems to refuse deliberately to involve himself in civil affairs and, not owning any kingdom but the divine spiritual one as his own, he let the civil government of the commonwealth go by unchanged.[10]

Locke does not only refer to Christ, the spiritual nature of his kingdom, and his refraining from any kind of political statements, but also to Paul as a genuine interpreter of it. "And the Apostle Paul, the teacher of the Gentiles," Locke continues,

> confirms the point, 1 Cor., ch. 7, where he teaches that the civil condition of men is not to be altered at all by Christian religion and liberty, but that bondservants, even though they were made subject to Christ, should still continue bondservants in their civil state and owe the same obedience as before to their masters. Nor is the argument at all different in the case of the prince and his subjects, since there appears not the faintest trace in holy Scripture of any commandment by which the power of the magistrate is diminished in any indifferent matters.[11]

Locke's reading of Scripture, it is clear, allows him sharply to separate between the worldly and the spiritual realm. This separation will become a key feature of his later political philosophy while he will no longer hold the view that the citi-

---

9 Locke, *Second Tract on Government*, 72.
10 Ibid.
11 Ibid.

zen's freedom of religious practice and belief can be limited with respect to "indifferent things."

In implicitly criticizing and abandoning his own previous view of the limitation of religious freedom in the *Letter Concerning Toleration*, Locke contributed significantly to the modern history both of the concept and of the practice of toleration. From a contemporary perspective, Locke's mature concept of toleration is with no doubt limited, too. For sure, he does not propose an absolute distinction between religion and politics. For example, he famously denied toleration to Catholics, Muslims, and, as has already been mentioned, atheists because the belief in the existence of God was not considered indifferent. For him, religious freedom—that is, both the freedom to believe and the freedom not to believe—is not yet a fundamental right of the individual human person. However, in comparison to earlier political philosophers such as Hobbes and to his own earlier ideas, Locke's *Letter Concerning Toleration* was indeed a great step forward in the history of understanding religious freedom.[12] While Hobbes attempted to solve the problems of religious conflict and civil war through unifying the political and the religious in the hand of one almost omnipotent sovereign, the Leviathan, a mortal God, Locke (whose early thought clearly exhibits Hobbesian elements) pursued a very different path and provided the outline of what Thomas Jefferson later called the "wall of separation of church and state."[13]

What is striking, to begin with, is the fact that already at the beginning of the letter, Locke refers to Paul's letters twice, namely to 2 Tim. 2:19 (which was then still considered to have been written by Paul) and to Gal. 5:21 (he also refers to Luke 22:25, 26, 32[14]). There is, therefore, a net of biblical references that seems to underline the compatibility of Locke's philosophical thought with scriptural teaching. Even though the biblical passages do not justify his arguments strictly speaking and play a rather illustrative role in the context of his argumentation, Locke does not merely pay lip service to the New Testament, but tries to do justice to its teaching from a philosophical position. According to his interpretation of Scripture, Christianity or, to be more precise, Christ does not allow persecution for reasons of doctrinal difference so that toleration of differences among Christians is necessary.

In his *Letter*, Locke provides the following definition of a church as the foundation for his reasoning:

---

[12] See not only Locke, *Two Tracts on Government*, but also Locke, *An Essay Concerning Toleration*.
[13] Hobbes, *Leviathan*. Thomas Jefferson used this formulation in 1802 in a letter to the Danbury Baptists, see Jefferson, *Political Writings*, 396–97.
[14] Locke, *A Letter Concerning Toleration*, 215, 217.

> Let us now consider what a church is. A church, then, I take to be a voluntary society of men, joining themselves together of their own accord in order to the public worshipping of God, in such a manner as they judge acceptable to Him, and effectual to the salvation of their souls.[15]

As Locke argues, freedom is, first of all, the presupposition for being a member of a (not *the*) church. This religious society has one fundamental purpose. This is the public worship of God. The end of this and, therefore, of a church lies in the salvation of one's soul. It does not concern political affairs. It does not fall under the responsibility of a church, so Locke thinks, to get involved with politics (even though belonging to a church has an important impact on politics). In his definition, Locke also emphasizes that the kind of worship that a church prefers depends on the judgment of its members, not on the decision of the magistrate and that it does not need to be private, but ought to be public.

The "voluntary society" of a church is, therefore, sharply to be distinguished from what Locke calls "commonwealth." It is defined as follows:

> The commonwealth seems to me to be a society of men constituted only for the procuring, preserving, and advancing their own civil interests. Civil interests I call life, liberty, health, and indolency of body; and the possession of outward things, such as money, lands, houses, furniture, and the like.[16]

That is to say that the commonwealth is not voluntary and concerns the "civil" life, or "interests," of its citizens. It thus has a completely different end than a church. On the basis of the essential differences between a church and the commonwealth, Locke substantially limits the power of the magistrate over the worship of the citizens of the state (and thus abandons the much stricter position of the *Two Tracts*).

In order to explain his views, he refers to God's commandments and to the nature of religious faith as a performance of freedom so that force from outside is, by definition, futile. He reasons not only that "the case of souls is not committed to the civil magistrate [...] by God,"[17] but also that

> the care of souls cannot belong to the civil magistrate, because his power consists only in outward force: but true and saving religion consists in the inward persuasion of the mind, without which nothing can be acceptable to God. And such is the nature of the understanding, that it cannot be compelled to the belief of anything by outward force. Confiscation of

---

15 Ibid., 220.
16 Ibid., 218.
17 Ibid., 218–19.

estate, imprisonment, torments, nothing of that nature can have any such efficacy as to make men change the inward judgment that they have framed of things.[18]

While a church ought to limit itself to spiritual affairs that are dependent upon one's freedom, and also needs to refrain from interfering in the worldly realm, the commonwealth must merely focus on necessary "civil interests" and should not to take responsibility for the salvation of its citizens.

As far as Locke's definitions of a church and of the commonwealth in the *Letter* is concerned, he does not refer to Scripture. He seems to imply that this definition can be understood on merely philosophical grounds. However, many other religions, to be sure, can propose a distinctly different understanding of the relation between a religious community and political society. Philosophically, too, a very different understanding of the relation between a church and the commonwealth could be possible, as Thomas Hobbes and the young Locke himself, among many others, have shown. There can be, as I would like to argue, no doubt that in the background of his definitions, so crucial for the history of liberal political thought and the development of the idea of religious freedom, stands Christianity. For Locke's reasoning in the *Letter* is deeply informed by Scripture. Particularly Rom. 13 where Paul argues that all political power comes from God, too, and that, therefore, the followers of Christ need to be obedient to political authorities, may well have played an important role for Locke.[19] While some interpreters such as Robert Filmer (against whose *Patri-*

---

18 Ibid., 219.
19 Rom. 13 reads as follows (in the King James version that Locke was familiar with): "1 Let every soul be subject unto the higher powers. For there is no power but of God: the powers that be are ordained of God. / 2 Whosoever therefore resisteth the power, resisteth the ordinance of God: and they that resist shall receive to themselves damnation. / 3 For rulers are not a terror to good works, but to the evil. Wilt thou then not be afraid of the power? do that which is good, and thou shalt have praise of the same: / 4 For he is the minister of God to thee for good. But if thou do that which is evil, be afraid; for he beareth not the sword in vain: for he is the minister of God, a revenger to execute wrath upon him that doeth evil. / 5 Wherefore ye must needs be subject, not only for wrath, but also for conscience sake. / 6 For for this cause pay ye tribute also: for they are God's ministers, attending continually upon this very thing. / 7 Render therefore to all their dues: tribute to whom tribute is due; custom to whom custom; fear to whom fear; honour to whom honour. / 8 Owe no man any thing, but to love one another: for he that loveth another hath fulfilled the law. / 9 For this, Thou shalt not commit adultery, Thou shalt not kill, Thou shalt not steal, Thou shalt not bear false witness, Thou shalt not covet; and if there be any other commandment, it is briefly comprehended in this saying, namely, Thou shalt love thy neighbour as thyself. / 10 Love worketh no ill to his neighbour: therefore love is the fulfilling of the law. / 11 And that, knowing the time, that now it is high time to awake out of sleep: for now is our salvation nearer than when we believed. / 12 The night is far spent, the day is at hand: let us

archa Locke wrote the *First Treatise*) have used this text as an argument in favor of the divine right of kings and against the very possibility of disobeying against political authorities, Locke proposes a different reading. For he interprets it in such a way that, while he still holds that "higher powers" come from God, one ought to distinguish firmly between the worldly and the heavenly kingdom (that is, acknowledge the secular character of the political and its autonomy) and also allow for civil disobedience in certain circumstances (that is, disobedience is allowed if the authority does not act lawfully).[20]

Locke's paraphrase and his notes of this passage neatly show how close he regards Paul to his own views as expressed in the *Letter*. According to Locke, Rom. 13:1–7 "contains the duty of Christians to the civil magistrate."[21] He particularly emphasizes

> that by being made Christians and subjects of Christs kingdom they were not by the freedom of the gospel exempt from any ties of duty or subjection which by the laws of their country they were in and ought to observe, to the government and magistrates of it though heathens, any more than any of their heathen subjects.[22]

Thus, belonging to the kingdom of Christ does not have immediate political implications. For Locke, as an avid reader of the New Testament, this kingdom is not of this world and Christianity, therefore, not a political religion. This is why Paul, as Locke reads him, refrains from commenting on political issues from a decidedly Christian position and only refers generally, or rather philosophically, to the divine origin of the "higher powers." For "how men come by a rightfull title to this power; or who has that title, he is wholy silent, and says noe thing if it."[23] In being silent about these issues and in not fusing the heavenly kingdom of Christ with any kind of worldly kingdom and vice versa, Paul, as Locke holds, follows the Gospel and Christ himself:

---

therefore cast off the works of darkness, and let us put on the armour of light. / 13 Let us walk honestly, as in the day; not in rioting and drunkenness, not in chambering and wantonness, not in strife and envying. / 14 But put ye on the Lord Jesus Christ, and make not provision for the flesh, to fulfil the lusts thereof."
20 For this see also Wainwright, introduction, 51.
21 Locke, *A Paraphrase and Notes on the Epistles of Paul*, 2:586.
22 Ibid.
23 Ibid., 2:587.

To have medled with that would have been to decide of civil rights, contrary to the designe and business of the gospel, and the example of our Saviour, who refused medling in such cases with this decisive question. Who made me a Judg or Divider over you? Luk. XII.14.[24]

The following note on Rom. 13:1–7 further explains Locke's view of the non-political and merely spiritual character of Christianity:

Whither we take *powers* here in the abstract for political authority, or in the concrete for persons de facto exerciseing political power and jurisdiction, the sense will be the same (viz) that Christians by virtue of being Christians are not any way exempt from obedience to the civil magistrats, not ought by any means to resist them, though by what is said ver. 3 it seems that St Paul meant here magistrates haveing and exerciseing a lawfull power. But whither the magistrates in being were or were not such, and consequently were or were not to be obeyed, that Christianity gave them no peculiar power to examine. They had the common right of others their fellow citizens, but had not distinct priviledg as Christians. And therefore we see ver. 7 where he enjoyns the paying of tribute and custome etc It is in these words. *Render to all their dues. Tribute to whom tribute is due; honour to whom honour* etc but who it was to whom any of these or any other dues of right belongd he decides not, for that he leaves them to be determined by the laws and constitution of their country.[25]

It is clear that Locke's definition of the church and of the commonwealth, as defined in the *Letter*, shows striking parallels to the view of Paul as explained by Locke. There can be, therefore, no doubt about a distinctly Pauline dimension of Locke's political thought. One could argue, of course, that he reads his own political philosophy into Paul's *Romans*. If that is the case, it still remains important that he *could* read his position into Romans and thus find support in Paul. It seems more plausible, however, that he was truly inspired by Paul. There is not only an Augustinian tradition of reading Paul that emphasized the genuinely non-political character of Christianity and among which Locke's *Letter* can be counted. His early *Two Tracts* clearly proof the informative impact of Paul himself on Locke. Furthermore, his later paraphrases and notes on Paul show that Locke considered revelation superior to reason.[26] It is for this very reason that when composing the *Letter Concerning Toleration*, he could presumably find not only an interesting parallel, but a crucial confirmation and a theological foundation of his political philosophy in Paul's letters.

---

24 Ibid.
25 Ibid., 2:588.
26 Wainwright, introduction, 31–32.

3 On the Pauline Foundations of Modern Liberalism

Political liberalism, one can argue, does not only have an impact on religion and politics in general and on Christianity in particular. Its very origin, the philosophy of Locke, is also deeply influenced by a Christian understanding of the relation, and, indeed, difference between worldly "higher powers" and the heavenly kingdom. If Paul's thought has been so important for the development of modern liberal political philosophy and, therefore, of modern liberal politics, two important questions remain that cannot easily be answered. I will only briefly mention them—as requiring further examination.

It could be the case, first of all, that Christianity did not only play a historically contingent role in the development of modern political liberalism, but also a constitutive role in envisioning the secular state and its autonomy as essentially different from a church and, consequently, from a concrete religion. Because Locke left questions of salvation to the churches, he could limit the commonwealth to the task of preserving the freedom of its citizens. He thus opened up the space of modern secular politics. The political, roughly speaking, guarantees freedom and is no longer in charge of the citizen's salvation or even of his or her happiness. However, if Christianity stands no longer in the background of political liberalism (as politics' other, as it were), the liberal state could be in danger of extending its own role in that it considers itself responsible for securing happiness or, even, for salvation and thus for more than simply, but importantly preserving the freedom of its citizens. Could the liberal state thus turn illiberal, that is, into an ideology of freedom? This danger has been addressed by liberal and left-wing critics of liberalism such as Jürgen Habermas or Jean-Claude Michéa.[27]

The second question does not concern Christianity in particular, but the philosophical theology that Locke presupposes. Contemporary theorists do not follow Locke in presupposing the existence of God in the context of political philosophy. There are, of course, very good reasons in not following him in his critique of atheism and atheists and in developing an understanding of freedom of religion, that comprises both positive and negative freedom of religion, that is, the freedom to believe and to practice a religion—and not to do so. But it remains an open question whether political thought does not, in the end, need some kind of philosophical theology, some framework within which its key concepts and practices can be understood and justified. It is an open question whether or

---

27 Cf. particularly Habermas, *The Future of Human Nature*. Cf. Michéa, *The Realm of Lesser Evil*.

not this can still be the minimal philosophical theology that Locke could still presuppose. Maybe something very different is necessary such as Derrida's thinking about the "mystical sources of authority"[28] or his messianic approach to history and, therefore, politics.

References

Agamben, Giorgio. *The Time That Remains: A Commentary on the Letter to the Romans*. Translated by Patricia Dailey. Stanford, CA: Stanford University Press, 2005.
Badiou, Alain. *Saint Paul: The Foundation of Universalism*. Translated by Ray Brassier. Stanford, CA: Stanford University Press, 2003.
Barth, Karl. *The Epistle to the Romans*. Translated by Edwyn C. Hoskyns, from the sixth edition. London: Oxford University Press, 1968.
Blanton, Ward, and Hent de Vries, eds. *Paul and the Philosophers*. New York: Fordham University Press, 2013.
Caputo, John D., and Linda Martín Alcoff, eds. *St. Paul among the Philosophers*. Bloomington, IN: Indiana University Press, 2009.
Derrida, Jacques. "Force of Law: 'The Mystical Foundation of Authority.'" In *Deconstruction and the Possibility of Justice*, edited by Drucilla Cornell, Michael Rosenfeld, and David Gray Carlson, 3–67. New York: Routledge, 1992.
Dunn, John. *The Political Thought of John Locke: An Historical Account of the Argument of the "Two Treatises of Government."* Cambridge: Cambridge University Press, 1969.
Frick, Peter, ed. *Paul in the Grip of the Philosophers: The Apostle and Contemporary Continental Philosophy*. Minneapolis, MN: Fortress Press, 2013.
Habermas, Jürgen. *The Future of Human Nature*. Translated by Hella Beister and William Rehg. Cambridge: Polity, 2003.
Heidegger, Martin. *The Phenomenology of Religious Life*. Translated by Matthias Fritsch and Jennifer Anna Gosetti-Ferencei. Bloomington, IN: Indiana University Press, 2004.
Hobbes, Thomas. *Leviathan*. Edited by Richard Tucker. Cambridge: Cambridge University Press, 1996.
Jefferson, Thomas. *Political Writings*. Edited by Joyce Appleby and Terence Ball. Cambridge: Cambridge University Press, 1999.
Locke, John. *Scritti editi e inediti sulla tolleranza*. Edited by Carlo Augusto Viano. Turin: Taylor, 1961.
Locke, John. *Two Tracts on Government*. Edited by P. Abrams. Cambridge: Cambridge University Press, 1967.
Locke, John. *A Paraphrase and Notes on the Epistles of Paul to the Galatians, 1 and 2 Corinthians, Romans, Ephesians*. Two Volumes. Edited by Arthur W. Wainwright. Oxford: Oxford University Press, 1987.
Locke, John. *The Second Treatise: An Essay Concerning the True Original, Extent, and End of Civil Government*. In *Two Treatises of Government and A Letter Concerning Toleration*, by

---

28 Cf. Derrida, "Force of Law."

John Locke, edited by Ian Shapiro, 100–209. New Haven, CT: Yale University Press, 2003.

Locke, John. *A Letter Concerning Toleration*. In *Two Treatises of Government and A Letter Concerning Toleration*, by John Locke, edited by Ian Shapiro, 211–56. New Haven, CT: Yale University Press, 2003.

Locke, John. *First Tract on Government*. In *Political Essays*, edited by Mark Goldie, 3–53. Cambridge: Cambridge University Press, 2004.

Locke, John. *Second Tract on Government*. In *Political Essays*, edited by Mark Goldie, 54–78. Cambridge: Cambridge University Press, 2004.

Locke, John. *An Essay Concerning Toleration And Other Writings on Law and Politics 1667–1683*. Edited with an introduction, critical apparatus, notes, and transcription of ancillary manuscripts by J. R. Milton and Philip Milton. Oxford: Oxford University Press, 2006.

Michéa, Jean-Claude. *The Realm of Lesser Evil: An Essay on Liberal Civilization*. Translated by David Fernbach. Cambridge: Polity Press, 2009.

Nietzsche, Friedrich. *The Anti-Christ, Ecce Homo, Twilight of the Idols and Other Writings*. Edited by Aaron Ridley and Judith Norman. Translated by Judith Norman. Cambridge: Cambridge University Press, 2005.

Strecker, Christian, and Joachim Valentin, eds. *Paulus unter den Philosophen*. Stuttgart: Kohlhammer, 2013.

Taubes, Jacob. *The Political Theology of Paul*. Translated by Dana Hollander. Edited by Aleida Assman and Jan Assmann in conjunction with Horst Folkers, Wolf-Daniel Hartwich, and Christoph Schulte. Stanford, CA: Stanford University Press, 2004.

Wainwright, Arthur W. Introduction to *A Paraphrase and Notes on the Epistles of Paul to the Galatians, 1 and 2 Corinthians, Romans, Ephesians*, vol. 1, by John Locke, edited by Arthur W. Wainwright, 1–99. Oxford: Oxford University Press, 1987.

Waldron, Jeremy. *God, Locke, and Equality: Christian Foundations in Locke's Political Thought*. Cambridge: Cambridge University Press, 2002.

Žižek, Slavoj. *The Puppet and the Dwarf: The Perverse Core of Christianity*. Cambridge, MA: The MIT Press, 2003.

Žižek, Slavoj, and John Milbank. *The Monstrosity of Christ: Paradox or Dialectic?* Edited by Creston Davis. Cambridge, MA: MIT Press, 2009.

Antonio Cimino
Europe and Paul of Tarsus: Giorgio Agamben on the Overcoming of Europe's Crisis

Abstract: In a recent interview published in the German newspaper *Die Zeit*, Giorgio Agamben analyzes the current political situation and outlines his own proposal for overcoming Europe's crisis. At the end of the interview Agamben seems to suggest a possible solution to the crisis by mentioning the Pauline notion of the ὡς μή, upon which he elaborates in his book *The Time That Remains*. In this paper, the author analyzes whether and to what extent Agamben's appropriation of the Pauline ὡς μή can provide a plausible and consistent answer to the political and philosophical problems that arise once we understand the logic of sovereignty in the light of the mutual implication of constituting power and constituted power. In this connection, the main question is whether a politics based on the ὡς μή is possible. Agamben's proposal for reenacting the Pauline ὡς μή within the context of Europe's current crisis cannot be considered revolutionary in the sense of modern revolutions. Agamben rejects any revolutionary attempts to change Europe because such attempts would remain caught up in the very circular dynamics of sovereignty that he wants to break out of. According to the author, the ὡς μή, however, does not succeed in breaking the circular logic of sovereignty because it is still caught within the logic of sovereignty. The ὡς μή is a suspension *within* the domain of sovereignty—not a sovereign suspension and exception but merely a spiritual, or inner, suspension and exception.

In a recent interview published in the German newspaper *Die Zeit*,[1] Giorgio Agamben analyzes the current political situation and outlines his own proposal for overcoming Europe's crisis. The interview is of great philosophical interest

---

[1] In the present essay, I will refer to the online version of the interview with Agamben: Radisch, "Europa muss kollabieren."

This paper results from my post-doctoral research project "The Truth of Conviction: Attestation, Testimony, and Declaration," financed by the Netherlands Organisation for Scientific Research (NWO). It is part of a larger project, "Overcoming the Faith–Reason Opposition: Pauline Pistis in Contemporary Philosophy" (project number 360–25–120), carried out at Radboud University and at the University of Groningen, The Netherlands. The present paper develops some ideas I have already outlined in my article "Agamben's Political Messianism in 'The Time That Remains.'"

because Agamben's analysis explicitly relies on a number of the innovative conceptual frameworks that he has introduced in major works such as *Homo Sacer* and *State of Exception*.² But more interestingly, at the end of the interview Agamben seems to suggest a possible solution to the crisis by mentioning the Pauline notion of the ὡς μή, upon which he elaborates in his book *The Time That Remains*.³ Thus, the interview turns out to be a valuable and clear follow-up overview to some of the most important and challenging perspectives Agamben has opened up during the last twenty years. As far as I can gather from this interview, one of the pivotal points of Agamben's position on the European crisis lies in his conception and repudiation of the relationship between "constituting power" and "constituted power."⁴ According to Agamben, the question of Europe's crisis has to be located in a broader horizon, which concerns our understanding of the political. Agamben plausibly argues that the notion of crisis as such should be put into question by scrutinizing not only its historical presuppositions but especially the way it is used in contemporary politics. Upon closer inspection of Agamben's critique of contemporary European politics, the crucial thesis can be read between the lines. More detailed accounts of this thesis are to be found in *Homo Sacer* and, above all, in *State of Exception*,⁵ where he maintains that the state of exception has become an increasingly pervasive paradigm of contemporary politics. In this context, crisis is nothing more than a label that covers up what is really at stake, that is, an enduring state of exception. Thus, Agamben's analysis of Europe's current crisis has to be examined in light of his account of the logic of sovereignty. In this paper, I intend to analyze whether and to what extent Agamben's appropriation of the Pauline ὡς μή can provide a plausible and consistent answer to the political and philosophical problems that arise once we understand the logic of sovereignty in the light of the mutual implication of constituting power and constituted power. In this connection, the main question is whether a politics based on the ὡς μή is possible.

Agamben's thoughts on the relationship between constituting power and constituted power, as they are formulated in the interview, can be summarized in two points. First, Agamben argues that there are two ways in which drastic political changes can be conceptualized in modernity. Either these changes

---

[2] Agamben, *Homo Sacer*; Agamben, *State of Exception*.
[3] See especially Agamben, *The Time That Remains*, 23–39.
[4] The interplay between constituting power and constituted power is already examined in *Homo Sacer*. See especially Agamben, *Homo Sacer*, 39–48. Agamben also conceives of that interplay in terms of the relationship between "the violence that posits law" and "the violence that preserves it," in accordance with Walter Benjamin's terminology. See Agamben, *Homo Sacer*, 40.
[5] See, for example, Agamben, *State of Exception*, 2.

can be thought of in terms of violent revolutionary events that subvert the established configuration of power relations or they can be conceived of in terms of new constitutional laws that substantially modify the given politico-juridical orders.[6] In the final analysis, the dynamics of such events or changes seems to correspond to the circularity between constituting power and constituted power.[7] Accordingly, constituting power, which assumes the shape of a certain political subject within a given historical situation, aims to destroy or modify constituted power, that is, a given politico-juridical order, which includes institutions, procedures, governmental entities, etc. But constituting power's attempts to destroy or change constituted power unavoidably lead to the establishment of a new politico-juridical order,[8] which in turn becomes the target of new forms of constituting power, and so on.[9]

---

[6] In the case of constitutional reforms, as Agamben pointedly stresses, the "paradox" that affects the relation between constituting power and constituted power becomes more apparent and shows its own intriguing nature: *"the constitution presupposes itself as constituting power* and, in this form, expresses the paradox of sovereignty in the most telling way. Just as sovereign power presupposes itself as the state of nature, which is thus maintained in a relation of ban with the state of law, so the sovereign power divides itself into constituting power and constituted power and maintains itself in relation to both, positioning itself at their point of indistinction." Agamben, *Homo Sacer*, 40–41.
[7] Agamben explicitly speaks of "the circular dialectic of these two forms of violence" (Agamben, *Homo Sacer*, 63).
[8] History has regularly provided various examples of such a circularity. Revolutions that claimed to emancipate oppressed human beings and to establish a new mankind destroyed old social and political orders but ended up in new forms of oppression.
[9] As far as I can see, this conceptual framework might serve *mutatis mutandis* as an explanatory model with reference to a number of phenomena, such as the origin, establishment, development, and decadence of religions and philosophical or scientific theories. The emergence of a more or less innovative philosophical trend implies the overcoming of a certain ("constituted") status quo in philosophical research; the establishment of a new status quo is followed sooner or later by attempts to overcome it. The transfer of the circular dialectic from politics to religion, philosophy, and science cannot be understood, however, in terms of mere analogy once one realizes that religion, philosophy, and science themselves can be considered powers and involve political features in the proper sense. Be that as it may, constituting power in politics, religion, philosophy, and science involves creative force, which weakens once constituting power passes into constituted power or assumes the shape of a conservative force. In what follows, I will ask the question to what extent one can see the relation between Paul's apostleship and the Jewish religion as well as the relationship between Paul and the Christian Church in the light of the circular dialectic of power. The answer to this question is of decisive importance both for understanding what is at stake in Agamben's reading of Paul and for testing the plausibility of his philosophical project.

Second, in the interview, Agamben lays emphasis on the need to break such a circularity, as he already does in *Homo Sacer* with reference to Benjamin.[10] In *Homo Sacer*, however, he does not give a detailed account of how it is possible to overcome or break the circular dialectic of power. In that context, he confines himself to elaborating on Benjamin's notion of divine violence and comes to the conclusion that this form of violence can be reduced to neither constituting power nor constituted power.[11] Nor can it be identified with sovereign power, because divine violence has to be seen as "the dissolution of the link between violence and law,"[12] while sovereign power is precisely the ultimate basis that underlies the interplay between constituting power and constituted power and allows for "the passage from the one to the other."[13] In other words, breaking the dialectic of constituting power and constituted power relies on the possibility of a power, or a violence, that does not adhere to the logic of sovereignty.

In the interview, Agamben does not elaborate on the notion of "divine violence" but calls this fourth kind of power—as distinct from constituting power, constituted power, and sovereign power—"destituent power" (*destituierende Kraft*) or "sublating power" (*aufhebende Kraft*).[14] Destituent power is supposed to escape the circular dialectic of sovereign power by overcoming the political framework of modernity, which, according to Agamben, relies on conflict. In the end, Agamben argues that the paradigm of conflict should be replaced with a new paradigm based on what he calls "escape" (*Ausweg*), or "exit," and "withdrawal" (*Rückzug*). In the present context, my concern is not to assess Agamben's proposal concerning specific political issues in contemporary Europe —in the interview, he explicitly refers to Greece's crisis and the role of Syriza— but to see it against the background of his reading of Paul. In fact, his understanding of destituent power and of a politics of exit or withdrawal is closely linked to his philosophical and political appropriation of the Pauline letters. At this juncture, it makes sense to highlight the implicit Pauline resonances of his analysis and to see the extent to which his Pauline proposal for overcoming Europe's crisis can withstand a number of the critical remarks one might formulate against it.

---

10 See especially Agamben, *Homo Sacer*, 63–67.
11 See ibid., 64.
12 Ibid., 65.
13 Ibid., 64.
14 As to the notion of destituent power, see the recent contribution by Agamben, "From the State of Control to a Praxis of Destituent Power." See also Agamben, *The Use of Bodies*, 263– 79, where Agamben discusses destituent potential precisely in the light of the Pauline ὡς μή.

The ideas of destituent power and of a politics of escape or withdrawal are directly linked to the concept of deactivation (*désœuvrement, inoperosità*), upon which Agamben elaborates in his book on Paul,[15] with particular reference to the notions of καταργεῖν and ὡς μή.[16] Indeed, it comes as no surprise that Benjamin's "divine violence" is rephrased by Agamben in terms of sublating, or destituent, power. For the politics of escape, which is supposed to rely on that power, is nothing but a way of deactivating the circular dialectic of sovereignty. In his commentary on the letter to the Romans, Agamben argues that the Hegelian notion of sublation (*Aufhebung*) derives from Luther's translation of the Pauline κατάργησις.[17] In this connection, the question arises whether the Pauline messianism can break or escape the circular dialectic between constituting power and constituted power on the basis of a messianic suspension, or deactivation, which is performed by means of the Pauline ὡς μή and κατάργησις. A positive answer to such a question would lead us to conceive of a politics of the ὡς μή as an alternative to the logic of sovereignty, that is, to the circular dialectic between constituting power and constituted power. A number of considerations, however, lead me to give a negative answer and to maintain that a politics based on the ὡς μή cannot constitute a solution for the overcoming of the circular logic of sovereignty.

If one applies the circularity of sovereignty not only to politics in a narrow sense but also to religious power as such—that is, to the way religion institutionalizes itself and ends up in the interplay of conflicting interests—Paul's apostleship can be viewed as a new (i.e., constituting) religious power that comes into conflict not only with Jewish law and institutions but also with diverging ways of understanding, institutionalizing, and practicing Christianity. Both well-known historical circumstances that come up in Paul's letters themselves—such as conflicts with other Christian fractions[18]—and other philosophical or theologico-political interpretations of Paul present him as a truly political thinker or activist who engages in conflicts and faces issues concerning power.[19] Paul is committed to political action both inside and outside of Christian communities. On the one hand, he is confronted with the Jewish political and religious tradition as well as with the Greco-Roman world, which includes both the pagan religions and the

---

15 See especially Agamben, *The Time That Remains*, 95–104.
16 I analyzed Agamben's appropriation of these notions in Cimino, "Messianic Experience of Language and Performativity of Faith."
17 See Agamben, *The Time That Remains*, 99.
18 See Dunn, *Jesus, Paul, and the Law*, 129–63.
19 See, for example, Nietzsche, *Twilight of the Idols. The Anti-Christ*, 166–67; Taubes, *The Political Theology of Paul*, 16–17; Badiou, *Saint Paul*, 20.

Roman Empire. On the other hand, he has competitors within Christianity itself. Such a political commitment can be read precisely in light of the circularity of sovereignty insomuch as Pauline Christianity is a constituting power that tries to break with the main constituted powers of that time (i.e., the established politico-religious orders in the Jewish, Roman, and Greek world) and to establish a new politico-religious order, that is, to redefine power relationships both inside and outside of Christianity.

It goes without saying that Agamben is fully aware that Paul has such a political commitment. Thus, his interpretive and philosophical strategy does not consist in depicting an apolitical Paul, who would escape the circularity of sovereignty by not becoming involved in political issues or conflicts. Quite the opposite, Agamben radicalizes Paul's political significance precisely by depriving it of political features in the narrow sense of the word. In other words, the political theory and action of Agamben's Paul relies on the politics of the ὡς μή, which does not commit itself to any specific political ideologies, identities, or actions.[20] According to Agamben, the politics of the ὡς μή is supposed to be radical insomuch as it does not attempt to establish a new social, political, and religious order or to posit a new ideology but is *"the revocation of every vocation."*[21] Thus, in accordance with Agamben's approach, one could say that Pauline politics is radical in the extent to which it gives up any revolutionary attempts and does not want to change society in the way in which revolutions are supposed to do, that is, by subverting the established configuration of power relations. All such radical political changes remain involved in the circularity of sovereignty because they rely on the creative forces of a new constituting power that sooner or later passes into a new constituted power. By contrast, the fruitful, paradoxical solution that the politics of the ὡς μή offers consists in the fact that it does not aim to destroy the constituted power of the Greco-Roman or the Jewish religious, cultural, and political order. Thus, the ὡς μή lets these orders be as they are by living or experiencing them *as not* being.

The politics of the ὡς μή, however, exposes itself to two fundamental objections. The first objection results from the historical considerations just mentioned. Seen in its own historical context, Paul's concrete political and religious practice attests to his willingness to establish new power relations and take decisions that have a more or less explicit political impact. In this connection, however, there is no need to unconditionally accept Nietzsche's, Taubes's, and Badiou's political or theologico-political readings of Paul. One can just refer to the

---

20 See Agamben, *The Use of Bodies*, 273–74.
21 Agamben, *The Time That Remains*, 23.

fact that Paul's apostleship implies a political commitment that, however, cannot be conceptualized merely in terms of the ὡς μή. Otherwise put, the ὡς μή as such cannot do justice to the complex meaning of Paul's interventions, which are supposed to face the specific and situation-related moral, social, and political issues that arise in Christian communities around the Mediterranean world at that time. Moreover, a further historical consideration undermines the political meaning of the ὡς μή. Let us concede that Paul shaped his apostolic and political action according to the principle of the ὡς μή. Let us also assume that the ὡς μή provides us with a genuinely new way of thinking and performing political action that might help us escape the circular logic of sovereignty. Nevertheless, as Agamben himself admits,[22] the history of the Church shows that Pauline messianism—or what Agamben deems Pauline messianism—has been ruled out. Thus, the Pauline politics of the ὡς μή did not prevent the Christian religion from being institutionalized and even becoming the oldest institution (i.e., constituted power) of the West, that is, from remaining within the circularity of sovereignty. From this viewpoint, Pauline messianism might be considered as one— under the circumstances, even the first—of the constituting powers that have characterized the history of the Church. Like many other more or less successful and serious attempts to reshape, refresh, or reform the Church, Pauline messianism acted as a new constituting power first, whose innovative force has been absorbed in a given constituted power. It is precisely the historical destiny of Pauline messianism that shows the extent to which it did not escape the circular dynamics of sovereignty. Thus, the history of the Church as a whole can be viewed as the history of a political entity that has been undergoing the more or less cyclic and circular dynamics of sovereignty, understood as the interplay between constituting power and constituted power. Pauline messianism and the related ὡς μή are part of this history.

The second objection results from what seems to be a contradiction intrinsic to Agamben's reading. As a matter of fact, the conceptual framework, or "epistemological paradigm,"[23] Agamben uses to single out the specific meaning of Pauline messianism—especially its essential component, i.e., κατάργησις—is Carl Schmitt's theory of the "exception,"[24] that is, the same paradigm he uses in *Homo Sacer* with a view to highlighting the logic of sovereignty.[25] As a matter of fact, Agamben extensively explains the analogies between the Pauline κατάρ-

---

[22] See ibid., 1–3 and especially 135.
[23] Ibid., 104 (translation modified).
[24] Ibid.
[25] See especially Agamben, *Homo Sacer*, 15–67.

γησις and the state of exception by comparing "the threefold articulation of the law in the state of exception with the state of the law in the horizon of messianic *katargēsis*."[26] If Paul's messianic κατάργησις is nothing but the deactivation, or suspension, of the Jewish law, then one can draw two conclusions.

The first conclusion is that Paul does not want to introduce a new political and religious order by destroying the constituted power of the Jewish law. In other words, in accordance with Agamben's reading, Pauline messianism does not act as a new constituting power. This might corroborate Agamben's claim concerning the ὡς μή as a way of escaping the circularity of sovereignty. But the second conclusion, which goes in the opposite direction, is that Paul's messianism remains captured by the logic of sovereignty insomuch as it only deactivates—or seems to deactivate—the Jewish law. Since the Pauline κατάργησις does not destroy, or abolish, but merely deactivates, or suspends, the old legal order, it still maintains a link to it in the form of a suspension or an exception.[27] Therefore, as far as I can see, Pauline messianism does not succeed in breaking the circularity of sovereignty—at least in the form in which it is presented and rephrased by Agamben. Pauline messianism is either a suspension of the constituted power or a new constituting power that aims to destroy the constituted, or already established, politico-juridical order. In both cases, the logic of sovereignty is neither overcome nor broken but, instead, confirmed and reinforced.

Although Agamben introduces his explicit use of Schmitt's paradigm of exception only in Chapter 5 of his book on Paul, the logic of sovereign exception, or suspension, is already at work in his analyses of the ὡς μή and the messianic vocation—albeit implicitly.[28] Let us elaborate on this crucial point. According to Agamben, the Pauline vocation performed by means of the ὡς μή is "*the revocation of every vocation.*"[29] Agamben understands "vocation" in Paul in terms of "a determinate factical condition"[30] in which individuals stand. In what way do the ὡς μή and the messianic revocation affect factical conditions, that is, the sta-

---

26 Agamben, *The Time That Remains*, 106.
27 See ibid., where an explicit connection is established between the structure of the Pauline remnant and the logic of exception. The conclusion Agamben draws could not be clearer: "The remnant is an exception taken to its extreme, pushed to its paradoxical formulation. In his rendering of the messianic condition of the believer, Paul radicalizes the condition of the state of exception, whereby law is applied in disapplying itself, no longer having an inside or an outside. With regard to this law that applies itself in disapplying itself, a corresponding gesture of faith ensues, applying itself in disapplying itself, rendering law inoperative while carrying it to its fulfillment." Agamben, *The Time That Remains*, 106–7.
28 See ibid., 23–24.
29 Ibid., 23.
30 Ibid., 24.

tus quo, including a determinate constituted configuration of power relations? Here, at first sight, three different ways of understanding the ὡς μή are possible, but Agamben explicitly excludes all of them.³¹ The first option is to understand the ὡς μή as a destruction of the factical condition. This is, however, not the case insofar as the ὡς μή does not alter the form or the content that defines the factical condition. The second option is to say that the ὡς μή replaces a concrete vocation with another vocation, but Agamben rejects this understanding too. In fact, the ὡς μή does not imply "substituting a less authentic vocation with a truer vocation."³² The third alternative is to conceive of the ὡς μή as "indifference"³³ towards a certain factical condition and its opposite; but this possibility, too, is ruled out by Agamben. Thus, the gist of the ὡς μή consists in the fact that the concrete conditions in which one stands are maintained but at the same time negated or nullified. As far as I can see, the only way of conceptualizing such a characteristic of the ὡς μή is to say that the ὡς μή works as a suspension, deactivation, sublation, or κατάργησις of the factical condition. The messianic way of life does not destroy or replace the status quo. Nor is it indifferent towards it. Instead, the individual that performs the ὡς μή is at the same time inside and outside the factical condition. She is inside insomuch as the factical condition is maintained. But she is outside it in that she lives this condition through the filter of the ὡς μή. But this is precisely the logic of sovereign exception, that is, of the "inclusive exclusion."³⁴ What this all amounts to is that, according to its inner logic, Agamben's Pauline politics of the ὡς μή does not claim to destroy a certain constituted power nor does it want to replace it with a new order of power relations—which would imply a new constituting power. Agamben's Pauline politics of the ὡς μή lets the status quo stand as it is by suspending, or deactivating, it.

It goes without saying that the suspension, or deactivation, implied by the messianic enactment of the ὡς μή cannot take place in the form of a sovereign suspension in the narrow sense of the word. Let us consider the example of the factical condition of being a slave. The fact that one experiences and lives her condition of being a slave *as not* being a slave does not mean that the concrete social and juridical condition of being a slave is suspended. The slave is not in a position to suspend her own being a slave without destroying the given constituted power. But destruction as such is incompatible with suspension. The suspension presupposes that the constituted power is maintained—albeit deactivat-

---

31 See ibid., 23–24.
32 Ibid., 23.
33 Ibid., 24.
34 Agamben, *Homo Sacer*, 21.

ed. Thus, since the messianic suspension, or deactivation, underlying the ὡς μή cannot be a sovereign suspension, it can only be an inner, or spiritual, suspension without any of the visible effects or alterations that happen, for instance, in the case of Spartacus. Spartacus's uprising can in fact be seen as an attempt to introduce a new constituting power by destroying the constituted power of the Roman Republic. It is a rebellion that can be associated *mutatis mutandis* with modern revolutions. This is not the case with the Pauline politics of the ὡς μή insofar as Paul does not aim to destroy the Roman Empire. Analogously, Agamben's proposal for reenacting the Pauline ὡς μή within the context of Europe's current crisis cannot be considered revolutionary in the sense of modern revolutions. As has already been stressed, Agamben rejects any revolutionary attempts to change Europe because such attempts would remain caught up in the very circular dynamics of sovereignty that he wants to break out of. Accordingly, if my reconstruction of Agamben's Pauline politics of the ὡς μή is correct, Agamben is right in maintaining that the ὡς μή does not constitute a further version of revolutionary constituting power. The ὡς μή, however, does not succeed in breaking the circular logic of sovereignty because it is still caught within the logic of sovereignty. The ὡς μή is a suspension *within* the domain of sovereignty—not a sovereign suspension and exception but merely a spiritual, or inner, suspension and exception.[35]

The conclusion of Agamben's interview with *Die Zeit* confirms my reconstruction, especially with regard to the two points that I have repeatedly emphasized. First of all, the conclusion corroborates my view that Agamben understands the Pauline ὡς μή as an inner, or spiritual, suspension. In fact, he depicts the messianic revocation enacted by means of the ὡς μή in terms of a force that is at work "within [*im Inneren*]" the vocation or in terms of an "inner urge [*inneren Drang*]." Second, the last lines of the interview allow us to see that in Agamben's reading there is indeed a truly substantive and consistent link between the Pauline κατάργησις and the ὡς μή, to the effect that they are two aspects of the same attitude, which is supposed to suspend, or deactivate, the constituted power as a given social, political, and economic order. Agamben does not claim that the overcoming of Europe's crisis relies on the possibility of changing our life or "manner of life" (*Lebensweise*). Instead, he argues that a different "form of life" (*Lebensform*) is needed. This is in full accordance with what he says in his book on Paul, namely, that the ὡς μή does not mean

---

[35] It would be interesting to explore similarities and differences between Heidegger's appropriation of Meister Eckhart's *Gelassenheit* and Agamben's reading of the Pauline ὡς μή, especially considering that both philosophers see in those attitudes an ethos appropriate to the crisis of modernity. Concerning Heidegger's thoughts on *Gelassenheit*, see Davis, *Heidegger and the Will*.

replacing a less authentic life with a more authentic life.³⁶ By mentioning the notion of a form of life,³⁷ Agamben means a deactivation, or suspension, of the social, juridical, economic, and even bodily factical conditions. His concern is not to destroy those conditions but to let them be *used* in a different way.³⁸ It is precisely at this juncture of the interview that he introduces one of the main results of his analysis of the Pauline ὡς μή, that is, the fact that the Pauline ὡς μή does not found any new identity or vocation but is the messianic revocation of every vocation.

Can the ὡς μή facilitate the overcoming of Europe's crisis given that it does not found any kind of identity (cultural, religious, political, etc.) but just lets us use our factical conditions and identities? On the one hand, I do not think Agamben's Pauline proposal can succeed in overcoming Europe's crisis. Despite his claims, the politics of the ὡς μή does not avoid the circular dynamics of power—at best the ὡς μή might found an attitude that enables one to withstand the crisis. On the other hand, however, Agamben's attempt to re-actualize the Pauline ὡς μή can and should serve as an example—regardless of whether it is successful or not—that makes us aware of one thing, among others, that is needed in our search for a solution to Europe's crisis, that is, a living reappropriation of Europe's cultural traditions. On this crucial point, which he has articulated more explicitly in a previous interview,³⁹ we can certainly agree with Agamben.

---

36 See again Agamben, *The Time That Remains*, 23.
37 The concept of form of life has played an increasingly decisive role in Agamben's most recent publications, which conclude the philosophical program outlined in *Homo Sacer*. See especially the third part of *The Use of Bodies*, which is devoted precisely to this concept. Another important source on the subject is Agamben, *The Highest Poverty*.
38 Regarding Agamben's account of the Pauline concept of "use" (χρῆσις), see Agamben, *The Time That Remains*, 26–39. See especially the crucial passage that establishes an explicit link between the ὡς μή and the χρῆσις: "The *hōs mē* therefore does not only have a negative content; rather, for Paul, this is the only possible *use* of worldly situations. The messianic vocation is not a right, nor does it furnish an identity; rather, it is a generic potentiality [*potenza*] that can be used without ever being owned. To be messianic, to live in the Messiah, signifies the expropriation of each and every juridical-factical property [...] under the form of the *as not*. This expropriation does not, however, found a new identity; the 'new creature' is none other than the use and messianic vocation of the old" (Agamben, *The Time That Remains*, 26). Concerning the use of bodies, see Agamben, *The Use of Bodies*, 3–94.
39 Schümer, "Die endlose Krise ist ein Machtinstrument."

References

Agamben, Giorgio. *Homo Sacer: Sovereign Power and Bare Life*. Translated by Daniel Heller-Roazen. Stanford, CA: Stanford University Press, 1998.
Agamben, Giorgio. *State of Exception*. Translated by Kevin Attell. Chicago, IL: The University of Chicago Press, 2005.
Agamben, Giorgio. *The Time That Remains: A Commentary on the Letter to the Romans*. Translated by Patricia Dailey. Stanford, CA: Stanford University Press, 2005.
Agamben, Giorgio. *The Highest Poverty: Monastic Rules and Form-of-Life*. Translated by Adam Kotsko. Stanford, CA: Stanford University Press, 2013.
Agamben, Giorgio. *The Use of Bodies*. Translated by Adam Kotsko. Stanford, CA: Stanford University Press, 2015.
Agamben, Giorgio. "From the State of Control to a Praxis of Destituent Power." In *Resisting Biopolitics: Philosophical, Political, and Performative Strategies*, edited by S. E. Wilmer and Audronė Žukauskaitė, 21–29. New York: Routledge, 2016.
Badiou, Alain. *Saint Paul: The Foundation of Universalism*. Translated by Ray Brassier. Stanford, CA: Stanford University Press, 2003.
Cimino, Antonio. "Messianic Experience of Language and Performativity of Faith: Agamben's Interpretation of Pauline Faith." *Freiburger Zeitschrift für Philosophie und Theologie* 61, no. 1 (2014): 127–40.
Cimino, Antonio. "Agamben's Political Messianism in 'The Time That Remains.'" *International Journal of Philosophy and Theology* 77, no. 3 (2016): 102–18.
Davis, Bret W. *Heidegger and the Will: On the Way to Gelassenheit*. Evanston, IL: Northwestern University Press, 2007.
Dunn, James D. G. *Jesus, Paul, and the Law: Studies in Mark and Galatians*. Louisville, KY: Westminster & John Knox Press, 1990.
Nietzsche, Friedrich. *Twilight of the Idols. The Anti-Christ*. Translated by R. J. Hollingdale. London: Penguin Books, 1990.
Radisch, Iris. "Europa muss kollabieren." *Zeit Online*, September 10, 2015. Translated from French by Andreas Hiepko. Accessed September 27, 2015. http://www.zeit.de/2015/35/giorgio-agamben-philosoph-europa-oekonomie-kapitalismus-ausstieg.
Schümer, Dirk. "Die endlose Krise ist ein Machtinstrument: Giorgio Agamben im Gespräch." *Frankfurter Allgemeine Zeitung*, May 24, 2013. Accessed October 21, 2015. http://www.faz.net/aktuell/feuilleton/bilder-und-zeiten/giorgio-agamben-im-gespraech-die-endlose-krise-ist-ein-machtinstrument-12193816.html.
Taubes, Jacob. *The Political Theology of Paul*. Translated by Dana Hollander. Edited by Aleida Assman and Jan Assmann in conjunction with Horst Folkers, Wolf-Daniel Hartwich, and Christoph Schulte. Stanford, CA: Stanford University Press, 2004.

Ward Blanton
The Invisible Committee as a Pauline Gesture: Anarchic Politics from Tiqqun to Tarnac

Abstract: This essay discusses a striking dimension of the political implications of the turn to Saint Paul by telling the story of the French collective Tiqqun, or the Invisible Committee, and its political manifestos, such as *Introduction to Civil War*, *This is Not a Program*, and *The Coming Insurrection*. As is shown, these manifestos demonstrate strong affinities with recent philosophical work on Pauline messianism. The call to a radical politics that speaks from these manifestos, as this essay argues, is marked by a strong Pauline legacy, especially as read through the lens of Agamben's *The Time that Remains*. The author does not only inform the reader about the Tarnac events and the particular political response to this French collective, but also explains in which sense the thought of this collective is Pauline as well as inspired by Francis of Assisi—much like the work of Agamben, such as developed in *The Highest Poverty*. Finally, Blanton shows how these Pauline resonances are first and foremost concerned with retrieving Paul's πίστις because the struggle that we can encounter in these movements is in fact a struggle to invent a contemporary Paulinist gesture in which the preservation or recuperation of a messianic πίστις is at stake.

> *Student:* I guess my question is kind of about radical politics, too. You know, like, there is this text I know you are aware of, *The Coming Insurrection*. It's making the rounds now and everyone on Znet is debating, "oh, it's nonsense" or "oh, it's great." And I was just wondering if you could say a few words about what you presume to be the importance or unimportance of *The Coming Insurrection* and also what your position is specifically on insurrectionary anarchism versus revolutionary politics.
>
> *Giorgio Agamben:* This book was written by friends of mine and so it's difficult to answer this question. But this is a peculiar instance of our present situation when every political, radical position which is outside the parliament is immediately nominated as terrorism, because these people—for the mere fact, fundamentally, of having written this book and for other things not sure at all and which are nothing like a terrorist crime—have been accused of terrorist association, and they risked twenty years of punishment. The problem is that one: today in Western, so-called democratic countries, every political action outside parliament is classified as terrorism. This is a great problem, and it has increased—we see it everywhere. Every political activity which is outside the parliament, precisely in the moment

when the parliament is destitute of any legitimacy—but precisely in this context—any activity outside parliament is equal to terrorism. That's the model of governance today.[1]

There is to date a carefully managed and perhaps actively suppressed news story about recent philosophical interest in the Pauline legacy. In a word, what are we to do with the evident Pauline affiliations of that anonymous authorial community, sometimes called Tiqqun and sometimes the Invisible Committee? This collective produced some of the most creatively trenchant—and also bestselling and frequently discussed—political manifestos of recent decades (for instance, *Introduction to Civil War*; *This is Not a Program*; *The Coming Insurrection*), and they did so by amplifying and resituating strong affinities with recent philosophical work on Pauline messianism. How has it gone unnoticed that their efforts to render a protreptic or conversionistic call to a radical politics are, in central and serially repeated respects, articulated through a Pauline legacy, especially the Pauline legacy as read through the messianic Paulinism of Giorgio Agamben (for instance, *The Time that Remains*)? By the same token, why is it that the Paulinism of these groups has not been discussed in relation to the fact that, soon enough after the publication of these widely circulated Paulinist manifestos, this group was threatened with the full force of new French anti-terrorist legislation after a major police raid of their commune at Tarnac in France? In his interaction with a perceptive student, Agamben formalizes this event as a name for the governance of our time. As an additional twist of Agamben's proclamation, must we not also say that—given the evident Paulinism of the Invisible Committee—our time is therefore also stranded within a Pauline tableau, one in which imperial forces once more threaten the small messianic collective?

Even Agamben's offhanded comments to the student repeat what is for him a Pauline and messianic tableau in which πίστις becomes the name for an anarchic zone within which positive law and constitutional promise are able to turn against each other, to split apart. In this case, the Invisible Committee is anarchic by definition in the sense that they have articulated a merely trusting solidarity which secedes from a representational form of governance glossed here by Agamben as parliamentarian. Indeed, Agamben often points out that this anarchic splitting apart of the order of law constitutes the modern period as definitively Pauline, this definitive repetition of a Pauline moment being that which,

---

[1] The transcription is taken from the lecture of Agamben and Butler, "Eichmann, Law, and Justice," 12:05 min., lecture at the European Graduate School. September 16, 2009. https://www.youtube.com/watch?v=bYzLcBO1ZwU.

as he writes, causes "the Schmittian thesis on political theology" to receive "further confirmation."² As Agamben elaborates:

> The caesura between constitutive and constituted power, a divide that becomes so apparent in our times, finds it theological origins in the Pauline split between the level of faith and that of nomos, between personal loyalty and the positive obligation that derives from it. In this light, messianism appears as a struggle, within the law, whereby the element of the pact and constituent power leans toward setting itself against and emancipating itself from the element of the *entolē*, the norm in the strict sense.³

Given the Pauline backdrop of the Invisible Committee and their active repression at the hands of parliamentarian officials, Agamben implies here that such a stark alternative is not just the "crisis" of contemporary governance but also the nomological crisis flagged up by Pauline messianism itself.

In the following pages, I would like to begin to counter what has been a strategic lack of reflection on such comparative questions by considering several aspects of the way—from anonymous authorial collective to demonized "terrorists"— the long and often surreal "Tarnac affair" brings to light one of the most wide-reaching philosophical efforts to invent a contemporary Pauline "gesture." This gesture would found neo-Paulinist communities effectively outside the reach of representational governance, just as they would make important claims about why this sphere elicits the aggressive response of an empire of representational governance.

1 Tarnac Affair

One reads the governmental and police documents about the Tarnac affair like those anxious ancient letters of Pliny to Trajan. Everywhere are so many civil servants desperately trying to conjure convincing links between the application of power in the field and its images of sovereignty back home in the architectures of the capital.

As you may recall, in 2008, 150 police officers descended on Tarnac, a scenic village of only 350 in the middle of France.⁴ Over the course of several days, the

---

2 Agamben, *The Time That Remains*, 118.
3 Ibid., 118–19.
4 The clearest and most comprehensive analysis of the Tarnac affair is to be found in the journalistic work of Dufresne, *Tarnac, magasin général*. The book is an extraordinary collection of interviews, reflections, and copies of official documents of interior ministers, police investiga-

massive police force arrested nine people, finally charging them with "associating with wrong-doers with terrorist aims."[5] In the rumor mill of the many of the periodicals covering these events along the way, other accusations sometimes popped to the surface, all articulating some threat of terroristic sedition or danger to the state. What is clearer is that police, and presumably anti-terrorism forces, had the Tarnac group under surveillance for an unspecified number of months before the arrests were made, and journalist David Dufresne provides convincing evidence of literally thousands of pages of police surveillance documents about Tarnac. According to some reports, the person named by police as the ringleader of the group, Julien Coupat, had previously come to the attention of French authorities after the FBI in the US alerted them that Coupat was present at a protest in front of the military recruitment station where reportedly a cyclist later left a small bomb. No one was injured in the ensuing blast, which broke windows at the recruitment station, but understandably the occurrence did receive a substantial amount of media coverage at the time. In France itself, not long before the arrests at Tarnac, someone had taken u-shaped bars (something like horseshoes, perhaps, though descriptions have been vague), hanging these on the electric lines of the TGV (or high speed train), an action which apparently disrupted communication between trains and which caused delays for thousands of travelers. According to some reports, Coupat and his girlfriend had been stopped and questioned by police shortly before the first train passed the obstructed section of line, and this just miles from where the bars were hung. Despite the entirely circumstantial nature of the evidence against them, the so-called Tarnac 9 were held via mechanisms of French anti-terror legislation, which had been passed rather recently under Nicolas Sarkozy. Most were released within days or weeks (though Coupat was held for six months) due to a lack of solid forms of evidence against them to substantiate these charges or indeed other suspicions.

2 Tracts of a Coming Metamorphosis

One reads the politics of their tracts like a peculiar new Corinthian correspondence, hovering somewhere between bluster, threat, utopianism, enthusiasm, banality.

---

tors, court proceedings. I rely on his work in the paragraphs which follow. In addition to innumerable newspaper and magazine articles, see also Paye, *L'emprise de l'image*.

5 See, for example, the phrasing of the newspaper article "Cabbage-Patch Revolutionaries?"

Despite (and perhaps because of) a lack of secure evidence against them, a major point of discussion by police and pundits alike during this period of arrest, questioning, evidence gathering, and the spinning machinations of mediated rumor mills was whether Coupat and his friends had in fact authored a book entitled *L'insurrection qui vient* (*The Coming Insurrection*), first published in 2007. Politicians made speeches extracting lines from this text as if to read aloud damning lines to bolster the criminal case against the Tarnac friends. Here were chapters in that perennially odd spectacle whereby politicians attempt to link a text to an act, not to mention an act which seems in any case not of the order to cause more harm than an annoying delay, a disruption of railway efficiency for the commuters. The question of authorship was the focus of many of the public governmental pronouncements about the group, however, and it was a line from *The Coming Insurrection* about the neutralization of the TGV line or high speed rail which became a runaway favorite for the governmental orators, cultural pundits, and talk show hosts:

> Information and energy circulate via wire networks, fibers and channels, and these can be attacked. Nowadays sabotaging the social machine with any real effect involves reappropriating and reinventing the ways of interrupting its networks. How can a TGV line or electrical network be rendered useless?[6]

To be sure, everywhere in France the governing elite seemed a kind of bustle of offense taken against *The Coming Insurrection* and its scathing critiques of contemporary culture, a culture the book depicts as a life-sapping social shipwreck in dire need of life-giving reorientation. Fear was expressed, and indeed called for, at the possibility that a home-grown, farm-town terrorist cell was in the making. After all, how else could one understand this line about the rendering "useless" of a TGV or high speed rail? Indeed, as Dufresne points out (not without a smile), was not someone at the commune reading a biography that saboteur Neil Ludd, a book not mentioned in the extensive police notes about the library of Julien Coupat?[7] In this archival policing, however, not even Dufresne notes that the discussion of rendering anything "useless" or "inoperative" is of course a crucial touchstone of the group's fascination with Paul's messianic writings, perhaps the most focused of the Paulinisms of *The Coming Insurrection*. Was

---

6 The Invisible Committee, *The Coming Insurrection*, 112.

7 Pointed out by Dufresne, the biography of the Luddite was one missed in the otherwise almost surreal fascination of the police to make lists of suspicious books at Tarnac (lists from Antonio Negri's *Books for Burning* to Tomothy Leary on chaos). For the description of the Luddite work, see Dufresne, *Tarnac, magasin général*, 37.

this public denunciation in parliament of those lines in the book not itself a declaration of war against the Paulinism of the Tarnac friends? After all, as we will show, the rendering "useless" of a network of everyday traffic is, in *The Coming Insurrection*, one of a panoply of wonders about how to unplug, through a kind of Situationist performance or *détournement*, the everyday function of all aspects of contemporary life. All this was with a view to the transformative wonder about how the new life, the new age, might "reappropriate" and "reinvent" our inherited identities and modes of living. And if the Pauline echoes are not already begun to resound, we should note that this panoply of strategies—the panoply that is *The Coming Insurrection*—are summarized in that book with repeated Pauline glosses on the τέλος of law as its law's odd suspension, neutralization, or productive uselessness. These wonders about the emancipatory messianic time of the TGV line would in other words be a kind of contemporary application of Paul's reflections on law, on identitarian right in relation to its structured traditions, or even on inherited everyday norms like food laws. On such evident comparative links, however, both the critics and defenders of the Tarnac 9 remained perfectly, awkwardly silent.

3 "Preparation for an Act" and its Archival Excavation

The affair boiled and bubbled over the edges of all its pots. Police memos circulated about "members of an ultra-Left movement of anarcho-autonomists."[8] The diffuse and expansive discursive traumas, and those thousands of surveillance reports, did eventually settle on a charge against members of the Tarnac collective: they were a "criminal association" preparing a "terrorist enterprise."[9] As one can imagine, the nature of the charge—both vague and pre-emptive—raised eyebrows, as did the application of that nomination which in recent decades is so often associated with pre-emptive interventions and sequestering: terrorism. In light of the pre-emptive charge, for example, Dufresne opens his massive journalistic account of the Tarnac affair with a citation of Philip K. Dick's *Minority Report*, that dystopian science fiction novel about policing which transforms it-

---

[8] See, e.g., Dufresne, *Tarnac, magasin général*, 1.
[9] The media proliferated many variations of the phrasing. Earlier discussions like those in Dufresne finally gave way to retrospective reflection on the accusations of terrorism and violence (e.g., in Seelow, "Tarnac : bataille procédurale autour de la définition du terrorisme.")

self into the management of the possible (and hence those who pre-emptively arrest criminals-in-the-making).

Jean-Marie Gleize also appropriates the charge itself as the title of his poetic provocations and meditative retrospectives in *Tarnac, un acte préparatoire (Tarnac, a Preparatory Act)*.[10] While Dufresne looks back to the sci-fi of Philip K. Dick for some orientation, Gleize also constructs extensive systems of illuminating references linking Tarnac—both its anarchist community of friends, its town church, and its town history—to the relevant legacy of Francis of Assisi. Gleize reads references to Assisi as through the diary of a priest of Tarnac, finding in him a figure of major relevance for the negative anthropology of the insurrectionist commune: "'if we had goods we would need weapons and laws to protect them. This is why we should possess nothing, nothing at all.'"[11]

Gleize's unique work affords a kind of poetic, material weight to "Tarnac" in the sense that he reflects equally on its textual, biographical, religious, political and natural histories. As he writes, in a quasi-biographical mode of his time in Tarnac and with the commune there:

> Tarnac flows through me like dust. Of the forest I first found three dark gray photos, very gray, steeped in fog. They will have to figure in the book, they will have to figure the invisible, the formless and blinding mass, what the child sees, what penetrates him without his knowing it.[12]

Indeed, it is this material density of traditions flowing through Tarnac, and of Gleize's own memories there, which makes his more mystical and poetic interventions so intriguing. What, after all, is the "act" at stake in the governmental question of "Tarnac"? Who or what is in dispute or under interrogation here? What act? Indeed, whose?

His exploration may be read as a profound and creative criticism of injustice toward the Tarnac writers inasmuch as Gleize's task explicitly and elaborately becomes a figuring of the invisible. This task of figuration, above all the figuration of an "act" which is yet to come, incorporates himself, the so-called "Invisible Committee," and indeed a longer theological tradition of corporate and spiritual bodies which preceded them both. Above all, for example, Gleize leads us back to the "preparatory" role of figuration to be encountered in both Francis of Assisi and Paul the apostle. Like the streams and moss and fog of Tarnac, in what way were Paul and Francis—indeed, Paul as read through Francis—crucial

---

10 Gleize, *Tarnac, un act préparatoire*.
11 Ibid., 47.
12 Ibid., 13.

"preparations" for the "act" which Tarnac has, apparently, almost become? Why does the figuration of the invisible for Gleize, not to mention the figuration of the Invisible Committee, necessitate these archival references to Francis and Paul?

In any case, Gleize consistently links the Tarnac anarchists to the religious history of the town which he then submits as through a diary of a priest:

> Tarnac 10/4/57 = The church conveys to francis in the introit of the mass: 'the world is crucified unto me' by our lord jesus Christ. That is, it no longer exists for me, just as I am myself crucified through this same jesus and no longer exist in the eyes of the world. For to exist, to be completely in our lord jesus Christ, is to be a new creature. Saint Paul says elsewhere: 'therefore if any man be in OSJC, he is a new creature: old things are passed away; behold, all things are become new.' This is all I have understood well in the famous passage from Paul's letter to the galatians. This moreover fits francis perfectly as he no longer existed for the world from the day he heard the words addressed to him by the Christ on the saint damian cross. This is also why we wanted to submit to the rule of Franciscan penitence, quite moderate gentle, of the third order, under the protection of our late lamented père gratian. It is therefore to some extent our feast that we celebrate today, since we are your children, o admirable, inimitable and seraphic francis.[13]

In naming such constellations, in bringing them to visibility, Gleize's poeticisms of Tarnac as an act in preparation deviate wildly from the usual bluster about the "politics" of the community. Here in the poetic—and as it were pre-political—underground Gleize hears the echoes of a Pauline voice in the radicalisms of Tarnac. In doing so, Gleize's meditative practice of figuration remains discernible in only the tiniest of marginal and minority commentators on the affair. To these filiations we must return, and it is worth saying that the linkage between Pauline messianic πίστις and later monastic orders like that of Francis remains a key part of Giorgio Agamben's larger genealogy of political life.[14] For the moment, however, it is worth taking a pause to consider some of the more hegemonic streams of cultural memory which took up the affair with such great gusto, as if they too were petrified in fear at the approach of the "act" of Paulinism.

4 The Pundits' Denunciation of the "Terrorists" at Tarnac

One hears his staged and self-serving rant like the sarcastic denunciation of a dangerously superstitious foreign cult by Juvenal.

---

13 Ibid., 47.
14 Agamben, *The Kingdom and the Glory*, 21–26; Agamben, *The Highest Poverty*, 46–47.

The Coming Insurrection was first published in English in 2009, a fairly quiet print run of the publisher *Semiotext(e)*. But the affair was destined to become tied into culture wars outside of France in such a way that what may have been a tempest in a foreign teapot would become elevated into a coming threat from abroad to the stability of the ways of life and good political sense at home. Strangely, it was such an affected reception, as if in panic and fury, by Glen Beck of Fox News which launched the little Semiotext(e) volume onto the list of major bestsellers in English. Beck set aside time in his editorial show for Fox News to denounce the book on air in July of 2009.[15] Beck's rhetoric was of course perfectly streamlined in keeping with the brand both of his show and of the Fox network. He included the requisite satirical jabs at the French, ominous statements about how "the disenfranchised" wanted to "bring down capitalism and the Western way of life," assertions that a movement of "Paris riots" was coming to America, and assurances that the book was intended to foment terrorist acts in the United States. As Beck spoke, an archive of unrelated news shots of burning cars and streams of threatening protestors rolled past on the screen behind him.

Beck warned against the dangerous manifesto but also urged that his audience should read the book in order to plumb the depths of the danger and violent inclinations of a new "radical left" in Europe. So sure was Beck about this advice that he himself promised in this same Fox News spot to read the book himself during his upcoming family vacation! No doubt the admission in this denunciation that he hadn't actually read the book is comical. Nevertheless, the comedic quality of Beck's satirical performance, however, should not belie that fact that effectively his condemnations were the same as those of the French government, namely, that the anonymous authorial collective was preparing for acts susceptible to the name terrorism.

Naturally, Beck claimed that *The Coming Insurrection* was the "anti-*Common Sense*" or the polar opposite of his own "revolutionary" book with the unwieldy title, *Glenn Beck's Common Sense: The Case of an Out-of-Control Government (Inspired by Thomas Paine)*. In Beck's anti-*Coming Insurrection*, we might say, readers were urged to consider, among other things, the "hand-out" prone Democrats as latter day British tax collectors who must be resisted by latter day patriots. Encouraging the Fox News audience to read *The Coming Insurrection* was of course also a clear indication that one needed to read Beck's own recent book in order to get the more fair and balanced view. And culture wars being what they are,

---

[15] "Fox News," YouTube Video 6:55, review of the Coming Insurrection by Glen Beck. Accessed at January 3, 2016. https://www.youtube.com/watch?v=ZKyi2qNskJc.

this modern Juvenal thus helped to launch his ostensible enemy onto the New York Times list of bestsellers, a list *The Coming Insurrection* soon conquered as its number one hit. The achievement owed a great deal to Glen Beck's denunciation and a great deal to the French government's very comparable reaction.

5 Paulinism's Hidden Transcript

Even while the Tarnac event was becoming a political and cultural affair of the first magnitude, and even as the affair set into motion these types of competition for the rights of valorized cultural legacies (for instance, "radical" or "revolutionary"), no one seemed to be willing to speculate on the oddly forgotten Paulinism of the Tarnac group and their associated writings.

One way to approach this issue of the hidden Pauline transcript (so to speak) in the Tarnac affair emerges through Giorgio Agamben's offhand response to the student question about *The Coming Insurrection*, cited above. Just naively, for example, it is interesting that Agamben calls the authors of *The Coming Insurrection* his friends. While I would argue that an Agambenian reading of Paul is everywhere evident in the creative and provocative *protrepsis* that is *The Coming Insurrection* of the Invisible Committee, perhaps the affinities between this authorial collective and the work of Agamben are even more evident in some of their earlier textual experiments (for instance, *Introduction to Civil War*). Indeed, even the earlier name of the authorial collective directly evoked the messianic practices of gathering fragments of redemption, *Tiqqun*. Linking two favorite topics of Agamben, for example, the "messianic" and "civil war" as the paradigm of contemporary political life, the earlier authorial collective summarized:

> Tiqqun is the becoming-real, the becoming-*practice* of the world. Tiqqun is the *practice* of the world. Tiqqun is the process through which everything is revealed to be practice, that is, to take place within its own limits, within its own immanent signification. Tiqqun means that each act, conduct, and statement endowed with sense—act, conduct and statement as *event*—spontaneously manifests its own metaphysics, its own community, its own *party*. Civil war simply means the whole world is practice and life is, in its smallest details, heroic.[16]

In fact, readers of these earlier writings could be forgiven for wondering whether Agamben himself had written parts of them, given that they are so steeped in his characteristic lines of questioning about messianism, empire, and the rise of a

---

[16] Tiqqun, *Introduction to Civil War*, 181.

biopolitical immanence of economic power. The point here is not at all to make an argument about the authorship of an anonymous and collective text, a speculation which would in any case be irrelevant for our purposes and without evidence. But the intellectual solidarities and the affinities of topic are worth understanding inasmuch as they point to the remarkable way in which Paulinism exerts over this literature such a massive gravitational force.

For example, in keeping with Agamben's agenda, Tiqqun's *Introduction to Civil War* promises a "*radically negative* anthropology" rather than a positive description of the stable ground of emancipatory critique.[17] The figures of this negative anthropology, moreover, are entirely oriented by the question of singularity or "form-of-life" which is opposed to the reduction of ourselves to a generic "bare life," a reduction which of course washes out our unique particularities or traits in ways that render us susceptible to abstractive managerialisms. Similarly, everywhere in Tiqqun's *Introduction to Civil War* we see an elaboration of those tactics of "suspension" of representational or juridical categories, those tactics which dominate Agamben's rendering of Paul, in whose hands the apostle becomes a kind of "classic" in the tradition of the "neutralization" (or rendering "inoperative") of juridical, identitarian, and representational forms.[18] Moreover, in some of the most important sections of the *Introduction to Civil War* are other favorite genealogical questions of Agamben which most directly bear on his philosophical reception of Paul, especially Foucault's analysis of the rise of biopolitics and the state as a servant of economy, a transformation the *Introduction to Civil War* articulates as a repetition of Christian theological themes.[19] Finally, just like Agamben's Paul book, we find in the *Introduction to Civil War* the group's main struggle articulated as the fight to inhabit singularities in relation to imperial abstractions which systematically neutralize these. They are, to repeat Agamben's Schmittian story about Paul, struggling for a gesture which convincingly feels like an opposition of the "spirit" of constitutive power over the "letter" of the constituted authority.

One could in fact read to good effect the *Introduction to Civil War* as a kind of application (or even cookbook version) of Agamben's study of Pauline messianism. For example, Agamben found in Paul thinker of virtual solidarities which were hit upon by Paul's efforts to "divide the division" which otherwise would separate, say, the Jew from the non-Jew.[20] The *Introduction to Civil War* therefore

---

17 See, e.g., ibid., 11–12.
18 See, e.g., his introductory remarks from his Berkeley lectures on *Romans*, in Agamben, *The Time that Remains*, 1.
19 Tiqqun, *Introduction to Civil War*, e.g., 111–21.
20 Note his comments in Agamben, *The Time That Remains*, 47–53.

becomes formally Pauline when it applies this tactic to contemporary nominations of in-groups:

> Every attempt to grasp a "people" as a form-of-life—as race, class, ethnicity, or nation—has been undermined by the fact that the ethical differences *within* each "people" have always been greater than the ethical differences between "people" themselves.[21]

This is not simply a reference to the Paulinism of a world in which "civil war" (rather than fighting against geographical outsiders) is the paradigm of contemporary politics. It is also a striking affirmation of the way that Paul names for these groups the key indication of what an "inoperative community" might look like.[22]

Thus, one could reasonably see the *Introduction to Civil War* as a kind of expansion and development of Agamben's earlier work on Paul. Paul becomes, in a word, the thinker of "civil war" *avant la lettre*, a thinker of that form of cultural conflict which, Tiqqun declares (and Agamben, too) is the most emblematic contemporary form of social reproduction. The thesis relates to the way all these texts assert that we are seeing at the moment the "sublimation"—or further abstraction—of nationalist and even actively colonialist forms of power. This new "empire" of power is emerging through new forms of global economic internationalism. Not so much a present representational power capable of enforcing its strategies as it is a diffuse and abstractive capacity to reorient the measures and metrics of life in endlessly proliferating ways, this imagined "empire" sets the stage on which the everyday "heroes" of neutralization and singularity—effectively so many Paulinists—will arise. And when they do, they will emerge replete with Paul's own κατέχον myth of the imperial repression of chaos. Note the *Introduction to Civil War*:

> Empire functions best when crisis is ubiquitous. Crisis is Empire's regular mode of existence in the same way that an insurance company comes into being only when there's an accident. The temporality of Empire is the temporality of emergency and catastrophe.
> ... Empire is not the crowning achievement of a civilization, the end-point of its ascendant arc. Rather it is the tail-end of an inward turning process of disaggregation, as that which must check and if possible arrest the process. Empire is therefore the katechon. "'Empire' in this sense meant the historical power to restrain the appearance of the Antichrist and the end of the present eon." (Carl Schmitt, *The Nomos of the Earth*,

---

21 Tiqqun, *Introduction to Civil War*, 31.
22 In addition to Agamben's work by that name, note the similarity of themes and the reliance on Paul in the philosophical work and analysis of "biopolitics" by Esposito, *Immunitas*; Esposito, *Categories of the Impolitical*.

59–60). Empire sees itself as the final bulwark against the eruption of chaos, and acts with this minimal perspective in mind.²³

It is as if the rulers of the present age realized that they are indeed undone, neutralized, a realization which spurs them to "sublimate" their weakness in this way, to supplement it with reference to this more opaque, abstract, and indeed mysterious form. The story is crucial, both for Agamben and for the Invisible Committee, as it often signals for them a shift from representational "law" and the juridical identities of an earlier nation state into something like an imperial and biopolitical immanence of "norms." This shift to a mysteriously uncontrollable immanence of this new sublimated power occurs, moreover, within the same tableau as Schmitt's κατέχον myth. In fact, in the *Introduction to Civil War* it appears in yet another gesture linking the Invisible Committee to the Pauline Thessalonian correspondence. Their gloss on Schmitt reads:

> What do we mean by the Imaginary Party? *That the Outside has moved inside*. The turning inside out happened noiselessly, peacefully, like a thief in the night. At first glance, it seems nothing has changed. ONE is simply struck by the sudden futility of so many familiar things, and the old divisions that can no longer account for what is happening are now suddenly so burdensome. ²⁴

Neither Agamben nor the Invisible Committee signal the specific comparison at this point, but it is worth reading such gestures as similar to what we find in the Pauline political theology of Jacob Taubes. Taubes was clear: the messianic inversions of Paul may be read as a Schmittianism "from below," an effort to appropriate and undermine the neutralizations of legal rights imagined to go along with empire or a sovereignty acting "from above" within the social food chain.²⁵ In other words, the Paulinists in view here are seeking gestures by which to appropriate from empire a subversive and self-protective or emancipatory version of empire's own move from the "letter" to the (sublimated) "spirit" of power.

Similarly, if for Agamben's paradoxical Pauline messianism "from below" "every vocation is a revocation," the singular community of Tiqqun's *Introduction to Civil War* faces the same paradoxes surrounding the impossible closure of self-identity²⁶:

---

23 Tiqqun, *Introduction to Civil War*, 126–27.
24 Ibid., 130.
25 See Taubes, *The Political Theology of Paul*, and discussions in Blanton, *A Materialism for the Masses*, 25–27.
26 For the formulation of paradoxical vocation as revocation, see Agamben, *The Time That Remains*, 23–26.

> The moment community tries to incarnate itself in an isolatable subject, in a distinct, separate reality, the moment it tries to materialize the separation between what is inside it and what is outside, it confronts its own impossibility. This point of impossibility is communion.[27]

Put differently, only the paradoxical and decidedly non-organic πίστις of a Pauline community can indicate the solidarity of the singular which the Invisible Committee is urging as a transformative panacea for our current life-destroying submissions to imperial fear and death. Or, in the language of Agamben's Paul, all our communities are such inasmuch as they remain alive to the messianic remainder, the "time that remains" to come. We might also point out that, like Paul, those singularities looked to as an escape from the global immanence of "empire" emerges in a Pauline mode—through solidarity with the *pariah:*

> All those who cannot or will not conjure away the forms-of-life that move them must come to grips with the following fact: they are, we are, the *pariahs* of empire. Anchored somewhere within us, there is a lightless spot, a mark of Cain filling citizens with terror if not outright hatred. ... there are the strays, the poor, the prisoners, the thieves, the criminals, the crazy, the perverts, the corrupted, the overly alive, the overflowing, the rebellious corporalities. In short, all those who, following their own line of flight, do not fit into Empire's stale, air-conditioned paradise. *Us*—this is the fragmented plane of consistency of the Imaginary Party.[28]

This zone of solidarity is, in good Pauline fashion, merely a matter of *pistis*, a zone where "friendships" can weave together a non-coercive and in some sense unmeasurable affiliation, their communicability emerging paradoxically on through the non-natural genealogies or even the incommunicability they indicate.[29]

In the end, the struggle to invent a contemporary Paulinist gesture will have been then about the preservation or recuperation of a messianic πίστις. As Agamben had declared earlier in his essay "In Praise of Profanation":

> The apparatuses of the media aim precisely at neutralizing this profanatory power of language as pure means, at preventing language from disclosing the possibility of a new use, a new experience of the word. Already the church, after the first two centuries of hoping and waiting, conceived of its function as essentially one of neutralizing the new experience of the word that Paul, placing it at the center of the messianic announcement, had called *pistis*, faith.[30]

---

[27] Tiqqun, *Introduction to Civil War*, 41.
[28] Ibid., 174.
[29] Ibid., cf. 179.
[30] Agamben, *Profanations*, 88.

Or, to conclude with the Paulinism of Tiqqun, this solidarity is a "formation" which is a "*contagious* formation" rather than a program to be implemented.[31]

Such is the Pauline gesture. *We* are the real children of Abraham, we the antagonists of empire whose trust simply is the invisible community—or, to say the same, the Invisible Committee.

References

Agamben, Giorgio. *The Time That Remains: A Commentary on the Letter to the Romans.* Translated by Patricia Dailey. Stanford, CA: Stanford University Press, 2005.
Agamben, Giorgio. *Profanations.* Translated by Jeff Fort. New York: Zone Books, 2007.
Agamben, Giorgio. *The Kingdom and the Glory.* Translated by Lorenzo Chiesa with Matteo Mandarini. Stanford, CA: Stanford, 2011.
Agamben, Giorgio. *The Highest Poverty: Monastic Rules and Form-of-Life.* Translated by Adam Kotsko. Stanford, CA: Stanford University Press, 2013.
Agamben, Giorgio, and Judith Butler. "Eichmann, Law, and Justice," 12:05 min., lecture at the European Graduate School. September 16, 2009. https://www.youtube.com/watch?v=bYzLcBO1ZwU.
Blanton, Ward. *A Materialism for the Masses: Saint Paul and the Philosophy of Undying Life.* New York: Columbia, 2015.
Dufresne, David. *Tarnac, magasin général.* Paris: Fayard, 2012.
Esposito, Roberto. *Immunitas: The Protection and Negation of Life.* Translated by Zakiya Hanafi. Cambridge: Polity Press, 2011.
Esposito, Roberto. *Categories of the Impolitical.* Translated by Connal Parsley. New York: Fordham, 2015.
"Fox News." YouTube Video 6:55. Review of the Coming Insurrection by Glen Beck. Accessed at January 3, 2016. https://www.youtube.com/watch?v=ZKyi2qNskJc.
Gleize, Jean-Marie. *Tarnac, un act préparatoire.* Paris: Éditions du Seuil, 2011. Translated by Joshua Clover, Abigail Lang and Bonnie Roy as *Tarnac: A Preparatory Act* (Berkeley, CA: Kenning Editions, 2014).
Paye, Jean-Claude. *L'emprise de l'image: De Guantanamo à Tarnac.* Paris: Yves Michel Éditions, 2011.
Seelow, Soren. "Tarnac: bataille procédurale autour de la définition du terrorisme." *Le Monde*, August 11, 2015.
Taubes, Jacob. *The Political Theology of Paul.* Translated by Dana Hollander. Edited by Aleida Assman and Jan Assmann in conjunction with Horst Folkers, Wolf-Daniel Hartwich, and Christoph Schulte. Stanford, CA: Stanford University Press, 2004.
The Invisible Committee. *The Coming Insurrection.* New York: Semiotext(e), 2009.
Tiqqun. *Introduction to Civil War.* Los Angeles: Semiotext(e), 2010.

---

31 Tiqqun, *Introduction to Civil War*, 174.

"Cabbage-Patch Revolutionaries? The French 'Grocer Terrorists.'" *The Independent* December 18, 2008. Accessed February 23, 2017. http://www.independent.co.uk/news/world/europe/cabbage-patch-revolutionaries-the-french-grocer-terrorists-1202334.html.

Gert-Jan van der Heiden and George van Kooten
Epilogue: Saint Paul and Philosophy—The Consonance of Ancient and Modern Thought

1 Introduction: How to Address the Philosophical Affiliations of Paul's Πίστις?

The sixteen essays in this volume reflect on, and discuss in detail important aspects of the threefold relation between Paul and continental philosophy, Paul and the Greco-Roman world, and Paul and political theology. Looking back on these contributions, in this epilogue we wish to consider what conclusions may be drawn from them and—by bringing these different interpretations into dialogue with one another—discuss what responses the volume may offer to the line of inquiry set out at the start of this project. As we noted in the introduction, our questions in this volume pertain first and foremost to the meaning and the impact of the notion of πίστις ("faith" or "belief") and Paul's πίστις language, both in the Greco-Roman world Paul inhabited and in the present-day philosophical discourse in which his letters are heavily debated. In particular, we are interested in how these two approaches to Paul's πίστις language can be brought into dialogue, and whether the essays in this volume indeed support a consonance between ancient and modern thought. The question of πίστις is a shared concern for all the contributions to this book, in which it is taken up in different ways and from different angles. Our introduction also suggested one specific direction the inquiry into the πίστις language of Paul might take, namely an interrogation of πίστις or faith against the background of the (in)famous distinction, sometimes presented as an opposition, between faith and reason. How does πίστις, and the usage of this term in Paul's letters, in the Greco-Roman world, and in the present-day philosophical reflection on Paul's thought, relate to notions such as reason, rationality, or rationalities? Do we find an opposition, a different kind of relation or, perhaps, rather a non-relation since they belong to different fields altogether?

If we consider how this more specific line of inquiry is addressed in this volume, we see a somewhat complex answer taking shape. The language of πίστις in Paul and in the Greco-Roman world does indeed have an epistemological dimension; however, as Teresa Morgan argues in her contribution, it is also used in relation to other ethical, social, psychological, and spiritual dimensions, which are concerned with πίστις in the sense of trust and trustworthiness—of God, of Christ, and of human beings. Moreover, from the point of view of the present-day philosophical turn to Paul, it becomes clear that the attention to πίστις is indeed of crucial importance. As Blanton writes in relation to the Invisible Committee, and Agamben as its source of inspiration: "In the end, the struggle to invent a contemporary Paulinist gesture will have been then about the preservation or recuperation of a messianic πίστις." Ultimately, this is one of the fundamental ways to capture and understand the present-day turn to Paul, to which this volume offers new insights: the interest in Paul concerns an attempt "to invent a contemporary Paulinist gesture" that indeed tries to revive, retrieve, and repeat (as in Heidegger's sense of *Wiederholung*) Paul's sense of πίστις. Yet it also seems —and we will clarify this further in this epilogue—that this retrieval of πίστις tends to emphasize the importance of the particular ethos or attitude to life with which it is presented in Paul's letters; there is much less concern with a theoretical-epistemological dimension of πίστις, although the latter is not absent from Paul's letters. Thus, there is a marked one-sidedness in the present-day philosophical approach to Paul. However, this one-sidedness allows the philosophers to concentrate on the issue of ethos and address it in different ways; the significance of this issue is multiplied in the analyses of trust, fidelity, oaths, ὡς μή ("as if not"), καταργεῖν ("to render inoperative" or "to deactivate"), the παρουσία ("the second coming") and so on.

In a sense, it is remarkable that philosophers today do not develop Paul's πίστις language in epistemological terms. Yet one should not forget that in philosophy, πίστις is always understood as subordinate to ἐπιστήμη, which is true scientific and theoretical knowledge. Therefore, πίστις has always been of lesser concern for the domains of ontology or first philosophy, in which only ἐπιστήμη is good enough. Moreover, in recent times, the notion of faith (and we are speaking here only about the vicissitudes of Paul's πίστις) has been turned into the opposite of reason, giving rise to the infamous opposition of (religious) faith and reason or knowledge. It is important to understand the implications of this opposition. Nietzsche's exclamations in *The Antichrist*, in which not Christ but Paul is one of the real targets, offers us a clear indication of what is at stake in this opposition. Although the influence of Paul in modernity is of course much more wide-ranging, as for instance Zaborowski's essay shows, Nietzsche's text provides one characteristic understanding of this opposition. And this in turn may offer an indication of why continental philosophers, who are often very well-versed in Nietzsche (and refer to Nietzsche's interpretation in their own reading of Paul), refrain from approaching faith in an epistemological register.

In *The Antichrist*, Nietzsche indeed characterizes faith as the true opposite of reason and its will to know. "'Faith' as an imperative," he writes, "is the veto against science—in praxi, the lie at any price ... Paul perceived that the lie—that faith was necessary."[1] And a few pages later, Nietzsche adds that "'faith' means not *wanting*-to-know what is true," thereby truly opposing faith and reason by their opposing wills. Science as the will to know is concerned with "the service of truth" which "is the hardest service" in which "almost everything on which the heart otherwise clings, our love, our trust in life, has had to be surrendered"; Paul's will of faith, on the other hand, as the will not to know, "makes blessed: consequently, it lies"—here, to be blessed means to be in a state of living that does not dare to confront the hardships to which science leads us and which is thus a bliss based on lies.[2] It is important to note that in this context, faith still belongs to the realm of epistemology; yet no longer as a lesser kind of knowledge (as πίστις was in relation to ἐπιστήμη), but as the *privation* of the will to know and the will to truth.

In contrast to this Nietzschean account of faith in *The Antichrist*, philosophers such as Badiou and Agamben emphasize that faith should first and foremost be understood from Paul's discussion of the law—not faith and *reason*, but faith and *law* is the appropriate pair of concepts in Paul's *Romans*. At the same time, they stress that faith is concerned with a particular ethos of the subject—whether it is Badiou's notion of fidelity or Agamben's account of faith as *performativum fidei*, as analyzed extensively by Peter Zeillinger in this volume. This ethos of faith is never characterized by them as *un*reasonable or as a will *not* to know; rather it concerns another realm than that of knowledge. It does, however, attest to a definite *non-conformity* to what is habitual, respected, or the general rule "in the world." This latter reinterpretation of faith will transform Nietzsche's famous account of Paul's rejection of "this world." In *Ecce Homo*, Nietzsche writes (not so much with respect to Paul as such but with respect to the Christian morality), "The concepts 'other world,' 'true world' invented in order to devalue the only world there is—in order to leave no goal, no reason, no task remaining for our earthly reality!"[3] Yet, if Paul's letters are read in this nihilistic key as affirming a world that is not, and thereby devaluing "the only world there is," it remains to be seen whether one captures the specific attitude

---

1 Nietzsche, *Ecce Homo and The Antichrist*, 151.
2 Ibid., 157, 155. For a more extensive discussion of how Nietzsche relates to the present-day readings of Paul, see, e.g., Van der Heiden, "The Experience of Contingency and the Attitude to Life."
3 Nietzsche, *Ecce Homo and The Antichrist*, 97.

to life Paul proclaims. Everything depends on what one means by, and reads into Paul's rejection of "this world."

This reference to the famous distinction between this world and the other world, which for Nietzsche is Platonist as well as Paulinist—since, as was already remarked in some of the essays collected in this volume, for Nietzsche Paul's Christianity is "Platonism for the people"—is interesting for one reason in particular. It shows, namely, that Nietzsche's battle with Paul concerns (a) the dishonesty of the latter's faith, which as "not-wanting-to-know" is a cowardly turning away from what is, and (b) the nihilism implied in such a rejection of this world. For Nietzsche, these two belong intrinsically together, and this may have attracted Nietzsche to Paul since these thinkers converge in their (supposed) nihilism. Consequently, for philosophers today the attempt to "invent a contemporary Paulinist gesture" cannot be limited to recalibrating the notion of faith and πίστις and rethinking it beyond the merely epistemological dimension in which Nietzsche positions it. Such an attempt must also address the accusation of Paul's nihilism. This latter task is even more important for philosophy today when one realizes that authors such as Heidegger, Badiou, and Agamben seem to have found in Paul an alternative mode of thinking to the metaphysical structure of philosophy that Heidegger termed onto-theology: For Nietzsche, if we reconstruct what he might have thought if confronted with this term, the onto-theological constitution is yet another version of philosophy's, Christianity's, and Paul's nihilism. This means that the recalibration of the notion of faith can only be truly effective if it is accompanied by an account of Paul's ontology that shows in what sense this ontology exceeds onto-theology and is not, in Nietzsche's sense of the term, nihilism. Moreover, formulated in these terms, as the contributions of the second part of this volume show, the questions are no longer solely a matter of present-day continental philosophy, but intersect with present-day research in ancient philosophy.

So where do these considerations leave us? Let us rephrase them in slightly different terms. If we ask what Paul's πίστις means today and, in particular, how this notion is related to—rather than merely "opposed to"—reason, reasonability, and rationality, we confront not two questions concerning the use of Paul's πίστις in Greco-Roman times and its reinterpretation in present-day philosophy, but rather three questions. The above unfolding of the basic line of inquiry put forward in the introduction suggests that a reflection on the results of this volume's sixteen essays may be divided into three parts, according to these three questions. The three are of course intrinsically connected, but this subdivision allows us to structure and systematize the results: (1) What is Paul's ontology? And in which sense can (or cannot) Paul's conception of the world be called onto-theological or, as Nietzsche would have it, nihilistic? (2) What is the meaning of πίστις language in Paul's letters and in the context of the Greco-Roman world? (3) How is this terminology used in present-day philosophy, and how does it offer an alternative to the Nietzschean claim that faith is nothing but the sheer privation of the scientific will to know? More positively, how is this usage conceived in terms of a confrontation with the law, of offering a particular sense of the political, and of inspiring us to devise a new ethos of commitment, conviction, and non-conformity? In the next sections, we will discuss these three sets of questions in turn.

2 Ontology and Μή-ontology in Paul's Letters

That there is an ontological concern in the present-day turn to Paul seems beyond doubt, even if this concern may indeed be focused first and foremost on the problem of a political ontology, as Ezra Delahaye suggests. Yet it is less clear what exact ontology the philosophers discern in Paul, and how we should assess their account of Paul's conception of reality.

An interesting point of departure for such a discussion can be found in Simon Critchley's reflections on the interpretations of Heidegger, Badiou, and Agamben. His reflections allow us to connect a number of themes and terms from the philosophical discussion on Paul's ontology. Critchley argues that the interpretation of authors such as Badiou, Agamben, and Heidegger negates reality, first of all, and that the ontology they find in Paul might best be conceived as *μή-ontology* (non-ontology).[4] This is an important suggestion, not least because the term "μή-ontology" is connected not only with Paul's notion of ὡς μή ("as if not") in 1 Cor. 7:29–30—as discussed in the work of both Agamben and Heidegger and addressed by a number of the essays in this volume—but also with Paul's rhetorical distinction between τὰ ὄντα ("the things that are") and τὰ μὴ ὄντα ("the things that are not") in 1 Cor. 1:28, which reads: "God chose what is low and despised in the world, things that are not (τὰ μὴ ὄντα), to reduce to nothing (καταργήσῃ) things that are (τὰ ὄντα)." This latter passage is central for Badiou and is explicitly addressed by him.[5] In fact, his most crucial comments on this passage are preceded by the affirmation that Paul's God cannot be thought in terms of what Heidegger called onto-theology: "Paul prescribes an anticipatory critique of what Heidegger calls onto-theology, wherein God is

---

4 Critchley was also a guest at the project in Nijmegen and with him we discussed Chapter 4 of his *The Faith of the Faithless*. For his account of μή-ontology, see ibid., 177–83.
5 Badiou, *Saint Paul*, 46–47.

thought as supreme being, and hence as the measure for what being as such is capable of."⁶ Paul's God, as Badiou suggests by subsequently referring to 1 Cor. 1:28, is not the measure of being, but rather the one who reduces "to nothing things that are" and chooses "things that are not." Moreover, this passage is of crucial importance to Agamben because Paul here uses the verb καταργεῖν, "to render inoperative," which plays a crucial role in Agamben's reading of Paul, as Antonio Cimino shows.

With these indications of what the "μή-ontology" of Paul refers to, we may immediately connect a number of important themes addressed in several essays in this volume: In Paul's vocabulary in *1 Corinthians* we find the important terms τὰ μὴ ὄντα ("the things that are not"), καταργεῖν ("to render inoperative"), and ὡς μή ("as if not"); in the immediate context of the latter term we also find the phrase τὸ σχῆμα τοῦ κόσμου τούτου ("the form of this world") which "is passing away" (1 Cor. 7:31). Other important terms here, drawn from the present-day philosophical vocabulary, include "onto-theology" and "nihilism," of which the term "μή-ontology" is reminiscent.

If we take these terms as our point of departure to reflect on the ontological problem in Paul, it seems reasonable to conclude on the basis of, for instance, the essays of Delahaye, Van der Heiden, Cimino, and Vedder that philosophers sense in Paul's letters an alternative to onto-theology, that is, to an approach to the cosmos or its form that does not affirm this form but rather problematizes it. In particular, Paul's proclamation of both the resurrection and the παρουσία evokes possibilities that are not acknowledged by the order of the world we inhabit. In addition, it makes sense to argue that in order to explore such an alternative for onto-theology, the philosophers pay special attention to the vocabulary in Paul's letters that seems to express a form of nihilism: God choosing τὰ μὴ ὄντα, "the things that are not"; the believers being advised to live their lives ὡς μή, "as if not" (for instance, to be married as if not being married); Paul proclaiming that τὸ σχῆμα τοῦ κόσμου τούτου, the present order of the world, is passing away; and so on.

When we are confronted with this observation that seems to support Critchley's suggestion that we are dealing here with a Pauline μή-ontology, two sets of questions arise. (1) First, are these philosophers reviving the sense of nihilism that Nietzsche ascribed to Paul? If so, in what sense is their reading different from Nietzsche? When they, unlike Nietzsche, attribute a positive value to Paul, are they reviving the Platonist-Marcionist core that Nietzsche rejected (as Critchley argues)? And if not, what form of nihilism (if any) do we encounter

---

6 Ibid., 47.

here under the seemingly well-chosen name of μή-ontology? (2) Secondly, is it actually convincing to deny that an onto-theology may be found in Paul? May the Stoic background of Paul perhaps offer other possibilities to read the various nihilistic passages, possibilities that do not reject the onto-theological structure in Paul's letters, as Van Kooten suggests? And what, then, are the philosophical consequences of such an argument?

(1) In order to address these questions, which allow us to explicate the ontological alternative found in Paul, we need first to clarify the terminology that is used here. Clearly, when Nietzsche describes Paul's Christianity as a form of Platonism for the people, this implies that the form of nihilism in Paul is the same as the nihilism Nietzsche discerns in Platonism, namely the rejection of this world in favor of a non-existing other or afterworld. Via the notion of God, as the name of a permanence of being that measures all that is, the Platonist dualism would subsequently be identified with what Badiou refers to as onto-theology. Thus, in this framework, what Nietzsche calls nihilism would be the very core of what Heidegger calls onto-theology. In the present-day debate, however, this identity is the very *status quaestionis* called into doubt by the philosophers. Yet to be able to open the debate, it seems that the philosophers feel compelled to start discussing the most nihilistic moments in Paul's letters— if they even *are* nihilistic moments.

It is important to capture the basic tenet of this latter remark—if they even *are* nihilistic moments. Whenever the question of non-being or nothingness is addressed in philosophy, one has to be aware that it is usually concerned with showing in what sense what is taken to be nothing is in fact not simply nothing. Consider, for instance, Plato and Aristotle who, when confronting the problem of non-being, do not deny the phenomenon, but rather try to understand how it is possible that certain forms of non-being appear as a variation of being. Their task was to capture why these forms they encountered were not simply nothing. Plato's *Sophist*, for example, offers the suggestion that one should think certain forms of non-being as being-different or being-otherwise in order to account for differences, and Aristotle's *Metaphysics* reinterprets certain forms of non-being in terms of potentiality to account for becoming. In both cases, we see a differentiation taking place: being is differentiated beyond mere identity and actuality. It might make sense to consider the present-day philosophers' attention to so-called nihilistic moments in Paul's letters in a similar light.

In fact, when we do indeed view the present-day philosophical readings of Paul in this light, we see a remarkably similar phenomenon: what initially appears to be nothing turns out to be a differentiation in being that cannot be reduced to "the things that are" or to "the form of this world," but rather constitutes an exception to this form, which is, however, more real than the present form of the world and the things that are something in the present order of the world. In fact, in this context, the reason why philosophers turn to Paul is not because he is "μή-ontological" as such, or because his conception of the cosmos and God is simply a variation of the onto-theological constitution of metaphysics ever since Plato (and thus deserves to be called nihilistic in a very precise sense of the word), but rather because Paul's letters attest to the fact that what appears to be nothing is in fact the very source of other possibilities of being. The things that are not turn out to be not-nothing, since they are chosen. What has no place in the order and the estimation of the world, and is counted or valued as nothing, turns out to be what remains as Van der Heiden suggests. In Heidegger's analysis of the παρουσία, it turns out that the παρουσία is not concerned with the end of time, that is, with the destruction of time and the destruction of the world, but rather that the very imminence and unexpectedness of this παρουσία—that it may come as a thief in the night—implies an intensification of the time of our lives and a qualitative change in how we experience our lives. Similarly, Agamben's attention to the ὡς μή and καταργεῖν is not concerned with the destruction of our vocations or of the things that are, but rather with disclosing that living does not coincide with the orders in which we live our lives, and that being does not coincide with the present order of form of the things that are. In this very precise sense, for Agamben Paul's ὡς μή is not a nihilistic structure but rather concerns an attitude of a certain indifference that does not destroy the believers' old vocations, but does show how the believers do not coincide with their vocations—these are not their identity—and thus allows them to use these vocations freely.

This is also a good moment to comment briefly on the issue of the best translation of Paul's ὡς μή, especially as Agamben and Taubes appear to differ here. Taubes translates this phrase from 1 Cor. 7:29–31 as "as if not": "as though they had none [as if they had none, *comme si*] … ."[7] As Frazier indicates in the discussion during our conference, the ὡς in the phrase ὡς μή should not be translated as an ontological term, as Taubes does, as "*comme si*," but rather as an axiological term, as "*dans la pensée que*," "considering that." Yet this correct remark is not unambiguously supported by Liddell, Scott, Jones's *Greek-English Lexicon* (LSJ), where the construction of ὡς μή followed by a participle in the case of the Subject is said "to mark the reason or motive of the action" and to ought to be translated as "as if," "as."[8] It is perhaps difficult to see how the ὡς

---

7 Taubes, *The Political Theology of Paul*, 53–54.
8 See LSJ s.v. ὡς C.I.1: C. "ὡς before I. Participles"; I.1 "with Participles in the case of the Subject, to mark the reason or motive of the action, 'as if,' 'as,' ὡς + participle / ὡς οὐκ + participle / ὡς μή + participle."

μή in 1 Cor. 7:29–31 marks the "reason" or "motive" of the actions described, but LSJ Lexicon seems to agree with Frazier's view that the ὡς μή alludes to an attitude, to an axiological, value-based consideration. Agamben, differently from Taubes, consciously steers away from the "as if." Following Heidegger, Agamben insists that the phrase ὡς μή should be translated as "as not," and not as "as if not" because the latter translation suggests that the phrase ὡς μή introduces something imaginary, un-real, as in the case of the expression "to act as if"; the one who acts "as if" merely simulates something and does not take it seriously.[9] So indeed, according to Agamben Paul's ὡς μή is not a nihilistic structure, but rather concerns an attitude of a certain indifference.

It is striking that Van Kooten's approach to the ὡς μή from Paul's Stoic background and its similarity to the ἀδιάφορα leads to a similar conclusion. By pointing out the Stoic background in Paul, Van Kooten not only dismisses a nihilistic or μή-ontological reading of the ὡς μή-structure, but also gives credence to, and a historical motivation for, Agamben's account of this structure in terms of an indifference. Concerning the resistance to a nihilistic or μή-ontological reading of Paul, we thus find crucial consonances between ancient and modern thought.

In more positive terms, the ontological alternative to both onto-theology and nihilism is connected to the idea of transformation, potentiality and contingency, since what remains in and through the seemingly nihilistic passages turns out to be what does not conform to the present form of the world: it does not destroy the world or the things that are, but allows them to be taken up in different ways than the form of the world prescribes. As Van der Heiden puts it: "The non-being of the world, of time and of human righteousness are taken up by Paul to demonstrate the non-conformity of what remains and to disclose what these remains keep in reserve: as sense of the being of the time, of the world and of the law as what-can-be-otherwise." This quote suggests that these ontological categories are taken up in a particular ethos or attitude to life, which is here described in terms of a non-conformity to the present orders, laws, and forms. The issue of the attitude to life that is heralded here will be discussed below, when we reflect on the third thematic line of inquiry on the particular attitude of faith.

(2) Notwithstanding the previous considerations, it remains to be seen to what extent the idea that Paul is truly beyond the onto-theological framework is in line with contemporary research on the work of the philosophy and culture

---

9 Agamben, *The Time That Remains*, 23–37; Heidegger, *The Phenomenology of Religious Life*, 86. As Baker nicely summarizes Agamben's discussion of the meaning of ὡς μὴ: "The small but all-important difference between negation as the 'as not' and as the 'as if' is the difference between messianism as already realized eschatology and as merely a point of view on another possible world" (Baker, "Paul and Political Theology," 303).

of the Greco-Roman world. In a number of essays, we encounter criticisms of elements of the present-day reception of Paul.

The imminence of the παρουσία, which is of fundamental importance for Heidegger's reading of Paul in light of the early Christian worldview, is relativized and contextualized by Morgan who writes: "*1 Thessalonians*' use of πίστις therefore suggests that Paul does not so much hold a view of the imminence of the second coming in this letter (cf. 1 Thess. 4:15, 5:6) which he later abandons, as that his sense of urgency and his sense of the diachronic nature of his mission are always in tension." This complicates the centrality of the sense of urgency at work in Paul's proclamation of the παρουσία and shows his attention to a history of institutionalization that is required in addition to this urgency.

Van Kooten directly addresses the question of onto-theology by showing how Paul's remarks in 1 Cor. 1 may be read in line with his affinity with the Stoics, for whom "all things come from God and return to God." This, as the final sentences from 1 Cor. 1 suggest, also applies to the things that are not (τὰ μὴ ὄντα): in this sense, for Paul *all* reality derives from God and there is hence no such thing as a *creatio ex nihilo*. Should one not say, then, that for this reason God is the very principle of all reality, and that it therefore seems highly problematic to discern in his letters (and especially in *1 Corinthians*) a critique of onto-theology, as some of the philosophers today attempt? The answer to this question is less straightforward than it may appear. In fact, rather than historically correcting the present-day philosophers, raising this question may open up a further line of inquiry that accentuates the true concerns in the present-day philosophical enterprise. Such a line of inquiry would definitely have to address the following ingredients. The verb καταργεῖν, which expresses how God dissolves the things that are (or renders them inoperative), is taken up philosophically in the German verb *aufheben*, as Agamben argues and as is reflected upon by Cimino.[10] This suggests that the Stoic-Pauline account of reality may be accounted for in terms of a particular dialectics in which God is not simply and only the measure of the things that are, but the provenance of both the things that are and the things that are not—and this means that God is also the critic and the dissolver of the things that are and of the present form of the world. This implies, first, that both philosophical and theological scholarship tend to reject the paradigm that Paul's letters offer a Gnostic-dualistic thought and are moving towards the paradigm of a more dialectical dimension to Paul's thought. In the context of modern philosophy, due to the analysis of onto-theology, this question of dialectics is subsequently understood in terms of the accentuated

---

10 Agamben, *The Time That Remains*, 99.

question of which type of dialectics one might discern in the Stoic Paul. Hence, such a future line of inquiry, inspired by the cross-fertilization of contributions on ancient and modern thought, would, for instance, have to address the question of whether such a dialectics is comparable to the movement of absolute spirit in Hegel's version of dialectics, or whether another form of dialectics announces itself here. Such a question would then have to be discussed, for instance, in light of Agamben's account of καταργεῖν and the difference it marks with Hegel's *Aufhebung*, as well as in light of Taubes's remarks on the difference between Paul's πνεῦμα and Hegel's world spirit. Such a confrontation between the models of dialectics offered by Hegel, Taubes, and Agamben's Paul, and a subsequent comparison with the Stoic-Pauline sense of God and spirit would be a following step in the dialogue between ancient and modern thought to capture the significance of Paul's letters today.

3 Πίστις Language in Paul and the Greco-Roman World

These reflections on Paul's ontology in light of present-day philosophy and Paul's Greco-Roman philosophical context prepare the ground for this volume's more particular interest in Paul's πίστις language. In order to connect the reflections on πίστις with the question of Paul's ontology, it might be helpful to take our departure from the insight we developed above that the present-day reading of Paul is marked by a continuous attempt to show how Paul, even in his seemingly most nihilistic moments, does not offer the type of nihilism Nietzsche finds in him. This continuous attempt is not limited to ontological concerns alone but stretches out to what we might call the epistemological status of Paul's notion of faith. As we noted in the opening pages of this epilogue, for Nietzsche faith is the opposite of reason, and he describes faith as "not *wanting*-to-know what is true": faith belongs to the space of knowledge, but only as a privation of knowledge. In *The Antichrist*, Nietzsche describes faith or belief (*Glaube*) in terms of "holding-something-for-true" (*Für-wahr-halten*).[11] In this way, he describes faith as an epistemological notion. This can also be observed elsewhere in Nietzsche's work: beyond the context of his account of Paul, too, Nietzsche conceives of *Glaube* as a form of *Für-wahr-halten* and its implications of the nihilism at

---

11 Nietzsche, *Ecce Homo and The Antichrist*, 139.

work in philosophy.¹² This holding-for-true or taking-to-be-true thus explicates faith (*Glaube*) as a form of propositional belief.

In light of this Nietzschean description of *Glaube* as *Für-wahr-halten*, it is interesting to note that Heidegger writes in his lectures on Paul: "The πίστις is not a taking-to-be true (*Fürwahrhalten*) … ; the πιστεύειν is a complex of enactment that is capable of increase."¹³ By using the same terminology as Nietzsche and by rejecting that this meaning is at stake in the specific passage he is discussing here (2 Thess. 1:3), Heidegger withdraws faith or πίστις from its epistemological context and points to the performative sense of faith and the way in which believers enact their lives and their faith. Πίστις thus reflects more a mode of living or a mode of being than a cognitive state. Although different philosophers read and interpret the notion of πίστις differently, it seems that they agree in their resistance to the Nietzschean stance in which πίστις concerns a particular cognitive stance of "taking to be true" or "holding for true" (and in the case of Paul's faith, for Nietzsche this means: despite and against what science as the real will to truth offers us). Yet, for Heidegger, Agamben, and Badiou, faith is not concerned first and foremost with holding something to be true. It belongs to a different sphere.

In this regard, the following remark by Heidegger is highly interesting:

> It is a decrease of authentic understanding if God is grasped primarily as an object of speculation. That can be realized only if one carries out the explication of the conceptual connections. This, however, has never been attempted, because Greek philosophy penetrated into Christianity.¹⁴

The metaphysical attention—effected by the Greek philosophical penetration into Christianity—to, for instance, the question of the existence of God as the highest being—can only be understood as a "decrease of authentic understanding," as Heidegger suggests. In his view, the real matter, for Paul, is not establishing the existence of a highest being as a metaphysical truth. He deems Paul to be concerned not with propositional beliefs but rather with the particular enactment of life that goes hand in hand with the name of God—and for Heidegger this means in the first place how to live one's life in accordance with the imminence of the παρουσία. Such a focus, as Badiou stresses, shows in what sense Nietzsche's analysis is inadequate: Paul does not shift the gravity of life into an otherworldly resurrection. Rather, as Badiou argues: "For Paul, the Resurrec-

---

12 See Nietzsche, *Nachgelassene Fragmente Herbst 1887*, 9[41], 9[97].
13 Heidegger, *The Phenomenology of Religious Life*, 76.
14 Ibid., 67.

tion is that on the basis of which life's center of gravity resides in life," that is, for Paul all depends on how life is lived in the here and now.¹⁵

One may argue that by addressing Paul's πίστις language in this way, present-day philosophers have neglected the epistemological sense that πίστις also has in his letters. Yet it is important to understand this neglect against the background of the specific sense this epistemological sense of faith had acquired in the nineteenth century in general, and in Nietzsche's reading of Paul in particular. Therefore, it makes sense to argue that these modern readers of Paul may be discovering a sense of the Greek language of πίστις and πιστεύειν that has otherwise been entirely lost in the conception of faith in the continental philosophical debate on Paul. If in this debate πίστις as a lesser form of ἐπιστήμη has indeed transformed into faith as the opposite of knowledge, the epistemological sense in which faith is understood—as holding to be true—deprives us of the basic tenet of πίστις in Paul. Moreover, once this ontological foundation of the Nietzschean conception of faith is problematized, faith has to be understood in another sense. One of the questions we set out to answer in this volume is whether the ancients' usage of πίστις language may help us to understand better how Paul's letters may indeed be a source for such a rethinking of faith beyond the epistemological dimension.

In general terms, as Françoise Frazier argues, the πίστις language used by Greco-Roman philosophers indeed covers a number of meanings besides the epistemological one: "in the sense of 'belief,' it is a kind of opinion, often opposed to knowledge; in the sense of 'confidence,' it is rather a state of the soul, a πάθος, which may be associated with self-assurance (θάρσος) or hope; in the sense of 'loyalty,' it is a virtue, which depends on justice." Even from a first, superficial glance at these three directions of meanings—belief, confidence, and loyalty—it is not difficult to see that much more than the first direction of meaning ("belief"), the present-day philosophical readings of Paul are concerned with finding those passages in which his πίστις language may be accounted for in terms of the other two ("confidence" and "loyalty"). If, indeed, we consider Paul's πίστις language from a scholarly perspective, as Morgan does in her contribution to this volume, we end up with the following result:

> Πίστις language is used to tell stories about the relationship between God and Christ and God, Christ and humanity; about the working of God's mercy, salvation, and the restoration of the faithful to righteousness; about the appointment of apostles to preach the gospel and their relationship with those they preach to; about how the faithful are chosen to accept the apostles' preaching; about how community members should live and relate to one another;

---

15 Badiou, *Saint Paul*, 62.

about how traditions and writings are authorized as objects and tools of πίστις. It is hard to conceive of any other lexical family in Greek that could have captured all these stories and bound them together into one grand, complex, (more or less) integrated system of thought and practice. Together with that of the other writers of the New Testament, Paul's and his followers' use of πίστις language integrated theology, ethics, ecclesiology and eschatology inextricably in early Christian thinking and ensured that πίστις, *fides*, and their translations into manifold later languages would become and remain central to every form of Christianity.

This means that any tendency to limit Paul's πίστις language to a sense of propositional belief, as is often done in the dominant general post-Enlightenment understanding of this term, tends to undermine the particular insight Morgan offers, namely that it is not so much the case that this language is used for theoretical purposes, describing what we do and do not believe to be the case, but rather that it is integrated into different practices that are related to each other. Anders Klostergaard Petersen explicitly confirms this when he writes in his contribution:

> In light of Paul's foundational worldview, the translation of πίστις Χριστοῦ/'Ιησοῦ as the steadfastness, commitment or faithfulness of Christ/Jesus is right to the point. Translations verging on modern ideas about "belief in" or "faith in" are in my view dubious by their anachronistic nature, presupposing as they do a later and stronger propositional concept of belief.

These comments by scholars of the Greco-Roman world clearly point to a basic consonance between the account of Paul's πίστις in ancient and modern thought. When we apply these general insights to see how this may lead to a fruitful interaction with the present-day philosophers, the contributions in this volume suggest at least two important points of contact and consonance between ancient and modern thought.

(1) If we consider the essay of Suzan Sierksma-Agteres, who examines how we should understand Paul's "justification by faith alone" axiom, it becomes clear that the combination of πίστις language with δίκη language (the language of justice) is not limited to Paul's letters, but is a common phenomenon in the ancient world. The combination of these terms in Paul may be understood as follows:

> Paul also proposes one common "law of πίστις" (Rom. 3:27). In light of these utopian, universalistic tendencies in Paul's Greco-Roman *Umwelt*, it seems more probable that Paul was, as the New Perspective argues, indeed arguing against Jewish—and Gentile—ethnocentrism.

This emphasis on the reading of Paul offered by the New Perspective on Paul, its emphasis on universalism and its criticism of the Lutheran account of Paul's justification by faith alone, is mirrored in Carl Raschke's contribution that rethinks the New Perspective's account in terms of Derrida's work on justice and righteousness. As in Sierksma-Agteres' contribution, Raschke argues that the Lutheran understanding of this Pauline axiom is untenable and that it should rather be understood in terms of what "Derrida himself reckons as a form of radical responsiveness and a sense of 'infinite' responsibility." Clearly such an affinity between what is found in the study of Paul in his Greco-Roman context does not imply that the ancient and the modern perspective simply fully converge, as Sierksma-Agteres illustrates with respect to Badiou: Although the theme of universalism and its relation to faith as fidelity, as investigated by Badiou, does have a definite similarity with her interpretation of Paul in his Greco-Roman context, it nevertheless also differs on important points. Yet the kinship between the two approaches indicates that moving away from a specific interpretation of πίστις in terms of epistemological concerns alone opens up Paul's πίστις language in such a way that the philosophical and the Greco-Roman significance of this language becomes clear. What we see here is that the question of universalism, justice, and fidelity become important markers in understanding how πίστις language—and in the texts of Sierksma-Agteres and Raschke especially in relation to δίκη language—may be interpreted beyond the sense of faith as explicated in the Lutheran context. As the Lutheran sense of "faith alone" has often been understood in terms of what is other than, or beyond the limits of reason, this Lutheran emphasis misses the point that Paul's usage of πίστις in relation to δίκη is concerned not so much with introducing a notion opposed to reason but rather with opening up a perspective of universalism (as Badiou suggests) or of responsibility (as Derrida suggests), in which πίστις concerns in the first place a sense of fidelity to both of these dimensions.

(2) Another important and fundamental elaboration of how Paul's notion of πίστις is reinterpreted by philosophers today is offered by Zeillinger. He shows how Agamben connects Paul's πίστις language to the phenomena of the oath and the ἐξομολόγησις, which Zeillinger describes as "an act meant to reveal both a truth and the subject's adherence to that truth; to do the ἐξομολόγησις of one's belief is not merely to affirm what one believes but to affirm the fact of that belief." As soon as one connects πίστις to practices of truth-telling, one obtains a very clear sense of what is at stake in the attempt to broaden the meaning of πίστις beyond the epistemological realm alone. When one is involved in an act to reveal the truth, there is always an epistemological moment involved because this act allows the truth to appear in the first place and thus communicates the truth to an audience. Yet it is important to note in what sense we

use "epistemological" here. First, the heart of the matter of such an act is not this knowing in itself. In particular, this understanding is not oriented towards a theoretical truth. Rather, what is fundamental for such acts is that they disclose and enact the "subject's adherence to that truth." Therefore, indeed, this truth is no longer a theoretical concern; rather it is concerned with what one might call a *conviction*, which the speaker does not simply "express", but to which the speaker attests, of which the speaker bears witness as being involved in it him- or herself. To say that a conviction is opposed to reason does not make any sense—one usually has all kinds of (good or bad) reasons for one's convictions. Yet to analyze a conviction in terms of these reasons *alone* would be to miss the particular mode of adherence, the πίστις involved in the subject's relation to a conviction, which is at work in every ἐξομολόγησις and truth-telling in Foucault and Agamben's sense of the word. Zeillinger's examination thus calls for further investigations along the lines of the work of Foucault, who analyzes παρρησία or truth-telling in the Greco-Roman context and explores how this work connects to Paul's πίστις. Agamben has some clear ideas about this, as Zeillinger quotes:

> When Paul, in Romans 10:6–10, defines the "word of faith" (*to rema tēs pisteōs*) not by means of the correspondence between word and reality but by means of the closeness of "lips" and "heart," it is the performative experience of veridiction that he has in mind ....

Looking back on the interaction between the present-day philosophical reinterpretation of Paul's πίστις and the repositioning of this term in the context of his letters and their Greco-Roman context, we see, first, how πίστις has a practical concern and, in particular, demands a certain ethos or attitude. In this way, πίστις is a term that is used beyond the mere theoretical-epistemological dimension, but without thereby being in opposition to reason. Secondly, the reasonability of πίστις cannot be reduced to external rules, orders, or laws alone: Paul's insistence on the law of πίστις refers to a non-external law and thus to a non-externality of πίστις. Thirdly, however, this non-externality should not be identified with a sheer subjectivist or individualistic choice. Rather, πίστις is interpreted as a notion, if we follow the suggestion of Agamben as well as of Badiou, that expresses a form of subjectification: it creates a subject of a particular practice—and in this sense, it is indeed necessarily communal rather than individual. Badiou interprets this as a practice of fidelity to the Christ-event that belongs to the community of believers, whereas Agamben interprets it as a practice of the believers that attests to their adherence to a conviction they publicly express; they do so to disclose their truth or conviction to the addressees of their attestations. It is this dimension of πίστις as ethos or attitude to life that we want to discuss in more detail in relation to the present-day philosophical readings of Paul in the next, final section.

4 The Ethos of Faith in Relation to Law and Politics

If πίστις is concerned with different kinds of practices that constitute the community as well as the subject, it may make sense to argue that the ethos of faith that speaks both from the analyses of Paul in his Greco-Roman context as well as from the present-day readings of Paul concerns first and foremost a form of trustworthiness and fidelity in a particular conviction that is brought forward by Paul's proclamation. Subsequently, one has to understand the notion of faith in a particular relation to what, in the second section of this epilogue, we referred to as Paul's ontology. In this final section, we would like to stipulate what precisely this understanding of faith means if we bring it into play with respect to the themes discussed above.

Let us start once again with Nietzsche's understanding of Paul's nihilistic ontology. One might say that this analysis depends on a simple dichotomy between this world and the other world and that, since according to Nietzsche the other world has no reality, faith as the attitude that rejects the earthly world and the life it represents and affirms the other world cannot be but nihilistic. In one sense, Nietzsche's bold claims may make sense: after all, isn't Paul's vocabulary based on a number of distinctions—such as flesh and spirit, death and life, and law and faith—that indicate the necessity of rejecting one term of the distinction while affirming the other one? And is it not also the case that, indeed, the positive terms "spirit," "life," and "faith" have to be understood from the resurrection of Christ, which for Nietzsche is the very proof that Paul resituates the true weight of (Christ's) existence in a realm beyond (Christ's) actual life? Yet the mere use of distinctions does not prove a nihilistic tendency in Paul.

First of all, as both Benjamin and Bloechl suggest, it is important to sense in Paul's attitude to life the element of *conversion*, both of himself and of the members of the communities to whom he writes. This means that above and beyond an analysis of the proper ontological issues at stake here—such as the afterlife, the resurrection, the end of the world, the παρουσία—Paul's distinctions are concerned with a very real distinction in the subject-position of Paul and his community members. A conversion, as Benjamin strikingly illustrates by referring to the logic of abandonment in some of the painted portraits of Paul, implies a change of identity and subject-position. Heidegger also emphasizes this point in his reading of *1* and *2 Thessalonians*, when he notes that Paul continuously appeals to the Thessalonians' having become.[16] Badiou understands the very distinction between life and death primarily in terms of this transformed subject-position, in which the death of the former subject-position is contrasted with the life of the present subject-position.

In line with Nietzsche, one might argue that this conversion may very well be very real to the subject, but this does not change the fact that this new subject-position is ultimately *nihilistic*, since it amounts to the very rejection of the world we inhabit: the new subject-position and its ascetic attitude to life is an enemy of life. Yet, as the present-day philosophers argue, Paul's "rejection" of the world involves more than, for instance, announcing the cosmological end of the world. The impact of these visions is to be found not in the particular ontological claims about the end of this world and the beginning of another world, but rather in another ontological issue, which, from a present-day philosophical point of view, is more urgent. The conversion and the subject-position to which it leads are concerned with adopting another perspective on the world. Whereas the world appears to us as "all there is," this other perspective challenges this appearance: the world, and that means its present form, its present order, its present laws, and its present rules, is *not* all there is. Rather than being grounded in a nihilism, the subject-position that adopts this other perspective only rejects the idea that the form, order, law, and rules of the world we inhabit encompass *the totality of what is possible*. When we look at the latter claim, it becomes much harder to argue, as Nietzsche does, that it is unreasonable and lacks honesty. In fact, Paul does not simply proclaim the existence of another world against all the odds and against reason. Rather, he argues that this order of the world is nihilistic in that it has no place for what is powerless, of low birth, lacks wealth, and so on—in short, for what appears to be nothing in this world—but that exactly these things that are not, τὰ μὴ ὄντα, are chosen to be.

Along this line of thought, it becomes clear why the distinctions introduced by Paul have *political* implications—and it is for this reason that the theme of political theology is so important in many of the present-day philosophers. In fact, and at this point Agamben might be not so far off in his insistence on the nature of the Pauline distinction: the distinctions Paul introduces *challenge* the distinctions that make up the form of the world (i.e., the distinctions between the wisdom and the folly of the world, between the powerful and the powerless, between the wealthy and the poor, and so on). In a certain sense, one might

---

[16] Heidegger, *The Phenomenology of Religious Life*, 65–67.

argue that Paul's faith concerns a proclamation as well as an argumentation for the contingency and the possible further differentiation of the distinctions that are operative in the world.¹⁷ As Terpstra writes, referring to Taubes:

> Contingency means that a distinction can always be challenged; another distinction can be drawn, or a distinction can be taken in a less strict way, and so on. This relates distinctions to the question of the exception: "The question is whether you think the exception is possible ... ."¹⁸

The thought of the exception is not, however, a thought that in and by itself is marked by the will not to know that Nietzsche ascribed to Christianity. In fact, it may be quite the contrary: in a given social order, an exception may very well exist but is often not so easily recognized or acknowledged. Exactly in such situations the ethos of truth requires people to speak out for the exception and the remainder. It is in this sense that Paul's universalism, as emphasized in different ways in this volume in reflections on both the New Perspective on Paul and the work of Badiou, indeed requires the ethos of faith and fidelity: a world order in which universalism and equality are not recognized or affirmed necessitates an engagement with and a fidelity to the idea of universalism, which includes the practice of telling this truth in a social environment in which it is not affirmed. Such examples also show that it does not make much sense to understand this ethos of faith in opposition to reason or to call it unreasonable. Rather, one would have to start explicating what reason and reasonable mean in this context. A given order of the world, and the discourses within which it describes and justifies its order, has its own rationality; and in light of this rationality, the ethos of faith appeals to a conviction or truth that can only emerge as being opposed to the rationality at work in these discourses of the world. The distinction between master and slave is a characteristic example of what we have in mind here: the meaning and rationale of the distinction between master and slave in ancient times are erased in Paul's proclamation because he argues that this distinction is irrelevant in light of the Christ or the messianic event. Distinctions may thus be the stuff which the order of the world is always made of, but these distinctions are not necessary but rather contingent. They can be destabilized and they can become irrelevant, but this does not happen overnight; it requires dedication, engagement, and fidelity. At the same time, it requires a corresponding practice of truth-telling, in line of what Agamben and Foucault suggest, by which the believer adopts a particular subject position, by which

---

17 Consider here also Ricoeur, "Paul apôtre."
18 Quote can be found at Taubes, *The Political Theology of Paul*, 85.

this subject intervenes in the existing discourses. In his reflections on παρρησία, which are also in the background of Agamben's account of ἐξομολόγησις, Foucault strikingly describes truth-telling as "irruptive ... which creates a fracture and opens up a risk: a possibility, a field of dangers, or at any rate, an undefined eventuality."[19] What Foucault calls "the field of dangers" does not only concern the possible dangers for the one who speaks in this way—for instance because his or her environment does not accept this threat to the given discourse; it also and mainly concerns the very uncertainty of the situation that will arise if this truth-telling is successful in its destabilization of the distinctions that order the given discourse. Yet, the ontological truth of this act of truth-telling is simply that the discourse and its guiding distinctions are contingent.

A similar strategy and a similar ontological concern is addressed by the philosophers in relation to Paul's concern with the passing away of the present form of the world. As Van Kooten insists in his account of this passage from 1 Cor. 7, this passage is indeed concerned with one of Paul's cosmological ideas. Yet, in addition, this cosmological truth requires and demands a particular ethos. Indeed, as Van Kooten suggests, this ethos of the ὡς μή—and one can immediately connect this with Paul's use of the verb καταργεῖν as discussed by Cimino—may be accounted for in terms of the Stoic conception of the ἀδιάφορα. Yet this is rather close to the present-day philosophical concern. Of course, the philosophers today are not simply Stoics and do not simply share the Stoic ontology. Yet what they do seem to be arguing is that in light of the passing away of the present form of the world, that is, in light of the contingency of this present form, the elements in the order that first seemed to matter are now seen in their indifference, and thus as things that can be used, as Agamben emphasizes. Here, an analysis of the Greco-Roman background, as attempted by Van Kooten, helps to understand what is at issue in the present-day reading: the cosmological occurrence of the ending of the world is no longer embedded in the particular ontological constellation Paul develops, but is rather interpreted in light of an account that emphasizes the contingency of the world. It is this contingency that also allows the present-day philosophers to challenge the present form of the world and its distinctions: faith is in this sense an ethos of non-conformity— "Do not be conformed to this world," as Paul writes in Rom. 12:2 (literally, "do not let yourself to be con-formed (μὴ συσχηματίζεσθε) to this present world era," using a verb that again includes the term σχῆμα of 1 Cor. 7:31). Further, this non-conformity is the reverse, to phrase it in Terpstra's terminology, of the attestation that the given distinctions are contingent, and that an exception is

---

19 Foucault, *The Government of Self and Others*, 63.

possible and a remainder can be made visible when the distinctions that are operative in the present form of the world are rendered idle and inoperative. Perhaps, looking back on Nietzsche's account of Paul, we might say that his Paul is the Paul who has given in to the dualistic Gnostic temptation, which is exemplified by the figure of Marcion, and which stresses the disconnectedness of this world and the other world. Perhaps one way to summarize the present-day philosophical account of Paul is as an attempt to show that Paul's letters, while harboring a Gnostic temptation, ultimately do not give in to this temptation: rather than offering a Gnostic dualism, these letters offer a Pauline dialectic that negates the present order of the world in order to contemplate the non-necessity of its form and thus its possible transformation, to which the ethos of faith corresponds.

References

Agamben, Giorgio. *The Time That Remains: A Commentary on the Letter to the Romans.* Translated by Patricia Dailey. Stanford, CA: Stanford University Press, 2005.
Badiou, Alain. *Saint Paul: The Foundation of Universalism.* Translated by Ray Brassier. Stanford, CA: Stanford University Press, 2003.
Baker, Gideon. "Paul and Political Theology: Nihilism, Empire and the Messianic Vocation." *Philosophy and Social Criticism* 41, no. 3 (2015): 293–315.
Critchley, Simon. *The Faith of the Faithless: Experiments in Political Ontology.* London: Verso, 2012.
Foucault, Michel. *The Government of Self and Others. Lectures at the Collège de France 1982–1983.* Translated by Graham Burchell. Edited by Frédéric Gros. New York: Palgrave Macmillan, 2010.
Heidegger, Martin. *The Phenomenology of Religious Life.* Translated by Matthias Fritsch and Jennifer Anna Gosetti-Ferencei. Bloomington: Indiana University Press, 2004.
Nietzsche, Friedrich. *Nachgelassene Fragmente Herbst 1887.* Werke. KGA Vol. VIII-2. Edited by Giorgio Colli and Mazzino. Berlin/New York: De Gruyter, 1978.
Nietzsche, Friedrich. *Ecce Homo and The Antichrist.* Translated by Thomas Wayne. New York: Algora, 2004.
Ricoeur, Paul. "Paul apôtre. Proclamation et argumentation." *Esprit* 292 (2003): 85–112.
Taubes, Jacob. *The Political Theology of Paul.* Translated by Dana Hollander. Edited by Aleida Assman and Jan Assmann in conjunction with Horst Folkers, Wolf-Daniel Hartwich, and Christoph Schulte. Stanford, CA: Stanford University Press, 2004.
Van der Heiden, Gert-Jan. "The Experience of Contingency and the Attitude to Life: Nietzsche and Heidegger on Paul." In *Rethinking Faith: Heidegger between Nietzsche and Wittgenstein*, edited by Antonio Cimino and Gert-Jan van der Heiden, 161–77. London: Bloomsbury, 2017.

About the Contributors

Andrew Benjamin is Professor of Philosophy and Jewish Thought at Monash University Melbourne and Professor of Philosophy and the Humanities at Kingston University London. His recent publications include: *Towards a Relational Ontology: Philosophy's Other Possibility* (Albany, NY, 2015), *Art's Philosophical Work* (London, 2015) and *Virtue in Being* (Albany, NY, 2016).

Ward Blanton is Reader in Biblical Cultures and European Thought at the University of Kent in Canterbury, for which he also teaches in Paris and Rome. His books include *A Materialism for the Masses: Saint Paul and the Philosophy of Undying Life* (New York, 2014), *Displacing Christian Origins: Philosophy, Secularity, and the New Testament* (Chicago, 2007) and (edited with Hent de Vries) *Paul and the Philosophers* (New York, 2013).

Jeffrey Bloechl is Associate Professor of Philosophy and founding director of the joint MA program in Philosophy and Theology at Boston College, as well as Honorary Professor Philosophy at the Australian Catholic University. His research and teaching concentrate in the areas of phenomenology, hermeneutics, philosophy of religion and philosophical anthropology.

Antonio Cimino is Assistant Professor at Radboud University, Nijmegen. He conducted research in Pisa, Tübingen, Freiburg im Breisgau, Fribourg, and Wuppertal. His main fields of research are metaphysics, contemporary European philosophy, practical philosophy, and philosophy of religion.

Ezra Delahaye is a PhD candidate in metaphysics and philosophy of religion at the Faculty of Philosophy, Theology and Religious Studies of Radboud University, Nijmegen. He holds a degree in philosophy from Radboud University and a degree in theology from Tilburg University. In his PhD project, he develops a new theory of subjectivity based on the contemporary philosophical readings of Saint Paul.

Françoise Frazier was Professor of Greek language and literature at the Université Paris Ouest-Nanterre till her death in December 2016. She was a leading scholar on Plutarch, and a collective volume of several of her Francophone articles on Plutarch's philosophy will be published in the Plutarch Studies series of Brill (edited by Lautaro Roig Lanzillotta and Delfim Leao; Leiden/Boston, forthcoming).

Gert-Jan van der Heiden is Professor of Metaphysics at Radboud University, Nijmegen. He holds a PhD in mathematics (Groningen 2003) and philosophy (Nijmegen 2008). He works mainly in the field of contemporary continental philosophy. His most recent monograph is *Ontology after Ontotheology* (Pittsburgh, PA, 2014).

George van Kooten is Professor of New Testament & Early Christianity at the University of Groningen. He received his degrees in Theology and Judaism of the Greco-Roman Period at the universities of Leiden (PhD 2001, MA 1995), Durham (MA 1995) and Oxford (MSt 1996).

His research interest is in the Greco-Roman context of early Christianity, and he is chief editor of the Ancient Philosophy & Religion series (Brill).

Teresa Morgan is Professor of Greco-Roman History and Nancy Bissell Turpin Fellow and Tutor at Oriel College, Oxford. Her major publications include *Literate Education in the Hellenistic and Roman Worlds* (Cambridge, 1998), *Popular Morality in the Early Roman Empire* (Cambridge, 2007), and *Roman Faith and Christian Faith* (Oxford, 2015).

Anders Klostergaard Petersen is Professor at the Department for the Study of Religion, Aarhus University. He has published extensively in the fields of late Second Temple Judaism, early Christ-religion, Greco-Roman philosophy and religion, and basic matters relating to theory, method, and the philosophy of science in the humanities and social sciences. During these years, he works copiously on biocultural evolution in the history of religions.

Carl Raschke is Professor of Religious Studies at the University of Denver, specializing in continental philosophy, art theory, the philosophy of religion, and the theory of religion. He is an internationally known writer and academic, who has authored numerous books and hundreds of articles on topics ranging from postmodernism to popular religion and culture to technology and society. He is current managing editor of *Political Theology Today* and senior editor for *The Journal for Cultural and Religious Theory*.

Suzan Sierksma-Agteres studied Greek and Latin language and culture at Leiden University (BA 2008 and MA 2012, cum laude) and Theology at VU University Amsterdam (BA 2012, cum laude). She is currently finishing her PhD thesis on the concept of πίστις in Paul's letters contextualised within ancient philosophical discourses.

Marin Terpstra is Assistant Professor in social and political philosophy and senior researcher at the Center for Contemporary European Philosophy, Radboud University, Nijmegen. In 1990, he obtained his doctorate with a dissertation on Spinoza's political philosophy, especially the concepts of *potentia* and *potestas*. His special interest is in philosophical problems concerning the tensions between politics and religion.

Ben Vedder studied theology in Utrecht and philosophy in Leuven. He wrote his dissertation on Heidegger and Scheler. He was Professor for systematic philosophy at Tilburg University and Professor of metaphysics and philosophy of religion at Radboud University, Nijmegen. From June 2013 onwards, he is emeritus professor. He published, among others, *Heidegger's Philosophy of Religion: From God to the Gods* (Pittsburgh, 2007).

Holger Zaborowski studied philosophy, theology, and classics at Freiburg, Cambridge, and Oxford Universities. After teaching at the Catholic University of America from 2005 until 2011, he now holds the Chair of History of Philosophy and Philosophical Ethics at the Catholic University of Vallendar, Germany. His research focuses on modern philosophy, ethics, philosophy of religion, and political philosophy. He is co-editor of the *Heidegger-Jahrbuch* and of the *Jahrbuch für Religionsphilosophie*. His most recent publications include *Menschlich sein: Philosophische Essays* (Freiburg im Breisgau, 2016) and *Tragik und Transzendenz: Spuren in der Gegenwartsliteratur* (Ostfildern, 2017).

Peter Zeillinger is assistant at the *Theologische Kurse* of the Austrian Bishop's Conference and lecturer for contemporary philosophy at the Philosophical Department of the University of Vienna, Austria. His work focuses on the threshold between theology, philosophy, political theory, and political theology. He has published numerous articles on the works of Jacques Derrida, Emmanuel Levinas, Michel Foucault and Alain Badiou. His recent work is centered on the topics of the event, on community-without-sovereignty and the political dimensions of alterity and time.

Index of Ancient Sources

Biblical Writings

Acts
5:38–39	52
7:53	53
9	50, 175
9:1–22	24
9:3–9	50
9:21	175
17:28	214
22	50–52
22:3	51
22:6–10	50

Col.
1:15	39
1:23	179
3:10–11	63
3:12	64

1 Cor.
1	11, 50, 54, 56, 62, 87, 125, 128, 133, 136–139, 141, 146, 152, 156, 158, 160–162, 167f., 175, 177, 232, 241, 245, 247, 255, 329, 334
1:10	255
1:17–29	87, 136
1:18–2:5	232
1:18–2:16	245
1:20	125, 128, 161
1:20–21	161
1:24	247
1:26–28	128
1:26–29	11, 133, 136, 160
1:27	125, 168
1:28	125, 136–139, 141, 146, 329
1:28–29	146
1:28–31	138f., 141
1:30	141, 156
2:1–5	11, 133–137
2:4–5	169
3:10	179
4:10–13	125
4:13	125
4:16	162
4:17	168, 181
5–7	56
7	9, 11, 58, 77, 81, 84, 88–91, 117, 125–127, 133, 146–161, 226, 273, 329f., 332, 344
7:1	89, 146, 149, 155f., 158
7:1–2	155, 158
7:2	9, 11, 77, 81, 84, 88, 90, 117, 126f., 133, 146–150, 154–161, 329, 332
7:5	158
7:6	146, 157
7:6–7	146
7:7	156
7:7–8	146
7:8	156
7:8–9	155
7:9	158
7:12	146, 157
7:14	158
7:17	89, 146
7:17–22	89
7:18–19	146
7:18–20	149
7:20	146
7:21–23	146
7:21–24	156
7:24	146
7:25	146
7:25–40	146
7:26	157
7:27–28	155
7:29	9, 11, 77, 81, 84, 88, 90, 117, 126f., 133, 146–150, 154, 156, 159–161, 329, 332
7:29–30	329
7:29–31	9, 11, 77, 81, 84, 88, 90, 126f., 133, 146f., 156, 161, 332

7:29–32	148–150, 154, 156, 160	**Eph.**	
7:31	125f., 150–152, 157, 161, 226, 273, 330, 344	1:3–5	181
		1:4	179
7:32–33	155	1:5	179
7:32–34	157	1:6	179
7:35	146, 157	1:7	179, 181
7:39–40	155	1:10	181f.
7:40	146	1:10–13	181
8:6	139, 162, 246	1:11	181
9	49	1:11–15	180
10:32–33	158	1:13	180f.
11:1	139, 162	1:15	179f.
11:12	139, 141	2:1	62, 178, 181
11:25	167	2:1–6	178
12	56, 62, 158, 177	2:4	179
12:9	177	2:4–6	178
12:12–27	158	2:5	179
12:12–30	56	2:5–10	182
12:31	56	2:7–9	178
13:6	156	2:11–12	62
13:7	57	2:15	181
14:18	54	3:2	274
15:1	175, 241	3:7–12	178
15:2–8	50	3:12	40, 178
15:11	241	3:14–15	139
15:24–28	152, 162	3:16	179
15:28	152, 161	3:17–19	179
15:42	162	4:1–16	179
15:50	162	4:2	179
		4:5	179f.
2 Cor.		4:11–13	180
3	237, 245	4:13	179
4:4	39, 161	4:15	179
4:6	24	5:2	179
4:13	241	5:25	179
5:5	242	5:28	179
5:7	242, 244	5:33	179
10:3–4	259	6:10–17	182
11:13–15	259	6:16	181
12:1	274	6:23	179, 182
12:2–3	54	6:24	179
12:20	255		
13:5	181	**Gal.**	
		1:4	171, 257
Deut.		1:6–9	177
32:20	223	1:11–16	50
		1:12	49, 169

1:13	175, 259	4:14	259
1:15–16	169	5:1	259
1:23	175	6:16	259
1:23–24	175	7:2–3	259
2	49, 110, 171f., 174, 181, 183	12:9	259
2:4	110		
2:15–21	171	**Jer.**	
2:16	40, 172f., 181	2:19	37
2:16–17	181	4:1	37
2:20	40, 171f.		
2:21	171	**Luke**	
3:7	173	4	56
3:10	173	6:20–36	53
3:11	173	12:39	68
3:12	173	22:25	289
3:14	173	22:26	289
3:17–19	122	22:32	289
3:18	173		
3:22	40	**Mal.**	
3:23–25	173	4:5	53
3:24	169		
3:28	9, 48, 81, 83, 85–87, 162, 280	**Mark**	
4:2	169	13:33–37	68
4:14	177		
4:19	177	**Matth.**	
5:5	224	4	56
5:6	181	5:20	272
5:7	177	5–7	53
5:14	57	22:40	57
5:21	289	24:42–44	68
5:22–23	177		
6:1	87, 176	**Phil.**	
6:2	57	2:8	171
6:6	176f.	3:9	40
6:9	176	3:19	64
6:10	176		
6:15	87	**Philem.**	
6:17	259	3:5–6	259
Gen.		**Rom.**	
1:26	39	1	13, 57, 60, 100, 124, 129, 139f., 145, 147, 152, 158, 161f., 168, 174, 179, 222–226, 253, 255f., 259, 262, 291–293, 344
Hab.			
2:4	173		
		1:11	255
Heb.		1:15	57
3:1	259	1:17–18	224

1:18	174, 222, 224, 226	9:4	57
1:18 – 3:20	222	9:16	259
1:18 – 32	174, 222, 226	9:27	124
1:19 – 20	140	9 – 11	123 f.
1:20	145	10	60, 100, 259
1:24	223	10:4	60
1:25	140, 161, 223	10:6 – 10	109, 340
1:26	223	10:9	100, 241
1:28	141, 223	11:5	124
1:29	224 f.	11:7	259
1:29 – 30	225	11:17 – 24	168
2	260, 271	11:25	253
2:17	260	11:36	139, 152
3	64, 120 f., 169, 183, 211, 224 f., 259, 338	12	13, 129, 141, 158, 223 f., 226, 344
3:9	120 f.	12:1 – 2	141
3:9 – 20	120	12:1 – 3	226
3:10	121, 259	12:2	129, 224, 344
3:20	169	12:4 – 5	158
3:21	224 f.	13	57, 147, 158, 262, 291 – 293
3:21 – 31	225	13:1 – 7	147, 158, 292 f.
3:22	40, 211, 225	13:5	158
3:24	224	13:8	57
3:25	224 f.	14	256
3:26	40, 224	15:20	179
3:27	225, 338	16:17	255
3:27 – 39	225	16:19	162
3:29 – 30	225	16:26	57
3:31	64		
4	122 f., 141, 276	**1 Thess.**	
4:3	276	1:4	168, 181
4:13	122	1:5	169 f.
4:17	141	1:6	162, 170
4:19	123, 141	1:7	169
4:23 – 24	141	1:8	169
5:19	171	1:8 – 9	170
5:20 – 21	169	1:9	167
6:8	241	1:10	170
7:6	57	2:1	170, 253
7:10	120	2:7 – 12	170
7:12	64	2:10	170
8	126, 162, 168, 181, 233	2:11	170
8:1	54	2:13 – 14	169
8:20	126	2:14	170
8:20 – 22	126	2:15 – 16	253
8:21	162	3:2	170
8:33	168	3:3	170

3:6–7	170	3:1	185
3:10	170	3:11	184
4	55, 68, 169, 334	4:9	185
4:15	169, 334	4:10	184
4:16	170	5:8	184f.
4:17	55	5:16	184
5	68, 76, 118, 167	6:2	184
5:2	68, 76, 118, 167, 170	6:10–12	185
5:6	55, 169, 334	6:21	185
5:9	168		
5:14	55	**2 Tim.**	
5:24	167f.	1:9	183
		1:9–10	183
2 Thess.		2:11	185
1:3	336	2:13	183
		2:14–19	185
1 Tim.		2:19	289
1:4	183f.	3:1–9	185
1:12	183	3:10	183
1:13	184	3:10–16	183
1:15	185	3:14–15	183
2:7	183	3:15	183
2:15	184	4:7	185

Other Ancient Sources

Aeschylus
Persae 818–31 227

Anonymous
apud Macarius Magnes, Apocriticus
4.1 153

Aratus
Phaenomena
96–136 214

Aristotle
De Anima
428a22–24 194
Ethica Nicomachea
1180–81 220
On Melissus
974a2–4 142
975a4–17 143

Posterior Analytics
90b14 193
Rhetoric
1355b35 193

Augustine
Contra Faustum Manichaeum
12.44 41
De Civitate Dei
4.31 215
7.5 215

Basil
De Fide, Prologue
8 (vol. 31, 677) 193

Catullus
Carmina
64.397–408 214

Cicero
De natura deorum
(On the Nature of the Gods)
1.3 219
2.87 152
De officiis
1.23 218
1.26 218
De oratore
2.343–34 218
De republica
1.2 218
2.26 215
2.61 218
3.8 218
3.27 218

Dio Chrysostom
Orationes
12.27 212 f.
12.28 212
12.29 213
74.10 218

Diodorus Siculus
Bibliotheca historica
11.66 218

Diogenes Laertius
Lives of Eminent Philosophers
7.1.101–2 154
7.1.104–15 154
7.1.137–38 140, 152
7.1.140 151

Diogenes of Oenoanda
Fragment
56 217

Dionysius of Halicarnassus
Antiquitates Romanae
2.75.1–4 215

1 Enoch
42.2 214
44.5 214

Epictetus
Diatribae (Discourses)
2.4.1–4 218
2.4.2–3 219
2.22.29–30 218
3.14.13–14 218
4.1.159 158
4.1.162 158
Enchiridion
24.4–5 218 f.

Euripides
Oedipus
fragment 543 227
fragment 545 227

4 Ezra
5.10 214

Flavius Josephus
Contra Apionem 259

Heraclitus
Homeric Problems
(Quaestiones Homericae/Allegoriae)
36.4 151
43.14 151

Hesiod
Opera et dies
174–201 214
276–80 213

Horace
Carmen Saeculare
57–60 216
Carmina
1.35.21 214

Iamblichus
On the Mysteries
V 26 202

Juvenal
Satirae
15.147–58 213
15.159 213

Macarius Magnes
Apocriticus
4.1 153

Marcus Aurelius
Meditations
11.1.2 151

Maximus of Tyre
Dissertationes
18.1 227

Ovid
Metamorphoses
1.90 213
1.129 214

Philo
On the Eternity of the Cosmos
76–77 144
78 144
Quaestiones et solutiones in Genesin
2.40 214

Philostratus of Athens
The Life of Apollonius of Tyana
(Vita Apollonii)
8.7.22–23 152

Pirkei Avot
1.16 52

Plato
Epistles
7, 351c 195
Laws
713d 220
713e–714a 220
716a 221
716c–d 221
720d 220
728a 221
732b–d 156
875c–d 220
957c 220
Phaedo
78b–84b 244

Phaedrus
230a 193
246a–49c 243
246a–b 243
246c 243
249c 244
249c–d 244
Republic
509d 193
514a–17a 242
517b–21b 242
521b 243
532e 195
611d–e 221
Theaetetus
176a–b 244
176b 200, 227
176b–c 221
176c 221
Timaeus
27b–c 201
27c 136f.
29c 192f.
37b 193
41d–47c 221
47b–c 205
90a–d 244

Plotinus
Enneads
3.8 198
3.8.6 198
4.7 193, 196
4.7.10 196
4.7.15 193
4.8 196
4.8.1 197
5.3.17 196
6.9 195
6.9.4 195f.

Plutarch
Adversus Colotem
1124D–E 221
1113C 143
Aemilius Paullus
2.6 218

Alexander
75.2 201
Amatorius
750C–51B 158
751B–54E 158
756B 192
764E 203
764F–65 A 203
769B 218
Aratus
43.4 191
Caius Marcius Coriolanus
38.3 191
38.4 191
Camillus
6.6 201
De Alexandri magni fortuna aut virtute
329 A–B 217
De E apud Delphos
393C 203
De Iside et Osiride
355C–D 193
359F 191
377F–78B 199
382D–E 199
382F–83 A 198 f.
De Pythiae oraculis
400 A 203
402E 191
409B 204
409C 203
409D 203
492B 200
De sera numinis vindicta
549B 200
549E 201
560C–D 193
560D 191
566D 200
De tranquillitate animi
477C 205
477D 205
477D–E 205
477F 205
Non posse suaviter vivi secundum Epicurum
1101C 191
1101E 204

1102 A–B 205
Numa
8.8 215
Quaestiones romanae et graecae
275 A (42) 213
Consolatio ad Apollonium
215B–C 193
De genio Socratis
591E 200

Porphyry
Ad Marcellam
24.377–82 202

Proclus
In Timaeum
1.212 202
On the Theology of Plato
1.25 194 f.

Pseudo-Andronicus of Rhodes
On Emotions
2.8.3 193

Pseudo-Seneca
Octavia
391–403 217
429–34 214

Seneca
Epistles
9.16 157
9.16–17 156
9.17 158

Sextus Empiricus
Adversus mathematicos
7.60 227

Silius Italicus
Punica
2.494–506 214

Sotah
15.18 52

SVF (Stoicorum Veterum Fragmenta)
1.351	155
1.361	155
1.365	155
2.557	151
2.580	140, 152
2.1009	151
3.128	155
3.137	155, 157

Tertullian
De praescriptione haereticorum
7.9–13	231

De paenitentia
10.1	102

Theognis
Fragment
1.1135–42	214

Theophilus
Ad Autolycum
1.4	142
2.4	142
2.10	142
2.13	142

Vergil
Aeneid
1.292–93	216
4.791–94	216

Eclogae
4.4–7	216

Xenophon
Memorabilia
4.4.10–18	36

Index of Names and Subjects

a priori 73, 145
abandonment 8, 341
Abraham 121–123, 141, 168, 173f., 181, 237, 276, 278, 280, 323
absolute spirit 335
Academy 231
act of faith 79, 100, 109
act of reading 72
actualization of life 68, 75–77
ἀδιάφορα (adiaphora) 11
ἀδικία (adikia) 156, 220, 223
aesthetics 234
affect 115, 304
after-effect 7
Agamben, Giorgio 4, 8f., 11, 14, 16f., 47, 57–60, 81f., 84f., 88–92, 95, 97–101, 103–112, 117f., 120–122, 124–129, 133f., 146–151, 153–157, 159–161, 254, 257, 260, 264f., 283f., 297–307, 309–311, 316, 318–322, 326–329, 332–334, 336, 339f., 342–344
ἀγάπη (agapē) 56, 59, 169
Age 13, 96, 231, 235, 237, 242, 279
ἀλήθεια (alētheia) 13, 183, 189, 191, 223
anarchic 310
anarcho-autonomist 314
animal rationale 96
announcement 75, 98f., 262, 322
anomial 58, 60
anthropocratic 259
anthropology 83f., 279, 315, 319
anti-Judaism 253
anti-metaphysics 160
anti-philosopher 11, 133–136, 148, 160, 229
anti-Semitism 253
anti-terrorist legislation 310
antinomial 60
ἀφωρισμένος (aphōrismenos) 98
apocalypticism 244, 264
apostle 3, 15, 86, 98f., 149, 183, 185, 209, 214, 254, 269, 274, 284, 315, 319
argumentation 16, 88, 121, 126, 134, 142, 153, 155, 157, 283, 289, 343

Aristotle 67, 73, 79, 130, 142f., 193f., 198f., 217, 220, 270, 280, 286, 331
ascetic 342
assurance 195, 197, 202, 337
Athens 135, 152, 231, 247, 258, 277
attestation 344
attitude 5, 7, 10, 62f., 68f., 111, 115, 117–119, 127, 129, 135, 146f., 151, 154, 158–161, 176, 179, 192f., 205, 215, 266, 306f., 326f., 332f., 340–342
attunement 63
Augustine 215, 254
authority 48f., 51f., 61f., 64, 106, 147, 169, 183, 193, 256, 260f., 274, 277, 287f., 292f., 295, 319
autonomy 280, 285, 292, 294
axial age 14, 231, 234f., 237–239, 242, 244–246

Babut, Daniel 190–193, 206
Badiou, Alain 4, 8f., 11, 13f., 16, 47, 59f., 81–83, 85–88, 90, 92, 109, 112, 117, 120f., 125f., 133–141, 145f., 148, 153, 159–161, 209f., 225, 228f., 254, 257, 264, 278–280, 283f., 301f., 327–329, 331, 336f., 339f., 342f.
bare life 58, 60, 319
Beck, Glen 317
behavior 80, 102, 184, 219, 228, 240, 276
belief 3, 13, 64, 100, 103, 166, 168, 170, 175, 190f., 193f., 196, 200, 205, 209, 239, 287, 289f., 325, 335, 337–339
believer 10, 57, 99, 115f., 123, 127, 275, 279, 304, 343
Bellah, Robert 235, 237
Benjamin, Walter 7, 82, 84, 100, 112, 148, 263, 277, 298, 300f., 341
Benveniste, Émile 106, 189
biopolitics 319f.
 – biopolitical 319, 321
body 54–56, 62, 64, 123, 144, 158, 180, 197, 200, 237, 242, 245, 255, 260, 276, 280, 290
body of Christ 55f., 158, 180, 255, 260

book 9, 13, 15f., 53, 67, 69, 86, 89, 92, 95, 99f., 104f., 107, 117, 123, 125, 151f., 216, 231, 239, 242, 253, 255, 264, 269f., 286, 297f., 301, 304, 306, 309, 311, 313, 315, 317, 319, 325
Bossuet, Jacques-Bénigne 41
Boyarin, Daniel 82
Brague, Rémi 265
Breton, Stanislas 5, 8, 47, 82–85
Brondos, David 269f.
Buber, Martin 36
Buddha 236
Butler, Judith 112, 310

Caesar 16, 276f., 279
calling. *See also* κλῆσις (*klēsis*) *and* vocation 54f., 89f., 141, 146, 149, 201, 264
capitalist society 265
Caravaggio 25–28, 38
care 13, 71, 73, 157, 161, 185, 215, 257, 290
cautiousness 201
Chantraine, Pierre 189
chosenness 168, 170, 181
Christ 8, 12, 15, 47, 49, 54–57, 59f., 62–64, 67f., 75–80, 83, 86, 117, 120, 125, 135, 137–139, 141, 152, 156, 158, 162, 165–176, 178–186, 211, 224, 227f., 232f., 237–242, 245–247, 251, 253–256, 259, 262, 270f., 273, 276, 278, 280, 284, 287–289, 291f., 301, 316, 326, 337f., 340f., 343
Christ-event 59f., 135, 137f., 141, 224, 340
Christian liberty 288
Christianity 4, 6, 8f., 47, 58f., 67, 74, 78f., 104, 107, 112, 145, 153, 186, 189, 211, 231, 233f., 238, 254, 259, 261f., 264, 284–286, 288f., 291–294, 301, 328, 331, 336, 338, 343
Christology 152, 165f.
– Christological 61, 64, 165, 275
χρόνος (*chronos*) 117f., 150
church 7, 16, 50, 56, 82, 142, 179, 254, 262, 269, 272, 275, 283, 289–291, 293f., 315f., 322
Cicero 105, 110, 152, 215, 218f., 273
cognitive science 235

collective 17, 48, 209, 212, 222f., 225, 228, 240, 279, 309–311, 314, 317–319
color 7
commitment 51, 53f., 59, 72, 104, 168, 180, 239f., 265, 302f., 329, 338
commonwealth 16, 62, 283, 288, 290f., 293f.
commune 310, 313, 315
communication 256–258, 263, 312
community 12, 55–57, 61, 64, 73, 75f., 98f., 102, 104, 107, 112, 116, 129, 158, 162, 165, 167–170, 173, 176f., 179, 181f., 184–186, 212, 215, 217, 225, 228f., 246, 252, 255f., 261, 264, 271–273, 276, 291, 310, 315f., 318, 321–323, 337, 340f.
comportment 10, 12, 84, 115f., 129, 165
concept 3, 5, 13, 15, 69, 74, 86f., 89, 96, 108, 120, 145, 148f., 167, 174, 177, 185, 191, 209f., 212, 219–221, 239, 252, 258, 260, 263, 269, 283, 287, 289, 301, 307, 338
condemnation 10, 115, 120, 122–124, 127, 130
conditions of possibility 79
confession 9, 95, 101, 103, 107, 109, 111f., 180
confession of faith 102
confidence 52, 173, 178, 190, 192–194, 198, 200, 213, 242, 337
Confucius 236
consciousness 169, 235
contemplation 12, 189, 196, 198–200, 205f.
content of faith 79
contingency 10, 115f., 118f., 121f., 126, 129, 258, 263f., 333, 343f.
contingent 116, 122, 145, 258, 294, 343f.
conversion 7, 53, 64, 78, 170, 180, 182, 202f., 341f.
conviction 3, 5, 14, 58, 100, 135, 142, 144, 171, 174, 194, 329, 340f., 343
cosmological 102, 139, 144, 151f., 342, 344

cosmos   123, 137–140, 142, 144f., 151–154, 157, 160–162, 216, 278, 330, 332
– σχῆμα τοῦ κόσμου (*schēma tou kosmou*)   10, 115, 126, 129, 147, 150–153, 157, 226, 330
Coupat, Julien   312f.
covenant   62, 120–124, 129, 167, 169, 182, 252f., 256, 259
creatio ex nihilo   138, 142–145, 334
creation   87, 111, 126, 138, 140, 142–145, 152f., 160f., 168, 179, 182, 222f., 274
Creator-God   252f.
credibility   112, 193
credit   106, 109, 178
crisis   10, 16, 111, 115–118, 120–122, 124, 126f., 157, 159, 161, 260, 273–275, 297, 300, 306f., 311, 320
Critchley, Simon   7, 116, 125, 329f.
crucifixion   15, 49, 181f., 271, 274, 276f.
cultural complexity   234
cultural evolution   14, 231, 233–235, 238, 242, 244, 246f.
custodian   173

Damascus   8, 47, 49–51, 53f., 86, 274, 278
deactivate. *See also* κατάργησις (*katargēsis*)   128, 304, 306, 326
deactivation. *See also* κατάργησις (*katargēsis*)   124, 127f., 301, 304f., 307
death   4, 15, 48–50, 52, 88f., 108, 120, 138, 141, 154, 169, 182, 185, 200, 216, 225, 240, 261, 276, 322, 341f.
deconstruction   272–274
Deleuze, Gilles   82f.
Derrida, Jacques   5, 15, 109, 112, 270–275, 277, 279f., 295, 339
dialectical   126, 160, 280, 283, 334
dialectical theology   283
dialectics   120, 161, 334
dialogue   4, 6, 200, 276, 325, 335
Diamond, Jared   236
Dick, Philip K.   314–315
difference   5, 9, 16, 51, 59–61, 69f., 80f., 83, 88, 101, 117, 140, 144, 151, 154, 158, 169, 195, 225, 227, 233, 235, 237, 240, 244–246, 259, 283, 287, 289, 294, 333, 335

δικαιοσύνη (*dikaiosunē*)   15, 156, 166, 173, 177, 213, 215, 218f., 224, 227, 269–272, 275f., 279
δίκη (*dikē*)   13, 212, 218–220, 222, 338f.
discourse   11, 13, 49, 53, 57, 71, 86f., 97–99, 104, 112, 135, 137f., 160, 162, 194, 203, 209, 216, 222, 224, 228, 233f., 258, 260, 276, 278, 325, 344
– Greek ~   6, 87f.
– Jewish ~   88
– Pauline ~   60f.
– regimes of ~   86
disobedience   292
– civil ~   292
distinction   3, 12, 15, 49, 96, 118, 121, 123f., 165, 195, 224f., 232, 237, 251, 253, 255–259, 261, 263, 265f., 270, 277, 289, 325, 328f., 341–343
divine violence   263, 300f.
division   89, 91, 126, 319
dogma   7, 77, 109
Donald, Merlin   235
Dostoyevsky, Fjodor   261
Dou, Gerard   32–34
δόξα (*doxa*)   12, 189, 191, 193f., 205
drawing   55, 183, 232, 285
dualism   3, 232, 237, 245, 261, 331, 345
Dufresne, David   311–315

ἐκκλησία (*ekklēsia*)   102, 179, 183
ἐλπίς (*elpis*)   13, 189, 191, 201, 205
empire   276–281, 311, 318, 320–323
– Roman ~   158, 276
enactment   78, 127, 305, 336
ἐνεργεῖν (*energein*)   128
Engberg-Pedersen, Troels   159, 232, 239
Enlightenment   3, 234, 237, 338
enthusiasm   119, 166, 312
Epictetus   156, 158, 218f., 233
epistemology   232, 234, 237–239, 242–245, 247, 327
ἐπιστήμη (*epistēmē*)   96, 326f., 337
ἐπιστροφή (*epistrophē*)   202
ἐποχή (*epochē*)   119, 121
equality   4, 14, 278, 286, 343
ἔρως (*erōs*)   13, 189, 191, 201

eschatology 15, 140, 186, 216, 264, 269, 333, 338
– eschatological 55 f., 58, 124, 139, 166, 216, 224 f., 228, 271, 273 f., 279, 283
eternity 80, 144
ethics 160 f., 169, 186, 211, 219, 234, 277, 338
ethnocentrism 211, 225, 228, 338
ethos 5, 10, 115 f., 118, 127, 129, 242, 306, 326 f., 329, 333, 340 f., 343 f.
εὐαγγέλιον (*euaggelion*) 49, 98, 175, 274 f.
εὐλάβεια (*eulabeia*) 201
Europe 16, 297, 300, 306 f., 317
εὐσέβεια (*eusebeia*) 201
event 8, 49 f., 59 f., 68, 79, 81, 86–88, 90 f., 99, 110, 116–118, 135, 137 f., 141, 204, 210, 224 f., 227, 229, 274 f., 277 f., 283, 310, 318, 340
evolution 176 f., 180, 214, 234 f., 238 f., 258
exception 86, 92, 97, 101, 123, 129, 166, 197, 263, 266, 297 f., 303 f., 306, 331, 343 f.
– sovereign ~ 304
exclusion 91, 305
existence 48, 54, 56, 70–72, 77, 106, 139–143, 191, 210, 234, 238, 243, 245 f., 251, 286, 289, 294, 320, 336, 341 f.
ἐξομολόγησις (*exomologēsis*) 95, 101, 103, 110, 339, 344
experience 8, 47, 50, 55, 61, 67–71, 73–75, 79, 86, 89, 96, 98, 102, 107, 109 f., 117–119, 126, 170, 195 f., 198, 204, 234, 254, 275, 279, 322, 332, 340
exploitation 154, 236, 276

face 8, 96, 224, 277, 303
facticity 8, 67, 69–77, 79
faith in Christ 56, 62 f., 165 f., 178, 210, 242, 252
faith. *See also* πίστις (*pistis*) 3–5, 8–10, 12–14, 47–49, 53–57, 59 f., 62 f., 75 f., 79, 95–101, 103–106, 109–112, 115–119, 122, 129, 135, 165 f., 170 f., 176–178, 180, 185, 189, 191 f., 194 f., 201 f., 209–211, 213–216, 218, 222, 224, 226–228, 239, 242, 252, 255, 271, 275 f., 280, 284, 290, 304, 311, 322, 325–329, 333, 335–341, 343 f.
faithfulness 165–168, 170–172, 183, 211, 214 f., 224 f., 227 f., 239, 242, 247, 276, 278, 338
– faithful 12, 54, 56, 63, 165, 167 f., 170, 172 f., 176 f., 180, 182–186, 202, 219, 225, 228, 240, 256, 276, 337
fidelity 5, 14, 59, 106, 190, 326 f., 339–341, 343
fides 9, 95, 105 f., 108–110, 112, 166, 186, 190, 215, 218 f., 239, 338
Filmer, Robert 291
flesh. *See also* σάρξ (*sarx*) 49 f., 54, 56 f., 62–64, 88, 123, 259, 341
form-of-life/form of life 306 f., 319 f.
formal indication 69, 73, 79
Foucault, Michel 9, 95, 99, 101, 103, 107–109, 112, 127, 319, 340, 343 f.
fragility 72 f., 78 f.
Francis of Assisi 17, 309, 315
Freud, Sigmund 82 f.
fulfillment 56 f., 60, 111 f., 118, 262, 273, 279, 304
fundamentalism 3
future 8, 16, 67 f., 76–80, 98 f., 112, 118, 150, 167 f., 196, 205, 210, 212, 215, 217, 228, 274 f., 335

Gamaliel 51 f.
Gautama Siddharta 236
gentiles 167 f., 173 f., 178, 183, 209, 222, 284
gesture 17, 57, 107, 125, 130, 304, 309, 311, 319, 321 f., 326, 328
Gleize, Jean-Marie 315 f.
glory 57, 139, 180, 216
Gnostic temptation 15, 251, 253 f., 265 f., 345
Gnosticism, Gnostic 15, 161, 251–254, 263–266, 334, 345
God 7, 11–15, 48, 50–57, 62–64, 73 f., 77, 84, 89, 100, 121 f., 124, 128, 133–142, 144–146, 149, 152, 156–158, 160–162, 165–184, 186, 193, 200, 202 f., 206, 210 f., 221–228, 240–242, 246 f., 251–253, 255, 257, 259, 261–263, 266, 271 f.,

274–277, 279f., 284, 286f., 289f., 292, 294, 326, 329–332, 334, 336f.
– from ~   11, 133, 138–141, 143–145, 152, 156f., 160f., 168f., 177–179, 185, 203, 205, 242, 291, 334
– to ~   11, 61, 78, 133, 138, 139, 140f., 152, 160f., 166f., 171, 173, 180, 182f., 202, 204, 221, 223, 225f., 240, 247, 255, 259–261, 276, 286, 290, 334
– through ~   152, 160, 179
– ~'s people/people of ~   121, 123f.
Golden Age   212, 214, 216, 219
Gospel   271, 288, 292
Gossaert, Jan   34
grace   49f., 60, 124, 178, 183, 193, 226, 269
Greek metaphysics   90

Habermas, Jürgen   294
Hadot, Pierre   193, 197f.
Havelock, Eric   219
Hays, Richard   165–167, 172, 174, 181, 240
Hegel, Georg Wilhelm Friedrich   80, 335
Hegelian   126, 161, 301
Heidegger, Martin   4, 8f., 47, 63, 67–80, 82–85, 92, 117–119, 125–127, 129, 137, 140, 148, 254, 283f., 306, 326, 328f., 331–334, 336, 342
Hellenism   13, 211, 231, 233, 235–237, 246
Hengel, Martin   13, 231
hermeneutics   9, 67f., 80, 269
– hermeneutic   7, 121
– ~ of religion   9, 67f., 80
– philosophical ~   67
– pneumatic ~   129
– political ~   256, 259
historicality   70, 72, 75, 77
historicity   8, 67–69, 74, 79
history   4, 7, 9, 13, 17, 48, 53, 59, 68f., 73f., 79, 95, 105, 112, 121–123, 160, 166, 168, 173f., 182, 189, 206, 212f., 215, 229, 231–234, 237, 241, 246, 252–254, 258, 260, 264, 273, 279f., 283, 287, 289, 291, 295, 303, 315f., 334
Hobbes, Thomas   289, 291
Hoffmann, Philippe   190, 201f.
holiness   64, 184

ὁμοίωσις θεῷ (homoiōsis theōi)   221, 228
ὁμολογία (homologia)   95, 100f., 109, 112
hope. See also ἐλπίς (elpis)   62, 64, 79, 97, 117, 166, 180, 190f., 201f., 204f., 210f., 227, 252, 263, 265, 337
horizon   61, 63, 79, 112, 298, 304
ὡς μή (hōs mē)   5, 7, 9, 11, 16, 58, 61, 67, 77, 79, 90, 126f., 129, 133, 146–150, 153, 156–160, 244, 287, 297f., 300–302, 304–307, 326, 329f., 332f., 344
hospitality   279
human existence   72, 76, 78
human facticity   8, 67, 74, 77
human life   58, 60, 72, 79, 117
humanities   234f.
humanity   12, 58f., 83, 125, 165f., 168, 171–174, 176, 178, 182, 186, 212, 214, 216f., 223, 228, 240, 279, 284, 337

Iamblichus   12, 189, 202
identitarian   314, 319
identity   7, 54, 58, 85, 87–91, 104, 121f., 124, 146, 197, 212, 215, 218, 251, 255, 263, 307, 321, 331f., 342
identity politics   85
image   7, 56, 72, 76, 182, 199f., 205, 280, 312
image of God. See also God   200
imitation   162, 221, 228
imminence   169, 332, 334, 336
imminent   90, 118, 126, 128, 157, 273
impotentiality   124, 129
in-between   89, 264f.
in Christ   15, 54f., 61, 63, 77, 85, 103, 125, 138f., 141, 161, 166, 168, 173f., 178, 180f., 183, 211, 225–228, 241, 253, 269, 271, 273, 280, 285, 303
inability   124, 129, 272
incapacity   64, 124, 128f.
incredulity   201
indifference   149, 154–156, 161, 305, 332f., 344
inoperativity, inoperative   57, 128, 304, 313, 319f., 326, 330, 334, 345
– ~ community   320
institutional distinction   256f., 261
intelligible   15, 195f., 201, 269, 280

interiority 237, 245
internal law 13, 209, 220 f., 225
Invisible Committee 16, 309–311, 313, 315, 318, 321–323, 326
Isaac 278
Israel 62, 167 f., 173 f., 236–238, 252, 276

Jefferson, Thomas 271, 289
Jennings, Theodore 15, 269–271, 273, 275 f.
Jeremiah 1
Jerusalem 49–52, 56, 231, 246 f., 277
Jesus Christ 47 f., 50 f., 53–55, 57, 62, 134, 139, 165–169, 171, 174 f., 181, 185, 211, 224 f., 239 f., 255, 261, 286
Jew 6 f., 14 f., 48, 51–54, 56 f., 59, 83–91, 120 f., 123 f., 126, 139, 142 f., 146, 165, 167 f., 174, 181, 183, 211, 214, 216, 218, 222, 225, 228, 233, 235 f., 238 f., 251–254, 256, 258 f., 262, 264, 266, 269–271, 279 f., 284, 299, 301 f., 304, 319, 338
Jewish law 53, 57, 120 f., 123 f., 126, 301, 304
Jewish tradition 252
Judaism 6, 13, 15, 50, 52 f., 210 f., 231, 233–237, 246, 269 f., 275
judgment 52, 64, 158, 196, 210, 214, 273 f., 290 f.
justice. *See also* δικαιοσύνη (*dikaiosunē*) *and* righteousness 6, 8, 13, 16, 67, 84 f., 122, 154, 156, 190, 200, 209–211, 213–222, 224 f., 227 f., 251, 270–277, 279, 283, 289, 303, 337–339
justification 13 f., 49, 100, 171, 185, 209–211, 226–228, 251, 256, 275, 338 f.

καιρός (*kairos*) 7, 68, 79, 98, 117 f., 150
Kant, Immanuel 284
κατάργησις (*katargēsis*) 301, 303–306
– καταργεῖν (*katargein*) 60, 90, 128, 301, 326, 330, 332, 334, 344
κατέχον (*katechon*) 320 f.
kerygma 175, 180
Kierkegaard, Søren 278, 284
kingdom 56, 260, 272, 274, 278, 280, 288, 292, 294

kingdom of God 280
κλῆσις (*klēsis*). *See also* vocation *and* calling 149 f.
knowledge. *See also* ἐπιστήμη (*epistēmē*) 69, 89, 179 f., 190, 193, 196, 212, 222 f., 243, 255, 326 f., 335, 337
Koester, Helmut 52

Lacan, Jacques 82 f., 85, 135, 148
lamentation 205
Laotse 236
law 5, 7, 10, 47, 51–60, 64, 84, 88–91, 103, 105–107, 109–111, 115 f., 119–124, 126 f., 129 f., 159, 166, 169, 172–174, 181, 209–211, 213, 219–221, 224–228, 255, 259 f., 263, 266, 270–275, 277–279, 288, 298–300, 304, 310 f., 314, 321, 327, 329, 333, 338, 340–342
– constitutional ~ 261, 299
– ~ of Moses/Mosaic ~ 57, 121, 173
– ~ of works 5, 120–122, 124, 129
leap 210
Lefort, Claude 280
letter 11, 48, 56 f., 62, 64, 75, 124–126, 128, 133, 139, 167–171, 174, 176–179, 181–183, 222, 224, 259, 289, 301, 316, 319, 321, 334
Leviathan 289
Levinas, Emmanuel 109, 112, 277
liberalism 14, 16, 253, 283, 285, 294
lie 58, 60, 64, 77, 104, 109, 140, 327
life 8, 12, 47–51, 53–56, 58, 60–63, 68–79, 83 f., 86, 88 f., 119 f., 127, 141, 146 f., 149, 154, 157, 159, 165, 169 f., 176–178, 180, 183, 185, 197, 200–202, 204–206, 213, 217, 220, 225, 227, 240, 251, 258, 261, 264 f., 276 f., 279, 284, 290, 305 f., 313, 316–318, 320, 322, 326–328, 333, 336, 340–342
– contemplative ~ 201
– ~ of faith 8, 47, 49, 63
light 5, 7, 10, 16, 50, 63, 69, 105, 118, 122, 126–129, 145, 154, 161, 182, 195 f., 202, 210, 212, 222, 224–226, 229, 234, 239, 243, 255, 265, 279, 283, 297–300, 302, 311, 314, 331, 334–336, 338, 343 f.
Locke, John 16, 283, 285–294

λόγος (*logos*)   97, 99, 108 f., 127, 155, 185, 192, 194, 199, 204, 221, 233, 237, 277
love. *See also* ἀγάπη (*agapē*) and ἔρως (*erōs*)   56 f., 59 – 61, 64, 69, 170, 178 – 181, 183 – 185, 191, 201 f., 215, 217, 254 f., 261, 266, 269, 278, 327
– ~ of Christ   179
– unconditional ~   64
loyalty   106, 190, 258 – 260, 262 – 264, 311, 337
Ludd, Neil   313
Luther, Martin   89, 275, 301
Lyotard, Jean-François   5, 109, 112

Mao Tse-Tung   264
Marcion   123, 252 f., 257, 345
– Marcionism   253, 265
– Marcionist   330
Marxism   264
– Marxist   84, 280
master   51, 68, 146, 343
Matlock, Barry   241
May, Gerhard   142 f., 190, 331
measure   13, 137 f., 141, 209, 221, 225 – 228, 330, 334
Mencius   236
μὴ ὄντα (*mē onta*). *See also* ontology   7, 11, 128, 136 – 141, 143, 160, 329 f., 334, 342
μή-ontology   329 – 331
mercy   12, 64, 106, 124, 165, 178, 186, 337
message   48, 75 – 77, 91, 97 – 99, 105, 111, 170, 175, 209, 225 – 227, 254, 257, 260, 262, 269, 286
Messiah   47, 90, 98, 111, 252, 307
messianic   9 f., 17, 84, 90, 97, 112, 252, 273 f., 295, 301, 304 – 307, 322
– ~ event   90 f., 120, 343
– ~ life   58, 149
– ~ time   58, 97 f., 112, 118, 314
messianism   14, 17, 264, 273, 301, 303 f., 309 – 311, 318 f., 321, 333
metahistorical narrative   212, 217, 222, 227
metahistory   13, 212, 218
metaphysics   5, 55, 68, 139, 161, 277, 318, 332
method   69 – 71, 82, 95, 270
Michéa, Jean-Claude   294

Middle-Platonism   190
μίμησις (*mimēsis*)   162
mind   13, 48, 53, 64, 98, 109, 141, 176 f., 179, 194, 205, 209, 213 f., 220, 223, 226 – 228, 235, 239, 255, 259, 265 f., 274, 290, 321, 340, 343
misuse   147, 151, 154
modernity   16, 252 f., 265, 283 – 285, 298, 300, 306, 326
monotheism   238, 245
mood   63
Morgan, Teresa   11, 165 – 168, 171 – 173, 175, 177, 179 f., 182, 184 f., 239, 241 f., 325, 334, 337 f.
mortification   141
Moses   57, 121, 238, 252
movement   11, 13, 60, 98, 133, 144, 148, 150 f., 189, 202, 232, 238, 279, 284, 314, 317, 335
μῦθος (*muthos*)   233, 237

narrative   11, 51, 124, 165 – 168, 170 – 178, 180 – 185, 212, 214, 219, 223, 240, 243
narrativity   166
Neoplatonism   12, 189 – 191, 194 f.
New Perspective   13, 209, 211, 225, 228, 269 f., 280, 338 f., 343
New Testament   5 f., 16, 50, 52, 68, 75, 166, 170 f., 176, 179, 186, 210 f., 253, 270, 280, 285, 288 f., 292, 338
Nicene Creed   144 f.
Nietzsche, Friedrich   82 f., 123, 135, 148, 238, 259, 284 f., 301 f., 326 – 328, 330 f., 335 – 337, 341 – 343, 345
nihilism   11, 124, 133, 147 f., 150, 328, 330 f., 333, 335, 342
– nihilistic   10 f., 115, 120, 126 – 128, 130, 133, 138, 144 f., 147 f., 153, 157 – 160, 327 f., 331 – 333, 335, 341 f.
nihilist   11, 133 f., 146
nomological crisis   311
νόμος (*nomos*)   174, 220, 271, 274 f., 277, 311
non-conformity   129 f., 327, 329, 333, 344
νοῦς (*nous*)   96, 198, 200, 220, 223, 226 f.
nullification   149 f.

oath 9, 12, 14, 95, 104–112, 165, 339
obedience 57, 147, 159, 170f., 220, 258, 276, 287f., 293
Old Testament 84, 123, 253
ὄντα (*onta*) 7, 11, 128, 136–138, 140f., 160, 205, 329
onto-theology 134, 136f., 139f., 145f., 148, 160, 328–331, 333f.
ontological inversion 138–140
ontology 5, 9, 11, 59, 74, 79, 81f., 84f., 87, 89, 91f., 133, 138f., 274, 326, 328–330, 335, 341, 344
order of the world 89, 117, 119, 125–129, 330, 332, 342f., 345

paradigm 4, 6, 298, 300, 303f., 318, 320, 334
pariah 322
παρουσία (*parousia*) 117f., 262, 273f., 276, 326, 330, 332, 334, 336, 341
παρρησία (*parrēsia*) 105, 108, 127, 340, 344
particularity 59f., 87
Pascal, Blaise 59
passing away 10, 84, 89, 115, 118, 126f., 129f., 147, 150–152, 160, 226, 273, 330, 344
πάθος (*pathos*) 190, 198, 337
Paul 3–11, 13–17, 47–61, 63f., 67f., 73–77, 80–92, 95, 97–101, 103–105, 109–112, 115–130, 133–141, 144–162, 165–179, 181–185, 209–211, 213f., 216–219, 221–229, 231–235, 238–242, 244–246, 251–266, 269–271, 273–276, 278–280, 283–289, 291–294, 297, 299–302, 304, 306f., 309, 313, 315f., 318–322, 325–344
Paul, deutero- 167, 185
Pauline gesture 323
Pauline politics 61, 302f., 305f.
Paulinism 17, 310, 314, 316, 318–320, 323
penance 9, 95, 101, 103f., 107, 110, 112
people 15, 50, 53, 56f., 63, 72, 76, 83, 86f., 89–91, 116, 121, 123f., 140, 162, 172, 180f., 192, 211, 215, 217, 220f., 223, 225, 227, 229, 243f., 251f., 254, 256, 259–262, 264, 266, 271, 274, 309, 312, 320, 328, 331, 343

performance 75, 96, 104, 106, 108, 110, 202, 290, 314, 317
performativity 10, 95, 100, 107–110
– performative force 271
– performative gesture 9, 95
performativum fidei 100f., 110, 112, 327
perjury 109f.
persecution 52, 175, 183, 185, 289
persuasion 203, 220, 290
Pharisee
– Pharisaic 47, 51f., 56
phenomenology 69, 73, 254, 283
– ~ of religion 73, 254
philosophy 3–6, 8–12, 16, 47f., 60, 67–74, 78f., 81, 89, 92, 130, 133, 135, 138, 143, 158, 189, 191f., 194f., 198–201, 203, 206, 210, 231–233, 238f., 242, 244–247, 263–265, 269, 272, 283–286, 288, 293f., 299, 325f., 328, 331, 333, 335f.
– ancient ~ 4f., 143, 232, 284, 328
– contemporary ~ 9, 81, 120, 210, 252
– Hellenistic ~ 284
– modern ~ 285, 334
φρόνησις (*phronēsis*) 79
piety 12, 52, 189, 201, 206, 214f., 218
πιστεύειν (*pisteuein*) 12f., 189, 195–197, 201, 231, 233, 235, 241, 246, 336f.
πίστις Ἰησοῦ Χριστοῦ (*pistis Iēsou Christou*) 165f., 171, 174
πίστις language (*pistis* language) 6, 11–13, 17, 165–168, 170–172, 176–178, 183f., 186, 189, 325f., 329, 335, 337–339
πίστις (*pistis*) 3–7, 9–13, 17, 95, 97–100, 103–106, 109f., 112, 115f., 165–185, 189–198, 200–202, 211–213, 215, 218, 222, 224f., 228, 231–233, 235, 239, 241f., 244, 246f., 271, 309f., 316, 322, 325–328, 334–341
πίστις Χριστοῦ (*pistis Christou*) 166, 178
πιστός (*pistos*) 167f., 171, 177, 183, 185, 214
Pitts, Andrew 241
Plato 12, 15, 130, 136f., 156, 189f., 192–195, 199–202, 205f., 219–221, 223, 226f., 233, 236, 242–245, 269–273, 276, 328, 330–332

Platonism 12, 158, 189–191, 193–195, 206, 219f., 229, 232, 238, 244, 259, 328, 331
Plotinus 12, 189, 191, 193, 195–198, 200–202, 206
plurality 55, 58–60, 65
Plutarch 12, 142f., 158, 189–195, 198–201, 203–206, 213, 215, 217f., 220f., 223, 225, 258
πνεῦμα (pneuma) 123, 129, 135, 255, 265, 335
ποιεῖν (poiein) 128
πόλις (polis) 15, 102, 258, 269f., 273, 276f.
πολιτεία (politeia) 276–278
political power 260, 287, 291, 293
political religion 292
political subject 299
political, the 6, 9, 16f., 56, 58, 62, 81, 92, 97, 125, 148, 253, 261, 265, 273, 276–279, 289, 292, 297f., 300, 302f., 309, 329
political theology 4f., 7, 14–16, 148, 251–254, 258–263, 269f., 277, 283, 311, 321, 325, 342
political theory 270
politico-juridical orders 299
politics 14, 16f., 57f., 62, 82, 91f., 97, 102, 125, 148, 166, 201, 253–255, 257f., 260, 265, 277f., 280, 283, 285, 288–290, 294f., 297–302, 305–307, 309f., 312, 316, 320
– ~ of escape 301
Porphyry 12, 153, 189, 200–203
Porter, Stanley 241
possibility 3, 8, 53f., 59, 63, 65, 67, 69, 71f., 74, 78f., 98, 104, 109, 118f., 122, 199, 201, 225, 240, 266, 278, 292, 300, 305f., 313, 322, 344
potentiality 90, 116, 119, 129f., 280, 307, 331, 333
power 87, 90, 100, 106, 109, 121, 128, 135, 137f., 140, 145, 169f., 177, 179, 182, 216, 220, 223, 247, 255, 262, 264–266, 270f., 280, 288, 290, 292f., 298–302, 304f., 307, 311, 319–322
– constituted ~ 297–306, 311
– constituting ~ 297–306
– destituent ~ 300f.

– dialectic of ~ 299f.
– economic ~ 319
pre-election 181
pre-Socratic philosopher 142, 234, 236
pre-structure of understanding 74
preaching 8, 12, 47–49, 51, 53, 58, 60, 63, 75–77, 165, 169f., 175, 180, 186, 254, 337
predestination 168
preferential indifference. See also ἀδιάφορα (adiaphora) 155f.
prejudice 74
prelaw 105, 111
preparation 174f., 245, 316
prepositional metaphysics 139, 152
presupposition 111, 123, 290
proclamation 75f., 118f., 121, 123, 126, 134, 136, 173, 175, 276, 310, 330, 334, 341, 343
Proclus 12, 189, 194f., 201f.
profession 89, 101, 109
– ~ of faith 101, 109
promise 53f., 57, 59, 62, 84, 108, 122, 124, 129, 166, 173, 262, 276, 280, 310
Providence 198, 206
provisional 73, 235, 276
ψυχή (psuchē) 255, 265, 269

quietism 147

rationality 3–5, 7, 198, 325, 328, 343
reading 7, 9, 15f., 54f., 57, 59, 61, 64, 72, 81–85, 89, 92, 95, 97–101, 103f., 111, 118, 121, 123, 146, 150, 156, 160f., 172, 175, 241, 252, 254–256, 262, 269, 274, 283, 285f., 288, 292f., 299f., 303f., 306, 313, 318, 321, 326, 330, 333–335, 337, 339, 342, 344
reason. See also λόγος (logos) and νοῦς (nous) 3–5, 10, 12, 64, 70, 81–83, 95–97, 108, 118, 138, 141, 144, 152, 155–157, 165, 169, 172, 180, 183, 192f., 195, 212, 220f., 231, 233, 252, 277, 279, 285, 287, 293, 325–328, 332, 334f., 339f., 342f.
reasonability 328, 340
recognition 103, 119

Reformation 269f., 275
relationship 9, 12f., 15, 74, 95, 107f., 148, 161, 165–177, 179, 181–184, 186, 219, 225, 231–233, 235f., 238, 240, 242, 244, 269, 274, 298f., 337
reliability 185
religion 3, 5, 8, 10, 13, 67–69, 73f., 79f., 83, 89, 95, 106f., 109–111, 190, 192, 201, 228, 231–234, 236f., 239, 242, 244–246, 258, 264, 270, 285, 288–290, 294, 299, 301, 303
religiosity 14, 74, 231, 244
religious behavior 80
religious liberty 287
remainder 120, 124, 322, 343, 345
remains 3, 9f., 12, 61, 67, 72, 106, 115f., 118f., 122, 124–127, 129f., 153, 160, 169, 183, 189, 244, 265, 275, 280, 293f., 304, 316, 322, 327, 332f.
– remnant 91, 124f., 161, 257, 304
Rembrandt 7, 27–44
reservation 160
resignation 147, 158
responsibility 102, 158, 258, 271, 275, 277, 290f., 339
responsiveness 275, 339
restoration 12, 98, 165, 186, 287, 337
resurrection 48, 60, 86, 88, 117f., 141, 169, 173, 181f., 185, 240, 260, 271, 274–279, 330, 336, 341
revelation 47, 49f., 57, 104, 110, 228, 231, 253, 261, 263, 274, 293
revocation. See also κλῆσις (klēsis) 90, 149, 302, 304, 306, 321
revolutionary event 299
rhetoric 11, 119, 124f., 133, 135, 160, 271, 317
Ricoeur, Paul 5, 82, 121, 343
Riegl, Alois 22, 32
righteousness. See also justice 12, 53, 64, 122, 130, 138, 156, 165, 172, 174, 186, 219, 221, 224, 227f., 270, 272, 275f., 333, 337, 339
Roman State 147, 158, 215
Rome 56f., 129, 215, 258, 264, 274, 276, 279
Rubens, Peter-Paul 22–25, 28

sacrifice 6, 192, 226, 240, 278
salvation 4, 12, 58, 100, 120, 122, 124, 128f., 165, 167f., 170, 174–176, 178, 180–183, 186, 202f., 210f., 223, 225, 262, 269, 276, 278, 287, 290f., 294, 337
Sanders, E. P. 211, 269f.
Sarkozy, Nicolas 312
σάρξ (sarx) 123
Saul 50, 53
Savior-God 252f., 257
Schmitt, Carl 15, 84, 251, 253, 260–265, 303f., 320f.
Scholem, Gershom 38
science 3, 8, 47, 68, 78, 299, 314, 327, 336
second coming 55f., 68, 75–80, 117f., 169f., 177, 260, 326, 334
Second Temple Judaism 14, 231–233, 238
secret 273
secular 117, 125, 128f., 261, 265, 273, 279, 285, 292, 294
seeing 7, 50f., 71, 92, 197, 239, 244, 320
self-emptying 64
self-love 61
self-reflexivity 237, 245
self-sufficiency 158
self-understanding 9, 67f., 175, 212
separation 90, 203, 210, 261, 285, 288f., 322
Siedentop, Larry 14
singularity 7, 275, 278, 280, 319f.
society 3, 107, 158, 166, 184, 219, 228, 257, 260, 266, 270f., 286f., 290f., 302
Socrates 136, 158f., 201, 220, 236, 243
solidarity 213, 310, 322f.
σοφία (sophia) 96, 247
sophist 192, 203
σωφροσύνη (sōphrosunē) 219, 227
soteriology 15, 269f., 275, 279
– soteriological 139
soul. See also ψυχή (psuchē) 12, 15, 48, 51, 189–191, 193, 195–200, 202f., 223, 227, 237, 243–245, 270, 284, 290, 337
sovereign power 277, 299f.
sovereign suspension 297, 305
sovereignty 14, 16, 107, 111, 259f., 277, 280, 297–304, 306, 311, 321
Spartacus 306

speech act 10, 95, 97, 100f., 107–110, 112
spirit. See also πνεῦμα (pneuma) 64, 123f., 129, 135, 168–170, 176f., 179f., 182, 185, 240, 242, 259, 319, 321, 335, 341
State 16, 58, 158, 162, 215, 298, 300
state of exception 260, 298, 304
steadfastness 239f., 338
Sterling, Gregory 139
Stoic metaphysics 160
Stoicism 232, 239
– Stoic 6, 11, 102, 133f., 138, 140, 143–145, 151–162, 193f., 217, 219, 259, 331, 333f., 344
subject 58, 70–72, 75, 86, 101–104, 107–110, 112, 135, 142, 159, 177, 210, 259, 278, 288, 307, 322, 327, 339–343
subjectification 103, 107, 109, 340
subjectivity 5, 60, 104, 171
suprarational faith 12, 189f., 194, 200
Supreme Being 200
suspension. See also ἐποχή (epochē) 90, 119, 121–124, 126f., 129, 297, 301, 304–306, 314, 319
Syriza 300

Tarnac affair 311, 314, 318
Tarsus 6, 16, 51f., 297
Taubes, Jacob 4, 11, 14, 16, 57, 82–85, 121, 123, 125, 133f., 146–148, 150, 153, 155–161, 251–254, 257, 260–266, 283f., 301f., 321, 332, 335, 343
Taylor, Charles 194, 202, 279
τέλος (telos) 60, 98, 199, 314
temperance 154, 215, 221, 227
temporality 5, 10, 58, 74, 79, 84, 90, 95, 97, 111f., 117f., 160, 320
– messianic ~ 9, 95, 97
tension 96, 111f., 149, 158f., 169, 219, 334
tensor 149
terrorist 309, 312–314, 317
Tertullian 101f., 107, 142, 231f.
testimony 107, 109
theocracy 253, 260
theocratic 259
theoretical attitude 69
θεωρία (theōria) 198
thief 8, 67f., 76, 118, 321, 332

threshold 100, 112
thrownness 74
time. See also χρόνος (chronos) 7, 10, 16, 53f., 61f., 68, 71, 76f., 79, 82, 88, 96, 98, 101, 103, 106, 110, 115–118, 121f., 124, 126–130, 138, 140, 144f., 147–150, 152f., 158–160, 167–169, 172, 174–177, 182–185, 209, 213–216, 218, 224, 228, 231, 233f., 236, 241, 243, 246, 254f., 257f., 260, 262, 264, 269f., 272–275, 277–279, 283, 302f., 305, 310, 312, 315, 317, 322, 327, 332f., 343
Tiqqun 17, 309f., 318–323
toleration 286, 289
Torah 52, 253, 271, 274
totalitarian temptation 265f.
tradition 64, 83, 96f., 99, 104, 136, 141, 168, 185, 192f., 213, 220, 231, 237, 252, 265, 270, 285, 287, 293, 301, 315, 319
transformation 10, 54, 62, 109, 115f., 118, 120, 123f., 128f., 228, 256, 264, 283, 319, 333, 345
Tronier, Henrik 238, 244
trust 106, 141, 156, 166, 168–177, 180f., 183, 190, 200, 213, 241f., 247, 323, 326f.
trustworthiness 5, 171f., 183, 185, 239f., 326, 341
trustworthy 105, 172, 180, 214, 218
truth. See also ἀλήθεια (alētheia) 5, 7, 11, 69, 76, 87f., 103f., 108–110, 133, 140, 145, 161, 175, 180, 191, 193, 199, 201–203, 210, 214f., 234, 238, 245f., 255, 258, 278f., 286, 288, 327, 336, 339f., 343f.

undeconstructible 270, 272f., 279
unfaithfulness 104
universal singularity 87
universality 5, 7, 55, 83, 87f., 91, 209f., 225, 228
unpredictability 8, 67f., 79
urgency 10, 115f., 129, 169, 334

Vattimo, Gianni 5
veridiction 14, 108f., 340
vernacular 62

violence 8, 47, 263, 277, 286, 298–300, 314
virtue 57, 177, 190, 201, 213, 215, 218f., 221, 233, 235, 243, 247, 270, 276, 286, 293, 337
vocabulary 118, 149, 210, 330, 341
vocation. *See also* κλῆσις (*klēsis*) *and* calling 150, 240, 247, 302, 304, 306f., 321
voluntaristic 145

Waldron, Jeremy 286
war 57, 150, 261, 264, 314, 318
– civil ~ 289, 318, 320
waste 10, 115, 125–128, 130, 262
way of being 70f., 150f., 271
weakness 128, 134, 138, 154, 255, 321
Weber, Max 89, 264
wisdom 11, 125, 128, 133–138, 156, 161, 177f., 183, 247, 252, 255, 262, 342
– ~ of God. *See also* God 136, 161, 178
– ~ of language 135f.
– ~ of the world 125, 128, 136, 161
withdrawal 60, 228, 261, 265, 300f.
witness 60, 183, 245f., 256, 340

Wittgenstein, Ludwig 135, 148
world. *See also* cosmos 3, 5f., 10, 12, 47, 49, 56, 58, 61–63, 68, 72f., 76–78, 84, 86, 89, 99, 106, 115–118, 122, 125–130, 136–138, 142, 144–148, 150–154, 156–162, 165f., 178, 181f., 185, 189, 191, 199, 205f., 213, 223, 226–229, 232, 235, 237–246, 251–255, 257–265, 271–274, 276, 279, 284, 287, 292, 301, 303, 316, 318, 320, 325, 327–331, 333f., 338, 341–344
– the other ~ 245, 265, 328, 341, 345
world spirit 335
world-view 148, 160, 238–240, 246
worldly calling 90
worship 57, 192, 204f., 215, 223, 226, 287, 290
Wright, N. T. 15, 211, 269f.

Xunzi 236

Yom Kippur 266

Žižek, Slavoj 5, 14, 16, 82f., 85, 283f.

www.ingramcontent.com/pod-product-compliance
Lightning Source LLC
Chambersburg PA
CBHW070058020526
44112CB00034B/1472